Time Out Guides Limited
Universal House
251 Tottenham Court Road
London W1T 7AB
Tel + 44 (0)20 7813 3000
Fax + 44 (0)20 7813 6001
Email guides@timeout.com
www.timeout.com

Editorial

Editor Ros Sales
Deputy Editor Rachel Howard
Consultant Lucy Wood
Listings Editor Emrah Güler
Proofreader Simon Cropper
Indexer Sam Le Quesne

Managing Director Peter Fiennes
Financial Director Gareth Garner
Editorial Director Ruth Jarvis
Deputy Series Editor Dominic Earle
Editorial Manager Holly Pick

Design

Art Director Scott Moore
Art Editor Pinelope Kourmouzoglou
Senior Designer Josephine Spencer
Graphic Designer Henry Elphick
Digital Imaging Simon Foster
Ad Make-up Jenni Prichard

Picture Desk

Picture Editor Jael Marschner
Deputy Picture Editor Tracey Kerrigan
Picture Researcher Helen McFarland

Advertising

Sales Director Mark Phillips
International Sales Manager Ross Canadé
International Sales Executive Simon Davies
Advertising Sales (CITY) Ajans Media
Advertising Assistant Kate Staddon

Marketing

Group Marketing Director John Luck
Marketing Manager Yvonne Poon
Marketing & Publicity Manager, US Rosella Albanese

Production

Group Production Director Mark Lamond
Production Manager Brendan McKeown
Production Coordinator Caroline Bradford

Time Out Group

Chairman Tony Elliott
Financial Director Richard Waterlow
Time Out Magazine Ltd MD David Pepper
Group General Manager/Director Nichola Coulthard
Time Out Communications Ltd MD David Pepper
Time Out International MD Cathy Runciman
Group Art Director John Oakey
Group IT Director Simon Chappell

Contributors

History Andrew Humphreys, David O'Byrne (*Great, but maybe no saint, Brotherly love?* Edoardo Albert; *Atatürk's new Turks* Ros Sales; *The mosque maker* Andrew Humphreys). **Istanbul Today** Jon Gorvett (*On the radio* Dorian Jones; *Istanbul by numbers* Richard Barbery). **People, Faith & Politics** Jon Gorvett. **Where to Stay** Emily Troutman, Andrew Humphreys (*Hotel hamams* Emily Troutman). **Sightseeing** Jon Gorvett (*Hard times in the harem* Andrew Humphreys; *Shopping the Bazaar* Ken Dakan; *The icon breakers* Edoardo Albert; *The ciy's narrator* Chris Watt; *Istanbul Modern* November Paynter). **Restaurants** Vanessa Able; *additional reviews* Yeşim Erdem Holland (*Summer loving, winter warming* Vanessa Able). **Bars & Cafés** Vanessa Able; *additional reviews* Yeşim Erdem Holland (*Hava narghile* Andrew Humphreys; *Up on the roofs* Dorian Jones; *Turkey's own brands* Yeşim Erdem Holland). **Shops & Services** Jody Sabral, Lucy Wood (*Mall life* Emrah Güler; *Beyoğlu's fashion passages* Vanessa Able; *The rug trade, Market day* Ken Dakan). **Festivals & Events** Jon Gorvett (*The new cosmopolitans* Yeşim Erdem Holland). **Children** Yeşim Erdem Holland. **Film** Lucy Wood. **Galleries** November Paynter. **Gay & Lesbian** Ken Dakan. **Hamams** Andrew Humphreys. **Music** Andy Footner (*Doing the Oryantal* Ken Dakan). **Nightlife** Attila Pelit. **Performing Arts** Attila Pelit. **Sport** Jon Gorvett (*Putting the boot in* Peterjon Cresswell). **Trips Out of Town** Jon Gorvett. **Directory** Attila Pelit.

Maps john@jsgraphics.co.uk, except p256 Communicarta Ltd.

Photography by Fumie Suzuki, except: page 12 Mary Evans Picture Library; page 15 akg-images; pages 16, 44, 50, 54, 60, 92, 118, 190 Jonathan Perugia; page 20 Topkapi Museum/The Bridgeman Art Library; page 22 The Bridgeman Art Library; pages 27, 97 Camera Press; page 162 Rex Features; page 185 Andreas Thiel/Doublemoon.

The following images were provided by the featured establishments/artists: pages 184, 188.

The Editor would like to thank Vanessa Able, *Time Out Istanbul* magazine and all contributors to previous editions of *Time Out Istanbul*, whose work forms the basis for parts of this book.

Contents

Introduction

Istanbul is several cities in one. Compare the smart shoppers flitting between the galleries and boutiques around Beyoğlu's European-style central drag, Istiklal Caddesi, with the modestly dressed and headscarved weekend picnickers in mosque gardens in conservative areas like Fener and Balat. Or the old men sipping glasses of dark tea in the recesses of the Grand Bazaar with sleekly dressed patrons sipping cocktails in smart bars along the Bosphorus or on Beyoğlu rooftops.

Compare also the historic Istanbul and the modern – it's a well-worn cliché but one that is impossible to escape with this city. As the centre of two great empires – Ottoman and Byzantine – Istanbul is steeped in a weighty heritage. At the same time, the modern city is possessed of an enormous, creative, forward-looking energy, with a young population open to foreign influences and ready to embrace change, but creative enough not merely to import it. Hence homegrown bands are at last finding their voice – and the right recording deals, while musicians from abroad play to packed houses; the 2006 Istanbul Biennial was the biggest ever in terms of international contributions, and local visitor numbers; people flock to cinemas to see foreign films during the International Istanbul Film Festival, while at least 30 new Turkish films were due to hit the screens in 2006.

Modern Istanbullus have a real appreciation for their roots, which means there's no danger of throwing out the old to welcome in the new. New bands may be forging their own modern Turkish identity, but everyone – old and young – still enjoys a night of traditional folk or *fasıl* music. Expect plenty of singing along and energetic dancing – possibly on the tables – in the *bağlama* bars and *meyhanes* of the city.

A respect for heritage is also evident in Istanbul's well-preserved historic buildings and monuments – and the Istanbullus who choose to spend time visiting them. If you're not yet an aficionado of Ottoman history, you probably will be after a few hours at Topkapı Palace, hub of the empire. Its pavilions are filled with imperial treasures ranging from heavily bejewelled *objets* to artefacts from Mecca; its beautifully decorated harem quarters are sizeable yet still manage to feel claustrophobic. And this is only one stop on the tour; there is so much more to see. The small Church of St Saviour in Chora, for example, is home to some of the best-preserved Byzantine mosaics and frescos in existence; and the architecturally outstanding mosques are open to all.

An appreciation of the past – both cultural and monumental – and a willingness to forge the old with the new are two of Istanbul's greatest assets. Both are vital factors in the creation of a city identity that is unique and always fascinating.

ABOUT TIME OUT CITY GUIDES

This is the third edition of *Time Out Istanbul*, one of an expanding series of Time Out guides produced by the people behind the successful listings magazines in London, New York and Chicago. Our guides are all written by resident experts who have striven to provide you with all the most up-to-date information you'll need to explore the city or read up on its background, whether you're a local or a first-time visitor.

THE LIE OF THE LAND

Istanbul is nightmarish when it comes to finding your way around. Streets can have two or more names, but quite often nobody seems to know what they are anyway; street signs are noticeable by their absence. Postal codes are not used outside the newer northern suburbs. Sometimes even building numbers are missing. Turkish addresses tend to be things like 'Across from the green mosque beside the old bridge'. But in most cases we have managed to provide a street name and number, and the name of the district. We have used the names of the main central districts (Sultanahmet, the Bazaar Quarter, Eminönü, Beyoğlu, the Asian Shore) as divisions in our Sightseeing section and in chapters that are organised by area.

ESSENTIAL INFORMATION

For all the practical information you might need for visiting the area – including visa and customs information, details of local transport, a listing of emergency numbers, information on local weather and a selection of useful websites – turn to the Directory at the back of this guide. It begins on page 216.

THE LOWDOWN ON THE LISTINGS

We have tried to make this book as easy to use as possible. Addresses, phone numbers, opening times and admission prices are all included in the listings. Information on public transport is given for destinations outside the central Beyoğlu area. However, businesses can change their arrangements at any time. Before you go out of your way, we'd strongly advise you to phone ahead to check opening times and other particulars. While every effort and care has been made to ensure the accuracy of the information contained in this guide, the publishers cannot accept responsibility for any errors it may contain.

PRICES AND PAYMENT

We have noted where venues such as shops, hotels, restaurants and theatres accept the following credit cards: American Express (AmEx), Diners Club (DC), MasterCard (MC) and Visa (V). A few businesses may accept other cards, or even travellers' cheques.

The prices we've listed in this guide should be treated as guidelines, not gospel. If prices vary wildly from those we've quoted, ask whether there's a good reason. If not, go elsewhere. Then please let us know. We aim to give the best and most up-to-date advice, so we want to know if you've been badly treated or overcharged.

TELEPHONE NUMBERS

To phone Istanbul from outside Turkey, first dial the international code 00, then 90 (Turkey's country code), then either 212 (the city code for Istanbul's European side) or 216 (the city code for the Asian side). Within Istanbul, if you are on the European side, only dial the city code if you are phoning the Asian side, and vice versa.

MAPS

The map section at the back of this book includes an overview map of the city, on pages 240-241. Detailed street maps are on pages 242-251. These now pinpoint specific locations of hotels (❶), restaurants (❶), cafés and bars (❶). Map references in the guide indicate the page number and the grid square on these maps. There is also a street index, starting on page 253. On page 256 you'll find a map to the Istanbul tram, metro and light metro systems.

LET US KNOW WHAT YOU THINK

We hope you enjoy *Time Out Istanbul*, and we'd like to know what you think of it. We welcome tips for places that you consider we should include in future editions and take note of your criticism of our choices. You can email us at guides@timeout.com.

There is an online version of this book, along with guides to over 100 international cities, at **www.timeout.com**.

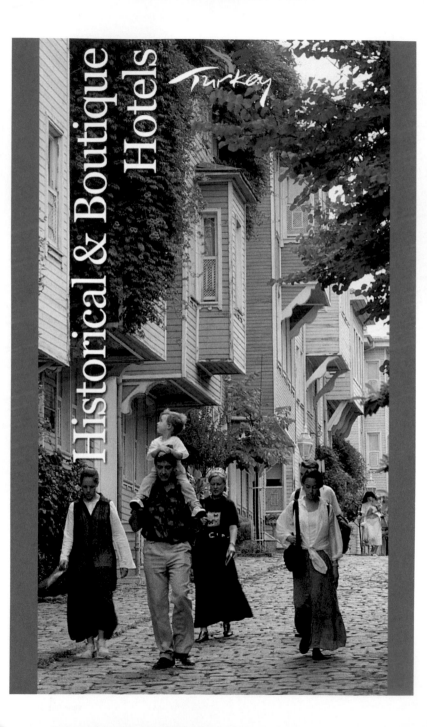

Historical & Boutique Hotels

Turkey

Historical & Boutique Hotels

Association of Historical & Boutique Hoteliers of Turkey

Historical & Boutique Hoteliers of Turkey (Ozbi) is an official association representing a group "hotels with distinct features" in Turkey. Member hotels are unique properties all independently owned and managed. The Ozbi hotels are usually small hotels offering guests a personal and intmate feeling.

Ozbi hotels are usually located in the city centers – within walking distance to city's landmarks. They may be remodeled mansions, reconstructed Turkish houses, or may exhibit distinctive architectural/design features that blend in with the surroundings they are a part of. They all possess exquisite character.

www.historicalhotelsofturkey.org

4G/4S

In Context

Botter House. *See p94.*

Atatürk with officials, 1921.

History

Two empires and a social revolution.

Few cities have occupied the imagination as Istanbul has. Fought over throughout its history by armies from Western Europe, the Middle East and Central Asia, capital and centre of two of the world's greatest empires, intriguing, perplexing and often frustrating, it captivates as few other cities can.

Most books will tell you that Istanbul is the only city in the world to straddle two continents, Europe and Asia. In fact it's the other way round: the history of the area defined what we now know as the continents. The unique geography of the 35-kilometre (22-mile) Bosphorus Strait, with its sloping shores running almost due north–south, must have suggested to early seafarers that this was indeed where two worlds met.

The 'cultural crossroads' was already well established by the fifth century BC, when Herodotus devoted much of his *Histories* to the conflict between Greece and Persia, East and West. His writings came to define the 'them and us' attitude that still dominates relations between Europe and Asia, and leads every writer to suppose that Istanbul must be a bridge between the two.

BLIND BEGINNINGS

Despite its geographical advantages, prehistoric finds around Istanbul have been scarce, probably due to the intensity of occupation that followed. Neolithic sites from about 7000 BC have been found near Kadıköy, and Bronze Age remains dated to 3200 BC unearthed in Sultanahmet; but these early chapters are blank pages waiting to be written.

Around 1600 BC, seafaring Greeks began to found colonies around the Aegean and Mediterranean. By 750 BC, they had passed through the Bosphorus and established settlements on the Black Sea coast of Anatolia and in the Caucasus. The 'clashing rocks' episode from the legend of Jason and the Argonauts was probably inspired by the voyage up the Bosphorus Strait. The first Greek settlement in what is now Istanbul was the colony of Chalcedon, founded around 675 BC in today's Kadıköy, a suburb on the Asian shore. According to Herodotus (the best source of classical soundbite), Chalcedon was dubbed 'the city of the blind', its founders having foolishly missed the clear geographical advantages of the opposite European shore.

Within less than 20 years, more clear-sighted parties had settled across the water on land now enclosed by the walls of Topkapı Palace. Roughly triangular, bounded on two sides by water, it was a natural fortress. To the north, the Golden Horn was a 6.5-kilometre (four-mile) long, deep-water harbour. The site offered access by sea to Africa, the Mediterranean, and the Black Sea, and lay at the crossroads of routes between Europe and Asia. It was destined to be a city of world importance. Its founding was attributed to a sailor by the name of Byzas, hence the name Byzantium.

Others were quick to recognise the strategic importance of the new city, and it was repeatedly taken by warring regional powers: first the Persians in 550 BC, then the Spartans, then the Athenians. The Byzantines quickly developed a skill for diplomacy and kept their predatory neighbours at bay through a series of shrewd alliances. When that failed, the city buckled down and dug in, successfully weathering a siege from Philip of Macedon in 340 BC.

Good judgement ran out in AD 196 when, after three centuries of independence as part of the Roman province of Asia, the Byzantines backed the wrong side in an imperial power struggle. After a prolonged siege, the stern emperor Septimius Severus had Byzantium's walls torn down, the city put to the torch and a fair chunk of the population put to death. Such a strategic location couldn't lie wasted for too long, and within a few years the emperor had rebuilt the city on a far grander scale with new temples, a colonnaded way and bigger walls. For all its pomp, like earlier Greek Byzantium, nothing of Severus's city has survived.

NEW ROME

By the end of the third century, the Roman Empire had become too unwieldy to govern effectively from Rome, and was subdivided, with part of the power shifted to Byzantium. The result was to create internal rivalries that ultimately could only be settled on the battlefield. In 324, Constantine, Emperor of the West, defeated Licinius, Emperor of the East, first in a naval battle on the Sea of Marmara, then on the Asian shore at a place called Chrysopolis, today's Üsküdar. With the empire reunited, Constantine set about changing the course of history, first by promoting Christianity as the official religion of the empire, then by shifting the capital from a jaded and cynical Rome to the upstart city on the Bosphorus. On 11 May 330, Constantine inaugurated his new seat of power as 'Nova Roma', a name by which the city has never been known since.

In Nova Roma, more popularly called Constantinople, the new uncontested emperor

had a city hitherto uncorrupted by power that he could make over as he saw fit. He embarked on a building programme, plundering the empire to bring in the tallest columns, the finest marble and an abundance of Christian relics, including the True Cross itself. He endowed the church of Haghia Irene (*see p66*) as the city's first Christian cathedral and commissioned a great palace, built adjacent to an extended hippodrome. To safeguard his capital, Constantine had new walls erected in an arc from near what is now the Atatürk Bridge over the Golden Horn, then looping south to present-day Mustafa Paşa, enlarging the area of the city fourfold. Other than a burnt and badly aged column, little physical evidence of Constantine's work survives, but he laid the foundations for an empire that was to endure for over 1,000 years.

'Presiding over a city of ruins soaked in its citizens' blood, Justinian needed to restore public faith.'

The beginnings were not auspicious. On Constantine's death in 337, achievement and stability ended. His three sons quarrelled over the succession and the empire was divided between Eastern and Western emperors, who sometimes co-operated but more often fought. Fortunately, Constantinople was largely unaffected by the ensuing two centuries of turbulence, and was even enlarged by the construction of new city walls during the reign of Theodosius II (408-50), completed just in time to halt Attila's advancing hordes. Rome was not so fortunate: it was ripped apart by tribes of Goths and Vandals from the north. With no rival, Constantinople was left to move towards a new era of greatness, reaching its apogee during the era of Justinian (527-65).

CROWD TROUBLE

Justinian's reign was marked by great confidence, which saw the empire extend across most of the Mediterranean coast, including the recapture of the lost dominion of Italy from the 'barbarian hordes'. But a great deal of the glory belongs to the emperor's supporting cast. He was fortunate in having at his service a supremely competent general, Belisarius, who takes credit for all military successes. Similarly exceptional was Justinian's wife, Theodora, a former street entertainer and prostitute.

Theodora is credited with saving her husband's skin when a revolt broke out among factions at the Hippodrome. Known as the

Great, but maybe no saint

It's rare for an emperor to earn the title 'the Great', even rarer for that same emperor to be a saint too. Granted, some modern scholars even debate the claim that Constantine the Great was the 'first Christian Roman emperor', as he may have clung to pre-Christian beliefs. And as far as claims to sainthood go, he is only recognised as such by the Orthodox and Eastern Catholic churches; his case isn't helped by the fact that he executed both his wife and son.

What nobody can dispute, however, is that Constantine gained control of a vast empire, created a New Rome in Byzantium, made Christianity a licit religion, and became the most powerful emperor of the late Roman period.

Constantine's mother, Empress Helena, was of humble stock. Helena was probably a tavern maid when she met an ambitious soldier called Constantius. She left her home town of Drepanum in Asia Minor to accompany Constantius on his campaigns, bearing him a son around 272. Constantius shot up the military and imperial ranks, eventually becoming commander of the Western Provinces of Gaul, Britain and Spain. On 25 July 306, he died in battle at Eburacum (York) and the legions promptly pronounced his son their emperor.

At the time, the sprawling Roman Empire was ruled by four emperors – two in the west and two in the east. Constantine and Maxentius became the new emperors of the west. In 312, a dispute between them took a bloody turn. Constantine and his troops marched across the Alps towards Maxentius's base in Rome; Maxentius set off with a far bigger army and prepared to do battle at the Milvian Bridge, on the Tiber. The night before the battle, according to one source, Constantine had a dream commanding him to place the sign of Christ on his soldiers' shields. Another chronicler claims he had a vision of a cross of light in the sky, above the words 'By this, conquer'. Whichever account is true, on 28 October 312 Maxentius's forces were routed by Constantine's army. Maxentius drowned while trying to flee across the river.

Constantine was now the undisputed emperor of the Western Roman Empire. Meanwhile, Licinius had fought his own battles to become sole ruler of the Eastern Empire. In February 313 the two emperors issued the Edict of Milan, which instructed the governors of all Roman provinces to stop the persecution of Christians, to restore all confiscated property to Christians, and to allow all citizens the freedom to practise whatever religion they wished. However, Licinius reneged on the Edict. Three battles later, Constantine became sole ruler of the entire Roman Empire in 324.

During the war with Licinius, Constantine laid siege to a city strategically located on a promontory of the Bosphorus. Whoever ruled this city was the master of maritime traffic in and out of the Black Sea, as well as commanding a key position on the trade routes between north and south, east and

Greens and the Blues, these factions originated in trade guilds and were a cross between political parties and gangs. Normally rivals, the Greens (lower-class radicals) and the Blues (upper-class conservatives) united in 532 to protest against the execution of some of their members. The subsequent uprising, buoyed on by chants of 'Nika, nika' ('Victory, victory'), plunged the city into chaos. Justinian, bags packed and in the hall, was all for fleeing, but Theodora persuaded him that it was 'better to die as an emperor than live as a fugitive'. In the event Belisarius, still only in his 20s, succeeded in trapping and massacring 30,000 rebels in the Hippodrome, thereby restoring civil order.

Left presiding over a city of ruins soaked in its citizens' blood, Justinian needed to restore public faith. His answer was to embark on a grand programme of reconstruction, providing for the city spiritually (he endowed over 40 churches) and practically – for example, providing the city with immense water cisterns, one of which still draws appreciative gasps from visitors (**Yerebatan Sarnıcı**, *see p72*). The crowning glory was the new cathedral, Sancta Sophia. In the eyes of contemporary chronicler Procopius, 'God allowed the mob to commit this sacrilege knowing how great the beauty of this church would be.'

Although the death of Justinian was followed by a prolonged period of decline, largely resulting from internal rivalries, Constantinople remained, as one Byzantine writer put it, 'the city of the world's desire'. There were plenty who acted on those desires. Slavs (581), Avars (617), Persians and Avars (626), Arabs (669-79

west. On 8 September 324, only weeks after his victory over Licinius, Constantine laid out the boundaries of his new city, which he called New Rome, and would later become known as Constantinople in his honour. This city was to be the centre of an empire for a thousand years after the fall of Rome.

These were undoubtedly great political achievements. However, Constantine's personal life was a little less illustrious. In 326, he executed Crispus, his illegitimate first son. Not long afterwards, the emperor got rid of his wife, Fausta, too – reputedly by dunking her in a scalding bath. The motivation for these murders is unclear. One theory is that Fausta accused Crispus of attempting to rape her, in order to ensure that her own sons succeeded to the throne. The hot-tempered Constantine flew into a rage, and promptly executed his son. When Constantine discovered that his wife had lied, he had no qualms about bumping her off, too.

So perhaps not a saint. But a great emperor, certainly.

and 717-18), Bulgars (813, 913 and 924), Russians (four times between 860 and 1043) and Pechenegs (1087) all marched on the city. Some armies were sufficiently daunted by the walls alone and quit before they'd begun to fight. Others persisted and laid siege. But all failed. Fortified defences were backed by the Byzantines' skilled and well-equipped navy and more unconventional deterrents such as 'Greek Fire', a mysterious liquid that was sprayed with devastating effect.

PICTURE PROBLEMS

Trouble was also brewing internally on the theological front when the iconoclast Leo III became emperor in 726. Iconoclasts believed literally in the first commandment, which forbids the worshipping of 'graven images'. Their stance was a complete break with the Greek tradition of adorning churches with elaborate frescoes and mosaics, and the veneration of icons and the relics of martyred saints. Thus began a 'dark age' of almost 120 years, during which churches were stripped of their decoration and those who stayed faithful to icons (iconodules) were forced to flee to distant monasteries or to worship in secret at risk of denunciation and death. The feud over icons burned on until 845, and it wasn't until 867 that the first new mosaic was unveiled in Haghia Sophia – that of the Madonna and child, still *in situ*. *See also p88* **The icon breakers**.

Religious problems of a different kind surfaced during the iconoclastic period when, in 800, the Roman pope crowned the Frankish leader Charlemagne the first Emperor of the West for over 400 years. This was followed

Süleymaniye Mosque. *See p80*.

by emissaries to Constantinople proposing a marriage between Charlemagne and the then Byzantine empress Irene. The aim was to re-unite the two halves of the Roman Empire, but the grandees of the Eastern church created by Constantine felt that they alone had the right to crown emperors. Unwilling to accept as supreme ruler an illiterate tribal leader unable to speak either Latin or Greek, they deposed Irene shortly after the emissaries' arrival.

A restoration in Byzantine fortunes came during the reign of Basil II (976-1025), who succeeded not just in holding the fort but also expanding the empire into Armenia and Georgia. A conscientious ruler, he was also incredibly harsh: he is best known for meting out one of the most horrific punishments that Europe has ever seen: in 1014, after taking 15,000 Bulgars prisoner, he had 99 out of every 100 blinded; the remainder were left with one eye to lead their fellow soldiers home. When he saw the ruined army that returned to his capital, Bulgarian Tsar Samuel is said to have collapsed and died two days later.

Basil's most significant contribution to history came in 989, the year when he gave his 25-year-old sister Anna in marriage to Vladimir, Prince of Kiev, in return for the pagan prince's promise to convert to Orthodox Christianity. This Vladimir did, then founded the Russian church and converted his subjects *en masse*, earning himself a sainthood in the process.

FRYING PAN OR FIRE?

The death of Basil marked a turning point in Byzantine fortunes, and the city entered a period of terminal decline. This was signalled to all when, in 1071, a combination of incompetence and treachery led to the annihilation of a Byzantine army at Manzikert in Anatolia. The victors were a new menace: the Selçuk Turks, who flooded across Asia Minor to the shores of the Sea of Marmara.

Meanwhile, to the west, Europe had emerged from its Dark Ages to become a patchwork of states owing religious allegiance to the Pope in Rome. Both the West and Byzantium were nominally Christian, but theological differences, coupled with the Western church's envy of its older and richer neighbour, meant any common cause was superficial. In 1054, a dispute between papal officials and the Patriarch of Constantinople had resulted in mutual excommunications. The animosity inaugurated the schism between the Roman and Orthodox churches that still exists today.

In its time of trouble, the empire fell into the hands of the scheming Ducas and Comneni families. They indulged their tastes for luxury, learning, and culture, making Constantinople perhaps the richest city in the world. It was also the most decadent, as the dynasties followed their penchant for intermarrying, intriguing, dethroning and murder. Where once Byzantine armies had conquered, the bloated and effete empire now relied on wealth and diplomacy.

Threatened by the Selçuk Turks, Byzantium was forced to enlist the aid of Latin armies as paid mercenaries. The Latins were crusading to recapture the Holy Lands lost to the Turks and, passing through Constantinople in 1097, they agreed to return to the emperor any formerly imperial territory that they might recapture. This was a promise they failed to keep. Instead, the crusaders set up their own Holy Land states. There followed 50 years of confused bruising between the Byzantine, Latin and Muslim armies, culminating in the Byzantines cutting crusader supply lines and enabling the Selçuks to retake lost territory.

Two or three relatively able emperors, notably John II (1118-43) and Manuel I (1143-80), applied clever diplomacy and judicious use of force to keep the empire intact and even extend its borders; but the good work was undone in 1185 with the accession of Isaac II. Isaac was totally incompetent and squandered the gains of the last 70 years. He was deposed by his brother Alexius III and imprisoned, but Isaac's son escaped and fled west, where he offered enormous sums of money to the armies massing in Venice for the Fourth Crusade, in exchange for helping his father and himself regain the imperial throne. With interest in a long and probably futile struggle in the Middle East never deep, the Latins needed little encouragement to accept.

Threatened with the vastly superior force of the crusaders, the Byzantines agreed to restore Isaac II to the throne. But Alexius III fled with the contents of the treasury and the crown jewels, leaving the reinstated emperor with no money to pay his mercenary allies. On 13 April 1204, the crusaders stormed Constantinople. They sacked the city, stripping it of its treasures and relics and sending them back west; the four gilded bronze horses that now stand over the doorway of St Mark's cathedral in Venice came from Constantinople's Hippodrome. What the crusaders couldn't strip away they destroyed, leaving the city in ruins.

The victorious Latins then appointed one of their own, Baldwin of Flanders, as emperor, and divided up the empire into a patchwork of fiefdoms and city states. Haghia Sophia and many Orthodox churches were converted to the Latin rite. The Latin state lasted until 1261 before the Byzantines mustered enough force to reclaim what remained of Constantinople.

Brotherly love?

Wielding absolute power in the most magnificent city on earth, as Emperor of Byzantium or Sultan of the Ottomans, might seem an enviable privilege. The Imperial reception rooms of the Byzantine Emperor had golden lions that roared and golden birds that sang. The Ottoman sultans were equally – if not more – ostentatious. Fanatical about tulips, Selim II once wrote to an official: 'I need 50,000 bulbs for my royal gardens…and I command you in no way to delay.' Yet despite this unparalleled luxury and privilege, there was a dark side to life in the imperial court. Since neither empire had a strict rule of primogeniture, getting to the top – and staying there – presented these capricious rulers with serious challenges.

Between the foundation and fall of Byzantium, there were 107 emperors. Only 34 of them died of natural causes; another eight were killed in battle. Sixty-five emperors were forcibly removed from the throne. Intrigue and assassination were common in imperial circles: emperors had no qualms about killing or mutilating potential claimants or conspirators, since failing to remain in power would generally result in blinding, banishment, or a long and painful death. (Since a deformed man could not be emperor, blinding was considered a more merciful alternative to murder.) When Emperor Andronikos I was overthrown, he was handed over to the mob, who broke his teeth, ripped out his hair, put out an eye, and chopped off a hand; he eventually died three days later.

Things were no better among the Ottomans. The death or decline of the reigning sultan triggered an intense power struggle among all the his brothers and sons. Given that the sultans had several wives and innumerable concubines, the number of claimants was extensive. Until the 17th century, the sultan's brothers were unlikely to get anywhere near the throne, since fratricide was one of the first acts committed by the new ruler. Garroting was the favourite method of disposing of unwanted siblings, a skill in which the palace mutes excelled.

After the 17th century, the sultan's brothers were confined to the Kafes, or Cage, a secluded building in the Inner Palace where they had no contact with the outside world apart from a few mute servants and barren women, who formed a harem for the imprisoned princes. Occasionally, one of them might be dragged out and abruptly appointed ruler of the Ottoman Empire. Ibrahim, the last surviving brother of Murat IV, had been a prisoner for 22 of his 24 years when a vizier came to tell him that Murat was dead and he was now Sultan. Ibrahim refused to open the door until Murat's corpse was produced. Ibrahim finally emerged crying: 'The butcher is dead!'

Sultan Ibrahim immediately set about making up for lost time. One source notes that: 'As Murat was wholly addicted to wine, so was Ibrahim to lust… He frequently assembled all the virgins, made them strip, and himself naked, ran among them neighing like a stallion, and ravish'd one or another.' The party couldn't last. Ibrahim was soon overthrown by the Janissaries. He was finished off by Kara Ali, the chief executioner, who strangled him with a garter.

OTTOMANS AT THE GATE

That the Byzantine state was able to survive for another 190 ineffectual years was down to the fact that the rival Selçuk empire had splintered into myriad warring *beyliks*, or fiefdoms. It was only a matter of time, though, before one *beylik* won out. By the first years of the 14th century a new power had emerged: the Osmanlı Turks, named after their first leader Osman, and better known to Westerners as the Ottomans. During the reign of their first sultan, Orhan Gazi (1326-62), the Ottomans conquered most of western Asia Minor and advanced into Europe as far as Bulgaria, establishing a new capital at Adrianople, now Edirne.

Constantinople had become a Byzantine island in an Ottoman sea. Inevitably, the severely weakened, ruined and depopulated city was confronted with a Turkish army at its walls. This first occurred in 1394, and again in 1400, 1422 and 1442. Each time the attacks were repelled, but this only forestalled the inevitable. Soon after becoming Ottoman sultan in 1452, Mehmet II constructed the fortress of Rumeli Hisarı on the European shore of the Bosphorus just north of the city. Fitted with cannons, it gave the Ottomans control of the straits and deprived Constantinople of vital grain supplies.

By April 1453, the Ottoman forces surrounding Constantinople numbered some 80,000; facing them were just 5,000 able-bodied men in a city whose population had fallen to less than 50,000. The Ottoman navy was anchored in the Sea of Marmara. However, it could not gain access to the Golden Horn because of a great chain that the Byzantines had stretched across its mouth from Galata castle to modern-day Sirkeci. But one night, several weeks into the siege, in an audacious move, the Ottomans circumvented the boom by hauling 70 ships on rollers up over the ridge above Galata and down to the water on the other side, so that by morning they were in the Golden Horn and up against the city walls.

On 27 May, Mehmet invited the last Byzantine emperor, named Constantine, like the first, to surrender. He refused. The final assault was launched two days later. The defenders on the walls threw back waves of attackers as they had many times before. This time, however, the besiegers forced an opening near the Golden Horn, and poured into the city in their thousands. By dawn it was all over, with an estimated 4,000 defenders lying dead. A contemporary account describes how 'blood flowed through the streets like rainwater after a sudden storm; corpses floated out to sea like melons on a canal'.

With the conquest of Constantinople, Mehmet, still only 21 years old, took the name 'Fatih', or Conqueror. He was apparently shocked at the ruined state of the once-great city. As he walked among the wrecked imperial palace, he is said to have recited lines from an old Persian poem: 'The spider spins the curtains in the palace of the Caesars, and the owl hoots its night call on the towers of Afrasiab.'

A MULTINATIONAL CAPITAL

Mehmet was intoxicated by the notion of Constantinople and its heritage as capital of Eastern and Western empires. It fitted his own imperial ambitions. Justinian's great cathedral, Haghia Sophia, was reconsecrated as a mosque, and the sultan attended prayer there the first Friday after the conquest. The Ottomans immediately set about repairing the damage sustained during the siege and the decay of preceding centuries. Defences were strengthened with a great citadel at Yedikule where the land walls met the Sea of Marmara, and a palace was constructed on the site of what is now Istanbul University. Mehmet ordered craftsmen and artisans from Bursa and Edirne to move to his new city. The sultan's *viziers* (ministers) were encouraged to build and endow the new capital with mosques and the beginnings of what would develop into the Grand Bazaar.

Efforts were made to repopulate the half-deserted city. Greeks, who had fled in the preceding years, were offered land and houses

and temporary tax exemption. Craftsmen, merchants and those who would enhance the city's wealth were invited regardless of race or religion. At a time when 'heretics' were being burnt alive in western Europe, the Ottoman regime granted all religions freedom of worship and the uncontested right to appoint their own religious leaders. Large numbers of Sephardic Jews expelled from Spain and Portugal took sanctuary in Istanbul, the only multinational, multi-faith capital in Europe.

On the Conqueror's death in 1481, a scuffle for succession was won by his elder son Beyazıt II, succeeded in turn by his son Selim I, known as 'the Grim' for his habit of having his grand viziers executed (inspiring the popular Ottoman curse, 'May you be a vizier of Selim!'). Though Selim's reign lasted only eight years, he presided over significant military victories, adding Syria and Egypt to the imperial portfolio. Further south, he saw off a Portuguese threat to Mecca and was rewarded with the keys to the Holy City, the sacred relics of the Prophet, and the title of Caliph, Champion of Islam. This made Istanbul not only the capital of one of the most powerful empires in the world, but, as it was still the home of the Orthodox Patriarchate, also the centre of two major religions.

> **'Pretenders to the throne were strangled with a silken bowstring, preferably by deaf mutes who would not hear their cries.'**

While Mehmet II made Istanbul the Ottoman capital, it was during the 46-year reign of Süleyman I (1520-66) that the city became a true imperial centre. A smug Süleyman described himself in his official correspondence as 'Sultan of Sultans, Sovereign of Sovereigns, Distributor Crowns, the Shadow of God on Earth, Perfecter of the Perfect Number.' These days, historians settle for 'Süleyman the Magnificent'. By the time of his death, he ruled an empire that covered North Africa, stretched east to India, and rolled from the Caucasus through Anatolia and the Balkans to Budapest and most of modern-day Hungary. Süleyman's armies reached the walls of Vienna in 1529, where they were turned back after an unsuccessful siege.

Key to Süleyman's military successes were the Janissaries, whose name comes from the Turkish *yeni ceri*, or 'new troops'. Originally entirely of Christian origin, selected boys were forcibly converted Islam and trained into a crack and fiercely loyal fighting force; they

Süleyman the Magnificent. *See p19*.

were richly rewarded in return. During the 16th century they were the most disciplined, well-armed and effective of all European armies, universally admired and feared. Later, though, their unchecked appetites for power and their lack of discipline would almost prove the empire's undoing.

Under Süleyman, Istanbul became synonymous with grandeur, the source of which was the imperial palace, Topkapı, founded by Mehmet the Conqueror, but gilded by the wealth, tributes and taxes from newly conquered territories. Severe and grave, Süleyman surprised all by falling under the spell of a slave girl, Haseki Hürrem, known universally as Roxelana due to her alleged

Russian origins. So besotted was Süleyman that in the early 1530s he married Roxelana and dispensed with the company of all other women. In 1538, as a further expression of devotion, he commissioned a promising young architect, Mimar Sinan, to construct the Haseki Hürrem Mosque complex as a birthday present.

This was Sinan's first major commission in Istanbul, launching a glorious career which was to span 50 years. During that time, he, more than any of the sultans or pashas, left his indelible mark on the city and indeed on most major cities of the Ottoman Empire (*see p21* **The mosque maker**).

THE RULE OF WOMEN

Süleyman should have been succeeded by his first son, Mustafa, an able soldier and administrator, but Roxelana schemed against it. Mustafa was not her son. She succeeded in convincing the sultan that he was traitorous and Süleyman had him strangled. Selim, Roxelana's son, became heir apparent.

Such bloodletting to secure the imperial throne was not uncommon. Although the sultanate always remained in the family – every ruler of the Ottoman Empire until its end was a descendant of Osman – the choice of which son or male relative would inherit the throne was left to 'the will of Allah'. More pragmatically, whichever of the sultan's sons happened to be in Istanbul, or got there first after the ruler's death, got the throne.

Succession was a matter of life or death, for Mehmet the Conqueror had declared, 'For the welfare of the state, the one of my sons to whom Allah grants the sultanate may lawfully put his brothers to death.' They were strangled with a silken bowstring, preferably by deaf mutes who would not hear their cries. The beautiful and elaborate tombs built to house the families of butchered children scarcely hid the brutality of the deed. Thus when Süleyman died on campaign in Hungary, the grand vizier sent a secret messenger to the preferred heir, Selim, then maintained the fiction that the sultan was merely ill. Once Selim was secure in Istanbul the vizier announced the sultan's demise.

Far from being 'Grim', like the first Selim, Selim II was known as Selim 'the Sot'. His rampant drunkenness rendered him useless as a ruler. The real power behind the throne was Nurbanu ('Princess of Light'), one of Selim's wives, who took control of both the harem and the palace, marking the beginning of an 80-year period referred to as 'the rule of women'. It was an era that saw weak sultans manipulated by their wives and their mother, the *valide sultana*, between whom there were often struggles for power (*see p71* **Hard life in the harem**).

Selim's drunkeness had fatal results: he drowned in his bath and the ruthless Nurbanu had four of his five sons killed, leaving her own child, Murat III, to succeed as sultan. When Murat died in 1595, his wife Safiye in turn had 19 brothers of her own son, Mehmet III, strangled. With Mehmet's successor, Ahmet I, the killing stopped, possibly out of fear of dynastic extinction.

From Ahmet's time, male relatives of the sultan were instead confined to the Kafes, literally 'cage', a closed apartment hidden deep inside the Topkapı Palace. Here they were kept in complete isolation, apart from a few concubines who had been sterilised by the removal of their ovaries. Guards whose eardrums had been pierced and tongues slit served the prisoners.

The mosque maker

If a poll was held to name the person who has made the single biggest contribution to the fabric of Istanbul, odds are the winner would be Mimar Sinan. He was chief imperial architect under Süleyman I 'the Magnificent' and two successive sultans. It's quite likely Süleyman would never have been considered quite so magnificent if wasn't for the legacy of Sinan.

Born around 1490 into a Christian family in central Turkey, Sinan was taken into the sultan's service as part of an annual levy of Christian boys. Trained as a military engineer, he served in seven of Süleyman's campaigns before being appointed chief imperial architect in 1538. He constructed his first mosque in Aleppo, Syria, that same year. By the time he died exactly 50 years later, he'd constructed an incredible 477 buildings, of which more than 100 were mosques. Pretty much single-handedly, Sinan wrote the rulebook for Ottoman architecture. It was Sinan who developed the typology of the imperial mosque as a single domed square surrounded by half domes and domed side aisles.

He exhibited this style exquisitely in **Süleymaniye Mosque** (*see p72*), which set the pattern for mosque-building for almost 200 years and continues to dominate the Istanbul skyline today. As with earlier mosques, the plan follows that of Hagia Sophia, with a huge dome flanked by two semi-domes. Sinan's genius was to support the whole structure on four piers, avoiding the need for additional columns or arcading, creating one immense, unified, enclosed space. From the outside, the profile is a beautiful confection of rippling semi-domes. The buildings of the surrounding complex are also perfectly proportioned.

Sinan's genius wasn't confined to huge imperial buildings. The **Sokollu Mehmet Paşa Mosque** (*see p74*) demonstrates his ability to work in difficult, confined spaces, the sloping

site proving no obstacle to designing one of the city's most stunning smaller mosques.

However, according to his own writings, Sinan considered the Süleymaniye merely 'good workmanship'. He was more proud of his **Selimiye Mosque** in Edirne: 'Architects of any importance in Christian countries consider themselves far superior to Muslims, because until now the latter haven't accomplished anything comparable to the dome of Haghia Sophia. Thanks to the All Powerful and the favour of the sultan, I have succeeded in building a dome for Sultan Selim's mosque that surpasses that of Haghia Sophia.'

Over 200 buildings credited to Sinan still stand, most in Istanbul or Edirne. Apart from Süleymaniye and Sokollu Mehmet Paşa Mosque, the most prominent in Istanbul are the **Rüstem Paşa Mosque** (pictured, *see p83*) and **Şehzade Mosque** (*see p84*).

Ladies of the harem, by a French photographer, 1896. Probably posed by prostitutes.

Although slightly more humane than the earlier fratricidal practices, confinement in the Kafes did little for the captives' mental health. Numerous sultans died prematurely without leaving an heir and their siblings were uniquely unsuited to rule, having spent most of their adult lives incarcerated. In the last years of the empire the problem grew more acute, as successive sultans had little experience of the outside world, or of government. Some simply emerged mad. *See also p18* **Brotherly love?**

THE TURNING POINT

In 1683 the Ottomans failed in a second attempt to take Vienna. This marked the end of Ottoman military successes and expansions and the beginning of a series of reverses. Within three years the imperial armies had lost Buda to the Austrians, and two years after that, Belgrade. More defeats followed. In less than a hundred years, times had changed from the days when Süleyman the Magnificent

was treated as a virtual god and all had to lower their eyes in his presence.

Pleasure-loving sultan Mehmet IV was accused of indifference to affairs of state and deposed by his vizier. His brother Süleyman was appointed instead, but, having spent 40 years in the Kafes, he refused to come out, believing that executioners were waiting to finish him off. He had to be coaxed from hiding like a skittish kitten.

The problem lay not just with addled sultans. In the absence of a strong figurehead, the Janissaries, once the sultan's finest troops, were now completely out of hand, threatening the sultan and killing ministers. Plagues were common. In 1603 a fifth of the population was wiped out, in 1778 a third. Such outbreaks had been eliminated in Europe by the early 1700s by the use of quarantines, but the fatalistic Turks accepted the epidemics as God's will.

Of the advances in science and technology that had begun to revolutionise Western societies and economies in the 18th century, the Ottomans were not only ignorant but arrogantly dismissive. One Turkish dignitary who visited a scientific lab in Vienna in 1748 described it as 'toys' and 'Frankish trickery'.

When Selim III took the throne in 1789, his position was perilous: disobedient guards, recurrent plague, economic decline, military defeats, moribund culture and a restless populace heavily taxed and suffering under poor administration. But he was at least sufficiently aware to know that he had to do something to remedy the empire's ills.

He looked to the West for inspiration. He established a consultative council and Western architectural influences started to appear at the palaces. More crucially, he attempted to reform the army. For this the sultan earned the enmity of the Janissaries, who felt their privileges were being threatened. They rose up in revolt, deposed Selim and murdered him.

'Mahmut banned the wearing of robes and turbans, except for the clergy.'

The Janissaries were finally crushed in 1826 by Sultan Mahmut II (1808-39), who had narrowly escaped from the palace with his life the day Selim had been killed. He went on to implement extensive and much-needed reforms, instigating what historian Philip Mansel calls 'revolution from above'. Local government was introduced to Istanbul for the first time, together with the city's first police and fire services. Quarantine and plague hospitals were established on his orders. He allowed the formation of limited companies and in 1828 brought an Italian conductor to train the imperial band to play Western music.

Mahmut appeared at public functions wearing Western clothes and, most striking of all, banned the wearing of robes and turbans, except for the clergy, introducing the crimson-wool fez from Morocco. This was soon taken to heart by the city, worn by all as a symbol of modernism. More than just a hat, the fez became, in the words of nationalist writer Falih Rifki Atay, 'part of the Turkish soul'. However, Mahmut's addiction to all things Western led to his untimely death – allegedly from cirrhosis caused by a love of champagne.

THE TANZIMAT ERA

Mahmut's successor, Abdül Mecit (1839-61), continued his father's reforming programme, resulting in what was to be a last blossoming of the Ottoman Empire. According to Philip Mansel, 19th-century Istanbul 'owed its grandeur to its defiance of nationalism'; as in the city of Mehmet the Conqueror, race and religion were not supposed to be an issue. Greek, Armenian, Kurd, Circassian, Turk, Christian, Muslim and Jew were all to be equal. To this end, two great imperial decrees of 1839 and 1856 were issued, forming the basis for what was known as *tanzimat* or 'the reforms'.

The sultan further embraced the new era by moving out of Topkapı and into a new Western-style imperial palace at Dolmabahçe. But the real hub of the city was the bridge built across the Golden Horn in 1845. The first bridge to link the two sides of the water, it became the most popular of places; every evening, show-offs from a dozen or more nationalities, would dress up like peacocks and promenade up and down the bridge. Between palace and bridge, the largely non-Muslim, European districts of Galata and Pera (modern-day Beyoğlu), originally founded as Italian traders' enclaves in Byzantine times, were rapidly developing into a new commercial and entertainment district centred on the Grande Rue de Pera, location for an increasing number of theatres, cafés, bars and hotels. Istanbul was shifting its locus from south of the Golden Horn to north.

In the middle of the 19th century, the city began to receive its first proper 'tourists', drawn by the oriental mystique of the capital of the Ottoman sultans. Almost immediately, the sightseeing circuit experienced by visitors today was set. Mark Twain road-tested these early attempts at tour guides in the late 1860s, and described his impressions in *Innocents Abroad*. Tourists dropped anchor in the Golden Horn and were rowed ashore to visit Haghia Sophia ('the rustiest old barn in Heathendom'), the Whirling Dervishes ('about as barbarous an exhibition as we have witnessed'), the Grand Bazaar ('a monstrous hive of little shops') and a hamam ('a malignant swindle'). Twain was, however, fascinated by the beggars – the three-legged woman, the man with an eye in his cheek, the man with fingers on his elbow. His verdict? 'Bismillah! The cripples of Europe are a delusion and a fraud. The truly gifted flourish only in the byways of Pera and Stamboul.'

Had Twain been visiting just 15 years later, his mood might have been improved by the opportunity to roll into Stamboul on the Orient Express, which pulled into Sirkeci station for the first time in October 1883.

Political reforms culminated in 1876 in the drafting of a constitution, and establishment the following year of the first Turkish parliament – albeit with very limited powers. In any case, it was short-lived. A year later, despite their defeat by the Turks and allies in the Crimean War just 30 year earlier, the Russians again seized Ottoman lands in the Balkans and Caucasus. Called to account, Sultan Abdül Hamit responded by dissolving parliament and ruling by decree from his new labyrinthine palace at Yıldız.

A paranoid ruler, he hid at Yıldız in constant fear of being bumped off, and had several close members of his family, as well as countless ministers, generals and other court officials, killed. British prime minister William Gladstone called him the 'Great Assassin'. The Turks simply called him 'Abdül the Damned'.

Reform had already progressed too far to allow this reversion to complete imperial rule. Small clandestine groups later known as 'Young Turks' kept up the pressure for change. Most were crushed, but one, the Committee of Union and Progress, based in Salonika, succeeded in seizing control of the Ottoman army in Macedonia. By 1908 the CUP was powerful enough to send a telegram to the ageing despotic sultan demanding the restoration of the constitution and parliament. Faced with a rebellious revolutionary army marching on Constantinople, Abdül Hamit acceded to their demands.

Atatürk's new Turks

'Happy is he who calls himself a Turk'.
Mustafa Kemal, 1933.

Every 10 November, at 9.05am, Istanbul comes to a halt for a minute's silence to mark the death of Mustafa Kemal Atatürk, 'father of the Turkish nation'. This is the man who took a nascent Turkish resistance after World War I and galvanised it into an army able to defeat the might of the Allies and regain Turkish lands. A man who unified disparate strands of a defeated Ottoman Empire to work towards his vision for an emerging – and radically new – Turkish nation.

After being on the 'wrong' side in World War I, it became obvious that the Allies had the destruction of the ailing and shrinking Ottoman Empire in their sights. The Arab lands were taken at the end of the war; by the end of 1918, the occupation of Thrace and Anatolia was under way. And – symbolically – the British occupied Istanbul.

Appointed Ottoman inspector of the Ninth Army in Anatolia, with a brief to discourage resistance, Mustafa Kemal proceeded to do the opposite. With amazing feats of energy and nerve, he emerged as an unassailable leader, able to bring the Allies back to the negotiating table in 1923. He used his stature to determine the future shape of the Turkish Republic that rose from the ashes of the Empire.

The new Turkish nation was to be totally 'modern'. Some of Atatürk's innovations would be politically inconceivable today – imposing a dress code that made men exchange fezes for hats, for example, or packing provincials off to performances by the newly founded state opera, would be seen as a demeaning apeing of the west by most post-colonial commentators. But

there was no such discourse around in 1927, when Atatürk explained: 'It was necessary to abolish the fez, which sat on the heads of our nation as an emblem of ignorance, negligence, fanaticism and hatred of progress and civilisation.' Atatürk's theory was simple: the West was advanced; Turkey would copy and reap the benefits.

Perhaps the most dramatic piece of social engineering was the adoption of the Roman alphabet – educated people became illiterate overnight and had to learn to read again, while a whole new generation grew up imbibing the new ideology to go with the new script.

Of course, appearing Western was not enough. State intervention in the economy and scientific progress would forge development; social and cultural changes completed the picture. The resulting modernity would become an integral part of a new and unique national identity.

Secularism was another central tenet of the new state, symbolised by the abolition of the caliphate in 1924 – in the face of opposition. Ottomans had not identified themselves as 'Turks'. Their language was Turkish, others called them Turks, but they saw their empire as Islamic, and the caliphate as a divine duty. There was support in some quarters for the idea of a sultan/caliph figure who would act as a sort of Muslim pope. Such an idea was anathema to Atatürk: the Kemalists insisted on the independence of the state from religion. However, this was not quite secularism as understood in the modern West. In Turkey, the state would exercise control over Islam and put it to its service. Here was another crucial marker of the Turkish identity, one that still has repercussions today.

Elections to the new parliament saw all but one of the seats won by the CUP, whose elected deputies included Arabs, Greeks, Jews, Armenians and Albanians. It took a pitched battle in Taksim Square to fight off the challenge of Islamic groups, but once that was won reforms were back on the agenda. What should then have been a period of rebirth was instead one of chaos and turmoil, as Europe saw the imminent demise of Ottoman rule as a chance to carve up what remained of its empire.

EMPIRE'S END

In 1911, Italy seized Rhodes and blockaded the Dardanelles. The following year the Balkan states launched their own offensive, which saw them take all Ottoman possessions in Europe and Bulgarian troops advance to within 40 kilometres (25 miles) of Istanbul. News that Russia, which had long coveted Istanbul and control of the Bosphorus Strait, had joined an alliance with Britain and France left Turkey with little option but to turn to Germany, and the two signed a formal alliance.

Despite a historic victory at Gallipoli, in which they stemmed the Allied invasion and forced a withdrawal, the country was on the losing side in World War I. In the aftermath, they could do nothing but watch as the former Ottoman Empire was divided up between European powers. The British and French took over the Arab lands, occupied Istanbul in 1919 and enthroned a puppet sultan there.

A Greek army occupied much of the remaining territory. Many in Greece had long aspired to the 'great idea' of retaking 'Constantinople' and making it the capital of a Greater Greece. This had support in high places, including from British cabinet minister Lord Curzon, who, in the face of clear evidence to the contrary, claimed that Muslims were in the minority in Istanbul. Greece was permitted by the European powers to occupy parts of the Aegean coast and eastern Thrace.

Turkish leaders in Istanbul seemed incapable of countering the threat. Groups of disillusioned soldiers began slipping out of the city, under the leadership of Mustafa Kemal, the young Turkish general who had masterminded resistance at Gallipoli. In 1919, Kemal led a revolt from the interior, declaring independence and forming a new government in Ankara. 'Henceforth,' he declared, 'Istanbul does not control Anatolia, but Anatolia Istanbul.' In other words: 'Turkey for the Turks.'

After two years of bitter fighting, the Turks forced the Greeks back to Izmir, which was all but destroyed in the final battle. It was a defining moment for the emergent Turkish state, which was now able to negotiate with the Allies on equal terms. In 1922, the sultanate was abolished and the reigning sultan reduced to little more than a ceremonial figurehead.

In fear for his life, the last sultan, Vadettin, fled Istanbul for Italy, with his son accepting the throne. In July 1923, the new state was strong enough to win back some of the territory lost through the treaty of Lausanne, paving the way for a complete allied withdrawal from Istanbul three months later.

LET THE GOOD TIMES ROLL

On 29 October 1923, just a few days after reoccupying Istanbul, Turkey adopted a new secular republican constitution, appointed Mustafa Kemal 'Atatürk' ('father of the Turks') as its president, and chose Ankara as its new capital. The latter was a bold break with almost 1,600 years of tradition, which saw the replacement of one of the world's most fabulous cities by a small, windswept, hillside town that lacked almost every modern amenity, but which was far enough from the new country's borders to make it secure from invasion. Within six months, the 1,300-year-old tradition of the sultanate was completely abolished, and the last members of the Ottoman dynasty were sent into exile, never to return.

Sweeping reforms followed. The European calendar was adopted, then the Swiss civil code and the Italian penal code – abolishing the role of religion in law. The fez – itself a fairly recent replacement for the turban – was banned in favour of Western hats, women were granted equal rights to men, and language reforms replaced Arabic script with the Latin alphabet. Later, in 1935, all Turks were obliged to adopt surnames; lists of suggested names were posted everywhere. The name Constantinople, still common in official and popular usage, was banned because of its imperial associations. The post office would only accept 'Istanbul' as an address on letters.

On a deeper level, Atatürk precipitated a sea change in national self-perception. Previously, 'Turk' was a term applied only to backward provincials; the cultured elite preferred to see themselves as Ottoman. From being the most international of cities, Istanbul rapidly became the most nationalistic.

Although supplanted by Ankara as the country's political powerhouse, Istanbul continued to prosper as the undisputed cultural and economic capital of the new republic. The Grand Bazaar remained the centre of commerce, while Pera – now renamed Beyoğlu – entered a wild and heady period buoyed by pro-Western reforms that allowed for previously unthinkable levels of freedom.

Added to the cocktail were a couple of hundred thousand White Russian refugees who had fled the far more po-faced Soviet revolution, including the odd genuine aristocrat. Russians were to dominate the cultural life of Beyoğlu for decades, opening cafés, bars and restaurants, and even introducing Istanbul to the 'jazz age' via a black American – a certain Mr Thomas – who had owned a famous bar in Tsarist Russia, but joined the exodus to the city of the Bosphorus, where he opened a dance hall.

'Atatürk may have moved the capital to Ankara, but his heart was in Istanbul.'

As a leader, Atatürk was the personification of good-time Turkey. A man of immense energy, he drank and gambled all night, napped for a couple of hours then got up to conduct the country's affairs. He may have moved the capital to Ankara, but his heart was in Istanbul. Atatürk died in 1938. His casket was placed in the throne room of Dolmabahçe Palace, where hundreds of thousands came to view the body. Crowds at the palace grew so disorderly that riot police charged and a dozen people were trampled to death. He was succeeded by Ismet Inönü, who had masterminded the Turkish forces in the war against Greece, but Atatürk's reputation has not been allowed to die: his image is still very visible all over Istanbul.

TURKIFICATION AND TURMOIL

At the renewed outbreak of war in Europe, Turkey opted to remain neutral. Battle did go on in Istanbul, however, as the city became the espionage capital of World War II. No fewer than 17 different intelligence agencies operated here; and half the population seemed to be making a living peddling information. Allied and axis spies would regularly dine at the same restaurants, such as Rejans (*see p121*), just off Istiklal Caddesi, where they would glare at each other across the room. Occasionally the rivalry would turn violent. In 1941 a bomb hidden by pro-Axis Bulgarian agents in the luggage of the British ambassador exploded shortly after he had arrived at the Pera Palas Hotel. The ambassador escaped unhurt, but six Turks were killed and the hotel lobby seriously damaged. To the chagrin of the British government, it was then sued for compensation by the Turkish authorities. The cracks in the marble on the walls of the lobby can still be seen today. For more on this period, read the excellent *Istanbul Intrigues* by Barry Rubin.

Packed with refugees from all over Europe, Istanbul was also something of a safe haven for

Jews escaping the Nazis. Purges in Germany had coincided with a reorganisation of Istanbul University, and by 1940 the institution employed some 120 Jewish exiles, many of them leaders in their respective fields.

However, Istanbul's indigenous religious minorities, who at the time still accounted for around one-third of the city's total population, were less fortunate. In 1942, on the pretext of combating war profiteering, the Turkish government introduced an 'asset tax', which was levied primarily on Jews, Armenians and Greeks. Fortunes accumulated over generations were wiped out overnight, as many were forced to sell off their assets to Muslims at a fraction of their worth. Thousands of those who were still unable to meet their payments were deported to labour camps in eastern Turkey. Although repealed in 1944 under pressure from the British, the tax dealt the minorities of Istanbul a crippling financial and psychological blow from which they have never recovered. The result was a steady flow of emigrants to Greece, the US and, after 1948, the new state of Israel.

Turkey finally entered the war on the Allied side in February 1945, in order to secure a seat at the United Nations when it was founded later that year. Turkey also sided with the West during the Cold War. Under pressure from its new allies, Turkey introduced parliamentary democracy; in 1950, in the first fully free elections, the Democrat Party (DP) led by Adnan Menderes swept to power with a huge majority. With the help of an economic boom assisted by anti-Soviet US aid, Menderes was able to reshape Istanbul with mass imports of cars and trucks and a programme of road-building implemented to accommodate them. Vast areas were flattened to make way for the broad concrete strips of Vatan Caddesi, Millet Caddesi and Atatürk Bulvarı.

But the boom proved short-lived. Menderes became increasingly nationalistic and authoritarian. In September 1955, he attempted to exploit tensions over Cyprus by encouraging anti-Greek protests in Istanbul. The protests became a riot and then a pogrom, as mobs attacked the Greek population, killing and looting. The police, apparently under orders not to intervene, stood back and watched. The pogrom sounded the death knell for the Greek community. Emigration accelerated. Today there are only 2,500 Greeks left in Turkey, fewer than the number of expatriate Britons.

In 1960, as Menderes moved to stifle all opposition to his rule, the military staged a coup and, in 1961, hanged Menderes and two of his senior ministers for treason. Although democracy was restored and a new constitution promulgated, the 1960s were characterised by a

Anti-Greek riots of 1955 hastened the end of the Greek community in Istanbul. *See p26.*

rise in political extremism, initially on the far left. Istanbul became the scene of mass demonstrations and terrorist attacks. The extreme right responded in kind. In 1971 the military intervened again, toppling the government and appointing an administration of technocrats.

But within a few years of the restoration of civilian rule, the streets of Istanbul were the battleground for a low-level civil war between left-wing extremists and far-right groups, who often worked in tandem with elements inside the security forces. Both groups conducted armed robberies to finance campaigns of assassinations, arrests, demonstrations and bombings. On 1 May 1977, unidentified gunmen opened fire on a leftist May Day rally in Taksim Square, killing 39 demonstrators. The violence escalated. By 1980, the daily death toll in Istanbul rarely fell below 20. A succession of weak coalition governments in Ankara seemed unable or unwilling to tackle the problem, with the prime minister Suleyman Demirel dismissing the anarchy as mere hooliganism. On 12 September 1980, to the relief of much of the population, the military seized power again.

For the next three years, Istanbul was under martial law. The ruling military junta banned public meetings, outlawed all existing political parties, closed newspapers and magazines, burned books and arrested tens of thousands of real or suspected political activists, many of whom were subjected to torture. The repression

took its toll on public sympathy for the military. When, in 1983, the junta restored civilian rule by allowing free elections, Turks rejected the military's preferred party and voted over-whelmingly for the broad-based Motherland Party and its founder Turgut Özal.

A NEW COSMOPOLITANISM

Faced with an economy that still closely resembled those found throughout Eastern Europe, Ozal implemented a series of market-oriented reforms that helped attract investment, but also brought widespread corruption and sleaze. As the Turkish saying goes, 'He who holds the honeypot is going to lick his fingers.' He also relaxed controls on religious organisations, allowing the creation of hundreds of religious-instruction schools that within a decade would become breeding grounds for Islamist extremism.

Ozal's economic reforms quickened the pace of urbanisation as millions of Anatolian peasants moved to major cities – particularly Istanbul – in search of a better life. They settled on the city fringes in *gecekondu* – literally 'night settlements', a term used to describe squatter houses put up overnight without permission. These newcomers swelled the population from three million in 1970 to approximately 12 million in 2003, changing the shape of the city. Istanbul has become a collection of villages with names such as 'little Gazientep' and 'little Sivas', named after the Anatolian towns from which most residents originate. In 2003, an estimated 500 peasants were still arriving in Istanbul every day from Anatolia.

Cheap labour from the *gecekondu* helped fuel the economic boom of the 1980s, although the spread of unplanned suburbs put an unbearable strain on the city's infrastructure, clogging roads and polluting out-of-town reservoirs, leaving some areas without water for weeks at a time. The new arrivals also brought with them the piety of the Anatolian villages, where many paid only lip-service to Atatürk's secularising reforms. In the local elections of March 1994, 40-year-old Tayyip Erdoğan became the city's first Islamist mayor in republican history. Erdoğan used his record as mayor of Istanbul – where even his opponents grudgingly admit he improved services – as a platform to enter national politics. He became prime minister in March 2003.

The city continues to grow, not just outwards but upwards. In the last two decades, a series of high-rise office blocks and luxury hotels have transformed the skyline. Many belong to large corporations that have grown rich on the back of Ozal's free-market reforms. Others have been constructed by Turkey's drug barons, who launder their profits from the lucrative heroin trade by pumping money into real estate. Over 80 per cent of the heroin entering Europe goes through Istanbul, much of it refined in temporary laboratories set up in the *gecekondu*, then smuggled across the border in trucks. Recently, smugglers have begun dealing in a new commodity: people. Nobody knows how many illegal immigrants are smuggled through Istanbul each year on their way to Europe, but estimates range from 150,000 to half a million.

Many of these migrants from Africa and Asia have stayed on to work in the city's vast, unregistered economy of factories, sweatshops, construction sites, bars and restaurants. Added to them is a massive influx of Eastern Europeans, who started arriving after the collapse of communism. Millions flocked to Istanbul to sell cheap consumer goods by day (and often themselves by night), transforming areas such as Laleli to the south of the Golden Horn into vast street markets.

In the meantime, the city has also regained much of its assertiveness and pride, becoming a regular venue for international conferences, cultural and sports events, and a seemingly permanent contender to host the Olympic Games. Ambition off the field has been accompanied by success on it, particularly in football. Galatasaray, one of the top three Istanbul teams, won the UEFA Cup in 2000. The European football authorities have just awarded Istanbul the right to stage another

prestigious final, the UEFA Cup final, in 2009. And the Formula One race track has already hosted two Turkish Grand Prix events.

After decades of neglect, money is being invested in preserving the city's battered heritage and upgrading its creaking infrastructure. A long-awaited metro system, promising relief from the worst of the traffic congestion, opened in 2000, tram and light railway lines are being extended, and construction of the Marmaray, a tunnel below the Bosphorus that will link the European and Asian shores, is finally underway. Although no one doubts that the city, for all its bewitching beauty, still has major congestion problems, there is visible progress in the right direction.

'Orhan Pamuk's Nobel Prize is a coup for contemporary Turkish literature.'

Other recent improvements to city life include cleaner streets, pedestrianisation projects, more trees and parks, and a clean-up of the Golden Horn. Cultural innovations have developed apace. But if local residents are enjoying a better quality of life, there is still much political tension to contend with. On 15 November 2003, two truck bombs hit different Istanbul synagogues. Five days later, there were two more explosions, this time directed at British targets – the British consulate and HSBC bank. Over 60 people were killed. The perpetrators claimed links with Al-Qaeda.

Meanwhile, Turkey's EU membership ambitions seem to be no nearer to realisation. The Turkish parliament has failed to ratify reforms in key areas, particularly the improvement of human rights and curbs on the political power of the military. This procrastination has reinforced opposition to Turkey's EU accession from some member states. France's lower house of parliament proposed a bill in 2006 that – if passed – would make it an offence to deny the Armenian genocide. Many see this as part of a concerted campaign to prevent Turkish accession.

In 2006, the Nobel Prize for Literature was awarded to Istanbul novelist Orhan Pamuk, who has written extensively about his native city. Reviled by nationalists, Pamuk's outspoken criticism of taboo issues, like the treatment of Armenians and Kurds, has got him into trouble with the Turkish state; he was tried (and acquitted) for 'insulting Turkishness'. But whether or not the Nobel jury's decision was politically motivated, the prize was recognised by Pamuk's friends and foes alike as a coup for contemporary Turkish literature.

Key events

Pre-history
7000 BC Neolithic fishing settlements at Kadıköy, Pendık and Yarımburgaz.
3200 BC Bronze Age settlement at Sarayburunu.
750 BC Greek sailors pass through the Bosphorus.

The Greek colony
675 BC Greek colony of Chalcedon founded in what is now Kadıköy.
658 BC Greek colony of Byzantium founded.
546 BC Byzantium falls to Persians.
129 BC Creation of Roman province of Asia Minor; Byzantium keeps independence.
AD 73 Byzantium incorporated into Roman province of Bithynia.
196 Byzantium sacked by Roman Emperor Septimius Severus.
324 Constantine defeats co-emperor,makes the city new capital of Roman empire.

From Eastern Rome to Byzantine Empire
326-330 Constantine christens city 'New Rome'. Instead it becomes Constantinople.
413 Theodosius II constructs new city walls.
537 Emperor Justinian dedicates new cathedral of Haghia Sophia.
745-7 Plague wipes out one third of the city.
976-1025 Reign of Basil II, longest reigning and most successful Byzantine emperor.
1071 Selçuk Turkish army conquers Anatolia.
1096 First Crusade reaches Constantinople, helps recapture lands lost to Selçuk Turks.
1147 Manuel I makes peace with Selçuks.
1204 Fourth Crusade sacks Constantinople.

Ottomans at the gate
1394-1442 Ottomans besiege the city of Constantinople four times.
1453 Mehmet II conquers the city and declares it capital of the Ottoman empire.
1492 Spain's exiled Jewish population invited by Beyazıt II to settle in Istanbul.
1517 Selim the Grim captures Cairo and appoints himself Caliph of all Islam.
1520-66 Reign of Süleyman the Magnificent.

Decline of the empire
1566 Beginning of the 'rule of women'.
1622 Janissaries murder Sultan Osman II.
1651-1783 Janissaries revolt 11 more times.
1778 Plague wipes out one third of the city's population.

1807-8 Janissaries wage civil war.
1813 Hundreds of thousands die of plague.
1826 Janissaries destroyed by Mahmut II.

Reform, repression and revolution
1839 Beginning of the 'Tanzminat' era.
1845 Galata bridge spans the Golden Horn.
1854-6 Crimean War and revolts against Ottoman rule in the Balkans.
1877 First Ottoman parliament.
1878 Russians sieze Balkans, Abdül Hamit closes parliament and rules by decree.
1883 Orient Express pulls into Istanbul.
1899 'Young Turk' groups formed in military.
1908 First elections. CUP emerges victorious.
1912 First Balkan war.
1913 Second Balkan war.

The Great War & aftermath
1914 Ottomans enter war on German side.
1918 Allied forces occupy Istanbul.
1919 Atatürk declares independent Turkey.
1922 After two years fighting Turks force Greeks out of Iznik. Sultanate abolished.

The Republic
1923 Allied occupation of Istanbul ends, Ankara declared capital of new republic.
1938 Atatürk dies.
1935-1941 Turkey provides safe haven for Jews fleeing German Reich.
1950 First democratically elected Turkish government.
1960 Prime Minister Adnan Menderes deposed in coup, hanged the following year.
1971 Instability in government and extremism prompts second army coup.
1980 Warring between left and right groups prompts military coup. Over 100,000 arrests.
1983-present Growth of shanty towns on the outskirts of Istanbul as migrants move in.
17 August 1999 Earthquake devastates parts of Istanbul and north-west Turkey.
November 2003 Over 20 die in suicide bomb attacks on synagogues. Bombs hit British consulate and HSBC bank, killing 58.
January 2000 Turkish novelist Orhan Pamuk acquitted of 'insulting Turkishness' for discussing the killing of Kurds and the Armenian genocide.
March 2006 Syrian national Loai al-Saqa on trial accused of masterminding 2003 terrorist attacks with support of al-Qaeda.
October 2006 Orhan Pamuk wins the Nobel Prize for Literature.

Istanbul Today

The city speeds towards the future, but knows where it comes from.

Forget the hippy trail, magic buses and *Midnight Express*. Istanbul today is a bustling and multi-centred metropolis that has gone through such a colossal makeover in recent years as to be unrecognisable as the 'eastern' city of 1960s and '70s traveller folklore. Istanbul now somehow combines the hippest contemporary styles with a history that goes back millennia – and a dedication to the secular with a strong backdrop of the religious. In short, the city is about as 21st century as it gets.

Anything goes in Istanbul – from global finance to whirling dervishes, rooftop bars to Byzantine mosaics. Growing out of a tiny hilltop settlement roughly where Topkapı Palace now stands, the metropolis now stretches along both the Asian and European shores so far that it swallows whole neighbouring villages and towns. With a population estimated between 12 and 15 million, Istanbul will officially take the mantle of Europe's largest city if Turkey ever joins the European Union. It will also be the city with the continent's youngest population, with the average age currently around 16.

Istanbul plays an enormous role in the Turkish economy too, responsible for much of the country's wealth and many of its jobs. It has acted as a magnet for migrants, investors, pirates and armies for some 2,700 years – and that is not about to stop now.

ALL CHANGE

Yet for all its history, the life that many Istanbullus lead now is really the result of some relatively recent changes. Ten years ago, entertainment in Beyoğlu was confined to a handful of *birahanes* and a couple of dodgy clubs, while a 'rock bar' skulking under Galata Bridge was the centre of edgy Istanbul bohemia. Now, there are more bars than that on a single side street off the main pedestrian drag, Istiklal Caddesi – and the variety among them is close to legendary. Istanbul as a city of nightlife has not so much grown as detonated, with the country's late, late baby boomers coming of age at the end of the 1990s and into the 2000s – then heading out to play.

The city's transformation has not just benefitted barflies either. A recent flourishing of the arts was crowned with the opening of Istanbul Modern in 2005, the Bosphorus-side venue that has joined a rash of galleries and museums opened since the new millennium. The metro many residents felt would never be finished is now functioning, and the Marmaray rail tunnel project will soon link the city's two continents. Istanbul also boasts the largest shopping mall, by square footage, in Europe; while the traditional Grand Bazaar has been relegated to little more than a giant, neon-lit souvenir shop. There's even a second airport – quite something considering that only a decade ago Turkey had larger provincial railway stations than Istanbul's Atatürk International Airport.

Speedy changes have often been the Turkish way. After all, Kemal Atatürk – the Republic's founder, who is still omni-present in busts and portraits – decided to change the country's alphabet more or less over lunch. Adopting a Western outlook and way of life was planned to take a little longer – but not much longer.

Likewise, the optimism inherent in such attempted transformations can be seen in the municipality's regular efforts to pave Istiklal Caddesi. A few days before the start of many international conferences and public holidays, the street is frantically ripped up and relaid with a new combination of cement and bricks. Since nowhere near enough time is ever allowed for this, the labourers toil heroically through the night – despite streams of drunken revellers who totter merrily past.

'Istanbul faces enormous strains as it grows.'

With luck, the new pavement is ready by the appointed date; yet, almost certainly, having been laid in such haste, it will need ripping up and relaying again soon after the delegates or holidaymakers have gone home. And there's the rub. Overnight changes may show great energy and enthusiasm, but often leave a question mark over just how much they've really taken hold.

On the radio

Acik Radio is like bouillabaisse soup, says its founder and director Omer Madra, because 'everything is in it.' Except for one thing: 'No pop music. We do every other music – world music, jazz, alternative, classical, anything a bit outside the mainstream.' Acik Radio, which means 'Open Radio', does have an amazingly eclectic programme, ranging from ancient music to cutting-edge electronica. Surprisingly, these incongruous genres blend well together.

But Acik is not only diverse in its choice of music. During the day, it hosts a variety of talk shows and current affairs programmes that underline the station's founding principles to strengthen democracy and support human rights. You might come across two 10-year-olds reviewing a new children's book, or a literature professor presenting a series on Don Quixote. Several programmes are presented in foreign languages by members of Istanbul's growing international community. For three years, the New York Times bureau chief presented his own blues session, which opened with the eccetric cry of 'Tarzan!'.

According to Madra, all the programmes have one thing in common: 'They try to read between the lines.' However, the station's 'anything goes' attitude often upsets the censorious Turkish authorities. After broadcasting a Bukowski novel, the station was banned for two weeks because of the 'lewd' language.

Acik was set up ten years ago during the media revolution that swept Turkey following the lifting of a state monopoly on broadcasting. Within a few months, thousands of radio stations opened across the country. In Istanbul alone, over 400 stations were launched; more than 200 are still broadcasting today.

Another unique feature of non-commercial Acik is that all the 120 contributors are volunteers. 'The term "amateurs" may sound negative, but amateurs know their subject best because they study it out of love. This is what our shows offer: passion and knowledge,' Madra explains. The station's growing audience, which is roughly 50 per cent women, obviously like what they hear. These loyal listeners provide around a third of Acik Radio's budget. If you get hooked too, you can tune into Acik back home on the web (www.acikradyo.com.tr) or through cable TV.

But Acik Radio's unexpected success has brought one disappointment for Madra. 'I set up this station so I could host my own programme, but until now I've been too busy. And I don't see that changing any time soon.

Fatih. *See p84.*

THE WEALTH GAP

Stray beyond the triangle of land bordered by the Bosphorus at the bottom and up to the Galata Tower, via Taksim, Cihangir, Teşvikiye, Esentepe and Etiler, and you will find that the rest of this vast, sprawling city can be of quite a different character. You don't need to go too far to find yourself on the 'wrong' side of the tracks – one street should normally do it. Istanbul is a city of highly visible wealth gaps, with super-clubs along the Bosphorus charging money for a margarita that would make even a Londoner blush – and for which your average Ahmet or Ayşe would have to blow a week's wages.

Despite these social divides, Istanbul is largely untroubled by the kind of crime that other big cities so often suffer. While street theft has been on the rise in recent years, Istanbul remains generally safe to walk around, even after dark. Istanbullus also retain that friendliness to visitors that has long since vanished from many other cities.

A SENSE OF PLACE

This is partly because there is a great pride among the city's inhabitants about the place where they live – even if most of them don't originally come from Istanbul. Turks generally give their hometown as the place where their family originates, leading to a variety of answers to the standard 'where are you from?' question that can stretch from Bosnia to Damascus. Like as not, they will never have been to such places in their lives, and were been born just up the road in an Istanbul hospital.

Yet only a tiny minority will claim to be 'from Istanbul', given that such a hometown would imply a pedigree stretching back generations – to Ottoman times at least. Perhaps among the 'old money' families of Nişantaşı, or among the residents of the vast *yalıs* on the Bosphorus one might meet such people, but this native aristocracy can be elusive. That doesn't stop the other, temporary residents – who go back only three or four generations – from puffing their chests with pride as they sweep their arm across the waterfront view and exclaim, 'Ah, Istanbul!'

CREDIT FOR GROWTH

Like many cities, Istanbul faces enormous strains as it grows, pulling in more and more of the world surrounding it. The end of the Cold War saw the Bosphorus reopen as a major waterway to the Black Sea ports, to Ukraine,

Istanbul by numbers

Moving
Number of commercial vessels that pass through the Bosphorus every year: 53,000
Number of ships carrying dangerous cargo that pass through the Bosphorus every 55 minutes: 1
Number of sunken ships in the Bosphorus: 24
Number of cars that cross the city's two intercontinental bridges daily: 345,212
Number of road vehicles in Istanbul: 1,800,000

Spending
Amount state auditors determined elite nightclub Reina rakes in on a single Friday night: $100,000
Number of people who live on less than $1 a day in Turkey: 136,000
Average bank balance of each Istanbul resident, in euros: 1,490
Ranking of Turkey in the world's most-taxed population list: 1
Ratio of tax paid to estimated taxable income undeclared in Istanbul: 1:1

Working
Average monthly salary of a married Turkish police officer, in euros: 520
Average monthly salary for an Istanbul doctor, in euros: 1,291
Number of Turkish citizens classified as poor: 6,308,000
Percentage of Turkish civil servants who live below the poverty line: 42.7
Percentage of people working in Turkey's finance and banking sector who are women: 50
Percentage of Turkish members of parliament who are women: 3.5.

Living
Number of apartments in Istanbul: 3,393,077.
Average number of people living in an apartment in Istanbul: 3.85.
Density of population per kilometre in Istanbul: 21,928.
Number of people who move to Istanbul every day: 500.
Average number of people who commit suicide annually in the city: 430.
Ranking of Istanbul in the worldwide 'Quality of Life' list: 76.

A popular destination for a day out: **Sultanahmet**. *See p65.*

Russia and Georgia. At the same time, the Turkic states of the former Soviet Union opened up, leading to a 1990s infatuation with the newly rediscovered 'cousins' of Azerbaijan, Uzbekistan, and beyond. People from these territories looked to Istanbul as a kind of promised land, a city of great wealth and opportunity. Meanwhile, as Turkey liberalised its economy and politics, Western businesses and professionals also made a beeline for the city, adding to the cosmopolitan mix.

Presiding over much of this has been another peculiarly Turkish phenomenon, the liberal Islamist city authority. Although the greater city council has been run since 1994 by one version or other of the country's ruling Justice and Development Party, which has Islamist roots, this has been no bar to the development of a liberal economy – or liberal attitudes towards drink, dress and decorum. That is, provided this liberal behaviour is confined to certain unspoken but widely understood geographical boundaries. No one will open a night club in Fatih; on the other hand, no one will mind you dancing in a bikini in Ortaköy. The Justice and Development Party has also made serious efforts to drive out some of the more corrupt practices of previous authorities.

Meanwhile, trade has boomed. Istanbul's financial district is a serious business hub; the new Manhattan-like skyline springing up in Levent, where banks and finance houses are building their head offices, is testament to this. And the strategic importance of the city has never vanished – although it has occasionally been forgotten. Istanbul, Constantinople, Byzantium –in their day, they were all the richest city on earth, and the reasons for their wealth have not all vanished. If you live at the crossroads between two continents, commerce comes naturally.

Of course, the stresses and strains of this ongoing expansion are obvious in the chaotic traffic, in the gradual elimination of all green space by concrete and ash block, in the architectural horror stories that abound. Even this glorious city of stunning skylines can take on a grim, ugly aspect at times. But take a drive over the Fatih Sultan Mehmet bridge at dusk, look down at the ferries, tankers and fishing boats chugging along the winding blue channel below, and up to the glimmering minarets and swooping seagulls overhead, and few cities can ever have looked so beautiful.

Like any great city, Istanbul is a place of contradictions – although here, the clash of opposites can be more acute. That sense of endless permutations is, of course, essentially what makes this city so fascinating and exciting. This expectant sense of unlimited possibilities also gives Istanbul a freshness, despite its ancient past. For many years, the city slumbered in a kind of post-war gloom – but now the lights are all back on.

Istiklal Caddesi.

People, Faith & Politics

Unravelling Istanbul.

For a city of around 12 million people – no one can quite keep count – Istanbul can still feel like a pretty small place. For a city of great traditions, it can also feel pretty modern. And for a city of the East, it can feel westernised. It's the largest city of a secular state, yet many of its citizens are pious Muslims. In short, Istanbul is as diverse as a plate of mixed *meze*.

Walk out the door and you can move from medieval to ancient to futuristic within a few paces. In a single day, you can watch Dervishes whirl, crawl around a Byzantine dungeon, take tea in an art nouveau café, sip Mojitoo in a trendy rooftop bar, then listen to the prayer calls of a hundred muezzin ripple around the hills of one of the oldest cities on earth.

Unsurprisingly, Istanbul attracts more than its fair share of clichés about bridges between continents and civilisations, worlds colliding and opposites attracting. In reality, contemporary Istanbul is much more of a complex jigsaw than a simple 'crossroads' between Europe and Asia.

Like the convoluted plots of the city's most famous author, Orhan Pamuk (*see p97* **The city's narrator**), the multi-layered, multiple cities within the city are Istanbul's assets. And these split personalities are real: they don't conceal one inner core of true identity. Peel away the layers and more layers are revealed, vestiges of 2,700 years of complicated and often bloody history.

YOUNG TURKS, OLD HABITS

Living with this eclecticism is an art that Istanbullus have, for the most part, perfected. At times, it simply means living with contradictions, focusing on one aspect of the city's character over another. Taken to extremes, it could mean that a young Turk might go out clubbing until dawn, but the following day will have tea and baklava with their extended family and discuss whom their older sister should marry. The guy wearing the Nirvana T-shirt with an encyclopaedic knowledge of British indie bands might think it's wrong for a woman to work outside the home. And who knows, that headscarfed woman hurrying home to cook her husband's supper could be late because she has just spent the afternoon with her lover.

Istanbul is a kaleidoscope, a city in which the picture can change dramatically in a few seconds, depending on where you're viewing from. The variety of images to choose from is growing too. Istanbul has a young population, which contributes to its raw energy and a sense of experimentation that sanitised western European capitals have often lost. This is a city with a hunger and a capacity for change, for embracing the new. A certain naivety may go along with this, but nonetheless there is a sense that these kids have never stayed out so late before. This isn't what dad – or even granddad – did.

These observations will not make sense to many, if not most, of the city's inhabitants, who take their city's multiple personality for granted, or simply do not mix much outside their own group. Just down the hill from Akmerkez, the upmarket mall favoured by the residents of Etiler's leafy avenues of villas, is a shanty town, or *gecekondu*, that was once a 'liberated zone' for a revolutionary Marxist party. As recently as 2001, its members were still on hunger strike in its woeful 'death houses'. Strike out just a little off the beaten track and you will find areas of the city where Kurdish is more widely spoken than Turkish. One such area is the working-class suburb of Gaziosmanpaşa, yet few of the residents here will ever set foot in 'old money' neighbourhoods, such as Nişantaşı and Teşvikiye.

A KALEIDOSCOPE OF CULTURES

Istanbul is a city of many ethnicities and religious groups. There are the Alevis, a religious community that is said to make up around 20 per cent of the city's population, but gets scant official recognition. Disregarded by most Sunni Muslims as not really Muslims at all, the Alevis' beliefs combine elements of Shia Islam with the animist religions of ancient Anatolia. Many of the city's bars and late-night dives reverberate to the music of the Roma, yet the gypsies themselves, who often inhabit the more run-down areas of Galata and Beyoğlu, are treated as outcasts.

Istanbul's other minorities include Laz from the Black Sea coast; remnants of the Greek Armenian and Jewish minorities; and a few Syriac Christians, a community centred on Mardin and Antioch, who still use a version

of the Bible in Aramaic, the language of Jesus and Mel Gibson movies. Venture down to Samatya, in Fatih, and you will meet Greeks and Turks, Christians and Muslims, living side by side – just as they coexisted throughout the city over centuries of Ottoman rule.

The large minorities of previous eras are gone now; the demography of modern Istanbul is instead a reflection of Anatolian migration: over the past 50 years, mass migration has made parts of the city more like a collection of villages, as pockets of people from the same region set up home in the same area.

RELIGIOUS SYNCRETISM

When it comes to religion, the boundaries between communities start to blur. The Greek Orthodox church of Saint George on a hilltop in Büyükada, the largest of the Prince's Islands, is a case in point. On the day of Assumption in August, tradition has it that infertile women should walk barefoot up the hill, tying a piece of string, paper or cloth to a tree as an offering to make their wish for a baby come true. Today, this tradition is still very much alive, but most of the women who make the pilgrimage are Muslim. There is a reverence among many for the 'old ways' – with Christian shrines sometimes seen as having more ancient mystical power than the mosque. Such openness to other ways is, once again, a product of longstanding coexistence.

Take a walk in a graveyard in one of the older mosques in the city, and you may notice some tiny shrines made of twigs and stones, hidden among the larger trees. You may even see someone praying there. This is about as far from orthodox Islam as it gets, yet the devotee is bound to be a faithful Muslim attempting to contact the dead, usually in the hope of finding out about the future. Just as Turks compulsively tell each other's fortunes from the grains of an upturned coffee cup – a ritual practised in humble homes and sophisticated salons alike.

REPUBLICAN RATIONALISM

Just as this kind of superstition is a far cry from the teachings of orthodox Islam, so it is the antithesis of the thinking of Mustafa Kemal Atatürk, the founder of modern, secular Turkey. Atatürk abolished the Caliphate, banned the dervishes, and pushed the imams and sheikhs out of politics. In their place, he hoped to install a new, Europeanised elite, leading a population for whom religion would be a strictly private matter (*see p24* **Atatürk's new Turks**).

The state still adheres to this system. Until recently, the ban on women wearing headscarves in public institutions, such as schools and universities, meant Istanbul's campuses were sometimes shrouded in tear gas, as protesting

Recreating the village in the city: sewing and socialising in Balat.

students in *hijabs* were given a taste of community policing, Turkish style. On national holidays, it is the turn of the secular squad to make their presence felt, marching beneath the flag and portraits of Atatürk, swearing to keep their beloved republic secular.

But, needless to say, when it comes to Istanbul it's not that straightforward. Islamists are also impressed by Atatürk. His face often looks down from portraits kept in the family home, next to a framed verse from the Qu'ran. Muslim women are grateful to him for giving them the right to vote. Bearded men revere him for protecting Turkey from the attacks of the infidel *ingililz* during the First World War, when he became a national hero.

Similarly, it is not uncommon to find more broadminded attitudes among those who vote for Prime Minister Recip Tayyıp Erdoğan's Islamist Justice and Development Party, than among supporters of the secular camp. This is particularly true of the army, which still sees itself as the guardian of secularism in Turkey, the role Atatürk assigned to it in the 1920s. To listen to some of the generals today, you could be forgiven for thinking that the kind of 'modernity' they have in mind is something akin to Mussolini's Italy. Meanwhile, many Islamists have embraced multiculturalism.

THE THING ABOUT SEX

Living with all these conflicting elements and contradictory beliefs at the same time requires a great deal of circumspection. To avoid cultural meltdown, there are many unspoken, but inviolable, social boundaries that keep things compartmentalised. Sexuality is, of course, one such area. Surveys show that many Istanbullus report finding the idea of living next to an unmarried couple worse than living next to an ex-convict. And there is a declared abhorrence of alternative sexuality within mainstream society. Yet behind these rigid attitudes lies a somewhat different reality. Transvestites and transsexuals are not just tolerated but actively enjoyed – as long as they stick to entertainment or prostitution; singers like Zeki Müren (a transvestite) and Bülent Ersoy (a transsexaul) enjoy huge following. Gay sex has actually been a part of the culture since time immemorial (note the popularity of gay hamams with married men). And far more unmarried couples cohabit than society will readily admit.

All this social compartmentalisation is part of the passion and energy of the city. Picture the scene: it's 4am in a club in Beyoğlu. People are already dancing on the tables when a local band takes to the stage. Outside the dark and smoky room, the first glimmers of the rising sun herald the call to prayer from a mosque down the street. At the same time, the female singer rips into a cover version of the Rolling Stones' 'Satisfaction', jumping off the stage into a sea of sweaty fans.

In some ways, this moment sums up this city of contradictions, just as it embodies the fact that this is a city that simply can't be summed up.

Where to Stay

Where to Stay

Ottoman-era boutique hotels in Sultanahmet, sheer luxury beside the Bosphorus or modern style in Beyoğlu.

As a long-standing tourist hotspot that has accommodated curious westerners since the mid 19th century, Istanbul is thick with places to stay in. For the very same reason, many of the city's hotels are rather well-worn. Even some of the five-star pick of the crop have been around since the 1950s and are seriously showing their age.

In some cases, age has been used to good effect. Istanbul has a nice line in 'Ottoman' boutique hotels. These are Ottoman-era houses

The best Hotels

For bold and eclectic design
The aptly named **Eklektik Guest House** (*see p52*).

For faded grandeur
The eccentric **Büyük Londra** (*see p55*) has wind-up gramophones and valve radios on display.

For sheer unrestrained luxury
There's no stinting on the opulence at the **Çırağan Palace Hotel Kempinski** or its new competitor **Hotel Les Ottomans** (for both, *see p57*).

For Ottoman inspiration on a small scale
Ayasofya Pansiyonları (*see p45*); **Empress Zoe** (*see p46*); **Ibrahim Paşa** (*see p47*); **Sarnıç** (*see p49*); **Yeşil Ev** (*see p45*).

For Ottoman inspiration on a grand scale
Hotel Les Ottomans (*see p57*).

For a drink
Yeşil Ev has an idyllic beer garden (*see p134*); the rooftop bar at the **Richmond Hotel**, Leb-i Derya Richmond, has magnificent views (*see p136*).

For seeing the sights on a shoestring
Hotel Hanedan and **Hotel Uyan** (for both, *see p49*).

and mansions, imaginatively converted into unique accommodation with period furnishings. In many cases, the original building has been entirely demolished apart from the facade, then reconstructed in concrete, so guests get nostalgic charm and all mod cons rolled into one. The first of these Ottoman guest-houses was **Ayasofya Pansiyonları** (*see p45*), founded and funded by the Turkish Touring and Automobile Association (TTAA). Committed to the promotion of Turkish culture, the TTAA went on to open several similar hotels; **Yeşil Ev** (*see p45*) is the pick of the bunch. Other businesses and individuals have picked up the baton, such as American Ann Nevans at the **Empress Zoe** (*see p46*), the charming **Ibrahim Paşa** (*see p47*) and **Sarnıç** (*see p49*).

THE DESIGN FACTOR
New openings since our last edition include three Bosphorus-side stunners: **Ajia** and **Sumerhan** (for both, *see p59*), both on the Asian side; and the super-opulent, super-priced **Hotel Les Ottomans** in Kuruçşme (*see p57*). Ajia and Les Ottomans are both converted *yalıs* (waterside houses). Sumerhan's premises were once a distillery. For all three, the waterside location is a huge selling point – the romantic setting is more important than proximity to the city centre. With the arrival of these, along with **Sofa** (*see p57*) in Nişantaşı, and the eclectically decorated and stylish **Eklektik** (*see p52*), the age of the design-led hotel has most definitely arrived in Istanbul.

LOCATION, LOCATION, LOCATION
There are basically two choices: south or north of the Golden Horn (the exceptions are the two hotels we list on the Asian side, *see p59*). Whichever you choose, expect to spend plenty of time in taxis, as most visitors split their time between the two areas. South of the Golden Horn means mosques, the Grand Bazaar, and all the major sights of Sultanahmet. This has traditionally been the centre for the city's budget and mid-range accommodation. Almost

> ❶ Green numbers given in this chapter correspond to the location of each hotel as marked on the street maps. See pp242-51.

The best views in the neighbourhood: **Hotel Uyan**. *See p49.*

all the cheapest options are on and around Akbıyık Caddesi and Utangaç Sokak, two parallel streets east of the Haghia Sophia. Increasingly, the area is moving upmarket and now has one of the best deluxe options in the **Four Seasons** (*see p43*). This is also the area in which you'll find all the Ottoman boutique hotels. Most Sultanahmet hotels have rooftop terraces and it's hard to beat morning coffee and croissants nestled between the domes of the Haghia Sophia and Blue Mosque – a classic Istanbul cleavage if ever there was one.

North of the Golden Horn is the business and entertainment district of Beyoğlu. There are plenty of backstreet mid-range places that put you right among the shops, restaurants, bars and clubs. They lack the views or romance of the Sultanahmet hotels, but are more convenient late at night.

Most of the city's high-rise, high-end options are clustered around Harbiye, an area of green parkland just north of Taksim Square. As well as being close to Beyoğlu, Harbiye is conveniently situated for shopping trips to the fashionable areas of Nişantaşı and Teşvikiye. All the culture of old Istanbul is

a ten-minute taxi ride away, although at the wrong time of day – morning and evening rush hours – that can stretch to half an hour or more.

PERA PALACE
Istanbul's most famous hotel, the Pera Palace – built in 1892 to accommodated guests from the Orient Express – was closed for renovations at the time of writing. In its old incarnation the PP was the epitome of faded elegance, a hotel with an incredibly romantic history; guests had included Sarah Bernhardt, Greta Garbo, Mata Hari, Alfred Hitchcock, Jackie Onassis and Agatha Christie (she wrote part of *Murder on the Orient Express* while staying here). We hope the new Pera Palace, due to reopen in late 2008, will retain its distinctive charms.

RESERVATIONS
In line with the basic economic principles of supply and demand, hotels don't come cheap in Istanbul. Competitively priced places book up quickly, particularly during the summer when they're choked with large tour groups, conventions and conferences. From May to September, Christmas, New Year and national

timeout.com

The hippest online guide to over 50
of the world's greatest cities

Yeşil Ev. *See p45.*

holidays (*see p227*) are the busiest times. Also beware of major cultural events like the various major international film, theatre and music festivals. At such times, you definitely need to book well in advance.

Plenty of hotels now take bookings online and there are also a few useful websites for online reservations, notably www.istanbul hotels.com, which brings together about 80 of the city's hotels and offers discounts for online booking. Alternatively, the website www.istanbul.hotelguide.net provides links to local hotel websites.

If you arrive without a reservation, there are several booking agents at Atatürk Airport in the international arrivals hall (at the opposite end to the tourist information desk). They have an extensive list of mainly three- and four-star hotels and don't charge any commission.

In all but a few of the high-end hotels, room rates include tax (18 per cent) and breakfast. Prices quoted below are high-season rates, which normally apply from the end of May to the beginning of September, at Christmas and New Year, and during national holidays. Outside these times you can expect a discount of up to 30 per cent. Rates are particularly open to bargaining in the mid-range and budget categories, especially if you can pay cash in foreign currency. Most places happily accept euros, dollars or sterling.

Conversely, payments by credit card can often incur a five per cent surcharge.

We have listed prices in this chapter in the currency quoted by the hotels themselves, usually euros, occasionally US dollars or YTL. Hotels in this guide are divided into the following categories: **Deluxe** (more than €200, or $270, a night for a double); **High-end** (€120-€200, $160-$270); **Mid-range** (€50-€120, $70-$160); **Budget** (€25-€50, $30-$70); and **Rock-bottom** (under €25, or $30).

South of the Golden Horn

Sultanahmet & Western Districts

Deluxe

Four Seasons
Tevkifhane Sokak 1, Sultanahmet (0212 638 8200/ fax 0212 638 8210/www.fourseasons.com/istanbul). Tram Sultanahmet. **Rates** $340-$530 single; $370-$560 double; $850-$3,500 suite (excluding tax). **Credit** AmEx, DC, MC, V. **Map** p243 N10 ❶
For 66 years this distinctive building, with its ochre walls and watchtowers, served as the infamous

Haghia Sophia. *See p65.*

Sultanahmet Prison; inmates included celebrated political prisoners. Sensitively renovated in 1986, the Four Seasons has held on to its position as one of Istanbul's best hotels. With its manicured gardens and elegant gazebo restaurant (Seasons Restaurant, *see p116*), the former prison yard has been transformed into an oasis of calm in the heart of bustling Sultanahmet. Cells have been replaced by 65 plush, high-ceilinged rooms and suites – a modest number that ensures intimacy and superlative service.
Bar. Business services. Concierge. Disabled-adapted rooms. Gym. Internet (wireless). Non-smoking rooms. Parking (free). Restaurants (2). Room service. Spa. TV.

High-end

Eresin Crown Hotel

Küçük Ayasofra Caddesi 40, Sultanahmet (0212 638 4428/www.eresincrown.com.tr). Tram Sultanahmet. **Rates** €150-€300 double; €450-€500 suite. **Credit** AmEx, DC, MC, V. **Map** p243 M11 ⓴
The Eresin Crown is unusual as a medium-sized, high-end hotel amid small 'Ottoman' boutique competitors in Sultanahmet: it's on the southern side of the peninsula, a stone's throw from Sultanahmet Mosque. Decor in the public spaces is pretty standard, of the marble and plate glass variety, but the hotel's unique selling point is its basement museum, containing 49 artefacts discovered when the hotel was being built. Some rooms are on the small side, but all are comfortable and well appointed, with jacuzzis; there are several suites. The Terrace Restaurant has amazing views over the city, the Bosphorus and Sea of Marmara. The Eresin is a choice worth considering if you want to be near the sights, but prefer accommodation with international-style features and facilities.
Bars. Business centre. Internet (wireless). Room service. Restaurants (2). TV.

Yeşil Ev

Kabasakal Caddesi 5, Sultanahmet (0212 517 6785/ fax 0212 517 6780/www.istanbulyesilev.com). Tram Sultanahmet. **Rates** €125 single; €165 double; €250 suite. **Credit** AmEx, MC, V. **Map** p243 N10 ❷
Flagship of the Turkish Touring and Automobile Association's fleet of restored Ottoman properties, the 'Green House' enjoys an unrivalled location on a leafy street midway between the Haghia Sophia and Sultanahmet Mosque. Entering this stately wooden mansion is like stepping on to the set of a 19th-century costume drama. Every room is decked out in reproduction furniture, complete with wood-panelled ceilings, creaky parquet flooring and antique rugs. The Sultan's Suite boasts its own hamam. The idyllic garden is one of the highlights, with a pretty pink pond, a fine café and beer garden (*see p134*) and the restaurant. With only 19 rooms, booking in advance is essential. Be sure to ask for a room on the first floor, overlooking the cobbled street – with no televisions in the hotel, you'll want the view. **Photo** *p43*.
Internet (wireless). Parking (YTL20 day). Restaurant. Room service.

Mid-range

Armada

Ahırkapı Sokak 24, Cankurtaran, Sultanahmet (0212 455 4455/fax 0212 455 4499/www.armada hotel.com.tr). **Rates** $80 single; $90 double; $225 suite. **Credit** AmEx, MC, V. **Map** p243 O11 ❸
Sandwiched between waterside Kennedy Caddesi and the suburban railway line, the Armada scores low on location, although it is only a ten-minute walk up the hill to sight-studded Sultanahmet. The real advantage is that most rooms have fantastic, uninterrupted Bosphorus views. Modelled on a row of 19th-century houses that once stood here, the building is now a bit stuck in the 1980s. The fancy lobby has a terrapin pond and café, while the 110 rooms, if not exceptional, are certainly comfortable and slightly bigger than the average Sultanahmet room.
Bars (2). Business centre. Concierge. Disabled-adapted rooms. Internet (wireless). No-smoking rooms. Parking (free). Restaurants (4). Room service. TV.

Hotel Ararat

Torun Sokak 3, Sultanahmet (0212 516 0411/ fax 0212 518 5241/www.ararathotel.com). Tram Sultanahmet. **Rates** €45-€75 single/double; €55-€75 room with view; €55-€80 triple; €75-€115 suite. **Credit** MC, V. **Map** p243 N11 ❹
Opened in 2000, Ararat's best feature is probably its location. Envious of the success of the nearby Empress Zoe, the young Turkish owners of Ararat recruited the same architect, Nicos Papadakis, to revamp their 11-room guesthouse. If the results aren't quite as inspired, the Ararat still breaks the mould with marbled walls and an orange and ochre colour scheme that works well with the dark, stained-wood floors. Rooms vary widely in terms of size and comfort – some are windowless boxes, while others have wooden four-posters with wonderful views of Sultanahmet Mosque. There's also a roof terrace for breakfast.
Bar. Internet (wireless). Parking (YTL15 day). Restaurant. Room service.

Ayasofya Pansiyonları

Soğukçeşme Sokak, Sultanahmet (0212 513 3660/ fax 0212 513 3669/www.ayasofyapensions.com). Tram Gülhane. **Rates** €70 single; €90 double; €140 suite. **Credit** AmEx, MC, V. **Map** p243 N10 ❺
In the 1980s, the Turkish Touring and Automobile Association reconstructed this row of nine clapboard houses dating from the 19th century. They were painted in pastel colours and furnished in period style. Rooms are all painted different colours and most have big brass beds. The setting is a dream: a sloping cobbled lane hidden between the high walls of Topkapı Palace and the back of Haghia Sophia. Breakfast is served in the pretty garden or gazebo of the Konut Evi, a four-storey annexe at the end of the alley. At night, the whole place is lamp-lit. Walt Disney couldn't create more magic.
Bar. Internet (wireless). Parking (free). Restaurants (2). Room service.

Citadel

*Kennedy Caddesi 32, Ahırkapı (0212 516 2313/
fax 0212 516 1384/www.citadelhotel.com).*
Rates €70 single; €90 double; €125-€150 suite.
Credit MC, V. **Map** p243 O11 **6**
Occupying a striking pink three-storey mansion, this
Best Western affiliate has 25 rooms and six suites
decked out in Barbie colours. The only thing
between you and the Sea of Marmara is – alas – six
lanes of speeding traffic. It's not far from the fish
restaurants of Kumkapı, though, and the conservatory bar and decent restaurant lessen the feeling of
isolation. Free airport pick-ups. **Photo** *p45.*
*Bar. Concierge. Internet (high-speed). Parking (free).
Restaurants (3). Room service. TV.*

Dersaadet

*Kuçuk Ayasofya Caddesi 5, Sultanahmet (0212 458
0760/www.dersaadethotel.com).* **Rates** €60-€85
single; €70-€100 double; €90-€130 triple; €120-€220
suite. **Credit** MC, V. **Map** p243 M11 **7**
In recent years, the Dersaadet (one of the many former names for Istanbul) has become one of the
most popular boutique hotels south of the Golden
Horn. The hotel's quaint wooden exterior and old-
fashioned decor (antique furniture, painted ceilings,
brass chandeliers) recreate the charms of the
Ottoman golden years. The 17 rooms on four floors
are all comfortable, although none have especially
remarkable views. The best room is the Sultan's

Suite, which has a low wooden ceiling, big windows and jacuzzi. There's a rooftop breakfast
terrace overlooking the Bosphorus and a café on
the ground floor. The place is owned and run by a
family that has been in the hotel business for the
last three generations.
*Bar. Internet (wireless). Restaurants (2). Room
service. TV.*

Empress Zoe

*Adliye Sokak 10, off Akbıyık Caddesi, Sultanahmet
(0212 518 2504/fax 0212 518 5699/www.emzoe.
com). Tram Sultanahmet.* **Rates** €70 single; €95
double; €100 triple; €105-€160 suite. 10% discount
for cash. **Credit** MC, V. **Map** p243 O11 **8**
Named after a racy Byzantine regent, the Zoe is one
of the best and quirkiest of the city's small hotels.
Its sunken reception area incorporates parts of a
15th-century hamam; the 'archaeological garden' –
ideal for breakfast or a beer – is idyllic. Bear in mind
that guests must be agile, as rooms are reached via
a wrought-iron spiral staircase. In contrast to the gilt
and frills of most other 'period' hotels, the Zoe's 19
small rooms are decorated in dark wood and richly
coloured textiles. A new wing of suites has recently
been added and the garden expanded. Add a fine
rooftop bar for a nightcap with a view and this place
is sheer class from top to bottom.
*Bar. Internet (wireless). Restaurant. Room
service. TV.*

The chain gang

A growing number of global chains have
branches in Istanbul (including the **Four
Seasons**, *see p43*; and **Kempinski**, *see
p57*). Apart from these two, don't expect
a great deal of character, but rest assured
that you'll get the same standard of service
and level of comfort you found at the same
chain's outlet in Dallas, Kuala Lumpur, or
anywhere else in the world.

The **Hilton Istanbul** (Cumhuriyet Caddesi,
Harbiye, 0212 315 6000, www.hilton.com,
map p247 P1) was the first of the modern,
high-rise blocks to brutalise the skyline.
Given the price bracket, it's far from
exceptional in terms of rooms, decor and
facilities, although the parkland setting is
a bonus. It's a ten-minute walk north of
central Taksim Square.

The **Hyatt Regency Istanbul** (0212 225
7000, Taşkışla Caddesi, www.istanbul.hyatt.
com.tr, map p247 P1) is to be commended
for keeping its building low-rise. The Hyatt
scores high on business facilities, with an
information library and private offices for
rent. There's also a luxury 'apart-hotel' with

its own separate check-in and elevators.
The hotel is a ten-minute walk north-east
of Taksim Square.

The **Mövenpick** (0212 319 2929,
Buyukdere Caddesi 4, www.movenpick-
hotels.com) towers above the business
district of Levent. People loyal to the
brand won't be disappointed; for that early
morning meeting, ask for a room with an
espresso maker.

The **Ritz-Carlton** (0212 334 4444, Asker
Ocaği Caddesi, www.ritzcarlton.com, map
p247 Q1) occupies the appalling blue-glass
tower block that dominates the city skyline.
The interior is bland, but facilities are good
and the Çintemani restaurant is excellent.
You'll need a taxi to get anywhere.

The **Swissôtel Istanbul The Bosphorus**
(0212 326 1100, Bayıldım Caddesi 2,
Maçka, www.swissotel.com, map p247 R1)
sits on the hillside above the Dolmabahçe
Palace. Rooms are exceptionally comfortable,
with gadgets galore. Sports facilities are
particularly good, as is the Japanese
restaurant, Miyako.

Ibrahim Paşa Hotel

*Terzihane Sokak 5, Sultanahmet (0212 518 0394/
fax 0212 518 4457/www.ibrahimpasha.com).
Tram Sultanahmet.* **Rates** €95 single/double;
€135-€175 deluxe. **Credit** AmEx, DC, MC, V.
Map p243 M11 **9**

Tucked round the corner from the Museum of
Turkish and Islamic Art, the Ibrahim Paşa is an emi-
nently likeable small hotel. It doesn't overplay the
old Ottoman card and instead is stylishly modern,
smart and bright, with just enough judiciously
placed artefacts (including some fascinating old photographs in the breakfast area) to remind you that
this is Istanbul. Rooms can be small, but judicious
use is made of space. The buffet breakfast is a daily
treat of wonderful cheeses, honey, bread, olives and
much more. Staff are helpful; the ambience calm and
relaxed. There are plenty of minarets and domes on
show from the rooftop terrace. **Photo** *p52.*
*Bar. Internet (wireless). Parking (free). Restaurant.
Room service. TV.*

Kariye Hotel

*Kariye Camii Sokak 18, Edirnekapı, Western
Districts (0212 534 8414/fax 0212 521 6631/
www.kariyeotel.com).* **Rates** €50-€70 single;
€70-€80 double; €80-€90 deluxe; €90-€100
suite. **Credit** AmEx, MC, V. **Map** p244 D4.**10**

Another 19th-century Ottoman residence stripped
down and dressed up by the Turkish Touring and
Automobile Association and pressed into service as
a hotel. There are 26 rooms, all done out in early
1900s fashion. The restaurant, Asitane (*see p117*),
is renowned for its authentic Ottoman cuisine. Next
door is the Church of St Saviour in Chora (*see p86*),
one of Istanbul's essential sights. But the big snag
is the location, out by the old city walls and about a
half-hour bus ride from Sultanahmet, or around
YTL10 in a taxi. But if you had a reason to be in this
part of town, this would be the place to stay.
*Bar. Concierge. Internet (wireless). Parking (free).
Restaurant. Room service. TV.*

Kybele Hotel

*Yerebatan Caddesi 33-35, Sultanahmet (0212 511
7766/fax 0212 513 4393/www.kybelehotel.com).
Tram Sultanahmet.* **Rates** €60-€70 single; €80-€100
double; €120 triple/suite. 10% discount for cash.
Credit MC, V. **Map** p243 N10 **11**

The Akbayrak brothers obviously have a thing
about vintage glass lamps – the interior of their hotel
is hung with 2,000 of them. The eccentricities continue: every room is crammed with kilims, candle-
stands, empty bottles and quirky knick-knacks.
Garish pink and green paint schemes heighten the
sense of fun. It all makes sense when you learn that
one of the brothers was formerly an antiques dealer,
while another spent three years with an Australian
circus. The 16 bedrooms are smallish, particularly
the singles, but they are comfortable enough and all
have fancy marble bathrooms. Breakfast is served
in a courtyard as colourful as a gypsy caravan.
*Bar. Internet (wireless). Parking (YTL10 day).
Restaurant. Room service.*

Sarnıç. *See p49.*

St Sophia
*Alemdar Caddesi 2, Sultanahmet (0212 528
0973/fax 0212 511 5491/www.saintsophia
hotel.com). Tram Gülhane.* **Rates** $70 single;
$90 double; $150 suite. **Credit** AmEx, DC, MC,
V. **Map** p243 N10 ⑫
In the shadow of the Haghia Sophia and across
the road from the Yerebatan Sarnıcı, this Best
Western affiliate is yet another conversion of a
19th-century house. Extensive renovations have
left it a bit over-polished and lacking in atmosphere. The 27 rooms have modern furnishings;
those on the top two floors have jacuzzis and balconies that overlook Justinian's great cathedral.
Service can be rather slow.
*Bar. Café. Internet (wireless). Parking (free). Room
service. TV.*

Sarniç
*Kuçuk Ayasofya Caddesi 26, Sultanahmet (0212
518 2323/www.sarnichotel.com).* **Rates** €45-€60
single; €60-€75 double; €80-€90 triple. **Credit** MC,
V. **Map** p243 M11 ⑬
Sarniç, the Turkish word for cistern, takes its
name from the fifth-century Byzantine cistern
beneath the hotel, which guests can explore from
9am to 6pm. Owned and managed by Eveline
Zoutendijk, a feisty Dutch lady (formerly of the
Four Seasons chain), Sarniç is a tightly run place
with ambitions above its modest appearance.
Think free wireless internet, fluffy towels, complimentary toiletries and an in-house massage
therapist. The 16 rooms are immaculate. The top-
floor terrace makes a scenic setting for breakfast
and four-course dinners that showcase regional
Turkish cuisine. Zoutendijk, a former Cordon Bleu
chef, also organises half-day cookery courses in
the hotel kitchen. The hotel is only a few minutes'
walk from the Hippodrome. **Photo** *p47.*
*Bar. Concierge. Internet (wireless). Massage.
Restaurant. Room service. TV.*

Turkoman
*Asmalıçeşme Sokak 2, off the Hippodrome,
Sultanahmet (0212 516 2956/fax 0212 516 2957/
www.turkomanhotel.com). Tram Sultanahmet.*
Rates €59-€79 single; €69-€99 double;
€89-€139 triple/suite. **Credit** AmEx, MC, V.
Map p243 M11 ⑭
'You can almost touch the exciting and amazing
Blue Mosque with your hands right through the
window of your room', according to the hotel website. And it's not too far wrong. Located just off the
Hippodrome and opposite the Egyptian obelisk, the
Turkoman's roof terrace does indeed have amazing views of the Sultanahmet Mosque, although in
the summer the mosque is hidden from the lower
floors by foliage. Bright, unfussy and very yellow
rooms verge on the tacky, but have brass beds, parquet flooring and big windows. Free one-way airport transfer is available for guests staying more
than three nights.
*Bar. Café. Concierge. Internet (wireless). Restaurant.
Room service. TV.*

Budget

Hotel Hanedan
*Adliye Sokak 3, Akbıyk Caddesi, Sultanahmet
(0212 516 4869/fax 0212 458 2248/www.hanedan
hotel.com). Tram Sultanahmet.* **Rates** €25-€35
single; €35-€45 double; €45-€65 family room.
10% discount for cash. **Credit** AmEx, MC, V.
Map p243 O11 ⑮
Hanedan is one of the smartest independent hotels
south of the Four Seasons. Clean, bright primrose-
yellow rooms with large beds draped with muslin
all have ensuite bathrooms with hairdryers and
heated towel rails. The three family rooms (a double
and two twins) have the best Marmara views. There
are more unobstructed views from the roof terrace.
It can be noisy on summer nights, when neighbouring hotels often host late-night rooftop parties.
Internet (wireless). Room service.

Nomade Hotel
*15 Ticarethane Sokak, Sultanahmet (0212 513
8172/fax 0212 513 2404/www.hotelnomade.com).
Tram Sultanahmet.* **Rates** €60 single; €75 double;
€90 triple. **Credit** MC, V. **Map** p243 N10 ⑯
The funky reception with comfortable, colourful
furnishing is perfect for watching the bustling pedestrian traffic outside, while the cushion-strewn,
flower-filled roof terrace is one of the prettiest in
Istanbul. Following a successful makeover in 2004
by a French interior designer, there are now 16 cosy,
uncluttered rooms with pastel walls, ethnic bed-
spreads, richly hued wall hangings and modern
bathrooms. Esra and Hamra, the French-educated
twins who run the place, ensure that standards
remain high and service is personal. They also run
the charming Rumeli Café across the road.
Internet (wireless). Restaurant. Room service. TV.

Side Hotel & Pension
*Utangaç Sokak 20, Sultanahmet (0212 517 2282/
fax 0212 517 6590/www.sidehotel.com). Tram
Sultanahmet.* **Rates** €20-€45 single; €30-€60 double;
€35-€70 triple. **Credit** V. **Map** p243 N11 ⑰
The hotel rooms are clean and well looked after, and
have ensuite bathrooms with shower cubicles (the
Istanbul budget norm is usually a showerhead that
falls straight on to the bathroom floor). Rooms vary
widely, so ask to look at a few before you make your
choice. Pension accommodation is more basic; the
cheapest room has a shared but clean bathroom.
There are two self-catering appartments for large
groups. Breakfast is served on the rooftop terrace.
There's free tea available in the rustic, wood-panelled foyer and a small book exchange.
*Internet (wireless). Room service (hotel rooms). TV
(hotel rooms).*

Hotel Uyan
*Utangaç Sokak 25, Sultanahmet (0212 516 4892/
fax 0212 517 1582/www.uyanhotel.com). Tram
Sultanahmet.* **Rates** €30-€40 single; €40-€50 double;
€80-€140 deluxe. **Credit** MC, V. **Map** p243 N11 ⑱

This attractive corner hotel in a 75-year-old building was renovated in 2002. There are 16 spacious standard rooms and ten suites spead over four floors. The standard rooms are simply furnished, with small bathrooms. Deluxe suites boast a jacuzzi and sound system in the bathroom. With so many similar places competing for business nearby, Uyan's main selling point is that it has the highest roof terrace in the neighbourhood, with views over the Sultanahmet Mosque. If you're not an early riser, avoid room 309, which lies directly underneath the breakfast room. The hotel offers free airport pick-ups.
Bar. Internet (wireless). Parking (€3 per day). Restaurant. Room service. TV.

Rock-bottom

Orient Hostel

Akbıyık Caddesi 13, Sultanahmet (0212 518 0789/ fax 0212 518 3894/www.orienthostel.com). Tram Sultanahmet. **Rates** YTL18-YTL20 dorm bed; YTL22.50 single; YTL32.50 deluxe. **Credit** AmEx, MC, V. **Map** p243 N11 ⑲
For years the Orient has been the mainstay of the Istanbul backpacker scene, base camp for a constant stream of wanderers tramping across Asia or through the Middle East. Besides the full range of budget traveller services, including cheap internet access, money-changing facilities and discounted airline tickets, the Orient has a lively social scene, with barbecues, belly-dancing and film nights. There is also a women-only dormitory.
Bar. Café. Internet. Restaurant.

Sultan Tourist Hostel

Terbıyık Sokak 3, off Akbıyık Caddesi, Sultanahmet (0212 516 9260/www.sultanhostel.com). Tram Sultanahmet. **Rates** YTL20 dorm bed; YTL35 single; YTL50 double. **Credit** MC, V. **Map** p243 N11 ⑳
Another backpacker staple, virtually next door to the Orient, the Sultan has bright and airy singles, doubles and mixed-sex dormitories, although having only a single shower/toilet on each floor is a major drawback. There's a restaurant up top, as well as a bar, pub, disco, games room with table tennis and darts, and computer centre.
Bar. Concierge. Internet. Parking (free). Restaurants (2). Room service. TV.

Yeşilköy

High-end

Polat Renaissance Istanbul Hotel

Sahil Caddesi, Yeşilköy (0212 414 1800/fax 0212 414 1970/www.polatrenaissance.com). **Rates** €170 single/double; €325 suite. **Credit** AmEx, DC, MC, V.
Our airport hotel of choice, the Polat Renaissance is a five-minute taxi ride from the terminal in the coastal suburb of Yeşilköy (it's 18 kilometres, or 12 miles, from the city centre). A 27-storey blue glass

skyscraper by the sea, the ultra-modern interior features a soaring central atrium. At least half the 390 rooms have views over the Marmara. All the facilities you would expect of a Marriott hotel, including a heated outdoor pool.
Bars (3). Business services. Concierge. Disabled-adapted rooms. Gym. Internet (wireless). Non-smoking rooms. Parking (free). Pool (1 indoor, 1 outdoor). Restaurants (5). Room service. Spa. TV.

North of the Golden Horn

Beyoğlu

Deluxe

Ceylan Inter-Continental

Asker Ocağı Caddesi 1, Taksim (0212 368 4444/fax 0212 368 4499/www.interconti.com.tr). **Rates** €325 standard room; €1,060 suite. **Credit** AmEx, DC, MC, V. **Map** p247 P1 ㉑
Formerly the Sheraton, the Inter-Continental is an 18-floor Goliath. The style is brash, the tone set by a golden staircase spiralling up from the lobby and a glitzy, palm-filled atrium. Decor aside, the hotel is well appointed, although most of the 335 rooms are a bit smaller than others in this price category. Those on the Club Floor (actually the top four floors) are preferable, but pricey. Mick Jagger, Liz Taylor and Roger Moore are some of the celebrities who have stayed in the four lavish Presidential Suites. The Safran restaurant and top-floor City Lights bar offer spectacular views but steep prices. The hotel is a ten-minute walk from central Taksim Square.
Bar. Business services. Concierge. Disabled-adapted rooms. Gym. Internet (wireless). Non-smoking rooms. Parking (free). Pool (outdoor). Restaurants (3). Room service. Spa. TV.

The Marmara Istanbul

Taksim Square, Taksim (0212 251 4696/fax 0212 244 0509/www.themarmarahotels.com). **Rates** €283-€303 single; €325-€345 double; €346-€1,240 suite. **Credit** AmEx, DC, MC, V. **Map** p249 P2 ㉒
A Taksim Square landmark , the Marmara is the place to stay if you want to be at the heart of the action. Turkish-owned (with sister establishments in Manhattan and all over Turkey), it isn't quite as polished as its international rivals. The street-level Marmara Café, with picture windows overlooking the square, is an established meeting place for the city's chic set (as is the flash gym). The glass-walled, first-floor Aqua Lounge, with its vast aquarium, is popular with businessmen socialising during conferences. The 410 rooms have the facilities and feel of a big chain hotel. Most have decent views, but the best lookout spot is from the top-floor Tepe Lounge.

Ottoman inspiration and modern style at the **Ibrahim Paşa**. *See p47.*

*Bars (3). Business centre. Café. Concierge. Gym.
Internet (wireless). Non-smoking rooooms. Parking
(free). Pool (outdoor). Restaurants (2). Room
service. Spa. TV.*

Divan Hotel

*Cumhuriyet Caddesi 2, Taksim (0212 315 5500/
fax 0212 315 5515/www.divanoteli.com.tr).* **Rates**
$230 single; $260 double; $425 suite. **Credit** AmEx,
DC, MC, V. **Map** p247 P1 ㉓
This 169-room hotel, part of a Turkish chain, benefits from a decent location just north of Taksim
Square. It's slightly old-school in appearance – very
1970s (which in Istanbul generally means it dates
from the mid 1980s) – but the interior is well looked
after. Rooms are large, but avoid those overlooking
the busy main road, Cumhuriyet Caddesi.
*Bars (2). Business services. Café. Concierge. Disabled-
adapted room. Gym. Internet (wireless). Non-smoking
rooooms. Parking (free). Restaurants (2). Room
service. Spa. TV.*

High-end

Richmond Hotel

*Istiklal Caddesi 445, Beyoğlu (0212 252 5460/fax
0212 252 9707/www.richmondhotels.com.tr).* **Rates**
$200 single; $230 double; $300 suite. **Credit** AmEx,
MC, V. **Map** p248 M4 ㉔
The Richmond is the only hotel on Istiklal Caddesi.
This scenic pedestrian street, lined with shops, cafés,
bars and plenty of grand old apartment blocks ripe
for conversion, has been oddly overlooked by hotel
developers – until now. The Richmond has retained
the building's historic façade, but ripped out the interior and replaced it with a spanking new structure.
What the interior lacks in style, the hotel makes up
for with a relaxed atmosphere and friendly staff.
Standard rooms are simple and streamlined, while
the executive suites cater mainly to business travellers. Trendy Leb-i Derya's new rooftop bar-restau-
rant (*see p136*) at the Richmond has upped its
position in the style stakes. The circular bar at the
centre is popular for cocktails.
*Bars (2). Business services. Café. Concierge. Disabled-
adapted rooms. Gym. Internet (wireless). Non-
smoking rooooms. Restaurants (2). Room service. TV.*

Mid-range

Eklektik Guest House

*Kadribey Cikmazi 4, Galata (0212 243 7446/fax
0212 243 7445/www.eklektikgalata.com).* **Rates**
€65-€100 double. **Credit** AmEx, DC, MC, V.
Map p248 M4 ㉕
This hip guesthouse on a quiet cul-de-sac is popular
with gay visitors, but the friendly and knowledgeable staff make everyone feel welcome. Each of the
seven rooms is beautifully decorated to a distinctive
theme: from clean lines, white walls and wood in the
Zen Room to drapes and ornate lamps in the Colonial

Where to Stay

Hotel hamams

Turkey is famous for its hamams, but for those who prefer their treatments more spa-like and less spartan, Istanbul hotels are opening their own, western-style spas – most include brand new Turkish baths for a western hotel take on the traditional hamam experience. Spa facilities aren't restricted to hotel guests, and a few hours' pampering can be a perfect pick-you-up. All the spas recommended below include an indoor pool, sauna, Turkish bath and steam room.

If you can't afford a $3,000-a-night room at the exclusive **Les Ottomans Hotel** (*see p57*), check into the basement Caudalie Vinothérapie spa instead. Facilities include a tiled hot tub and indoor pool with natural light filtered through the glass bottom of the above-ground pool. For around $100 a day, visitors can use the pools, exercise equipment, sauna (with flat-screen TV), steam room, Turkish bath and 'salt

inhalation therapy' room. There's even a meditation room, complete with a cascade of lavender-infused water. Best of all, indulge in one of the treatments using grape-based Caudalie products.

Another luxury hotel that's big on spa treatments is the **Çirağan Palace Kempinski** (*see p57*). In summer, you can take full advantage of your environment by booking a poolside massage in a private cabana with views of the Bosphorus. A vast range of treatments using Decléor products is available. The Traditional Çirağan Body Scrub ($100) is pure bliss.

An Asian-inspired ambience, expert staff and Molton Brown products are the hallmarks of the Laveda Spa at the **Ritz-Carlton** (pictured, *see p46*). One of the city's most exclusive spas, its menu features a Traditional Turkish Hamam treatment, including massage ($70).

Room. There is also a terrace with views over the Bosphorus. Staff will arrange tours, transportation or restaurant bookings. For late risers, continental and Turkish breakfast is served all day.
Concierge. Internet (wireless). Parking (free). Room service. TV.

The Madison Hotel

Recep Paşa Caddesi 23, Taksim (0212 238 5460/fax 0212 238 5151/www.themadisonhotel.com.tr). **Rates** €70 single; €90 double; €250 suite. **Credit** AmEx, MC, V. **Map** p247 P1 ❻

North-west of Taksim Square, between Tarlabaşı Bulvarı and Cumhuriyet Caddesi, are a series of quiet streets that are home to a handful of good mid-range hotels, including this one. The Madison is a modern four-star place with decent-sized rooms. Insipid colour scheme aside, there's little cause for complaint. Bathrooms are small but clean and pracitcal, decked out in marble, and some thoughtful person has even thought to put an extra telephone next to the toilet. The indoor pool-side bar is a relaxed place to hang out.
Bar. Concierge. Gym. Internet (wireless lobby access). No-smoking rooms. Parking (free). Pool (indoor). Restaurant. Room service. Spa. TV.

Taksim Square Hotel

Sıraselviler Caddesi 15, Taksim Square (0212 292 6440/fax 0212 292 6449/www.taksimsquare hotel.com). **Rates** €70 single; €80 double. **Credit** AmEx, DC, MC, V. **Map** p249 P2 ❼

Bang in the centre of town, this modern, high-rise hotel is modestly priced but lacks charm. Just 32 of the 87 rooms have a view across the rooftops to the Bosphorus; in the rest, guests have to be content with looking down on the street life on busy Sıraselviler and the diners on the rooftop terrace of Burger King opposite.
Bars (2). Business services. Café. Concierge. Disabled-adapted room. Internet (wireless). Restaurants (2). Room service. TV.

Taksim Suites

Cumhuriyet Caddesi 49, Taksim (0212 254 7777/ www.taximsuites.com). **Rates** €190-€210 single suite; €210-€236 double suite; €354 penthouse. **Credit** AmEx, MC, V. **Map** p247 P1 ❽

Operated by the Divan hotel chain (*see p52*), these self-catering suites make an ideal base for business people. Japanese minimalism meets Swedish chic in the elegant, open plan interiors decorated in neutral shades. Fully equipped with everything from a microwave to a fax machine, the five options range from a 45sq m (480sq ft) studio to a 109sq m (1,150 sq ft) penthouse with remote-controlled skylights and Bosphorus views. Additional treats include breakfast in bed (or the Taksim Lounge), jacuzzis, fitness room, wireless internet, and accommodating staff who will buy your groceries if you leave a shopping list at reception. Another plus is the excellent location minutes from Taksim Square.
Business services. Concierge. Gym. Internet (high-speed). Room service. Spa. TV.

Budget

Avrupa

Topçu Caddesi 30, Talimhane, Taksim(0212 250 9420/fax 0212 250 7399). **Rates** YTL60 single; YTL80 double. **Credit** MC, V. **Map** p247 O1. ❾

In business since 1966, the Avrupa has a cheerful orange, green and yellow colour scheme. The unfussy rooms with small ensuite bathrooms are good value. There's a breakfast room but no restaurant or bar – not really a problem when you're so close to Taksim Square.
Room service. TV.

Büyük Londra Hotel

Meşrutiyet Caddesi 117, Tepebaşı (0212 245 0670/ fax 0212 249 1025/www.londrahotel.net). **Rates** €50 single; €60 double; €150 'super' rooms. **Credit** AmEx, MC, V. **Map** p248 M3 ❿

The Londra was built in 1892, so it's roughly the same age as the nearby Pera Palas (*see p40*). But whereas the Pera Palas is like a sleep-in museum, the Londra is homely and eccentric. Caged parrots peer dolefully out from their cages on the windowsills in the lounge-bar (*see p135*). Portable coal burners, wind-up gramophones, valve radios and plenty of other ancient junk clutter the corridors. Hemingway stayed here in 1922, sent by the *Toronto Daily Star* to cover the Turkish war of independence, and the place is still favoured by artists, writers and film crews. Some of the 54 rooms are a little down-at-heel, but they are clean. The upper floors have 'super' rooms with double glazing, plush carpets and jacuzzis.
Bar. Internet (wireless lobby access). Room service. TV.

Monopol

Meşrutiyet Caddesi 223, Tepebaşı, Beyoğlu (0212 251 7326/fax 0212 251 7333). **Rates** YTL50 single; YTL80 double; YTL100 suite. **Credit** MC, V. **Map** p248 M4 ⓫

The Monopol is the best of a row of otherwise rather nondescript mid-range hotels. Despite the early 1980s appearance, the hotel has actually been open for less than ten years. The 75 rooms, all with ensuite bathrooms, are a decent size and well equipped. The desk staff make the effort to be friendly and speak good English.
Internet (wireless lobby access). Room service. TV.

Residence

Sadri Alışık Sokak 19, off Istiklal Caddesi, Beyoğlu (0212 252 7685/fax 0212 243 0084). **Rates** YTL70 single; YTL100 double; YTL120 suite. **Credit** AmEx, DC, MC, V. **Map** p247 O3 ⓬

The Residence is a bit difficult to find as it's tucked away on a narrow side street, but it's worth the effort. The rooms, though small, are bright and well equipped. The location is great too, right among the bars of Beyoğlu.
Bar. Restaurant. Room service. TV.

Bentley. *See p57.*

Vardar Palace Hotel

Sıraselviler Caddesi 54, Taksim (0212 252 2888/fax 0212 252 1527/www.vardarhotel.com). **Rates** €48-€60 single; €60-€75 double. **Credit** AmEx, MC, V. **Map** p249 O3 ③

Two minutes from Taksim Square, the 40-room Vardar occupies a drab-looking 19th-century building on Istanbul's sleaziest strip, where Sıraselviler narrows to almost canyon-like proportions. Inside, however, the hotel is bright, pleasant and deserving of its three-star status, although the airiness of the high-ceilinged rooms is sabotaged by a dark colour scheme. Front-facing rooms can get noisy.
Bar. Concierge. Internet (wireless). Parking (free). Restaurant. Room service. TV.

Villa Zurich

Akarsu Yokuşu Caddesi 44-46, Cihangir (0212 293 0604/fax 0212 249 0232/www.hotelvillazurich.com). **Rates** €60-€80 single; €75-€100 double; €120-€150 sea view. **Credit** AmEx, MC, V. **Map** p249 O4 ③

Ten minutes' walk down Sıraselviler Caddesi from Taksim Square, in the *yabancı* (foreigner) neighbourhood of Cihangir, the Villa Zurich is conveniently close to the centre but pleasantly removed from all the hustle. The area itself is worth exploring – a lively mix of local shops and tea houses mixed with hip cafés and gourmet delis. The Villa Zurich is vaguely European in character, with 43 comfortable, if unremarkable, guest rooms. Unfortunately, the popular rooftop bar means that the only rooms with a view are now very noisy.
Bar. Concierge. Internet (wireless). Non-smoking rooms. Parking (free). Restaurant. Room service. TV.

Nişantaşı & Şişli

Deluxe

The Sofa Hotel

Teşvikiye Caddesi 123, Nişantaşı (0212 368 1818/fax 0212 359 9117/www.thesofahotel.com). **Rates** €470 single; €530 double; €590-€1,420 suite. **Credit** AmEx, DC, MC, V

The Sofa Hotel offers minimalist chic in the heart of Nişantaşı's upmarket shopping and dining area, and is also within walking distance of the Istanbul Convention and Exhibition Center. The design-led bedrooms are comfortable, and the well-equipped bathrooms feature rainshowers, natural soaps and fluffy bathrobes. There's a decent spa and fitness room, and the in-house restaurant serves up mod Med cuisine in handsome surroundings.
Bar. Business services. Café. Concierge. Disabled-adapted rooms. Gym. Internet (wireless). No-smoking rooms. Parking (YTL15 day). Restaurant. Room service. Spa. TV.

Bentley Hotel

Halaskargazi Caddesi 75, Harbiye (0212 291 7730/fax 0212 291 7740/www.bentley-hotel.com). **Rates** €200 single; €240-€280 double; €400-€800 suite. **Credit** AmEx, MC, V.

Istanbul's first (self-proclaimed) 'hip' hotel, the Bentley's minimalist chocolate-and-cream lobby looks like the reception area of an upmarket ad agency. Rooms are similarly smart and understated. Best options are the corner rooms with curving glass walls (a pity there's not much of a view). The two penthouse suites have wine minibars, plasma TVs and espresso machines. One comes with an adjacent single room suitable for a nanny or bodyguard. Despite the stylish amenities you would expect from a member of the Design Hotels group, beware of noisy rooms and occasionally indifferent staff. **Photo** p56.
Bar. Business services. Concierge. Gym. Internet (high-speed). Non-smoking roooms. Parking (free). Restaurant. Room service. Spa. TV.

Bosphorus Villages

Deluxe

Çırağan Palace Hotel Kempinski

Çırağan Caddesi 32, Beşiktaş (0212 258 3377/fax 0212 259 6687/www.ciraganpalace.com). **Rates** $240-$1,400 standard room; $1,480-$2,360 suite. **Credit** AmEx, DC, MC, V.

The hotel is an annexe to a 19th-century palace on the Bosphorus built for Sultan Abdülaziz, an ill-fated ruler who killed himself with a pair of scissors in one of its chambers. In 1908, the palace became the seat of parliament, but burned down two years later. In 1986, following an ambitious restoration, parts of the original complex were incorporated into this super-luxurious, 315-room extravaganza belonging to the Kempinski chain. Only 12 suites are in the palace itself, along with the restaurants (Laledan serves great seafood; Tuğra showcases Ottoman cuisine) and public rooms. The latter are worth a look for the bizarre decor, described by one journalist as 'post-Orientalist psychotropic'. All other bedrooms are in the annexe. Be sure to ask for a sea view. In summer, take advantage of the stunning outdoor infinity pool, which appears to flow into the Bosphorus. **Photo** p57.
Bars (2). Business centre. Concierge. Disabled-adapted room. Gym. Internet (wireless). Non-smoking roooms. Parking (free). Pools (1 indoor, 1 outdoor). Restaurants (4). Room service. Spa. TV.

Hotel les Ottomans

Muallim Naci Caddesi 168, Kuruçşme (0212 287 1024/fax 0212 287 6061/www.lesottomans.com). **Rates** €1,200-€5,400 suite. **Credit** AmEx, DC, MC, V.

Opened in spring 2006, this all-suite hotel is designed to lure celebrities, heads of state and millionaires bored of the Çırağan Palace. In an impeccably restored white wooden *yalı* (mansion), the style is Oriental opulence – to excess. Think brocade drapes, Arabic-script inscriptions and giant chandeliers. With just 12 suites, the emphasis is on exclusivity. Butler, yacht and limousine service are all part of the package. The Passionate Suite is, of course,

billed as the perfect honeymoon destination – with feng shui to 'add a completely new freshness and purity to your life as a couple'. There's an intimate Ottoman restaurant with an impressive cellar and a fabulous Caudalie spa (*see p53* **Hotel hamams**).
Bar. Business services. Concierge. Gym. Internet (wireless). Non-smoking roooms. Parking (free). Pool (indoor). Restaurant. Room service. Spa. TV.

High-end

Bebek Hotel

Cevdet Paşa Caddesi 34, Bebek (0212 358 2000/ www.hotelbebek.com). **Rates** $190 street view; $295 water view. **Credit** AmEx, MC.

Far from the centre and the sights, this is primarily a business hotel. From the outside, the four-storey building is nothing special, but inside the 21 suites are all gleaming dark wood, brown leather, pink marble and rattan furniture. The real wow factor here is the view, and half the rooms have balconies over the Bosphorus. Is it worth the extra $105? We'd have to say yes. However, if you get stuck with a room overlooking the street, you can enjoy the same view from the waterfront bar downstairs. Beware of Bebek in the summer, when the traffic into town can be agonisingly slow. **Photo** *p59.*
Bars (2). Café. Concierge. Internet (wireless). Parking (free). Restaurant. Room service. TV.

Princess Hotel Ortaköy

Dereboyu Caddesi 10, Ortaköy (0212 227 6010/fax 0212 260 2148/www.ortakoyprincess.com). **Rates** €118 single; €148 double; €308-€444 suite. **Credit** AmEx, DC, MC, V.

Few people other than those doing business up in nearby Levent and Maslak choose to stay in Ortaköy, but if scurrying around the mosques isn't on your agenda, this rather bland option is worth considering. A modern hotel with 82 generously sized rooms, its most appealing feature is probably its proximity to the waterfront bars, cafés and fish restaurants. You can avoid the traffic that clogs Istanbul's roads by catching a ferry down the Bosphorus to the sights in Sultanahmet.
Bar. Business services. Café. Concierge. Gym. Internet (wireless). Non-smoking rooms. Parking (free). Pool (outdoor). Restaurants (2). Room service. Spa. TV.

Mid-range

Galata Residence

Felek Sokak 27, off Bankalar Caddesi, Karaköy (0212 292 4841/fax 0212 244 2323/www.galata residence.com). **Rates** €90 for an apartment for two; €140 for an apartment for four (excluding tax). **Credit** MC, V. **Map** p246 M6 ⑤

An apartment hotel with history. The house formerly belonged to the Kamondos, an important Levantine banking family, who gave their name to the sculpted steps that lead up to the residence from Voyvoda Caddesi. The solid brick building later served as a

Çırağan Palace Hotel Kempinski. *See p57.*

An idyllic Bosphorus setting: the waterfront bar at the **Bebek Hotel**. *See p58.*

Jewish school. It is now split into 15 comfortably furnished apartments, which sleep four. Smaller two-bedroom apartments are available in the next building. The decor is homely in an old-fashioned way, with four-poster beds, vintage armchairs and sofas. Each apartment has a fully equipped kitchen, but there's also a restaurant on the roof and a bare-brick café in the vaulted cellar. It is close enough to walk across the bridge to Eminönü and the bazaar, but just downhill from the Galata Tower and Beyoğlu.
Café. Internet (high-speed). Parking (free). Restaurant. Room service. TV.

Camping

Ataköy Tatil Köyü

Rauf Orbay Caddesi, off Ataköy Tatil Köyü, Bakırköy (0212 559 6014/fax 0212 560 0426). **Rates** $10 per tent (two-man); $6 per caravan; $2.50 extra for car. **Credit** DC, MC, V.
On the Marmara coast about 15 kilometres (10 miles) from the centre, this campsite is conveniently situated near Ataköy train station, from where there are regular trains into Sirkeci. The site is clean and has good facilities, including a tennis court, pool (summer only) and bar, although make sure you don't get a pitch too close to the noisy road.

Asian Shore

Deluxe

Ajia

Ahmet Rasim Paşa Yalısı, Çubuklu Caddesi 27, Kanlıca (0216 413 9300/fax 0216 413 9355/ www.ajiahotel.com). **Rates** €250-€800 double; €430-€700 suite. **Credit** AmEx, DC, MC, V.

The first boutique hotel on the Asian Shore, Aija opened in 2004 to great acclaim. Aijia is Japanese for Asia, and the Zen influence is palpable in the 16 sleek, pared down rooms, whose style successfully contrasts with the traditional exterior of this restored waterfront mansion (or *yalı*) that once belonged to a pasha. It's little wonder that the Ajia is a favourite venue for weddings and honeymoons – the remote setting oozes romance. Helpful staff can arrange boat trips. The drawback? Prices are pretty steep. But if you're prepared to splash out, book one of the split-level deluxe suites overlooking the Bosphorus.
Bar. Concierge. Disabled-adapted rooms. Internet (high speed). Non-smoking rooms. Parking (free). Restaurant. Room service. TV.

Sumahan

Kuleli Caddesi 51, Çengelköy (0216 422 8000/ fax 216 422 8008/www.sumahan.com). **Rates** $220-$395 double; $290-$395 suite. **Credit** AmEx, DC, MC, V.
This converted distillery, dating from 1875, enjoys a fabulous waterfront setting in Çengelköy, a sleepy fishing village way off the tourist radar. The far-flung location can be an asset or annoyance, depending on whether you want to kick back and enjoy the luxurious amenities, or get to the centre of town in a hurry. The architect owners have created polished contemporary interiors featuring grey marble, exposed stonework, and picture windows with extraordinary views of mosques and minarets shimmering beyond the Bosphorus bridge. Many rooms come with mini-hamams. Kordonbalik restaurant dishes up superlative seafood – at a price.
Bar. Business services. Café. Concierge. Disabled-adapted rooms. Gym. Internet (high speed). Non-smoking rooms. Parking (free). Restaurant. Room service. Spa. TV.

Sightseeing

Introduction

Read this first.

Istanbul is sightseeing heaven. You want churches? It has plenty. Mosques? The city has maybe the world's finest. Bazaars? The biggest. Palaces? In abundance. And that's before you get to the fortresses, city walls, underground cisterns, public baths, museums, parks, and islands. For sheer volume of sights, Istanbul gives London, Paris or Rome a run for their money.

The topography is confusing for newcomers, involving three land masses, two on the European side of the Bosphorus – divided by the Golden Horn – and one on the Asian shore. There's no uptown or downtown, inner circle or any other convenient way to read the city. Its street patterns are irregular; generations of development without urban planning have created a city almost devoid of straight lines and right angles. Buildings crowd sightlines, every now and again opening up to expose a view that takes you completely by surprise. In such a set-up there's no such thing as a wrong turn, only alternative routes.

THE HISTORIC HEART

Most of the sights that could properly be described as unmissable – either because they're really famous or simply because you couldn't avoid them if you tried – are in and around **Sultanahmet** and the **Bazaar Quarter**, which together constitute the city's historic centre. This is the ancient walled capital of the Byzantines and the Ottomans. If this is your first time in Istanbul, this is where you're going to be spending the greater part of your waking hours (and your sleeping hours, too, because most hotels are here). The area occupies the highest part of a fat thumb of land enclosed by the Sea of Marmara and the Golden Horn. Its spine is **Divan Yolu**, the main drag and tram route. With stops beside the main mosques and bazaars, the tram is the best way to get around this side of town.

South of Divan Yolu there's little of interest, but to the north the streets slope precipitously down to the waterside district and transport hub of **Eminönü** beside the **Golden Horn**. Here the tram terminates, over the road from a wharf busy with ferries departing for destinations up the **Bosphorus** and over to the **Asian Shore**.

Beyond the Bazaar Quarter are the **Western Districts**, conservative neighbourhoods such as **Fatih**, **Fener**, **Balat** and, further afield, **Eyüp**. Few visitors make it out here, but there are several worthwhile monuments, notably the Byzantine **Church of St Saviour in Chora** (*see p86*) and the **city walls** (*see p87*).

► For boat trips to the Upper Bosphorus, see p206.

Don't miss Sights

Roman engineering
Three hundred and thirty-six underground columns and an eerie upside-down head of Medusa make the **Yerebataban Cistern** (Sarnıcı) unforgettable. *See p72.*

Ottoman power centre
Topkapı Palace was the hub of Ottoman power for more than three centuries. Its pavilions house everything from stunning jewels to a harem. *See p68.*

Great imperial mosque
The silhouette of **Sultanahmet Mosque**, with its six minarets, is elegant and unmistakeable. *See p72.*

Sinan's small masterpiece
Dazzling colourful tiling is key to the beauty of the small Rüstem Paşa Mosque, the work of celebrated Ottoman architect Sinan. *See p83.*

Istanbul from the water
Cruise down Bosphorous and admire the city skyline. *See p206.*

Byzantine splendour
The well-preserved mosaics and frescoes at the **Church of St Saviour in Chora** are perhaps the most important surviving examples of Byzantine art. *See p86.*

Oriental experience
The **Grand Bazaar** is everything most people imagine the 'exotic East' to be. *See p78.*

Sightseeing

0381 → Four Feathers
4831 – Medical Annual 1901
3566 – My Poultry
0231 – Eyes of Horus
0232 – Land of the horizon
0002 – European Reformation
0175 – Oldest code of laws
2180 – Dartmoor
1248 – Owd Bob
2704 – Finches
2490 – Spiritual Despotism
2691 – Canvasser's Handbook
2857 – (Rebellion)
0422 – Last Things ⟵ ?
0134 – Data of Ethics
0435 – Erchie & Jimmy Swan
4023 – Six-Pointer Buck
2989 – Helcrad
4027 – Le Savant Du Foyer
2985 – The Most of S.S. Perelman
0105 – Hist. Technology
2799 – Blinds, Curtains & Cushions

109
⟨ Our British Empire by Leacock

Devon & Cornwall

Fener. *See p85*.

Crossing the Golden Horn

Sultanahmet (south of the Golden Horn) is great for sightseeing during the day, but Beyoğlu (north of the Golden Horn) is the place to be come nightfall.

To get to Beyoğlu from Sultanahmet, take the tram downhill to Sirkeci station, where you can catch another tram across Galata Bridge and down to Kabataş. From there, the new metro will speed you up the hill to Taksim Square, Beyoğlu's uptown hub.

Alternatively, get off the tram at Karaköy and take the one-stop, 19th century Tünel, an underground funicular that clatters up the steep slope to Tünel Square at the southern end of Istiklal Caddesi. This long, paved boulevard, running between Tünel and Taksim, is the backbone of the whole area. All Beyoğlu destinations are reachable from Istiklal Caddesi, or from Tünel and Taksim.

For this reason, we have not listed transport details for Beyoğlu destinations. An old-fashioned tram usually runs between Tünel and Taksim. It was out of service at the time of writing, but should be up and running some time early in 2007.

There's also a bus (T4) from Sultanahmet Square to Taksim, but it only departs every half hour. An alternative is to walk down the hill and across the Galata Bridge, then take the funicular to Tünel, all of which takes a good 30-40 minutes.

The simplest and fastest option is to flag a cab, which will take about ten minutes from Sultanahmet Square to Taksim Square – traffic permitting – and should cost in the region of YTL5-YTL9.

For a detailed map of the tram, funicular and metro system, *see p256*.

PLACES TO PLAY

The Golden Horn bisects European Istanbul, but the two parts are linked by a number of bridges including, most prominently, the Galata and, further west, the Atatürk. North of the Golden Horn is the 'modern' city, developed largely in the 19th century. Ground zero is **Beyoğlu**, the place to play after sightseeing. Beyoğlu subdivides into several smaller neighbourhoods (including, from south to north, **Galata**, **Tünel**,

Hasırcılar Caddesi. *See p82.*

Asmalımescit and **Galatasaray**), all linked by **Istiklal Caddesi**, a long, pedestrian boulevard whose narrow off-shoots are filled with shops, cafés, bars, clubs and restaurants.

At its north end, Istiklal Caddesi empties into **Taksim Square** – large and charmless, it's recommended only as a place to pick up a taxi. North of Taksim are the newer districts of **Harbiye**, **Şişli**, **Nişantaşı** and **Teşvikiye**, where middle-class Istanbullus shop, eat and socialise. Further north still (reachable by metro), **Etiler** and **Levent** are where the real money's at; go clubbing here and your bank manager will know about it.

The string of neighbourhoods down by the water are sometimes referred to as the 'Bosphorus villages'. **Ortaköy**, **Arnavutköy** and **Bebek** are picturesque clusters of attractive wooden villas, folksy shops and markets, open-air cafés and restaurants. There's not much in the way of major sights, but these neighbourhoods are definitely worth a wander. They are linked by bus services or, better still, you can travel here by ferry (*see p99*).

Ferry is also the best way to go to get over to the **Asian Shore**'s two main neighbourhoods, **Kadıköy** and **Üsküdar**. There is no significant change in character here. Instead, the Asian Shore is a vast dormitory for Istanbullus who commute to jobs on the west side of the water. Real estate is cheaper, and it's less crowded than urban European Istanbul. The character of the Asian Shore is heavily shaped by large numbers of immigrants from the Turkish provinces.

Sultanahmet

Picture-postcard surroundings that give you plenty to write home about.

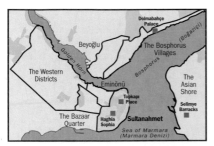

Sultanahmet is the 'proper' Istanbul: the one with the slim minarets pointing skywards and the domes – the 'Orient' of the Turkish Delight ad. It's a scenic thumbnail of land surrounded by sea on three sides. Surrounding its famous mosques are palaces, museums and assorted historical oddments, testament to a heritage that encompasses the birth, youthful exuberance, mature middle age and drooling dotage of not one but two great empires: the Byzantine and Ottoman.

Focal point for disgorging tour buses and feeding ground for taxis, **Sultanahmet Square** (Ayasofya Meydanı) is the obvious place to begin. Most of the city's major monuments are just a few minutes' walk from here, including the **Topkapı Palace**, the underground cistern **Yerebatan Sarnıcı**, **Sultanahmet Mosque** (visible across the park) and the **Museum of Turkish & Islamic Art**. Most notably, the square also acts as a forecourt to what for close to a thousand years was the greatest church in Eastern Christendom, the **Haghia Sophia** (Ayasofya in Turkish). After the Turkish conquest it served for five centuries as the chief mosque of the Ottoman empire, and is now open to all as a museum.

Haghia Sophia (Ayasofya)

The third sacred building on the site to bear the name, the existing Haghia Sophia ('Divine Wisdom') was dedicated on 26 December AD 537 by Emperor Justinian. He had come to power less than a century after the fall of Rome, and was eager to prove his capital a worthy successor to imperial glory. Approached by a grand colonnaded avenue beginning at the city gates, Justinian's cathedral towered over all else and was topped by the largest dome ever constructed – a record it held until the Romans reclaimed their pride just over a thousand years later with Michelangelo's dome for St Peter's (1590). In the meantime, Justinian's dome took on almost fabled status. It was of such thin material, wrote the chroniclers of old, that the hundreds of candles hung high within would cause it to glow at night like a great golden beacon, which was visible to ships far out on the Marmara Sea.

Adding to the wonder, the church served as a vast reliquary, housing a pilgrim's delight of biblical treasures, including fragments of the True Cross, the Virgin's veils, the lance that pierced Jesus' side, St Thomas' doubting finger, and a large assortment of other saintly limbs, skulls and clippings.

All this was lost in 1204, when adventurers and freebooters on Western Christendom's Fourth Crusade, raised to liberate Jerusalem and the Holy Lands, decided they would be

Haghia Sophia.

Istanbul on foot Sultanahmet

Begin at Karaköy Square for a stroll across the Golden Horn into Sultanahmet. It takes imagination to see **Galata Bridge** as it was in its golden era, a time when Edmondo de Amicis, an Italian writer who visited the city in the 1870s, gave a literary snapshot of the bridge's human comings and goings in his *Constantinople*. At that time the bridge was the centre point of the multicultural Ottoman Empire, and flowing across it were Albanians in petticoats with pistols at the ready, Maltese ladies in black *fadetta*, Tartars wearing sheepskin, European ambassadors, necromancers, eunuchs busting skulls making way for the lunchtime social runs of the aristocratic Turkish *hanims* in their charge, and porters limping along under hundreds of pounds of firewood. These days you're much more likely to see amateur fishermen lining the rails, selling their catch to sandwich vendors; there is also a lively line of touristy restaurants and bars on a lower level between the road and the water. It's still a classic Istanbul walk, though, and an exhilarating one.

Straight ahead on the Sultanahmet side of the bridge lies the **Yeni Camii**, or New Mosque, so called because, as a 17th-century construction, it was a relatively late addition to the skyline.

From here, hit the Misr Carsi, the **Egyptian Bazaar**, also known as the Spice Bazaar. As well as shops selling Turkish delight, 'Turkish Viagra', and backgammon boards, the market is also home

equally content with a treasure-grabbing raid on the luxurious capital of their Eastern brethren. At Haghia Sophia they ripped the place apart, carrying off everything they could, and added insult to thievery by infamously placing a prostitute on the imperial throne.

Further destruction was narrowly avoided in 1453, when the Ottoman Turk armies, led by Mehmet II, breached the walls of the city of Constantinople and put its Byzantine defenders to flight. Those who took refuge in the church were slaughtered, but the conquering sultan to a clutch of quality delis, as well as spice and coffee merchants.

Loop back on to Residaye Caddesi and, with the Golden Horn on your left, head up Muradiye Hudavendigar, which becomes Alemdar Caddesi. You will pass the flouncy hat entrance of the **Sublime Porte**, once the home of the Ottoman Grand Vizier, but now relegated to the headquarters of the Istanbul governor. Today, the Porte's wan look says little about what used to happen at this juncture of road. Here the Grand Vizier held the dangerous job of wielding true power, while the sultans retreated to the harem, went to seed on wine nominally denied to the Muslim masses, or – in the case of 'Mad Ibrahim' (1640-48) – took to **Alay Koksu**, the polygonal kiosk across from the Porte, where the demented sultan would take potshots at pedestrians with a crossbow. Beyond lies the gate to **Gulhane Park**, where picnickers and sweethearts while away the afternoon. Further up the hill, Istanbul's showcase pieces come tantalisingly into view.

At the top of Alemdar Caddesi, the road leads into Sultanahmet Square. Here, you are at the epicentre of historic Sultanahmet. To the left lies **Haghia Sophia**; **Sultanahmet Mosque** is ahead, visible on the other side of the square past a lovingly attended park with fountains and flowers, a popular place for weekend picnickers. **Topkapı Palace** is around the bend off Soğukçeşme Sokak. There are more sights in this area than can be seen on one visit (it's easy to spend a day at Topkapı Palace). Before deciding what to visit, it might be time for a rest in the mosque's gardens. Alternatively, the **Hippodrome**, on the other side of Sultanahmet Square, is a place of greenery and park benches, with a road encircling the park that follows the old chariot tracks. A good place in which to find a shady spot, enjoy an ice-cream, and conclude our walk.

allegedly rounded on a looting soldier whom he found hacking at the marble floors, telling him: 'The gold is thine, the building mine.'

Haghia Sophia may have been spared, but it was lost to Christianity. The Friday after the conquest, the church resounded to the chant,

'There is no god but Allah, and Mohammed is his Prophet'. For the church had already been converted into a mosque.

The basilica acquired the addition of four minarets, from which to deliver the Muslim call to prayer. The construction of these minarets was staggered; only two are matching. In 1317, a series of unsightly buttresses was deemed necessary when the church seemed to be in danger of collapse. These aside, what you see today is essentially the church exactly as it was in Justinian's time.

At the death of the Ottoman Empire, with plans afoot to partition Istanbul along national lines, both the Greeks (on behalf of the Eastern Church) and the Italians (on behalf of the Western Church) lobbied for Haghia Sophia to be handed over to them. In Britain, a Saint Sophia Redemption Committee was formed. The Ottoman government posted soldiers with machine guns in the mosque to thwart any attempt at a Christian coup. An expedient solution was effected by the leaders of the new Turkish republic in 1934, who deconsecrated the building and declared it a museum. This action remains controversial, with Islamists periodically calling for it to be restored as a mosque. Comparing the pristine state of the neighbouring mosques with the shabby state of Haghia Sophia, you can't help wondering if they have a point.

THE CATHEDRAL TODAY

At least the cathedral's interior remains impressive, particularly the main chamber with its fabulous dome, 30 metres (98 feet) in diameter. The other extraordinary interior feature are the mosaics. Plastered over by the Muslims, they were only rediscovered during renovations in the mid 19th century. Some of the best decorate the outer and inner narthexes, which are the long, vaulted chambers inside the present main entrance. The non-figurative geometrical and floral designs are the earliest and date from the reign of Justinian. Further mosaics adorn the galleries, reached by a stone ramp at the northern end of the inner narthex.

At the eastern end of the south gallery, just to the right of the apse, is a glimmering representation of Christ flanked by the famous 11th-century empress, Zoe, and her third husband, Constantine IX. One of the few women to rule Byzantium, Zoe married late and was a virgin until the age of 50. She must have developed a taste for what she discovered, going through a succession of husbands and lovers in the years left to her. On the mosaic in question, the heads and inscriptions show signs of being altered, possibly in an attempt to keep up with her active love life. En route to see Zoe is a slab marking the burial place of Enrico Dandalo, doge of Venice, a leader of the Fourth Crusade, and the man held responsible for persuading the Latins to attack Constantinople. Following the Ottoman conquest of the city, it is said that his tomb was smashed open and his bones thrown to the dogs.

Haghia Sophia
Ayasofya Camii Müzesi
Sultanahmet Square (0212 522 1750). Tram Sultanahmet. **Open** 9am-5pm Tue-Sun, plus 1st Mon of every month. Galleries close 1hr earlier. **Admission** YTL10. **Credit** AmEx, DC, MC, V. **Map** p243 N10.

Topkapı Palace

Directly behind Haghia Sophia are the walls shielding Topkapı Palace. Part command centre for a massive military empire, part archetypal Eastern pleasure dome, the palace was the hub of Ottoman power for over three centuries, until it was superceded by Dolmabahçe Palace in 1853. For lavish decor and exquisite location, it rivals Granada's Alhambra. At least half a day is needed to explore Topkapı; given the high entrance fee you might want to take a full day to get your money's worth. If you're pushed for time, the must-see

Gardens of **Sultanahmet Mosque**.*See p72.*

features are the Harem, Imperial Treasury and the views from the innermost courtyard.

The entrance t the palace is via the **Imperial Gate** (Bab-ı Hümayün), erected by the Sultan Fatih in 1478 and decorated with niches that during Ottoman times were used to display the severed heads of rebels and criminals. The gate leads into the first of a series of four courts that become more private the deeper żinto the complex you penetrate. The **First Court** was public and not considered part of the palace proper. It housed a hospital and dormitories for the palace guards, hence the popular name, Court of the Janissaries. Off to the left is the church of **Haghia Irene** (Aya Irini Kilisesi), built by Justinian and thus a contemporary of Haghia Sophia. It has the distinction of being the only pre-Ottoman-conquest church in the city that was never turned into a mosque. Closed most of the time, the church serves as a concert venue during the International Istanbul Music Festival (*see p163*).

Still in the First Court, down the hill to the left, is the superb **Archaeology Museum**, but the palace proper is entered through the Disneyesque gate ahead. Tickets can be bought just before you reach the gate, beside the Executioner's Fountain, where the chief axeman would wash his blade after carrying out his grisly work. The heads of his victims were also displayed on top of the truncated columns on either side of the fountain.

A semi-public space, the enormous **Second Court** is where the business of running the empire was carried out. This is where the viziers of the imperial council sat in session in the divan, overlooking gardens landscaped with cypresses, plane trees and rose bushes. Where once there would have been crowds of petitioners awaiting their turn for an audience, nowadays there are queues lined up waiting to get in to the **Harem**, an introverted complex of around 300 brilliantly tiled chambers on several levels, connected by arcaded courts and fountain gardens. Unfortunately, access is limited: you must wait to join a group that leaves every half-hour and is led through no more than a dozen chambers by an official guide. It's not the ideal way to see the place – locked in a crowd and herded around – but it's the only way. Tickets are sold separately, from a window located beside the Harem entrance. (*See also p71* **Hard times in the harem**).

Around from the Harem ticket window, a low brick building topped by shallow domes is the former **State Treasury**, present home of an exhibition of arms and armour, which is interesting for the contrast between cumbersome, bludgeonly European swords

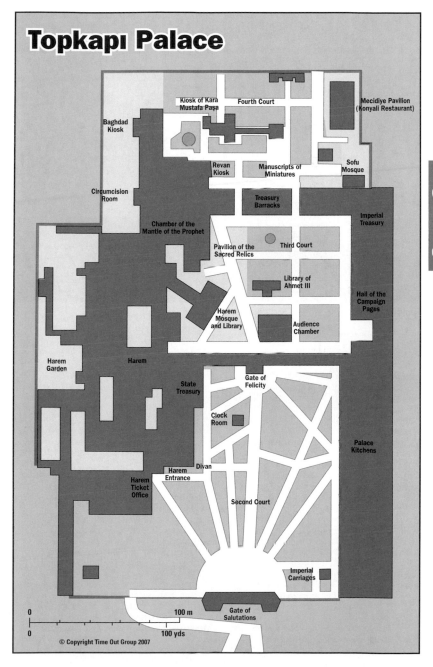

Topkapı Palace

Kiosk of Kara Mustafa Paşa

Fourth Court

Mecidiye Pavilion (Konyali Restaurant)

Baghdad Kiosk

Revan Kiosk

Manuscripts of Miniatures

Sofu Mosque

Circumcision Room

Treasury Barracks

Imperial Treasury

Chamber of the Mantle of the Prophet

Pavilion of the Sacred Relics

Third Court

Library of Ahmet III

Hall of the Campaign Pages

Harem Mosque and Library

Audience Chamber

Harem Garden

Harem

State Treasury

Gate of Felicity

Clock Room

Palace Kitchens

Divan

Harem Entrance

Harem Ticket Office

Second Court

Imperial Carriages

0   100 m

Gate of Salutations

0   100 yds

© Copyright Time Out Group 2007

Topkapı Palace: opulent hub of the Ottoman Empire.

and the lighter, more deadly-looking Ottoman model. Across the gardens, a long row of ventilation chimneys punctuates the roof line of the enormous kitchens, which catered for up to 5,000 inhabitants of the palace. They now contain a collection of ceramics, glass and silverware, much of it imported from China and Japan via Central Asia, along the legendary Silk Route. The earliest pieces are Chinese celadon, particularly valued by the sultans because it was supposed to change colour when brought into contact with poison.

All paths in the Second Court converge on the **Gate of Felicity** (Bab-üs Saadet), the backdrop for an annual performance of Mozart's *Abduction from the Seraglio*. The gate also gives access to the **Third Court**.

The Third Court was the sultan's own private domain. Confronting all who enter is the **Audience Chamber** (Arz Odası), which is where foreign ambassadors would present their credentials, until the room's role was supplanted by the Sublime Porte (*see p81*). Although the sultan would be present on such occasions, he would never deign to speak with a non-Turk and all conversation was conducted via the grand vizier.

To the right is the **Hall of the Campaign Pages** (Seferli Koşusu), whose task it was to look after the royal wardrobe. They did an

excellent job: there's a perfectly preserved 550-year-old, red-and-gold silk kaftan worn by Mehmet II, conqueror of Constantinople.

Things get even more glittery next door in the **Imperial Treasury** (Hazine). Many of the items here were made specifically for the palace by a team of court artisans, which at its height numbered over 600. A lot of what's displayed here has never left the confines of the inner courts. Not that too many people outside the sultan's circle would have had much use for a diamond-encrusted set of chain mail or a Koran bound in jade. Items like the Topkapı Dagger, its handle set with three eyeball-sized emeralds (one of which conceals a watch face), are breathtaking in their excessiveness, vulgarity and sheer uselessness.

From the ridiculous to the sublime: the final and **Fourth Court** is a garden with terraces stepping down towards Seraglio Point, the protruberance of land that watches over the entrance to the Golden Horn. Buildings are limited to a bunch of reasonably restrained pavilions, while the views over the Bosphorus are wonderful, as are the sea breezes on a sun-beaten summer's day. The very last building to be constructed within the palace, the **Mecidiye Pavilion** (Mecidiye Köşkü), built in 1840, houses a restaurant and café, notable for its covetable terrace seating.

Topkapı Palace

Topkapı Sarayı
Bab-ı Hümayün Caddesi, Gülhane (0212 512 0480/
www.topkapisarayi.gov.tr). Tram Gülhane or
Sultanahmet. **Open** May-Sept 9am-7pm Mon, Wed-
Sun. Oct-Apr 9am-4pm Mon, Wed-Sun. **Admission**
YTL10. **Harem** YTL10. **Credit** AmEx, DC, MC, V.
Map p243 O9. **Photo** p70.

Archaeology Museum

Arkeoloji Müzesi
Osman Hamdi Bey Yokuşu, Topkapı Sarayı, Gülhane
(0212 520 7740). Tram Gülhane. **Open** 9am-5pm
Tue-Sun. **Admission** YTL5 (incl Museum of the
Ancient Orient & Tiled Pavilion). **Credit** MC, V.
Map p243 O9.

The collection of classical antiquities displayed here
is world-class and – rare for Istanbul – well lit and
well-labelled. Within the grounds of Topkapı Palace,
the museum was founded in the mid 19th century in
an attempt to staunch the flow of antiquities being
spirited out of the country by foreigners to fill the
museums of Europe. The exhibits were originally
housed in the Tiled Pavilion (see p72) until the
commissioning of a new building, since extended on
three occasions to keep up with the growing
contents. Even so, the bulk of the collection remains
in storage due to lack of space and funds.

Greeting visitors is a grinning statue of Bes, a
demonic Cypriot demigod of inexhaustible power
and strength, qualities required of anyone hoping to
get through even a fraction of the 20 galleries within. Starting with the pre-Classical world, they cover
5,000 years of history, with artefacts gathered from
all over Turkey and the Near East and grouped
thematically. Highlights include a collection of sixth-
to fourth-century BC sarcophagi from a royal
necropolis at Sidon, in modern Lebanon, of which
the finest is known as the Alexander Sarcophagus
because of the scenes of the Macedonian general's
victory at Issus (333 BC) adorning its side panels.

Sightseeing

Hard times in the harem

From its inception in around 1540 until its
dissolution in the early 20th century, the
Topkapı harem was home, prison and entire
world to almost four centuries of palace
women. The word means 'forbidden', a ruling
that applied to all men except the sultan,
the princes and the eunuch guards. Women
had no problem getting in, but once admitted
they were in for life. Most entered as slave
girls presented to the sultan as gifts: it was
forbidden to make slaves of Muslims, so
they were all Christians or Jews. Circassian
girls who came from what is now Georgia
and Armenia were favoured because of their
fair skin, although even the fairest was still
only valued at a fifth of the price of a good
horse. The girls were converted to Islam
and 'palace-trained', which means they were
taught to sing, dance, play instruments and
to give pleasure of a more tactile kind.

But notions of the harem as a sensual
hothouse are misplaced. It was a highly
competitive and cut-throat environment in
which each girl sought to catch the eye of
the sultan or a prince and so secure a better
station. At any one time, a dozen or so girls
would be chosen as imperial handmaids
and bedmates. Giving birth to the sultan's
child ensured exalted status. If it was a boy,
there was even the chance he might one day
become sultan and his mother valide sultana,
'mother of the sultan' – the most powerful
woman in the land. At such high stakes, with
the sex came violence as the women
manoeuvred, plotted, poisoned and knifed
their way up the harem hierarchy. A mother
with the sultan's child was particularly
vulnerable – Murat III (1574-95), for example,
fathered 103 children, only one of whom was
ever going to make the throne.

All the while, harem girls also had to court
the favour of the present valide sultana,
responsible for selecting girls for the sultan,
while avoiding the displeasure of the kizlar
ağasi, the chief black eunuch. These latter
characters were the go-betweens for the
sultan and his mother and so privy to all
palace secrets. At the same time, physically
and psychologically mutilated as they were,
the chief black eunuchs tended to be a
dangerous combination of corrupt, scheming
and vindictive. Some of them got their kicks
by stuffing girls in sacks, loading them into a
boat, and dumping them into the Bosphorus,
usually on the instructions of the valide
sultana (although Sultans Ibrahim and Murat
II are both alleged to have ordered their
entire harems drowned, one out of boredom
the other through paranoia).

Alev Lytle Croutier sums it all up very nicely
in her fine book Harem: The World Behind
the Veil, describing it as a world of 'frightened
women plotting with men who were not men
against absolute rulers who kept their
relatives immured for decades'. Far from
being a palace of sensual delights, the
Topkapı harem must have been more of a
nerve-shredding chamber of horrors.

Up on the first floor, 'Istanbul Through the Ages' is a summary of the city's history presented through a few key pieces, including a serpent's head lopped off the column in the Hippodrome (*see p73*) and a section of the iron chain that stretched across the Bosphorus to bar the way of invaders. One great innovation is a small children's area, complete with low cabinets. The museum also occasionally holds special exhibitions – check *Time Out Istanbul* magazine for details.

Outside in the museum courtyard is a Troy-style Wooden Horse, while across from this stands the **Tiled Pavilion** (Çinili Köşk), which dates back to 1472 and the reign of Sultan Mehmet II, Ottoman conqueror of Constantinople. Built in a Persian style, it was an imperial viewing stand that overlooked a large gaming field, now occupied by the main museum building. The pavilion displays some outstanding samples of Turkish tiles and ceramics from the Seljuk and Ottoman periods, dating from between the end of 12th century and the beginning of 20th century.

To the south, beside the main entrance, is the **Museum of the Ancient Orient**, containing antiquities from the Mesopotamian, Egyptian and Hittite cultures, including some wonderful monumental glazed-brick friezes from the main Ishtar Gate of sixth-century Babylon. There is also the world's first peace treaty (1283 BC), a clay tablet signed by the Hittite king Hattushilish III and Egyptian pharaoh Rameses II that ended a lengthy conflict between the two ancient rival empires.

The Cisterns

Running downhill from Topkapı's Imperial Gate, **Soğukçeşme Sokak** is an example of urban set design. Formerly a row of dilapidated wooden buildings, the street was demolished in the 1980s and recreated in concrete, disguised under pastel-painted weatherboard panelling. Intended to evoke the atmosphere of Ottoman Istanbul, the 'old houses' are one long, straggly, boutique hotel (*see p45* **Ayasofya Pansiyonları**), apart from one which contains Istanbul Library.

Following the tram tracks back uphill leads to a right turn and a lone, single-storey building that sits over the entrance to the **Yerebatan Sarnıcı** (Basilica Cistern), the grandest of several underground reservoirs that riddle the foundations of this part of the city.

A second cistern, the **Binbirdirek Sarnıcı** (the 'Cistern of 1001 Columns', although there are only 224) is also open to the public.

Binbirdirek Sarnıcı

Imran Ökten Sokak 4 (0212 518 1001). Tram Sultanahmet. **Open** 9am-9pm daily. **Admission** YTL10. **Credit** AmEx, DC, MC, V. **Map** p243 M10.
Like the more famous Yerebatan cistern, this one is a Byzantine forest of pillars and brick-vaulted ceilings, but sadly the restorers have put in a false floor that halves the original height of the chamber (a well at the centre illustrates the original floor level). No one has yet figured out what to do with the place and it currently unsuccessfully accommodates a couple of cafés, a bar and a restaurant. The admission fee gets you a free drink.

Yerebatan Sarnıcı

Yerebatan Caddesi 13 (0212 522 1259/www. yerebatan.com). Tram Sultanahmet. **Open** 9am-5.30pm daily. **Admission** YTL10. **Credit** MC, V. **Map** p243 N10.
Built by the Emperor Justinian at the same time as the Haghia Sophia, it was forgotten for centuries and only rediscovered by a Frenchman, Peter Gyllius, in 1545 when he noticed that people in the neighbourhood got water by lowering buckets through holes in their basements. It's a tremendous engineering feat, with brick vaults supported on 336 columns spaced at four-metre (13-foot) intervals. Prior to restoration in 1987, the cistern could only be explored by boat (James Bond rowed through in *From Russia With Love*). These days there are concrete walkways. The subdued lighting and subterranean cool are especially welcome on hot days. Look for the two Medusa heads at the far end near the entrance, both recycled from an even more ancient building and casually employed as column bases. There's a café down here and a platform on which occasional concerts of classical Turkish and Western music are performed; check with the ticket office for further details.

Sultanahmet Mosque

Seductively curvaceous and enhanced by a lovingly attended park in front, Sultanahmet Mosque is Islamic architecture at its sexiest. Commissioned by Sultan Ahmet I (1603-17) and built for him by Mehmet Ağa, a student of the great Sinan, this was the last of Istanbul's magnificent imperial mosques, the final flourish before the rot set in. It provoked hostility at the time because of its six minarets – such a display was previously reserved only for the Prophet's mosque at Mecca – but they do make for a beautifully elegant silhouette, particularly gorgeous when floodlit at night.

By contrast, the interior is clumsy, marred by four immense pillars, disproportionately large for the fairly modest dome they support (especially when compared to the vast yet seemingly unsupported dome that caps Haghia Sophia). Most surfaces are covered by a mismatch of Iznik tiles: their colour gives the place its popular name, the Blue Mosque.

A part of the mosque complex, the **Imperial Pavilion** now houses the entirely missable **Vakıflar Carpet Museum**. In the north-east corner of the surrounding park is the *türbe* or

Sultanahmet Mosque.

Tomb of Sultan Ahmet I. It also contains the cenotaphs of his wife and three of his sons, two of whom, Osman II and Murat IV, ruled in their turn, Ahmet being the sultan who abandoned the nasty Ottoman practice of strangling other potential heirs on the succession of the favoured son.

Sultanahmet (Blue) Mosque

Sultanahmet Camii
At Meydanı Sokak 17 (0212 518 1319). Tram Sultanahmet. **Open** *9am-1hr before dusk (prayer time) daily. Sound & light show May-Oct, just after dusk daily.* **Admission** free. **Map** p243 N11. **Photo** *p68.*

Vakıflar Carpet Museum

Vakıflar Halı Müzesi
Sultanahmet Mosque (0212 518 1330). Tram Sultanahmet. **Open** *9am-noon, 1-4pm Tue-Sat.* **Admission** YTL2. **No credit cards.** **Map** p243 N11.
What was once the Imperial Pavilion in the outer courtyard of Sultanahmet Mosque, used by the sultan whenever he visited for prayers, is now a display space for an extensive collection of carpets from all over Turkey. The setting is appropriate, considering that until quite recently most of these carpets and rugs lay inside working mosques, but presentation is sparse, lighting is poor, and the whole enterprise is handicapped by meagre funding. This is done much better at the Museum of Turkish and Islamic Art; the Vakıflar is only for committed rug enthusiasts.

The Hippodrome & South

On the north-west side of the Sultanahmet Mosque, a strip of over-touristy tea-houses and souvenir shops fringes the **Hippodrome** (At Meydanı), formerly the focal point of Byzantine Constantinople.

At one time, this ancient arena was used for races, court ceremonies, coronations and parades. Originally laid out by the Roman emperor Septimius Severus during his rebuilding of the city, the arena was enlarged by Constantine to its present dimensions. The modern road exactly follows the tracks of the old racing lanes. Now little more than an elongated park circled by traffic, the Hippodrome does retain an odd assortment of monuments, which stand on what was the *spina*, the raised area around which chariots would have thundered.

Closest to the mosque is an **Egyptian obelisk**, removed from the Temple of Karnak at Thebes (now Luxor). The obelisk was originally carved in around 1500 BC in order to commemorate the great victories of Pharaoh Thutmosis III. In a self-congratulatory mood, the Byzantine emperor Theodosius had the obelisk moved to Constantinople in AD 390, where it was set upon a marble pedestal and sculpted with scenes of himself and his family enjoying a day at the races.

Next to the obelisk is the bronze **Serpentine Column** (also known as the Spiral Column), carried off from the Temple of Apollo at Delphi, where it had been set to commemorate Greek victory over the Persians in 480 BC. When it was brought to the Byzantine capital by Constantine its three entwined serpents had heads, but each was decapitated over the years. One detached head survives and is displayed in the Archaeology Museum. A third monument, known as the **Column of Constantine**, is a pockmarked and crumbling affair, once sheathed in gold-plated bronze, but stripped by the looting Fourth Crusaders.

Overlooking the Hippodrome is the grand **Museum of Turkish and Islamic Art**, while down the hill from its south-west corner is the **Sokollu Mehmet Paşa Mosque**, another tour de force by Sinan.

The streets around here twist and turn between creaky wooden buildings – a delight to explore. Head south, downhill toward the sea, for the **Küçük Haghia Sophia Mosque**.

Following Küçük Ayasofya Caddesi back uphill leads past the very worthwhile **Mosaic Museum** and the Ottoman-era shopping centre, the **Arasta Bazaar**, beyond which a sunken terrace café where you can puff an afternoon away with a *narghile*.

Küçük Haghia Sophia Mosque

Küçük Ayasofya Camii
Küçük Ayasofya Caddesi, Sultanahmet. Tram Sultanahmet. **Open** prayer times only, daily.
Admission free. **Map** p243 M12.
Also known as 'Little Haghia Sophia' because of its resemblance to Justinian's great cathedral. Like its larger namesake, it was originally a church, in this case dedicated to Sergius and Bacchus, the patron saints of the Christianised Roman army. Also like its namesake, it's not much to look at from the outside, but possesses a fine interior, including a frieze honouring Justinian and his wife, Theodora. There's also a very pleasant garden which has an adjoining café.

Mosaic Museum

Büyüksaray Mozaik Müzesi
Arasta Çarşısı, Torun Sokak 103, Sultanahmet (0212 518 1205). Tram Sultanahmet. **Open** *Winter* 9am-4.30pm Tue-Sun. *Summer* 9am-6pm Tue-Sun. **Admission** YTL5. **No credit cards**. **Map** p243 N11.
Behind Sultanahmet Mosque and slightly down the hill towards the Marmara is a small, 17th-century shopping street, built to provide rental revenue for the upkeep of the mosque. It has been converted into a cluster of tourist shops, the Arasta Bazaar. Leading off here is a prefabricated hut that is the unlikely home of a fantastic archaeological find. Uncovered in the mid 1950s, it's an ornamental pavement belonging to the Byzantine Great Palace

(Büyüksaray), which stood where the mosque is now, and probably dates from the era of Justinian. The surviving segments depict mythological and hunting scenes, with pastoral idylls disturbingly skewed by bloody depictions of animal combat: elephant versus lion, snake versus gazelle, stags and lizards being eaten by winged unicorns. It's also worth a visit for the informative wall panels, particularly the pictorial reconstructions of how the Byzantine palace quarter would have looked.

Museum of Turkish & Islamic Art

Türk ve Islam Eserleri Müzesi
At Meydanı 46, Sultanahmet (0212 518 1805). Tram Sultanahmet. **Open** 9am-4.30pm Tue-Sun. **Admission** YTL5. **Credit** MC, V. **Map** p243 M10.
Overlooking the Hippodrome, the museum occupies the restored 16th-century palace of Ibrahim Paşa. A Greek convert to Islam, Ibrahim was the confidant of Süleyman I and in 1523 he was appointed Grand Vizier. When his palace was completed the following year, it was the grandest private residence in the Ottoman Empire, rivalling any building of the Topkapı Palace. When Süleyman fell under the influence of the scheming Roxelana (*see p20*), he was persuaded that Ibrahim had to go, and the vizier was strangled in his sleep.

The palace was seized by the state and has variously been used as a school, a dormitory, a court, a barracks and a prison, before being restored as a museum. The well-planned collections, all housed in cool rooms around a central courtyard, include carpets, manuscripts, miniatures, woodwork, metalwork and glasswork. Items range from the earliest period of Islam through to modern times, all presented chronologically and geographically, with full explanations provided.

On the ground floor, a gallery showcases modern Turkish and foreign artists. There's an interesting ethnographic section, including a recreation of a *kara çadır* or 'black tent', the residence of choice for many of the nomadic Anatolian tribes who developed the art of the *kilim*. Upstairs, the Great Hall contains what is reckoned to be one of the finest collections of carpets in the world.

There's also an excellent café in a shaded courtyard, with a covered terrace overlooking the Hippodrome next to it.

Sokollu Mehmet Paşa Mosque

Sokollu Mehmet Paşa Camii
Şehit Mehmet Paşa Sokak 20, Sultanahmet (0212 518 1633). Tram Eminönü or Sultanahmet. **Open** 7am-dusk daily. **Admission** free. **Map** p243 M11.
One of Sinan's later buildings (constructed between 1571-72), this mosque has been widely praised by architectural historians for its skilful handling of an uneven, sloping site. If you manage to get inside (hang around long enough, and somebody will usually turn up with a key), notice the lovely tiling and painted calligraphic inscriptions, set among vivid floral motifs. If you don't, the ornate ablution fountain in the courtyard is also beautiful.

The Bazaar Quarter

Welcome to the world's oldest shopping centre.

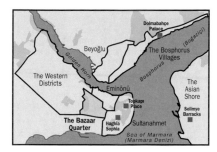

For centuries, this was where the gears of an empire's economy clashed, with sellers from Damascus and Yemen bartering hard with buyers from Anatolia, the Balkans and the Aegean. A cacophony of multilingual haggling and braying camels, it was the oriental bazaar *par excellence*. While nowadays the **Grand Bazaar** is given over to a more decorative tourist trade, the experience can still be shopping as a contact sport: a million and one touts with goods that range from the cheesy to the literary. In the surrounding streets, Istanbul's masses still do the real business, descending on the nearby markets to do their weekly shopping.

To get to the Grand Bazaar from Sultanahmet Square, follow the tram lines west up Divan Yolu.

Divan Yolu

Narrow, sloping, partially cobbled and given over to purring trams, the street known as Divan Yolu is modestly attractive. There's little indication that this was formerly the ancient Meşe, or Middle Way, the main thoroughfare of Byzantine Constantinople and, later, Ottoman Stamboul. It ran from the imperial centre (today's Sultanahmet) due west over the city's seven hills to the Topkapı Gate. From Byzantium, the Meşe continued all the way to Durres (Durazzo) on the Albanian coast. A large marble sliver at the bottom of Divan Yolu, in the small park behind the Yerebatan Sarnıçı, is all that remains of a Byzantine triumphal arch, known as the **Milion**, which originally marked the point from which all distances were measured.

Modern Divan Yolu is defined by tacky souvenir shops, cheap eateries, money exchange bureaux and bucket-shop travel agencies, with the odd smattering of antiquity. On the corner with Babıali Caddesi is a small, well-tended cemetery with the **Tomb of Mahmut II**. Over the road and down a side street is the **Theodosius Cistern**, sitting under the 'Eminönü Belediye Başkanlığı' building. The **Basın Müzesi** (Press Museum) is rather dull, but has a popular café on the ground floor. Next door, on the corner with Vezirhanı Caddesi, the big, bulbous, yellow-faced dome belongs to the **Çemberlitaş Hamam** (*see p182*). The buildings fall back here to create a small, pigeon-infested plaza, marked by the equally scruffy **Burnt Column**. Otherwise known as the Hooped Column, this easily overlooked pillar is, in fact, one of the city's oldest monuments. Erected by Constantine to celebrate the city's inauguration as new imperial capital in 330, the column was topped by a statue of the emperor until this was destroyed in an 1106 hurricane. Its present blackened state is the result of one of Istanbul's periodic fires. The iron hoops are structural reinforcements that were added in the fifth century and replaced in the 1970s.

By now Divan Yolu has turned into **Yeniçeriler Caddesi**, which is lined with a string of small mosques, tombs and *medreses* (theological schools), a couple of which have small courtyards that double up as **narghile cafés** (*see Hava Narghile p132*). From here, the Grand Bazaar is immediately to the north.

Theodosius Cistern

Şerefiye Sarnıçı
Piyer Loti Caddesi, Sultanahmet. Tram Sultanahmet.
Open 9am-5pm Mon-Fri. **Admission** free.
Map p243 M10.
This unrestored Byzantine reservoir is what the more famous Yerebatan Sarnıçı would have looked like before it was cleaned up for tourists.

Tomb of Mahmut II

82 Divan Yolu, Sultanahmet. Tram Sultanahmet.
Open 9.30am-7pm daily. **Admission** free.
Map p243 M10.
Mahmut II (1808-39) was the sultan who crushed the Janissaries. He must have been a formidable force in the harem, too, for he produced 15 sons and 12 daughters, many of whom are now crammed into the domed tomb with him.

Sightseeing

Grand Bazaar

The Grand Bazaar (in Turkish *Kapalı Çarşı*, or 'Covered Market') is a world apart. A maze of interconnecting vaulted passages, the bazaar has its own banks, baths, mosques, cafés and restaurants, a police station and post office, not to mention thousands of shops, all glittery and fairy-lit in the absence of natural light. Since the rise of the mall it's no longer the biggest shopping centre in the world, but it can still claim to be the oldest.

Part of the building dates back to the ninth century, when it was used as something akin to a Byzantine ministry of finance. Trading proper started in 1461, a mere eight years after the Turkish conquest of Constantinople. The Ottomans ushered in a new economic era, with the city at the centre of an empire that stretched from the Arabian deserts almost to the European Alps. Mehmet the Conqueror ordered the construction of a *bedesten*, a great secure building with thick stone walls, massive iron gates and space for several dozen shops. This survives in modified form as the **Old Bedesten** (*İç Bedesten*), at the very heart of the bazaar. It remains a place where the most precious items are sold, including the finest old silver and antiques. The **Sandal Bedesten** was added later; named after a fine Bursan silk, it was filled with textile traders. It now hosts a carpet auction at 1pm every Wednesday, which is a real crowd-pleaser.

A network of covered streets grew up around the two *bedestens*, sealed at night behind 18 great gates. Whenever the economy was booming, the market would physically expand, only to be cut back by frequent fires. As the Ottoman Empire started to decline after 300 years of wealth, so did the legendary splendour of the bazaar. In 1894, a devastating earthquake hit the traders particularly hard. It wasn't until the 1950s that the bazaar began to revive, as the new republic found its economic footing. These days, it's taking tentative steps into the 21st century with chic boutiques, hip cafés, and even a website (www.kapalicarsi.org.tr).

Much of the current prosperity comes from gold, of which nearly 100 tonnes is sold in the bazaar each year. Then there are the 'black bag' shoppers from the former Soviet Union, so called because of their habit of filling several bin bags with cheap clothing. Among the sea of inessential knick knacks, tacky souvenirs, nasty leather jackets, hookah pipes and hippy outfits, there are some attractive, unusual, and high quality goods to be had; you just have to know where to look and be prepared to haggle (*see p78* **Shopping the bazaar**).

AROUND THE BAZAAR

If you can find your way out of the east side of the bazaar, you emerge into daylight beside the **Nuruosmaniye Mosque**.

From here, follow **Mahmut Paşa Yokuşu** north. This market street is given over to the rag trade: it's lined with wholesalers knocking out fake Lacoste T-shirts and imitation Levi's jeans in salubrious basement workshops. The street's great stone archways lead into numerous *hans*, medieval merchant hostels with storage rooms and sleeping quarters built around a central courtyard.

To the north, the bazaar extends much further than the limits of the covered area, spilling over into a crazed warren of narrow streets that zigzag all the way to the districts of Tahtakale and Eminönü (*see p81*) beside the Golden Horn. If you're lost, just keep heading downhill. On the way, you'll see the contemporary bazaar at its most frenetic.

Exit the Grand Bazaar on the west side for **Çadırcılar Caddesi**. At No.27 is a large derelict courtyard graced with a mosaic of **Yunus Emre**, a 13th-century Sufi poet ('God is our professor and love is our academy', quoth he). Ascend the staircase to be greeted by wholesaler Ahmet and his stock of Central Asian kaftans, Pakistani fabrics, shamanistic artefacts and jewellery at prices you won't find anywhere else in the bazaar.

West of Çadırcılar, in Sahaflar Çarşısı Sokak, is the **Booksellers' Bazaar**, a lane and courtyard where the written word has been traded since early Ottoman times. Because printed books were considered a corrupting European influence, only hand-lettered manuscripts were sold until 1729, the year the first book in Turkish was published. Today, much of the trade at this historic bazaar is in textbooks (the university is nearby), along with plentiful coffee table volumes and framed calligraphy for the tourists. Sadly, the booksellers now have to compete with itinerant merchants peddling everything from Byzantine coins to used mobile phones.

Nuruosmaniye Mosque

Nuruosmaniye Camii
Vezirham Caddesi, Beyazıt (0212 528 0906).
Tram Beyazıt or Çemberlitaş. **Open** 10am-7pm daily. **Admission** free. **Map** p242 L9.
Constructed on one of the seven hills within the walls of former Constantinople, this was the first mosque in the city built in the style known as Turkish Baroque. Istanbul historian John Freely describes the architecture as possessing a 'certain perverse genius'. Certainly, the courtyard shaded by plane trees is lovely. The extensive manuscript library is also worth a look.

Grand Bazaar.

Sightseeing

Shopping the Bazaar

Walk away. Be prepared to walk away if you want to escape being harangued into a raw deal by whichever of the 5,500-odd vendors in the Grand Bazaar you happen to be dealing with. Shopkeepers cajole and entreat passers-by in a dozen languages, determined not to permit visitors to indulge in such a non-commercial activity as sightseeing. Remember, you're not dealing with sales clerks paid by the hour but most likely the owners themselves, or at least a trusted brother or nephew. Their rents have to be paid in gold – a hefty seven kilos per year for shops on the main avenue.

Fortunately, the perception that hardcore hustling is bad for long-term trade has finally started to sink in. Visitors will find the Grand Bazaar a kinder, gentler place than it was a few years ago. But even the sagacious Mehmed the Conqueror, who founded the covered bazaar in the 1460s, would have been surprised by the plasma screens overhead in the bazaar's 65 alleys, piping the greatest hits of the Turkish Tourist Board and cheesy pop tunes.

THE PRACTICALITIES

Serious shoppers should come armed with a notepad, a calculator and plenty of time – three hours is about the minimum needed for a purchasing expedition here. When you find something you like, jot down the price and the location of the seller. Then find the item elsewhere and get more quotes. Continue for as long as you have the patience. Use the calcuator to work out exchange rates.

Don't assume that wildly varying prices for the same item is a rip-off. Shopkeepers price their goods according to their needs. Someone may require ready cash to pay overheads or buy new stock and will be happy to settle for a quick, cheap sale. Also, it's not true that large, sleek shops in busy central locations always charge more. Even though they pay higher rents, higher turnover often allows them to lower prices.

BARGAINING ETIQUETTE

When bargaining, start somewhere well below your ideal price, because the shopowner will start well above his. Hopefully, you can meet in the middle. Remember that it is considered bad form to walk away empty-handed after an elaborate bargaining process.

WHERE TO BUY WHAT

There are over a dozen main gates into the Grand Bazaar. At least five of them open on to **Kalpakçılar Caddesi**, an opulent east–west thoroughfare lined with gleaming jewellery shops. On this street, you'll also find **Pako** (at No.87), the place for some of the city's best handbags and purses.

South of Kalpakçılar is the **Kürkcüler Çarşısı**, filled with leather jackets and coats. It's also where you'll find **Yörük** (*see p155 The rug trade*), a highly recommended little carpet shop, located at the base of some steps leading up and out of the bazaar.

For more carpets visit the **Rabia Hanı** at the eastern end of Kürkcüler Çarşısı. **Tradition** at No.11 is another well stocked and hassle-free option.

Running north from Kalpakçılar Caddesi, **Kolonçılar Sokak** is lined with shops that peddle a typical mix of souvenirs, ceramics, tea sets, silks, water pipes, chess sets and carved wood. It crosses **Keseciler Caddesi** (location of the quality rural crafts shop **Derviş** (*see p157*) before making a beeline for the ancient heart of the bazaar, the **Old Bedesten**. (Check out the Byzantine eagle carved into the stone on the outside face of its eastern entrance.) In here, the atmosphere is hushed, almost scholarly – a suitable setting for dealers in Ottoman-era prayer beads, icons, chess sets, firearms, pocket watches, painted miniatures, snuff boxes and Soviet memorabilia. The museum quality is enhanced by the display of a brass diver's suit, art nouveau jewellery and a meerschaum pipe that took an artisan a whole year to carve – proudly displayed below a photograph of an admiring Hillary Clinton.

On the north side of the Bedesten is **Halıcılar Caddesi**, no longer 'the Street of the Carpet Sellers', but instead the front line of gentrification, with quaint **Café Fes** and **Café Sultan** selling Illy coffee and fresh flowers, plus **Abdulla** (*see p157*), that uses chic packaging to shift traditional products.

West along Halıcılar are some more alternatives to carpets, notably at **Galeri Apollo** (No.22-6), a shop stocked with silky-soft goat-hair rugs and calf-skin hides, hand-stitched into patchwork designs.

Halıcılar connects to **Yağlıkçılar Sokağı**, a long, wide, street running north–south and the place for belly-dance costumes, incredible fabrics, lamps, knitwear and more unnecessary souvenirs.

Off Yağlıkcılar is the tranquil **Cebeci Hanı** and, beyond, the **İç Cebeci**, where a large open courtyard is ringed by a second floor, lined with antique and metalwork shops, plus a few places selling fabulous Central Asian fabrics and garments.

To visit the most beautiful *han* in the bazaar, head east from Yağlıkcılar along **Perdahcılar Sokağı**; at the end follow the signs for **Zincirli Hanı**, the lair of the Grand Bazaar's most famous carpet dealer, **Sisko Osman** (*see p155* **The Rug Trade**).

Grand Bazaar

Kapalı Çarşı
Beyazıt (0212 522 3173/www.karpalicarsi.org.tr).
Tram Beyazıt or Çemberlitaş. **Open** 8.30am-7pm
Mon-Sat. **Map** p288 L9.

TIME OUT
Outside the southern entrance to the Old Bedesten are **Julia's Kitchen** (Keseciler Caddesi 92), a great breakfast stop, and **Köşk** (Keseciler Caddesi 98-100), which serves traditional *sulu yemek* (home cooking) dished up from bains-marie, The **Şark Kahvesi** (at the corner of Yağlıkcılar and Fesciler Caddesi) is an old-style coffee-house, decorated with wondeful pictures of old fellows on flying carpets. The courtyard of the **İç Cebeci Hanı** has an excellent kebab shop and a tea house where off-duty merchants spend a serious amount of time over games źof cards. **Havuzlu Lokantasi** (Gani Çelebi Sokak 3) is a basic, old fashioned joint that does fine kebabs. Remember that all cafés and restaurants in the bazaar shut by 6.30pm.

Sightseeing

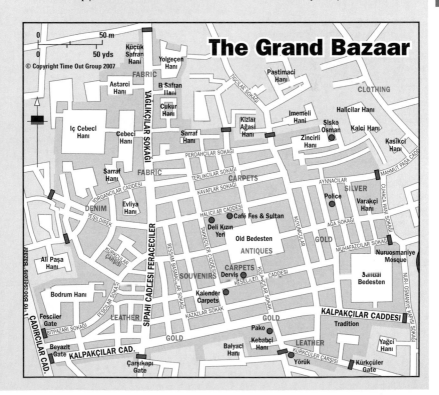

Beyazıt Square

A large, irregularly shaped plaza west of the bazaar, Beyazıt Square was the site of the forum in Roman times. It regained importance when the early Ottomans built a palace here, which served as the pre-Topkapı seat of power until it burnt down in 1541. Other significant Ottoman structures still stand, notably the **Beyazıt Mosque**.

Facing the mosque is the monumental gate to **Istanbul University**, previously the Ottoman Ministry of War. In the 1960s and 1970s, the campus was a favourite battleground for both left and right, and is still a centre for political protest, with bullets occasionally whizzing across the square. As a result, the university grounds and **Beyazıt Tower**, built in 1828 as a fire lookout (the construction of many buildings in wood made fire a constant hazard) and a prominent city landmark , are currently off limits to all but accredited students.

To the left of the monumental gate is a small *medrese*, which was originally part of the Beyazıt Mosque complex but is now occupied by the **Calligraphy Museum,** sadly in a sorry state of decline.

Follow either of the roads that hug the university walls to reach the architectural perfection of the **Süleymaniye Mosque**. Outside its compound wall, in a walled, triangular garden to the north, is the modest **Tomb of Sinan**, designed by the occupant himself. The mosque's 500-year-old kitchens are now employed by **Darüzziyafe**, where you can have a rather unexceptional lunch in an exceptional setting. Also worth a visit is the neighbouring **Lalezar** tea-house, which occupies a sunken courtyard with a marble fountain, comfy cushioned seats along the walls, and *narghile* to puff on.

Beyazıt Mosque

Beyazıt Camii
Beyazıt Square, Yeniçeriler Caddesi. Tram Beyazıt. **Open** 10am-final prayer call daily. **Admission** free. **Map** p242 K9.
Built in 1501-06, this was the second great mosque complex to be founded in the city. The first, the Fatih Mosque (see p84), was destroyed, which makes Beyazıt the oldest imperial mosque in town. In effect, it's the architectural link between the Byzantine Haghia Sophia – the obvious inspiration – and the great, later Ottoman mosques such as Süleymaniye. The sultan for whom it was built, Beyazit II, is buried at the back of the gardens. Still in use, the mosque is full of market traders at prayer times. Outside is the Sahaflar Carsisi (book bazaar), where Sufi booksellers tout travelogues and novels in many diffferent languages.

Calligraphy Museum

Vakıf Hat Sanatları Müzesi
Beyazıt Square, Beyazıt (0212 527 5851). Tram Beyazıt. **Open** 9am-4pm Tue-Sat. **Admission** YTL3; photo permit YTL10; video permit YTL20. **No credit cards. Map** p242 K10.
A sad reminder of the perishable nature of human endeavour, this limited celebration of one of the principal arts of the Ottoman Empire now reeks of rotting manuscripts. Forbidden to portray living beings by their religion (although this was not always strictly adhered to), Islamic artists developed alternative forms of virtuosity. Calligraphy was regarded as a particularly noble art because it was a way of beautifying the text of the Qu'ran. But the sanctity of the text placed restrictions on the flourishes that could be added. Not so with the sultan's *tuğra*, or monogram, which incorporated his name, titles and patronymics into one highly stylised motif – the precursor of the modern logo.

Despite the museum's dearth of labelling, there's plenty of stuff that's worth seeing. The tile art is excellent and there are a number of brilliantly illuminated Qu'rans dating from the 13th to 16th centuries. The museum also has a pleasant courtyard that features stone-carved calligraphy. During Ramadan, the Dar'ül-Kurra in the courtyard is open to visitors; it contains some holy relics of the Prophet Muhammed.

Süleymaniye Mosque

Süleymaniye Camii
Tiryakiler Çarşısı, off Prof Sıddık Sami Onar Caddesi, Süleymaniye. Tram Beyazıt or Eminönü. **Open** 9am-7pm daily. **Admission** free. **Map** p242 K8.
Completed in 1557 under Süleyman the Magnificent, this stunning mosque is arguably the crowning achievement of architect Mimar Sinan. Built on Istanbul's highest hill, it is visible for miles. The approach is along Prof Sıddık Sami Onar Caddesi, formerly known as 'Addicts Alley' because its cafés sold hashish. This is no longer the case, although the area's tea houses are still very popular student hangouts. The low-rise, multi-domed buildings surrounding the mosque are part of its *külliye* (compound), and include a hospital, asylum, hamam and a soup kitchen.

Walk through the gardens and arcaded courtyard, whose columns allegedly came from the Byzantine royal box at the Hippodrome, until you enter the mosque – remarkable for its soaring central prayer room, illuminated by some 200 windows. The interior decoration is minimal but effective; it includes stained glass added by Ibrahim the Mad and sparing use of Iznik tiles (which Sinan would later use profusely at the Rüstem Pasha Mosque, just down the hill; *see p83*).

Behind the mosque are several *türbes* (tombs), including Süleyman's own beautifully restored grave. Haseki Hürrem, the sultan's influential wife, a former slave known as Roxelana (*see p20*), is buried beside him.

Eminönü & the Golden Horn

Gourmet delis and chugging ferries.

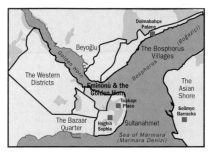

If Sultanahmet is the Istanbul of postcards, Eminönü is the Istanbul of ferry schedules. The commercial hub of the old city and a port since Ancient Greek times, its bustling waterfront leads back to a maze of alleys, mosques and the **Egyptian Bazaar**.

To get here from Beyoğlu, cross the Galata Bridge. From central Sultanahmet, ride the tram north to Eminönü, or follow the tramlines on foot (a ten-minute walk from Sultanahmet Square). The route curves sharply around the walls enclosing **Gülhane Park**. Formerly part of the grounds of the Topkapı Palace, the park is now rather dismal, with more concrete than grass. It contains a dire little zoo and, one for connoisseurs of lost causes, the **Tanzimat Museum**, whichcommemorates the liberalising reforms proclaimed from this spot by Sultan Abdülmecid in 1839, then roundly ignored by one and all (*see p23*).

Back on the tram tracks, just west of the Gülhane stop, is an ornate monumental gateway with a rococo roof: this is the historic **Sublime Porte** (Bab-ı Ali). At one time, this was the entrance to the palace of the grand vizier, the true administrator of the empire during the dotage of the sultans. Foreign ambassadors were accredited to the 'Sublime Porte', and the term became a synonym for the Ottoman government. The current gate dates from 1843 and is now the entrance to the headquarters of the provincial government.

Opposite, jutting out of a corner of the Gülhane Park wall, is the **Alay Köşkü**, an elaborate platform from which the sultans would observe parades or, in the case of Ibrahim the Mad, take potshots with a crossbow at passing pedestrians.

END OF THE LINE

After Gülhane, the tramlines descend to **Sirkeci Station** (Sirkeci Istasyonu). On its completion in 1881, this was the eastern terminus for trains from Europe, including the Orient Express. Its street-facing façade has been disfigured by modern additions, but the waterfront profile retains an element of grandeur. Despite the station's relegation to the status of suburban shuttle hub (the only international trains are to Thessaloniki and Bucharest), the original **Orient Express restaurant** beside platform one remains

Tasty treats on **Hasırcılar Caddesi**. *See p82.*

Rüstem Paşa Mosque – a sublime sanctuary above a shopping centre. *See p83.*

largely intact (*see p117*). Sadly, it's too fancy for the commuters and tends to be empty.

Opposite the station, more than holding its own against the neighbouring McDonald's, **Konyalı** (Mimar Kemalettin Caddesi 5, 0212 513 9610) is a Turkish institution. Commuters cram this basic takeaway joint that specialises in pastries, both savoury *börek*, stuffed with minced meat or cheese, and sweet varieties filled with crushed nuts and doused in syrup. Just past Konyalı the tram tracks swing left, terminating at Eminönü, grandly signposted by the **New Mosque**.

New Mosque

Yeni Camii
Eminönü Meydanı, Eminönü (0212 527 8505).
Tram Eminönü. **Open** 7am-dusk daily.
Admission free. **Map** p243 M8.
Construction on the mosque began in 1598, but suffered a setback when the architect was executed for heresy. It was eventually completed in 1663, after the classical period of Ottoman architecture had passed. It is nonetheless a regal structure, particularly uplifting seen floodlit from a taxi after a night on the town. The fact that it is so obviously a working mosque tends to keep visitors at bay, but nobody objects to non-Muslims entering.

Tanzimat Museum

Tanzimat Müzesi
Gülhane Park (0212 512 6384). Tram Gülhane.
Open 9am-5pm Mon-Fri. **Admission** free.
Map p243 O9.
The exhibits here amount to little more than a wall of portraits, a waxwork bust and some yellowing imperial decrees, all housed in a small wooden hut that's easily mistaken for a public toilet.

The Egyptian Bazaar

In front of the New Mosque is a pigeon-plagued plaza busy with itinerant street sellers and dominated on its south side by the high brick arch leading into the **Egyptian Bazaar**, otherwise known as the Spice Bazaar. The market was constructed as part of the mosque complex, and its revenues helped support philanthropic institutions. The name derives from its past association with the arrival of the annual 'Cairo caravan', a flotilla of ships bearing rice, coffee and incense from Egypt.

While the bazaar's L-shaped vaulted hall is undeniably pretty, at first glance its 90 shops seem to be hustling nothing more than an assortment of oily perfumes, cheap gold and sachets of 'Turkish Viagra'. It's a tourist trap, to be sure, but to dismiss it out of hand is to miss one of the world's finest delis: make a beeline for **Erzincanlılar** (shop No.2) for delicious honeycomb and the mature hard Turkish cheese known as *eski kaşar*. Other food shops worth checking out are **Pinar** (No.14) for excellent *lokum* (Turkish delight); **Antep Pazarı** (No.50) for pistachios, nuts, honey-covered mulberries and dried figs stuffed with walnuts; and **Güllüoğlu Baklavacısı** (No.88) for pastries. Showing where the spice bazaar is probably headed, **Özel** (No. 82) has pretty, cheap scarves. One other reason to visit the market is to lunch at **Pandeli's** (*see p117*), a famous Greek-run restaurant up a steep flight of steps just inside the main entrance.

Running west from the market, **Hasırcılar Caddesi** is one of the city's most vibrant and aromatic streets thanks to a clutch of delis (*see p153* **Namlı Pastırmacı**), spice merchants and coffee sellers, including **Kurukahveci Mehmet Efendi** (*see p151*), where caffeine addicts queue at the serving hatch to purchase the own-brand bags of beans.

Further along the street, look out for the arched doorways where flights of stairs lead up to the **Rüstem Paşa Mosque**, built in 1561 for a grand vizier of Süleyman the Great.

TAHTAKALE

The view from the Rüstem Paşa's forecourt is dominated by a large dome, which belongs to the nearby **Tahtakale Hamam Çarşısı**, a 500-year-old bathhouse in the process of being converted into a 21st-century shopping centre. At the time of going to press, most of the shop units had yet to be let, but there is a pleasant café occupying the main domed chamber.

This area north of Hasırcılar Caddesi is known as Tahtakale. Its streets heave with locals out to snap up bargain clothing, underwear and household accessories. Women shop here to top up their dowries, picking up linens, bedwear, lingerie and towels. This is also the place to buy the traditional circumcision outfits that consist of a crown, a white satin cape, and a golden staff. Local traders also do a brisk business in wood and wickerware, handmade wooden spoons and coat-hangers, knives and tools. **Tahtakale Caddesi** is renowned for its 'portable stalls' manned by shifty gents peddling pirated CDs, DVDs, smuggled electronics and cigars. At the first whisper of police, stalls are snapped shut and the owners all leg it.

Egyptian Bazaar

Mısır Çarşısı
Yeni Camii Meydanı, Eminönü (0212 513 6597).
Tram Eminönü. **Open** 8am-7pm Mon-Sat.
Map p243 L8.

Rüstem Paşa Mosque

Rüstem Paşa Camii
Hasırcılar Caddesi 90 (0212 526 7350). Tram
Eminönü. **Open** 9am-dusk daily. **Admission** free.
Map p242 L7.

Above the shops, (whose rents pay for its upkeep), the mosque is invisible from the street. It's quite a city secret, although it's one of the most beautiful mosques built by Sinan (*see p21* **The mosque maker**). Smaller than most of his works, it's also set apart by its liberal and dazzling use of coloured tiles. The first-floor forecourt, with its colonnaded canopy and potted plants high above the crowed alleys, is one of Istanbul's loveliest hideaways. **Photo** *p82.*

The Golden Horn

Eminönü is the departure point for ferries up the Bosphorus, across to Asia and out to the Princes' and Marmara Islands. A few services also head up the Golden Horn, an inlet of the Marmara some 7.5 kilometres (five miles) long. The maritime traffic here is frantic, as hulking vessels skirmish with tiny motorboats for berthing positions. Pedestrian traffic is intense too – watch your wallet.

Mingling with the smell of diesel is the whiff of deep-frying fish. This comes from the small boats moored at the dockside, cooking up their day's catch of small fry for sale in sandwiches.

The best place to observe the hustle and bustle is from the **Galata Bridge**, the vital link between the two sides of European Istanbul. The current structure, an unsightly concrete ramp with four steel towers at its centre (they're supposed to raise the bridge, but don't work) replaces a much-loved earlier bridge. This one, was built in the 1980s to accommodate growing traffic. Its saving grace is the lower deck of restaurants, bars and tea-houses right on the waterfront that provide ring-side seating for cheap beers and boat-watching.

Galata Bridge.

The Western Districts

Another Istanbul: modern faith and historic religious heritages.

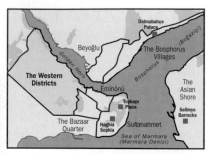

West of Sultanahmet and the Bazaar Quarter lies the sprawling Western District – an ancient, melancholy collection of neighbourhoods that make up one of the most religious areas in the city. In **Fatih**, **Fener** and **Balat**, headscarves, chadors and the baggy *şalvar* trousers worn by devout men are much in evidence. Often neglected by Western visitors, the area is rich in atmosphere and monuments, peppered with churches, synagogues and Greek Orthodox schools – a reminder that until early last century, around 40 per cent of Istanbul's population were Christians and Jews.

Two highlights in this area are the **Church of St Saviour in Chora**, one of the city's most dazzling Byzantine monuments, and the mosque at **Eyüp**, a major pilgrimage site with stunning views down the Golden Horn and across to the Asian Shore.

Fatih

Immediately west of the Bazaar Quarter, Fatih is easy to reach by tram from Sultanahmet. Hop off at the Üniversite or Laleli stop and walk north, past rows of leather and suede shops, to the **Şehzade Mosque**, the first royal complex built by Sinan (*see p21* **The mosque maker**).

Beyond the gardens of the mosque is the mighty **Aqueduct of Valens**. Constructed by the Roman emperor Valens in the fourth century AD, the aqueduct channelled water from the lakes north of the city to Istanbul's cisterns up until the late 19th century. For a city often under siege, a reliable water supply was critical. These days, the aqueduct forms a dramatic entrance to the city as modern Atatürk Bulvarı passes beneath its two-tiered arches.

Huddled in the shadow of the aqueduct is the attractive little Medrese of Gazanfer Ağa, now the **Cartoon Museum**. A short walk further north is what's now known as the **Zeyrek Mosque**, but was once the Byzantine Church of the Pantocrator. Ten minutes' walk due west is one of the most significant, and under-explored, historical sites in the city: the **Fatih Mosque**. On Wednesdays, the streets around the mosque throng with **Fatih Pazarı**, a vast street market. From the Fatih Mosque follow Darüşşafaka Caddesi north; turn right onto Yavuz Selim Caddesi past the fifth-century **Cistern of Aspar** (now a sports complex) to the **Selim I Mosque** (Yavuz Selim Camii).

Cartoon Museum

Karikatür ve Mizah Müzesi
Kavacılar Sokak 12, off Atatürk Bulvarı, Şehzadebaşı (0212 521 1264). Tram Laleli or Üniversite. **Open** 9am-4.30pm Tue-Sat. **Admission** free. **Map** p242 H8.
Set in a beautiful 17th-century *medrese*, this is one of the city's more unusual museums. Where instructors once lectured students in Islamic philosophy, they now give lessons in illustration, engraving and screen-printing. The permanent collection, with pieces dating back to the 1870s, illustrates the long-standing popularity of caricature and satire in Turkey. One of the most recurring themes is the insidious influence of the West. Temporary exhibitions are devoted to Turkish and foreign cartoonists. The museum also hosts Turkey's only humour library and an archive open to the public upon request.

Fatih Mosque

Fatih Camii
Fevzi Paşa Caddesi, Fatih. Metro Emniyet. **Open** 9am-dusk daily. **Admission** free. **Map** p245 G7.
Fatih Mosque is a popular place for pious picnickers. The vast 18th-century baroque structure is built on the site of the Church of the Holy Apostles, burial place of most Byzantine emperors, including Constantine. The church was already in ruins by the time Mehmet II conquered Constantinople. He used it as a quarry for a mosque built in 1470 to celebrate his victory (*fatih* means 'conqueror'). Most of Mehmet's original structure was destroyed by an earthquake in 1766; all that remains is the courtyard and parts of the main entrance. The tomb of the Conqueror stands behind the prayer hall.

Selim I Mosque

Yavuz Sultan Selim Camii
Yavuz Selim Caddesi, Fatih. Bus 90, 99A. **Open** 8am-dusk daily. **Admission** free. **Map** p245 G5.

It may have been built to commemorate Sultan Selim the Grim, nicknamed for his habit of executing senior officials on a whim, but this little-visited mosque is one of the most beautiful in the city, with a lovely courtyard and terrace overlooking the Golden Horn.

Şehzade Mosque

Şehzade Camii
Şehzadebaşı Caddesi, Saraçhane, Şehzadebaşı. Tram Üniversite or Laleli. **Open** 9am-dusk daily.
Admission free. **Map** p242 H8.
Completed in 1548, Sinan dismissed his first royal mosque complex as 'apprentice work'. It is named after Prince Şehzade Mehmet, son of Suleyman, who died suddenly and prematurely. He is buried in the complex. The square courtyard is as big as the interior of the mosque. The combination of the square plan and the central dome surrounded by four half domes is unprecedented in Islamic architecture.

Zeyrek Mosque

Zeyrek Camii
Ibadethane Sokak, Küçükpazar. Metro Laleli. **Open** 9am-dusk daily. **Admission** free. **Map** p242 H7.
Built in the 12th century for the wife of Emperor John II Comnenus (1118-43), the Byzantine Church of the Pantocrator became the imperial residence during the struggles with the Latin crusaders. It was turned into a mosque after the Muslim conquest of Constantinople. Although in a deplorable state of disrepair, it retains some fine internal decoration, including exquisitely carved door frames and marble mosaic floors which, if you're lucky, one of the caretakers will reveal by drawing back the carpets. Archaeological oddities are displayed on a terrace overlooking the Golden Horn, which belongs to the swish Zeyrekhane restaurant.

Fener & Balat

Until the early 20th century, Fener was primarily Greek, while Balat was mainly Jewish. Although lacking major monuments, these are fascinating areas in which to wander.

The most picturesque approach to the two districts is on foot from the Selim I Mosque (*see p84*), which is a ten-minute taxi ride from central Sultanahmet.

From the mosque head downhill past the red-brick Fener Greek School for Boys. A little below and to the left is the only Byzantine church still in Greek hands, the **Church of Panaghia Mouchliotissa**. Immediately north of the church is the stretch of Byzantine sea wall breached by the crusaders in 1204. East along Incebal Sokak is the **Greek Orthodox Patriarchate**, an unprepossessing walled compound that has been the world centre of Greek Orthodoxy for the past 400 years.

Back west along **Yıldırım Street** are some of the city's finest old Greek residences, including the Fener Mansions, which date from the 17th and 18th centuries. Most are in a terrible state of dilapidation. Only one is presently occupied, housing the first dedicated womens' library (**Kadın Kütüphanesi**) in Turkey.

Equally unique is the church of **St Stephen of the Bulgars**, one of Turkey's only examples of neo-Gothic architecture.

THE JEWISH QUARTER

Inland from St Stephen, the streets take on a grid pattern in what used to be Istanbul's main Jewish district. It is home to the city's oldest synagogue, the **Ahrida Synagogue**. Around the corner is the fascinating Armenian Orthodox Church of **Surp Hireşdagabet** (Holy Archangels). Heading south-west, towards the city walls, is the **Church of St Saviour in Chora**, now a museum featuring extraordinarily well-preserved Byzantine frescoes and mosaics.

Ahrida Synagogue

Ahrida Sinagogu
Kürkçüçeşme Sokak 9, Balat. Bus 35D. **Open** by appointment with the Chief Rabbi (0212 243 5166).
Map p245 F3.

Fatih Pazarı. *See p84.*

Daily life in **Balat**. See p84.

Founded by Macedonians from the town of Ohrid (of which 'Ahrida' is a corruption) in the 15th century, the synagogue's congregation later comprised the city's Sephardic Jewish community who had fled Spain during the inquisition. The synagogue is still used by the Sephardic community, many of whom speak the medieval Spanish dialect Ladino. The wooden dome, restored in 17th-century baroque style, is exquisite.

Church of Panaghia Mouchliotissa
Kanlı Kilise
Tevkii Cafer Mektebi Sokak, Fener (0212 521 7139).
Bus 55T. **Open** 9am-5pm daily. **Admission** free.
Map p245 G4.

Otherwise known as St Mary of the Mongols, this 13th-century church was erected in honour of Princess Maria, daughter of Emperor Michael VIII, who was married off to the khan of the Mongols. It was reputedly spared conversion into a mosque thanks to a Greek architect employed by Mehmet II; a decree issued by the Conqueror to this effect has pride of place in the church.

Church of St Saviour in Chora
Kariye Müzesi
Kariye Camii Sokak 26, Edirnekapı (0212 631 9241). Metro Ulubatlı or bus 37E, 38E, 91O toVefa Stadium. **Open** 9am-4.30pm Mon, Tue, Thur-Sun. **Admission** YTL10. **Map** p244 D4.
Often overlooked because it's so far off the beaten track, for Byzantine splendour this church (also known as the Kariye Mosque or Museum) is second only to Haghia Sophia. Built in the late 11th century, its celebrated mosaics and frescoes were added when the church was remodelled in the 14th century. Depicting all manner of Christain iconography, from the Day of Judgement through to the Resurrection, the works here are arguably the most important surviving examples of Byzantine art in the world, both in terms of their execution and preservation. Ironically, this Christian art owes its excellent condition to the church's conversion to Islam in the early 16th century, when the frescoes and mosaics were covered over. They remained concealed until their rediscovery in 1860. The Kariye Hotel at the end of the street is also worth visiting for its excellent Ottoman restaurant, Asitane (*see p119*). **Photo** *p88*.

Church of St Stephen of the Bulgars
Mürsel Paşa Caddesi 85-8, Fener (0212 521 1121). Bus 55T. **Admission** free. **Map** p245 G3.
Erected in 1871 for Istanbul's Bulgarian community, this church is still used today by Macedonian Christians. It is constructed entirely from prefabricated iron sections, cast in Vienna and shipped down the Danube to Istanbul.

Church of Surp Hireşdagabet (Holy Angels)
Kamış Sokak, Balat. Bus 35D. **Open** Thur am services only. **Admission** free. **Map** p245 F3.
Tentatively dated to the 13th century, this church was taken over by the Armenians in the early 17th century. Although much of the current structure dates from 1835, the side chapel and *ayazma* (sacred spring) are original Byzantine features. The congregation is composed almost exclusively of headscarved Muslim women – many devout Muslims take both Christian and Jewish rituals very seriously as 'precursors' of Islam. The church is famous for one thing: every 16 September, a miracle cure is reputedly bestowed on one member of the congregation. Muslims with birth defects or incurable illnesses from all over Turkey crowd the church, hoping to be the lucky one.

Greek Orthodox Patriarchate

Fener Rum Patrikhanesi
Sadrazam Ali Paşa Caddesi, Fener (0212 525 2117).
Bus 55T. **Open** 8am-5pm daily. **Map** p245 G4.
The central section of the seat of Greek Orthodoxy
is permanently closed in memory of Patriarch
Gregory V, who was hanged from it in 1821 as punishment for the outbreak of the Greek War of
Independence. The main Church of St George is
unremarkable save for three unusual free-standing
mosaic icons. During celebrations for Orthodox
Easter, the church attracts hundreds of pilgrims
and provides a focal point for the dwindling Greek
community of Istanbul.

City walls

Constructed during the reign of Theodosius II
(408-450), the walls of Constantinople are the
largest Byzantine structure that survives in
modern Istanbul. Until the Ottoman conquest
in 1453, these walls withstood invading armies
for over 1,000 years, resisting siege on more
than 20 occasions.

The walls encompass the old city in a great
arc, stretching some 6.5 kilometres (four miles)
from the Golden Horn to the Sea of Marmara.
Together with the sea walls that ringed
Constantinople, they constituted Europe's
most extensive medieval fortifications.

A triumph of engineering, the walls comprise
inner and outer ramparts with a terrace in
between. The outer wall is two metres (seven
feet) thick and around 8.5 metres (30 feet) high,
with 96 towers overlooking the 20-metre (70-
feet) moat. The five-metre (16-feet) wide inner
wall is around 12 metres (40 feet) high and is
studded with another 96 towers.

Large sections of the walls have been
rebuilt in recent years, drawing criticism
from scholars for inappropriate use of modern
materials, but the restored sections are
undeniably impressive.

WALL WALKING

There are several ways to get to the walls,
depending on which part you want to visit. It's
possible to walk the whole length, along both
the inside and outside, although care should be
taken as some sections are deserted apart from
vagrants. The best place to begin is on the
Marmara coast at **Yedikule**. Take a bus from
Eminönü (80) or Taksim (80T) or, for a more
scenic ride, a suburban train from Sirkeci to
Yedikule. The train passes under the ramparts
of Topkapı Palace and winds in and out of what
remains of the southern sea walls.

On the Marmara shore, the walls begin with
the imposing **Marble Tower** on a promontory
by the sea. It has served as both an imperial
summer pavilion and as a prison. You can

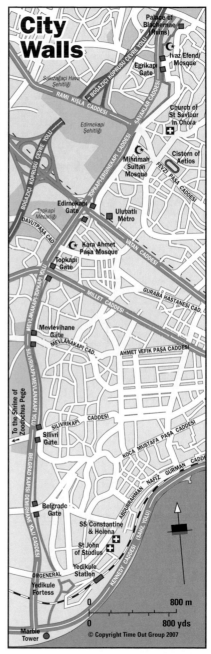

The icon breakers

In the eighth and ninth centuries, a Byzantine empire faced with the onslaught of expansionist Islam was also torn apart by an internal controversy: whether or not it was permissible to paint images of Christ and the saints. Whether icons should be created or destroyed was the hot theological topic of the day. From the vantage point of the 21st century it's easy to say that the Byzantines should have united against the outside threat rather than wasting energy on an internal clash of ideologies. But the empire believed it had a divine mission. This dilemma was central to how that mission would be carried out, and went to the core of Byzantium's definition of itself.

When Emperor Leo III removed an image of Christ from above the doors to the imperial palace in 726, it sparked riots and deaths. However, the emperor was not to be dissuaded. In 730, Leo deposed the patriarch of Constantinople and ordered the removal or destruction of all icons in the city. All resistance was violently suppressed. This ruthlessness must have been effective, for precious few icons painted before the eighth century have survived.

What prompted Leo to plunge his empire into a virtual civil war? The answer lies partly in the Byzantine struggle against Islam. The Byzantines saw success or failure as marks of God's favour or disfavour. Encroachment on Christendom by the aggressively iconoclastic Muslims led some to assume that God had forsaken them because the veneration of icons was an idolatrous contravention of the second commandment, desecrating Christ's divinity by depicting him in human form.

The icon-worshippers developed an underground resistance movement, hiding icons from the imperial troops in monasteries. They found a powerful spokesman in St John of Damascus, a Christian who was chief councillor to the Ummayad rulers of the city. Safely out of the emperor's reach (or so he thought), John wrote in defence of icons. He pointed out that iconographers were only painting what God himself had done: become flesh and blood in the person of Christ. According to the iconoclasts' logic, he argued, the first and greatest idolater was therefore God himself. Infuriated, the emperor allegedly forged a letter in which John offered to betray Damascus to the Byzantines. An unamused Caliph had John's hand cut off.

The icon controversy raged on for over a century, outlasting four religious councils that provided ecclesiastical back-up, several emperors and two empresses. It was these female rulers who eventually decided the case. Empress Irene was the first to reverse the iconoclast policy of her predecessors, and in 843 the Empress Theodore proclaimed the restoration of icons. Since then, the first Sunday of Lent has been celebrated as the triumph of Orthodoxy.

Go into any Orthodox church today and the first things that strike you are the glorious icons, glittering in the candlelight: icons and the faith and art that surround them survived, and it's hard to imagine the Orthodox Church without them. Had the iconoclasts prevailed there would have been none of the later Byzantine religious imagery gloriously preserved in Istanbul – in the **Church of St Saviour in Chora** (*pictured*).

still see the chute through which executed corpses were dumped into the sea.

On the other side of the coastal road is the near-pristine **Gate of Christ**, the first of 11 fortified gates. On the northern side of the railway line is **Yedikule Fortress**, whose entrance is in the north-east wall.

From Yedikule to the **Belgrade Gate** (Belgrad Kapısı) and onwards to the **Silivri Gate** (Silivri Kapısı) it is possible to walk along the top of the walls or on the terrace below. Near the Silivri Gate is the **Shrine of Zoodochus Pege** ('life-giving spring'). The **Mevlevihane Gate** bears several inscriptions, including one in Latin boasting how Constantine erected the final phase of the walls in 'less than two months'. Further north beyond Millet Caddesi stands **Topkapı Gate**, or Cannon Gate.

North of Topkapı the walls descend into the Lycus river valley, now the six-lane Vatan Caddesi. This low-lying stretch was particularly difficult to defend, and it was here that the besieging Ottomans finally broke through in 1453. Over 500 years later, the battlements here remain in the worst state of repair. A little to the north, Mehmet the Conqueror made his triumphal entry into the city through **Edirnekapı** (Edirne Gate). A plaque on the south side of the gate commemorates the event.

Approaching the Golden Horn, the city walls end at the Byzantine **Blachernae Palace**.

Blachernae Palace

Anemas Zindanları
Ivaz Ağa Caddesi, Ayvansaray. Bus 5T, 99A. **Open** 9am-7pm daily. **Admission** YTL2. **Map** p87.
First constructed around AD 500, the palace was extended in the 11th and 12th centuries, by which time it had become the favoured imperial residence. It's now mostly in ruins. The best-preserved sections are the brick-and-marble three-storey façade, the Palace of the Porphyrogenitus, and five floors of tunnels and galleries below the Ahmet tea garden, which were cleared of rubble in 1999 for a film shoot and are rather awesome in their medieval splendour.

Shrine of Zoodochus Pege

Balıklı Kilise
Seyit Nizam Caddesi 3, Silivrikapı (0212 582 3081).
Tram Seyitnizam. **Open** 9am-4pm daily.
Admission free.
Originally an ancient sanctuary of Artemis, the first church was built over the 'life-giving spring' here in the early Byzantine era. Destroyed and rebuilt many times, the present structure dates from 1833. The shrine itself is a pool containing 'sacred' fish, said to have leapt into the spring from a monk's frying pan on hearing him say that a Turkish invasion of Constantinople was as likely as fish coming back to life.

Yedikule Fortress

Yedikule Müzesi
Yedikule Meydanı Sokak, Yedikule (0212 585 8933).
Yedikule Station from Sirkeci or bus 80, 80T. **Open** 8am-5pm Mon,Tue, Thur-Sun. **Admission** YTL5.
Map p87.
Impressively restored, this Byzantine 'castle of the seven towers' was remodelled by the Ottomans. Its western face incorporates the Golden Gate (now bricked up), a triumphal arch erected around AD 390. The vertiginous battlements offer wonderful views.

Eyüp

Beyond the city walls, a mile west along the shore of the Golden Horn, is the village of Eyüp (pronounced 'eh-oop'). Historian John Freely describes its traditional image as a 'peaceful backwater devoted to religion and death'. These days, the place is on the verge of being absorbed by suburbia, but for the time being it retains both rural and spiritual qualities courtesy of two large, wooded hills above the village whose slopes are free of development by virtue of being devoted to the dead.

The area's popularity as a burial spot derives from the **Eyüp Mosque**, the holiest mosque in Istanbul, and the third-most sacred site in Islam after Mecca and Jerusalem. Its holy status comes from being the - reputed - burial place of Eyüp Ensari, companion and standard-bearer of the Prophet Mohamed. His tomb is adjacent to the mosque and boasts a gold-framed footprint of Mohamed and some fancy Iznik tiling. A constant trail of pilgrims queue to supplicate themselves before the cenotaph. A vast *külliye* (complex) surrounds the mosque, with most buildings dating to 1458 and the reign of Mehmet the Conqueror. Non-Muslims are welcome, but visitors should dress modestly. Headscarves are available for women.

Running north from Eyüp's main plaza is an attractive shopping street full of bakeries and interesting food shops. From the top end, flag a taxi and ride all the way up the hill to the **Pierre Loti Café** (*see p134*), named for the 19th-century French romantic novelist who lived in Eyüp for several years. You'll be dropped at a modern tourist development with fantastic views from its terrace, but for something with more charm (and equally good views) follow the path down the hill to a modest tea shop with rickety tables beneath the trees.

GETTING THERE

Take the No.99 bus from Eminönü bus station to Eyüp. It's a 15-minute ride. Alternatively, you can catch a ferry from Eminönü, stopping off at Kasımpaşa, Fener and Balat en route. The first ferry departs Eminönü at 7.20am, with hourly departures until 8pm.

Beyoğlu & Beyond

The heart and soul of the modern secular city.

Like Istanbul itself, Beyoğlu is an area with boundaries that are hard to define, but for our purposes the area includes everything up the hill from the Golden Horn, all the way to **Taksim Square**. Since most streets are too narrow and twisted for traffic (but that doesn't mean cab drivers don't try their luck), the best way to explore the various neighbourhoods that make up Beyoğlu is on foot. Lost? Ask someone to point you in the direction of **Istiklal Caddesi**, where the entire city goes to work, shop and play, making it one of the liveliest streets on earth.

A tram usually runs along its length, from Tünel to Taksim; it was out of commission at the time of writing, but should be back in business early in 2007. We don't list transport details for individual destinations in Beyoğlu; for information on getting around, *see p63* **Crossing the Golden Horn**.

GALATA AND PERA

Historically, the district went by two different names: Galata, for the hillside just north of the Golden Horn, and Pera, denoting what's now the lower Istiklal Caddesi area. Occupied by foreigners since Byzantine times, these trading colonies across the water from the walls of Constantinople proper were founded by merchants from Genoa and Venice. After the Ottoman conquest in the 15th century, it was to Galata that the European powers sent their first ambassadors. By the 17th century, Galata/Pera was a substantial city in its own right, with a multiethnic population known collectively as Levantines. Among them were Italians and many other significant communities, defined thus by a Turkish chronicler of the time: 'The Greeks keep the

taverns; most of the Armenians are merchants or money-changers; the Jews are the go-betweens in amorous intrigues and their youths are the worst of all the devotees of debauchery.'

OLD PERA TO NEW

It was during the 19th century that the area acquired its present character. The increased use of iron and brick, instead of the traditional wood, made it feasible to construct buildings that could survive the fires that regularly ravaged the city.

After the foundation of the Republic in the 1930s, the area officially became known as Beyoğlu and blossomed with new restaurants, theatres and concert halls. Older residents still speak wistfully of never daring to go to Istiklal Caddesi without a collar and tie. World War II brought a discriminatory wealth tax that hit the Christians and Jews hard (Muslims were exempt). As a result, many left for Greece, America or Israel. In the 1950s and '60s, political tensions caused most of the remaining Greeks to depart. In their place came a flood of poor migrants from Anatolia, and Beyoğlu gradually lost its cachet.

By the late 1980s, Istiklal Caddesi and the area around it was run-down, sleazy, even a little dangerous. That began to change in late 1990 after the simple measure of turning it into a pedestrian precinct. The subsequent transformation has been swift and continues apace. Newly reopened **Passage Markiz** on lower Istiklal Caddesi, a five-storey complex of shops, bars and restaurants, is a marked contrast to the cut-rate clothing, music and bookshops currently associated with Beyoğlu. This is the place to pick up Cuban cigars, imported wines, Mont Blanc pens and tailored shirts. It's book-ended by an AFM cinema and Sony store just before Taksim Square. Two narrow lanes behind the Galatasaray Lycée also got a makeover recently, when no fewer than 24 derelict buildings were converted into cafés, bars, galleries, restaurants and a boutique hotel, collectively marketed as the **Rue Française**.

Galata

Echoing its mercantile origins, Galata remains almost completely commercial. There's even a row of ships' chandlers still trading along Yüzbaşı Sabahattin Evren Caddesi.

Location, location, location

With real estate prices rocketing and old-school dives closing, Beyoğlu is not the rough and ready bohemia it once was. The boom in trendy cafés and bars, exclusive restaurants and clubs has turned the district into the city's hottest destination for many Turks and foreign residents. Covetable 19th- and early 20th-century apartments have been gobbled up wholesale by Istanbul's growing band of property developers.

Just ten years ago, most locals would never have dreamed of living in run-down Beyoğlu, which hadn't seen any major building development since the 1930s. The violent anti-Greek riots of the 1950s and '60s cleared out most of the area's original inhabitants; their apartments were often taken over by Anatolian squatters or sweat-shops run by local racketeers. But through the layers of pigeon droppings and mould, these grand old apartments, hotels and banks continued to attract those with a more discerning eye. Given the rapid rise in Istanbul's population, the revival of down-town Beyoğlu was only a matter of time.

Property values in the district are rising by up to 25 per cent a year. Many owners are now foreigners, especially in expat-heavy **Cihangir**. In 2006, an 80-square-metre ground-floor flat in the district was going for around YTL117,000, with a rental value of about YTL1,200 a month. A per-square-metre rate of YTL2,900 is typical, but the better the Bosphorus view, the higher the price.

Çukurcuma, the shabby chic antique district nestled between Çihangir and Istiklal Caddesi, is also heating up. Meanwhile, **Galata** is already a lost cause for anyone looking for a bargain. Even **Tarlabaşı**, one of the city's grimmest, poorest areas, commands premium prices these days.

Even so, it is still just about possible to pick up a decrepit historic building with great potential for a less-than-exorbitant price. For property-obsessed Brits, one of the pleasures of Beyoğlu is hunting them out. But be warned: the local *emlakçı*, or estate agent, has a keen sense of what these places are worth – and will be more than anxious for his or her 10 per cent commission.

Çukurcuma.

Sightseeing

Yerebatan Sarnici. See p72.

All roads lead to **Istiklal Caddesi**. *See p90.*

Central to the area's history, and easily the most distinctive landmark north of the Golden Horn, the conical-capped **Galata Tower** has spectacular views from its pinnacle.

Just downhill from the Galata Tower on **Camekan Sokak**, Beyoğlu hospital is a large building with a vaguely gothic tower. It was built in 1904 as the British Seaman's Hospital, designed by Percy Adams, better known as architect of London University's Senate House. The tower afforded clear sightlines to incoming ships, allowing them to signal news of any illness on board, an important consideration in the days before ship-to-shore radio.

Around the corner on **Galata Kulesi Sokak** stands the former British consular prison: the Ottomans allowed favoured nations to imprison their own nationals, adn this is where the British convicts were banged up. The building has been put to imaginative use as the charming and quirky Galata House restaurant (*see p125*).

On the same street is the former parish church of Galata's Maltese community, the **Dominican Church of St Peter and Paul**. It's a superb neo-classical affair built by the Swiss-born Fossati brothers, dating from 1841 but containing a number of much older relics.

From the 18th century onwards, it was the bankers of Galata who kept the declining Ottoman Empire afloat, albeit at ruinous rates of interest. **Voyvoda Caddesi**, at the bottom of Galata Kulesi Sokak, was the city's banking centre. Although the financial institutions have since moved out, the street is still lined with imposing 19th-century mansions.

Running up from Voyvoda, the curvaceous **Kamondo Steps** are named after the local Jewish banking family who paid for their construction. Part staircase, part sculpture, they were immortalised in the early 1960s in a famous photograph by Henri Cartier-Bresson. Galata's long Jewish legacy is celebrated at the western end of Voyvoda Caddesi at the **Jewish Museum** (*see p100*), housed in the beautifully restored Zülfaris Synagogue.

South of Voyvoda, **Perşembe Pazarı Caddesi** boasts some fine 18th-century merchants' houses, while 100 metres (320 feet) west on Fütühat Sokak stands the only remaining Genoese church, now the **Arap Mosque**. Just to the north on Yanıkkapı Sokak are more Genoese remains in the shape of the **Burned Gate** (Yanık Kapı), the only remaining gate from the old city walls. It still bears a plaque with St George's cross, symbol of Genoa.

Arap Mosque

Arap Camii
Fütühat Sokak, Galata. Open 9am to dusk daily. **Admission** free. **Map** p246 L6.
Built between 1323 and 1337, and dedicated to St Dominic and St Paul, this was the largest of Constantinople's Latin churches. In the early 16th century, it was converted into a mosque to serve the Moorish exiles from Spain, which is possibly how it got its current name, the 'Arab mosque'. Despite extensive alterations, the design is clearly that of a typical medieval church, complete with apses and a belfry.

Galata Tower

Galata Kulesi
Galata Square (0212 293 8180). **Open** 9am-8pm daily. **Admission** YTL10. **No credit cards**. **Map** p246 M5.
Originally named the Tower of Christ, this watchtower was built in 1348 at the apex of fortified walls. After the Ottoman conquest, it was used to house prisoners of war and later became an observatory; during the 19th century, it was a lookout post to watch for the fires that frequently broke out in the city's largely wooden buildings. In the 1960s, the tower was restored and a horribly cheesy restaurant and nightclub were added. They have barely changed since, and both are very much missable, but it's worth paying the rather hefty entrance fee to ascend to the 360-degree viewing gallery, with commanding views of the entire sprawling metropolis.

Tünel

Opened in 1876, the one-stop **funicular** that runs from Karaköy up to **Tünel Square** at the southern end of Istiklal Caddesi is, after London and New York's systems, the third-oldest passenger underground in the world.

Tünel, the area around the upper station, is currently in transition from shabby neglect to arty affluence. The proliferation of stylish businesses such as KV Café (*see* p135), occupying a 19th-century Italianate passage opposite the funicular, extends as far as Sofyalı Sokak, which is lined with fine bars and restaurants, such as Sofyalı 9 (*see* p125).

Around the corner from Tünel Square, on Galip Dede Caddesi, is a dervish lodge, the **Galata Mevlevi-hanesi**, that also goes by the name of the Museum for Classical Literature.

Galata Mevlevihanesi

Galip Dede Caddesi 15, Tünel (0212 245 4141).
Open 9.30am-4.30pm Mon, Wed-Sun. **Admission** YTL2. **Map** p248 M5.

This is the only institution in Istanbul dedicated to the Whirling Dervishes that is open to the public. A peaceful courtyard leads through to the octagonal *tekke* (lodge), a restored version of the 1491 original, which contains various musical instruments and beautifully illuminated Qu'rans. Also within the complex is the tomb of Galip Dede, a 17th-century Sufi poet after whom the street is named.

Istiklal Caddesi

Originally known as Cadde-i Kebir (the high street), and later La Grande Rue de Pera, Istiklal Caddesi gained its present name, 'Independence Street', soon after the founding of the Republic. In character, it remains resolutely pre-republican, thanks to some wonderful early 20th-century architecture. The **Botter House** at Nos.475-477 is an art nouveau masterpiece by Raimondo D'Aronco, built for Jean Botter, Sultan Abdül Hamit's tailor. His daughter offered to leave the building to the city council, but the authorities refused to guarantee its preservation and since her death it has become dilapidated. A few doors up, at No.401, the **Mudo Pera** has an art nouveau interior of highly polished wood.

The street's churches are more restrained, often hidden from the street – the result of a restriction forbidding non-Muslim buildings from appearing on the skyline that held sway until the 19th century. The oldest is **St Mary Draperis** at No.429, a fairly humble building from 1789 that once served as the Austro-Hungarian embassy. This stretch of Istiklal is lined with former embassies, some still serving as consulates, others converted to new uses.

West of the main street is the lively neighbourhood of **Asmalımescit**, home of the city's low-rent art scene. The back streets are full of studios and galleries, as well as countless laid-back cafés, bars, and cheap eateries. Its western boundary is Meşrutiyet Caddesi, address of the swish new **Pera Museum**, as well as the famed **Pera Palas Hotel** (*see p40*), with its Orient Express associations and celebrity-filled guest book.

Pera Museum

Pera Müzesi
141 Meşrutiyet Caddesi (0212 334 9900/www.pera muzesi.org.tr). **Open** 10am-7pm Tue-Sat; noon-6pm Sun. **Admission** YTL7; YTL5 concessions; free under-12s. **Credit** *café & gift shop only* MC, V. **Map** p248 M3.

In an 1893 building that formerly housed Istanbul's famous Bristol Hotel, this new, well-run museum combines permanent exhibitions, art galleries, an auditorium, shop and café. Exhibits range from the arcane – a collection of Anatolian weights and measures – to the decorative: Kütahya tiles and ceramics. There is a major collection of 17th- to 19th-century European Orientalist art. Also look out for work by Osman Hamdi, including his most famous painting, *The Tortoise Trainer*.

Galatasaray

Hardly big enough to constitute a district, Galatasaray refers to the streets surrounding the **Galatasaray Lycée**, founded in 1868. The current building, which dates from 1907, includes the small **Galatasaray Museum**, dedicated to Istanbul's top football team, which started life at the school.

The slight widening of Istiklal in front of the Lycée is known as **Galatasaray Square**. Recently, it has become the venue for political demonstrations, notably by the 'Saturday Mothers', relatives of the many political activists who have 'disappeared' in the past 20 years. Such demonstrations are illegal, and the 'mothers' are often met by armoured riot police.

Beyoğlu nightlife once revolved around the *meyhanes* (Turkish tavernas) of Çiçek Pasajı (Flower Passage), an arcade in what was originally the Cité de Pera building (1876). Its heavily restored façade faces the school gates. These days, it's almost exclusively frequented by tourists, a beautiful setting for an over-priced, mediocre meal (*see p120* **Çiçek Pasajı and Nevizade Sokak**). The adjacent Balık Pazarı (Fish Market) is lined with shops fronted by wooden trays of piscine still-life on ice. On the east side of the market passage at No.24A, hidden behind big, black doors, is the Armenian Church of the Three Altars – it's rarely open, but take a look inside if you get the chance.

Botter House. *See p94.*

Prime real estate on **Persembe Pazarı**. See p93.

Just beyond the fish market is **Nevizade Sokak** (*see p120*), the liveliest and loudest dining spot in town, crammed full of pavement restaurants. On the west side are two old arcades, the **Avrupa Pasajı** and **Aslıhan Pasajı**: the former is a mini Grand Bazaar, the latter is full of second-hand book and record shops. The *pasajı* lead through to Hamalbaşı Caddesi and the **British Consulate** (1845), designed by Charles Barry, architect of the British Houses of Parliament, but completed by W.S. Smith in neo-Renaissance style. The building was bombed in November 2003, in an attack that killed British Consul-General Roger Short and over a dozen others.

The Çiçek Pasajı is the most famous of a host of covered arcades leading off Istiklal Caddesi. A few steps south is **Aznavur Pasajı**, with three floors of teenybopper's bedroom accessories (incense and candles, comics and clubwear). A few steps north is **Atlas Pasajı,** which has more eccentric stock – anything from furry lampshades to tribal masks. (*See also p150* **Beyoğlu's fashion *pasajs*.**) The Atlas also has a fine bar in Sefahathane (*see p138*).

The side streets sloping south of Istiklal Caddesi at this point filter down into the appealingly decrepit district of **Çukurcuma**, whose twisting alleys are rife with fascinating antique and junk shops. Among the dealers of carved wedding chests and period furniture are some dim, dusty cubbyholes that offer delightfully off-beat finds such as a temporary London bus stop or cigarette tins painted with scenes of Old Stamboul.

Galatasaray Museum
Galatasaray Lisesi, Istiklal Caddesi 263 (0212 249 1100). **Open** 1.30-3pm Wed. **Admission** free. **Map** p248 N3.
The official museum of the Galatasaray School sports club, now more famous for its football team. Barely more than a trophy room, the exhibits include photographs, memorabilia and cases crammed with medals and prizes. Microscopic opening hours (which are not always reliable, either), make this one of the world's most difficult museums to visit.

Taksim

If Çiçek Pasajı represents old Beyoğlu, the new Beyoğlu is focused on the stretch of Istiklal Caddesi north of Galatasaray, which stretches all the way to Taksim Square. Here, arcades, churches and period architecture give way to malls, mega-stores and multiplexes, as well as endless bars and cafés. Always thronging with shoppers, it feels like Istanbul's Oxford Street.

The city's narrator

Orhan Pamuk has never been shy about giving out his home address, even though the Nobel Prize-winning novelist received death threats and faced imprisonment after speaking out about two Turkish taboos: the Armenian genocide, which the government denies, and the ongoing persecution of the Kurdish minority in the south-east.

Some conservative critics argue that it was his outspoken dissidence that won Pamuk the world's highest literary accolade. In fact, the prolific Pamuk has long been celebrated for his polished prose and Byzantine plot development, as well as his outspokenness. The Turkish authorities might have secretly been infuriated, but the public – or at least the left-leaning intelligensia – relished this international recognition for one of the nation's best-loved writers.

Pamuk's last name (which means 'cotton' in Turkish) appears above the front door of his childhood home, Pamuk Apartmanı in Nişantaşı, which he called 'the centre of my life' in his 2004 memoir, *Istanbul: Memories and the City*. The family lost the apartment due to dwindling fortunes when Pamuk was a child - a period that inspired his first novel, the three-generation saga *Cevdet Bey and his Sons* – but Pamuk eventually bought it back.

Nişantaşi had changed drastically in the interim, with corner shops giving way to designer boutiques. *The Black Book*, Pamuk's complex 1990 novel about a young lawyer searching for his missing wife, features a Nişantaşi apartment playfully called The-Heart-of-the-City, which is probably modelled on Pamuk's own.

Pamuk now has an office in cosmopolitan Cihangir, the neighbourhood where his family relocated after they lost their Nişantaşi home. Journalists often describe how the bay window in his office perfectly frames two minarets rising from the local mosque; they see a symbolism in the contrast between Pamuk's secular space and a religious world beyond. Pamuk rejects the idea: 'I hate both the concept and the reality of a Muslim world clashing with the West.'

Yet contradictions, if not clashes, are very much a part of Istanbul's identity, and identity is a major theme of Pamuk's writing. 'Istanbul's fate is my fate', he writes in *Memories and the City*. 'I am attached to this city because it has made me who I am.' Pamuk has done for Istanbul what Joyce did for Dublin: the mysteries of human nature lurk around every corner of the city in his brilliant evocations of his birthplace.

At its north end, Istiklal Caddesi runs into **Taksim Square**. The name comes from the stone reservoir (*taksim*) on the west side. Built in 1732 on the orders of Mahmut I, the *taksim* was at the end of a series of canals and aqueducts that brought water down from the Belgrad Forest (*see p208*).

Despite such picturesque associations, the giant square is one of the world's uglier plazas – little more than a snarled-up transport hub with a small park attached. Even so, the square is regarded as the heart of modern Istanbul and symbol of the secular Republic. So much so that in 1997, when the short-lived Islamist government unveiled plans to build a huge mosque on an adjacent lot, they were forced to backtrack in the face of public uproar. Instead, the municipality decided on a YTL730,000 fountain for the site, complete with a blaring sound system and dancing lights.

Beyond Beyoğlu

Harbiye & Şişli

North of Taksim, there is little to capture the visitor's imagination in the residential neighbourhoods of Harbiye and Şişli, save for a couple of museums celebrating Turkey's military conquests and republican ideals.

Atatürk Museum
Atatürk Müzesi
Halaskargazi Caddesi 250, Şişli (0212 233 4723). Bus 46H. Metro Osmanbey. **Open** 9am-4pm Tue-Sat. **Admission** free.
In northern Şişli, a short bus ride from Taksim Square, is a candy-pink Ottoman house in which Mustafa Kemal once stayed. It now contains three floors of memorabilia of the great Atatürk, from his astrakhan hat to his silk underwear. There's even a wine-stained tablecloth on which he bashed out the new Turkish alphabet over a picnic lunch in 1928. The top floor holds a large collection of propaganda paintings from the war of indepedence, depicting scenes of Greek brutality, with the flag of the perfidious British occasionally fluttering in the background. It's a wonder the Greek soldiers were ever taken seriously, as they advanced into battle in pleated mini skirts and scarlet slippers adorned with fluffy pom-poms.

Military Museum
Askeri Müze ve Kültür Sitesi
Vali Konağı Caddesi, Harbiye (0212 233 2720). Bus 46H, 46KY, 69YM/Metro Osmanbey. **Open** 9am-4.30pm Wed-Sun. **Admission** YTL3. **No credit cards.**
The sheer size and wealth of this place says as much about the military's continued clout in Turkey, as it does about the country's bloody history. For many years, this was one of the few

national museums to enjoy substantial funding, so the collection is nothing if not comprehensive. However, all but the most hardened military enthusiasts will suffer serious battle fatigue long before the interminable procession of rooms and corridors comes to an end. Definitely worth seeing are the gloriously colourful campaign pavilions of the Ottoman sultans, created from embroidered silk and cotton. Upstairs, in the 20th-century section, there's a decent display dealing with the 1915 Gallipoli campaign, plus some bizarre furniture constructed out of bayonets and gun parts. For sheer morbidity, nothing beats the car in which the Grand Vizier Mahmut Şevket Paşa was assassinated while travelling along Divan Yolu in 1913. The number of bullet holes shows that the gunmen left little to chance.

Hasköy

Heading along the banks of the Golden Horn from Beyoğlu, the coastal road is lined with increasingly shabby houses and scruffy little parks where local families hang out. School buses regularly make the journey to Hasköy to visit the **Rahmi M Koç Museum**. This unusual transport museum is worth the ride if you have car-crazy kids with you. If you don't fancy taking a bus, a taxi from Eminönü or Taksim Square takes around 15 minutes. The splendidly eccentric **Miniaturk** (*see p167*) is only a couple of miles further down the coast.

Rahmi M Koç Museum
Rahmi M Koç Müzesi
Hasköy Caddesi 27, Hasköy (0212 369 6600/ www.rmk-museum.org.tr). Bus 47, 54HM, 54HT. **Open** 10am-5pm Tue-Fri; 10am-7pm Sat, Sun. **Admission** YTL7. *Submarine* YTL4. **No credit cards.**
Founded by the eponymous industrialist, this converted 18th-century foundry on the waterfront is a showcase for the assorted obsessions of one of the wealthiest men in Turkey. The collection includes halls after hall of antique trains, trams, boats and planes. There's even a submarine moored in the Golden Horn. Many exhibits have moving parts that can be manually activated by buttons or levers; there's a walk-on ship's bridge with a wheel, sonar machines and alarm bells. Try to visit on a Saturday or Sunday, when all the working models are in action.

Across the road from the main complex, a domed workshop makes a quaint setting for more industrial curios including the forward section of a US airforce bomber shot down in 1943 and recovered from the seabed off Turkey's coast some 50 years later. Everything is fully labelled in English.

The museum has two top-class eateries in the pricy **Café du Levant**, modelled after an old-fashioned Parisian bistro, and **Halat** (*see p119*), a fish restauarant with tables on the wharf.

The Bosphorus Villages

Parks, palaces, and castles by the sea.

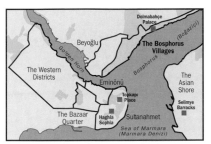

Running along the banks of one of the world's busiest waterways, a chain of waterfront parks, palaces, and *yalıs* stretches from the Galata Bridge as far as the fortress of Rumeli Hisarı.

Several buses run the route, including 22, 22R and 25E from Eminönü. The new metro line (from Taksim) or the new tram (from Eminönü) to Kabataş also place you at a convenient point on the coastal road. A more relaxed way of travelling is to take one of the half-hourly ferry services from Eminönü, stopping at Beşiktaş, Ortaköy and Bebek. Unfortunately, these commuter services only run in the mornings (around 8-10am) and evenings (around 5-8pm).

Karaköy

Karaköy has been a port since Byzantine times, when the north shore of the Golden Horn was a separate settlement – Galata (*see p90*) – distinct from the rest of Constantinople. Much of the maritime traffic has since moved out, and Karaköy is being cleaned up, but it still has several monuments reflecting its grittier past.

The area also has a refreshingly diverse array of religious monuments. One street inland from the harbour, on Kemankeş Cadessi, is the district's oldest building, the **Yeraltı Mosque**. Not far from here is the **Jewish Museum**, housed in a restored synagogue, and further inland are a couple of curious churches. The Russian Orthodox Church of **St Andrea** on Balyoz Sokak is on the top floor of what appears to be a 19th-century apartment building, but was actually built as a monastery. The monks have long gone, but the church has experienced a revival thanks to the Russian tourists who have arrived en masse since the collapse of the Soviet Union. Around the corner

is the **Church of St Panagia** belonging to the tiny Turkish Orthodox sect, which broke away from the Greek church in the 1920s. Mass here is said in the Karamanlı Turkish dialect.

GUNS AND SMOKE

North along **Kemeraltı Caddesi**, the road passes in the shadow of the slightly sinister **Tophane**. A former Ottoman cannon foundry built during the reign of Mehmet the Conqueror, the current building, with its distinctive row of ventilation towers, dates only to 1803. Recently renovated, it's now used as an occasional arts and exhibition centre.

Opposite are two impressive mosques. **Kılıç Ali Paşa Mosque** is named after a famed admiral who was born in Calabria, captured by pirates, and then, after gaining his freedom, entered Süleyman's navy and rose to become the commander of the entire Ottoman fleet. The mosque was built in 1580 by the celebrated architect Sinan, who was by this time in his 90s.

Jewish Museum. *See p100.*

Istanbul Modern

Istanbul's long-awaited contemporary art museum, Istanbul Modern, opened in its doors in December 2004. Housed in a former customs warehouse on the waterfront in Karaköy, which had been used as a venue for two of Istanbul's Biennials, the two-storey museum has a whopping 8,000 square metres of exhibition space. A large, site-specific piece from the eighth Biennial (curated by Dan Cameron) remains – a shattered glass staircase hung from steel chains, created by Monica Bonvicini. Likewise, Richard Wentworth's installation of hundreds of books suspended over the library, for the *Centre of Gravity* exhibition, proved so popular that it stayed.

The museum's permanent collection, displayed in themed groupings on the first floor, consists primarily of modern Turkish painting. Criticised for lack of edge, this collection has yet to make a real impact on either the local or global contemporary art scene. But observers are hopeful that there will be changes in direction when David Elliot, former director of Tokyo's Mori Museum, takes up his new post as director in January 2007.

The varied programme of changing exhibitions on the ground floor, curated by Rosa Martinez, has already proved more successful. Shows like 'Venice-Istanbul', the first time that part of the Venice Biennial has been exhibited in another city, have helped put the museum on the global art map. These exhibitions have also introduced major international artists, including Anish Kapoor, Juan Munoz and William Kentridge, to a local audience. Similarly, temporary exhibitions have allowed for more curatorial approaches to contemporary Turkish art.

One of the museum's galleries is dedicated exclusively to exhibitions of photography; another is devoted to video art, showcasing work by the likes of Sam Taylor-Wood and Fischli and Weiss, alongside local artists such as Şener Ozmen and Erkan Ozgen. The in-house cinema screens an interesting mix of Turkish and international art-house movies and experimental shorts.

The museum's restaurant has proved a big hit in its own right. Stunning views across the Bosphorus to the minarets of Sultanahmet and out to the Marmara Sea just about justify bumped-up prices for decent bistro fare.

Istanbul Modern

Meclis-i Mebusan Caddesi, Liman İşletmeleri Sahası, Antrepo No.4, Karaköy (0212 334 7300/www.istanbulmodern.org). Tram Karaköy. **Open** 10am-6pm Tue, Wed, Fri-Sun; 10am-8pm Thur. **Admission** YTL7; YTL3 concessions. **Free** for all Thur. **Credit** MC, V.

A little farther north is **Nusretiye Mosque**, built in the late 1820s in baroque style by Kikor Balyan, an Armenian architect whose sons would later design the nearby **Dolmabahçe Palace**. Behind the mosque is the city's current 24-hour hotspot, a row of cafés specialising in narghiles (*see p132* **Have narghile**).

The main road continues past the port. Just up the hill is **Inönü Stadium**, home of Beşiktaş football club (*see p199*). Towering over the stadium is the monstrous, high-rise Ritz-Carlton hotel. High-rollers book suites overlooking the stadium when there's a big match on.

Yeraltı Mosque

Yeralti Camii
Kemankeş Cadessi. Tram Karaköy. **Open** varies. **Admission** free. **Map** p292 N6.
Often called the Underground Mosque because it's buried beneath a 19th-century wooden mansion, the low, vaulted interior is supported by 54 columns, built on the remains of the Byzantine castle of Galata, which guarded the entrance to the Golden Horn. From here, a great chain was stretched across the waterway, blocking access to enemy ships in times of siege. The upper part of the castle was demolished following the Ottoman conquest, and the remaining lower floor – formerly a prison – was converted to a mosque in 1757.

Jewish Museum

Türk Musevileri Müzesi
Karaköy Meydanı, Perçemli Sokak (0212 292 6333/ www.muze500.com). Tram Karaköy. **Open** 10am-4pm Mon-Thur, 10am-2pm Fri, Sun. **Admission** YTL5. **No credit cards**. **Map** p292 M6.
Housed in the immaculately restored Zülfaris Synagogue (in existence since 1671, but dating in its present form to the early 19th century), a collection of well-presented objects, documents, photographs and storyboards (in English) tells the story of over 500 years of Jewish presence in Turkey. The Jews first arrived in the Ottoman Empire fleeing the

pogroms of Christian Europe. They have made significant contributions to Istanbul life, particularly in the financial sector. An ethnography section presents costumes and accessories related to circumcision ceremonies, dowries and weddings. **Photo** *p99*.

Beşiktaş

A celebration of just about everything awful about 19th-century European design, the excessively opulent **Dohlmabaçe Palace** is on most tour group itineraries. Many of its dubious treasures are now housed in the **Depot Museum** next door. Passing the palace, the road is flanked by colonnades of plane trees leading to **Beşiktaş**, an unsightly concrete shopping and transport hub with a statue of Atatürk for a centrepiece. It wasn't always this way: this used to be a quiet suburb of dignified terraced houses and plush mansions. The last remaining terrace is on **Spor Caddesi**, built to house the staff of Dolmabahçe Palace.

Despite having no real harbour, Beşiktaş has strong nautical connections, on display in the **Naval Museum** beside the ferry terminal. Nearby is the tomb and statue of Hayrettin Paşa, the Ottoman admiral known as Barbarossa. His tomb is only open to visitors on April 4 and July 1. Nearby **Mimar Sinan University Museum of Fine Arts** houses Turkish 19th and 20th century painting.

The Depot Museum

Depo-Müze
Dolmabahçe Caddesi, Dolmabahçe Palace, Beşiktaş.
(0212 236 9000 ext 1339). Bus 25E, 28, 40, 56.
Open 9am-5pm Tue, Wed, Fri-Sun. **Admission** YTL3. **No credit cards. Map** p293 R2.
Opened in 2004 to commemorate the 150th birthday of Dolmabahçe Palace next door, this rambling collection of pieces salvaged from the palace's storage rooms is housed in what used to be the imperial kitchens. Everything from crystal tumblers to copper cauldrons, samovars to silver candlesticks, French vases to Japanese porcelains are stuffed into this Ottoman time warp. Many of these antiques have been rescued from the palace cellars, which have regularly flooded over the last few decades.

Dolmabahçe Palace

Dolmabahçe Sarayı
Dolmabahçe Caddesi, Beşiktaş (0212 236 9000).
Open *May-Oct* 9am-4pm Tue, Wed, Fri-Sun. *Nov-Apr* 9am-3pm Tue, Wed, Fri-Sun. **Admission** YTL15. *Harem* YTL10. **Credit** MC, V. **Map** p293 R2.
Irrefutable evidence of an empire on its last legs, Dolmabahçe Palace was built for Abdül Mecit by Karabet Balyan and his son Nikoğos. It was completed in 1855, whereupon the sultan and his household moved in, abandoning Topkapı Palace, which had been the imperial residence for four centuries. The outside is overwrought enough – though the

façade of white marble is striking when viewed from the water – but it's trumped by the interior, the work of French decorator Sechan, who worked on the Paris Opera. 'Highlights' are the 36-metre-high throne room with its four-tonne crystal chandelier (a gift from Queen Victoria), the alabaster baths, and a 'crystal staircase' that wouldn't look out of place in Las Vegas. Atatürk died in Dolmabahçe in 1938, although his apartment is not on the tour itinerary. Visitors are only allowed into the palace, which is still used for state functions, in guided groups.

Mimar Sinan University Museum of Fine Arts

Mimar Sinan Üniversitesi Istanbul Resim ve Heykel Müzesi
Barbaros Hayrettin Paşa Iskelesi Sokak, off Beşiktaş Caddesi, Beşiktaş (0212 261 4299). Bus 25E, 28, 40, 56. **Open** 10am-4.30pm Mon-Fri. **Admission** free.
The decrepit state of this poorly signposted museum, housed in a waterside mansion, suggests that few visitors find their way here. Shame, because the collection of Turkish art on display in the high-ceilinged halls includes some fine pieces. It all dates from the mid 19th- to mid 20th- century, mostly Orientalist in style. Look out for several notable works by Osman Hamdi Bey, one-time director of the Archaeology Museum. To find the museum, walk down the side-street south of the Naval Museum, pass through the gateway with the armed guard, cross the waterfront plaza and turn right at the end; it's the building on the left.

Naval Museum

Deniz Müzesi
Barbaros Hayrettin Paşa Iskelesi Sokak, off Beşiktaş Caddesi, Beşiktaş (0212 327 4345). Bus 25E, 28, 40, 56. **Open** 9am-12.30pm, 1.30-5pm Wed-Sun. **Admission** YTL3. **No credit cards.**

Dolmabahçe Palace.

Sightseeing

Yildiz Chalet Museum.

Announced by a roadside garden full of big guns, the museum is housed in two separate buildings on the Bosphorus. The larger building holds an extensive collection of model ships, mastheads and oil paintings, along with plenty of booty captured from British and French warships sunk during the abortive Dardanelles campaign of World War I. Upstairs are commemorative plaques to Turkish sailors killed on duty from 1319 to the Cyprus war of 1974, as well as the battle flag of Barbarossa, the notorious 16th-century pirate. Downstairs, you'll find just about everything that wasn't nailed down on Atatürk's yacht, the *Savarona*, including a set of silver toothpicks.

The smaller building houses an impressive collection of Ottoman caiques. At one time, these elegant vessels were as symbolic of the city as the gondola is to Venice. Back then, boats rivalled the horse and carriage as the common mode of transport. The sultans' caiques were rowed by Bostancı, an imperial naval unit that doubled as palace gardeners. The largest caique on display, a 1648 model, required some 144 Bostancı to power it along. The oarsmen were apparently required to bark like dogs as they rowed, so that they wouldn't overhear the sultan's conversations. An enterprising Black Sea firm has made modern replicas that convey tourists to the city's smarter hotels, although, regrettably, the banks of oarsmen have now been replaced by an outboard motor.

Yıldız

To the north-west of Beşiktaş are the extensive grounds of **Yıldız Palace**, a sprawling complex of buildings of which only a small part is open to the public. On Yıldız Caddesi is one of the most striking monuments in the city, the **Şeyh Zafir Complex**. Comprising a tomb, library and fountain, it commemorates an Islamic sheikh but is designed in art nouveau style by Raimondo D'Aronco.

YILDIZ PARK
A little further along, a side road leads off Yıldız Caddesi into **Yıldız Park**, formerly the grounds of **Yıldız Palace** and now a pleasantly overgrown hillside forest. Sadly, the small tea house built for Abdül Hamit, of which he was the sole patron, is long gone, but there are several former imperial pavilions, including the Şale Pavilion, a D'Aronco-designed building set in private gardens at the top of the park, now open to the public as the **Yıldız Chalet Museum**. While wandering through the park, you might want to stop at the **Imperial Porcelain Factory** and the **Malta Köşkü**, an 1870 pavilion in which Sultan Abül Hamit had his brother Murad imprisoned. It now makes an attractive café-restaurant, with a terrace overlooking the Bosphorus.

Across from the park entrance, between Yıldız Caddesi and the Bosphorus, is what's left of the **Çırağan Palace**. Last of the Ottoman imperial palaces, it was built for Abdül Aziz who died there (probably murdered) in 1876, two years after it was completed. In 1908, it was restored to house the Ottoman parliament; but it burnt down in 1910 and remained a shell until it was rebuilt as a hotel by the Kempinski chain.

Imperial Porcelain Factory
Yıldız Parkı içi (0212 260 2370). Bus 25E, 28, 40, 56. **Open** 9am-noon, 1-6pm Mon-Fri. **Admission** YTL1. **No credit cards**.
Sultan Abdulhamid II established Yıldız Porcelain Factory in 1890 at the suggestion of the French ambassador Paul Cambon, to provide a ready supply of fancy china for the Ottoman palace. Today, it mass-produces rather cheesy souvenirs in another splendid building designed by the prolific Italian architect Raimondo D'Aronco.

Yıldız Chalet Museum
Yıldız Şale Müzesi
Palanga Caddesi 23, Yıldız Parkı (0212 259 4570). Bus 25E, 28, 40, 56. **Open** 9am-5pm Tue, Wed, Fri-Sun. **Admission** YTL4 Tue, Wed; YTL2 Fri-Sun. **No credit cards**.
The obligatory tour takes you down long, dark, musty corridors leading to 60 rooms furnished with ornate furniture. The Grand Salon, a massive court

chamber, now stands empty but for a line of chairs that highlight the sense of lost grandeur.

Yıldız Palace

Yıldız Sarayı
Yıldız Caddesi (0212 258 3080). Bus 25E, 28, 40, 56. **Open** *Mar-Sept* 9.30am-4pm Mon, Wed-Sun. *Oct-Feb* 9am-3pm Mon, Wed-Sun. **Admission** YTL2. **No credit cards.**

Most of the palace dates from the late 19th century when the paranoid Sultan Abül Hamit II ('Abdül the Damned') abandoned waterfront Dolmabahçe for fear of attack by foreign warships. The sultan was so fearful for his safety that no architect was allowed to see the complete plans for the new palace, and the labourers who built it were forbiden to communicate. Only the sultan knew the location of all the secret passages. He never slept in the same suite two nights running and placed large objects in the palatial passageways to obstruct any would-be assassins. The rooms open to visitors contain porcelain, furniture and some of Abdül Hamit's possessions, including the carpentry set he used to while away his time after he was deposed in 1908.

Ortaköy

Long a thriving social and commercial centre, Ortaköy is a refuge from the crush of the inner city. In the 17th century, Ottoman chronicler Evliya Çelebi noted with a hint of disdain, 'The place is full of infidels and Jews; there are 200 shops, of which a great number are taverns.'

Today, this appealing neighbourhood's narrow, cobbled streets are closed to traffic, its low-rise houses painted in pastel shades. There's a pretty waterfront plaza overlooked by the **Mecidiye Mosque**. Set dramatically on a promontory jutting into the strait, the mosque was built for Sultan Abdül Mecit in 1854 by Nikoğos Balyan, the architect responsible for the Dolmabahçe. Happily, the mosque avoids the vulgarity of the palace; this is one of the most attractive baroque buildings in Istanbul.

Beside the ferry landing, waterfront **Ortaköy Square** (Iskele Meydanı) is fringed with open-air cafés and restaurants (*see p127 and p142*). The tight nexus of streets inland from the square has been over-gentrified and filled with gift shops. At weekends it's the venue for a popular **craft market**.

Nearby are the twin domes of a 16th-century hamam, yet another work by Sinan. Recently restored, it now houses a restaurant.

North of Ortaköy, the road passes under the kilometre-long **Atatürk Bridge**, finished just in time for the Turkish Republic's 50th birthday celebrations in 1973. Beyond the bridge is a string of exclusive nightspots, where Istanbul's socialites and celebrities strut their stuff (*see p194* **Bosphorus bling**).

Arnavutköy

Arnavutköy, the 'Albanian Village', is far more low-key than Ortaköy, and has yet to be spoilt by an influx of venture capital. In Ottoman times, the local population was not Albanian, as the name would imply, but predominantly Greek and Armenian. It's overwhelmingly Turkish today, but a small community of Greeks still lives around here, celebrating mass at the Orthodox **Church of Taxiarchs** in the backstreets. Next to the church is a small chapel containing a sacred spring, or *ayazma*, which is down some marble stairs.

Arnavutköy's picturesque wooden *yalıs* overlook the shore, although the traffic sweeping past detracts from the effect. Many local businesses occupy these 19th century houses with lace-like trim, pulpit balconies and elaborate ornamentation. As more and more of them are renovated, Arnavutköy is rapidly taking on a fairytale appearance.

Supposedly enjoying official protection, this architectural heritage has ironically long been under threat from the government itself – plans for a third Bosphorus bridge threatened to rip apart the neighbourhood with great concrete supports. However, opposition from local residents has swayed officials towards a less contentious tunnel project.

Bebek

Just north of Arnavutköy, a small white lighthouse marks **Akıntı Burnu**, a promontory jutting out into the straits, named after the strong current that swirls and eddies past the shore. It's a favourite spot for local fishermen who cast out from the shore, but also trawl from rickety wooden boats, battling against a flow so brisk that in days gone by sailing ships often had to be towed around the point by porters.

From Akıntı Burnu it's a ten-minute stroll along a broad, seaside promenade to the next 'village', Bebek. Ranged around a bay backed by wooded hills, this attractive, affluent suburb has the air of a Hampstead-on-Sea.

Beside the small waterfront park is a handsome, white art nouveau mansion. Still in service as the **Egyptian consulate**, it was designed by D'Aronco, who would be mightily aggrieved by its cluster of satellite dishes and general state of dilapidation.

At the top end of the park is Bebek's tiny ferry station and an equally diminutive brown stone mosque dating from 1912. Next door, **Bebek Café** is as basic as they come, but it's a pleasant, unaffected place for a coffee. Round the corner, the high street is a bit of a let-down, lined with modern buildings, including a

Sightseeing

Istanbul on foot
Karaköy to Dolmabahçe

To explore this part of the city, begin at Karaköy Square. Head up busy Haracı Caddesi, then on to Karaköy Caddesi before taking a detour right on to Necatibey Caddesi, and right again to Tulumba Sokak. At the bottom of the street, at the corner of Kemankes Caddesi, one road back from the shore, is the underground **Yeraltı Mosque**. Buried beneath a 19th-century wooden house, the mosque has been described by John Freeley, the most eminent Istanbul historian writing in English, as a 'strange and sinister place'.

From the ragged shore lined with fish restaurants, private and municipal ferries run back and forth across the Bosphorus from **Karakoy Iskele**. It was around this spot that Byzantine emperors stretched a chain across the Golden Horn to keep enemy ships from accessing the city's waterways.

Bustling Karaköy Caddesi is a warren of kiosks selling all manner of electronics. These slip away as the street ascends uphill to Galata. The road forks to the right, becoming Kemeraltı Caddesi, home to several churches. **St Benoit** is on the left, and **St Gregory** is further down on the right.

On the left, past Bogazkesen Caddesi, as it intersects with Necatibey Caddesi, lies the last incarnation of a series of Ottoman munitions foundries that occupied the **Tophane** site. This boxy number, built by Selim III in 1803, with eight domes and scrub growing on the roof, now hosts wedding receptions and occasional art exhibitions.

On the right is the baroque **Nusretiye Mosque**. The Balyans, a family of Armenian architects active in Istanbul during the 18th and 19th centuries, built both the mosque and Dolmabahçe Palace up the road. Past the mosque, cafés set back in the park appeal to those in need of a *narghile* fix. Slump into a bean-bag and have a smoke, or keep walking.

You are now in a convenient spot to take the new tram from Tophane a couple of stops to Kabataş. From here, it's not far along the coastal road to the neo-baroque fantasy that is **Dolmabahçe Palace**, which stretches the length of nearly three football pitches along the water's edge. In 1453, Mehmed the Conqueror, chose this spot – then a small inlet – to haul 70 ships up into Beyoğlu using mules, and down to the Golden Horn, thus avoiding the chain slung across the straits by the Byzantines.

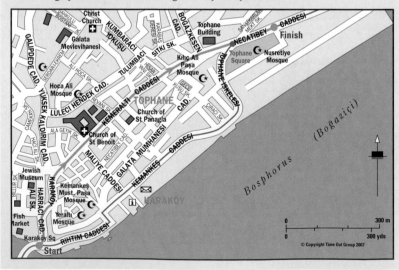

prominent McDonald's, and choked by traffic. In 2006, Bill Gates was spotted eating breakfast in these parts. Among the shops selling silk ties and antiques is **Meşhur Bebek Badem Ezmesi**, specialising in marzipan, beautifully displayed in hardwood cabinets.

Follow any of the streets leading uphill off the high street and almost immediately you're surrounded by greenery and wooden terraces. Head up **Hamam Sokak** opposite the park and after a few minutes' walk you'll find **Café de Pera**, a welcoming place to take a break.

From Bebek, a wooden promenade winds north towards the fortress of **Rumeli Hisarı**, a ten- to 15-minute walk. Before the castle, a sign points up a steep road beside the **Kayalar Mezarlığı**, one of Istanbul's oldest Muslim cemeteries, to the **Aşiyan Museum**.

Aşiyan Museum

Aşiyan Müzesi

Aşiyan Yolu, Bebek (0212 263 6986). Bus 25E, 40. **Open** 9am-4.30pm Tue, Wed, Fri, Sat. **Admission** free.

This attractive wooden mansion was the retreat of celebrated poet Tevfik Fikret (1867-1915), who built it himself. Although the literary exhibits don't amount to much, the views from the upper-storey balconies are wonderful.

Rumeli Hisarı

Rounding the headland north of Bebek brings you face to face with the imposing fortress of **Rumeli Hisarı** and below it, the suburb of the same name. The sleepy village is an unlikely setting for the **Fatih Mehmet Bridge**, which at 1,096 metres (3,634 feet) is one of the longest suspension bridges in the world. Completed in 1988, it spans the straits at the same point where King Darius of Persia crossed with his army via a pontoon bridge in 512 BC.

Just before the small central square of the village is another oddity, **Edwards of Hisar**, an upper-crust tailor more suited to Savile Row.

Two bus stops north of Rumeli Hisarı is **Emirgan**, famous for its tulip gardens (best visited in late April or early May), and home to the excellent **Sakıp Sabancı Museum**. The museum is about 100 metres beyond the pencil-sharp minaret of the **Hamidiye Mosque**.

Rumeli Hisarı Fortress

Rumeli Hisarı Müzesi

Yahya Kemal Caddesi, Rumeli Hisarı. Bus 25E, 40. **Open** 9am-4.30pm Tue-Sun. **Admission** YTL3. **No credit cards**. **Map** p207.

Consisting of three huge towers joined by crenellated defensive walls, the fortress was raised in a hurry as part of Mehmet II's master plan to capture Constantinople. Facing the 14th-century castle of Anadolu Hisarı (already in Ottoman hands)

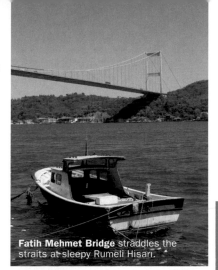

Fatih Mehmet Bridge straddles the straits at sleepy Rumeli Hisarı.

across the Bosphorus' narrowest stretch, Rumeli Hisarı was designed to cut maritime supply lines and isolate Constantinople from its allies. For this, it earned itself the evocative nickname Boğazkesen, the 'Throat-Cutter'. Designed by the sultan himself, work was completed in August 1452, just four months after it commenced. Garrisoned by Janissaries and bristling with cannon, Rumeli Hisarı proved its effectiveness immediately: a Venetian merchant vessel that attempted to run the blockade was promptly sunk.

Having helped secure the Ottoman conquest of Constantinople, the castle lost its military importance and was downgraded to a prison. The castle was restored by the government in 1953. Today, visitors are free to clamber around the walls, enacting childhood fantasies. An open-air theatre in the courtyard hosts popular musical events throughout the summer (*see p191*).

Sakıp Sabancı Museum

Istinye Caddesi 22, Emirgan (0212 277 2200/ http://muze.sabanciuniv.edu). Bus 22, 22RV, 25E. **Open** 10am-7pm (no entry after 6pm) Tue-Sun; 10am-10pm Wed. **Admission** YTL3, YTL1 concessions. **No credit cards**. **Map** p207.

Owned by one of Turkey's wealthiest businessmen, this museum is housed in a fabulous villa right on the shores of the Bosphorus, built for Egyptian royalty in the 1920s. The steeply sloping lawns are scattered with stone treasures on loan from the Archaeology Museum. Inside are two floors of exceptionally fine ceramics and calligraphy, with informative English texts. A modern extension in glass, steel and marble holds a collection of 19th- and 20th-century Turkish art that unfortunately fails to do justice to its coolly elegant surroundings: the paintings play second fiddle to the panoramic views. However, the museum occasionally hosts major touring exhibitions by the likes of Picasso and Rodin, which pull in big crowds.

The Asian Shore

Istanbul's alter ego.

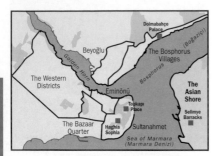

It's not like those 'Welcome to Asia' signs beside the Bosphorus Bridge go unnoticed, but some Istanbullus' eyes might glaze over if you mention that over-used tourist board strapline, 'One City – Two Continents'. Historically, 'Stamboul' only comprised the area within the Byzantine Walls on the European side. Only in the last 20 years have the disconnected villages of the Asian shore coalesced into the sprawl of suburbs that make up Asian Istanbul.

Though lacking the European city's richness, the Asian shore is pleasantly less hectic. The two main centres of **Üsküdar** and **Kadıköy** offer shopping with a regional slant and a sprinkling of historic sights. North of Üsküdar, the settlements along the Asian Bosphorus still resemble the quiet fishing villages they so recently were.

THE GREENER SHORES
While most sights of interest date from the past 100-odd years, the area's history goes back a very long way. The oldest settlement in the Istanbul metropolitan area, Chalcedon, was discovered near Kadıköy and dates from neolithic times, much earlier than anything on the European side. The first Greek city was also founded at Kadıköy in 675 BC – 17 years before the founding of Byzantium.

Separated by water from their more powerful European neighbour, the Asian settlements suffered over subsequent millennia; the ruthless antics of various invading armies explains the lack of substantial early remains. Before the 19th century, only Üsküdar saw any significant development. That changed in 1852 when a steam ferry company, Şirket-i Hayriye

(literally 'the good deeds company'), started plying its trade across the straits. Rich Levantines from Beyoğlu began constructing elaborate summer mansions along the shore to the south and east of Kadıköy.

For the first 50 years of the service, the ferries were all products of British shipyards. In fact, trade between the Ottoman and British empires was at such a level that by the end of the 19th century the Kadıköy suburb of Moda was more or less an English colony. Under the republic, most of the mansions were demolished and replaced by apartment blocks. These retained their garden settings, which gives the Asian shore, especially between Kadıköy and Bostancı, a greener, more suburban feel than the European side.

GETTING THERE
Although two great suspension bridges now span the straits, the best way to get here is by boat. Between 6am and midnight, ferries depart every 15 minutes from Eminönü (just west of Sirkeci station), Karaköy and Beşiktaş for both Üsküdar and Kadıköy. The crossing takes around 20 minutes.

Kadıköy

No trace remains of the Greek or Byzantine settlements of Chalcedon, but modern Kadıköy does retain many hints of its 19th-century incarnation as an area largely settled by Greeks and Armenians. To visitors arriving by ferry, this isn't immediately apparent as the two most visible buildings, Kadıköy Municipality and the local theatre, are in an unlovely modernist style.

Bear right for the main Söğütlüçeşme Caddesi and cut into the alleys beside the **Mustafa Iskele Mosque**. This is the old bazaar, an area of narrow streets lined with tiny two- and three-storey buildings, many dating from the 19th century. Some of the best food shopping in Istanbul is on offer here. At the top end of **Yasa Sokak** are delis stocking a huge range of regional Turkish produce. A few steps south on **Mühürdar Caddesi**, opposite a small Armenian church, **Esmer Ekmek** bakes on the premises in a wood-fired oven.

Other than the bakery, Mühürdar is almost completely given over to booksellers, most specialising in academic textbooks. Narrow, sloping **Dumlupınar Sokak** boasts more book shops, including, at No.17, **Greenhouse Books**, run by Charlotte McPherson, an American who offers tea and coffee as well as a large English-language stock.

Güneşlibahçe Sokak has more great food shops, including one devoted exclusively to honey, another to olive oil, and some fantastic fishmongers. One block east, **Dellalzade Sokak** is lined with antique shops.

The area has a lively café and bar scene centred on **Kadife Sokak** – it's the Asian shore's (slightly downmarket) answer to Beyoğlu, with the feel of a student quarter. It's worth aiming to be here on a Tuesday or Sunday for the market, which fills the streets north of the bull statue, a local landmark on **Söğütlüçeşme Caddesi**, the main drag.

Beyond the cinema, Kadıköy gives way to the posher suburb of **Moda**. A few minutes' walk south is the popular waterfront promenade, with a tiny ferry terminal designed in late-Ottoman revival style by Vedat Tek.

SOCCER AND SHOPPING

East of Kadıköy is **Rüştü Saraçoğlu Stadium**, home of Fenerbahçe football club (*see p199*). Although currently eclipsed by

Galatasaray, Fener is traditionally one of Turkey's top three teams, with a massive fan base among the lower middle classes. Such is the fanaticism of local supporters that their neighbourhood is often referred to as the 'Republic of Fenerbahçe'.

Behind the stadium is **Bağdat Caddesi**, one of the city's best-known streets. For much of its length it's an unremarkable swathe of asphalt, but passing through the plush suburb of **Suadiye** it is lined with upmarket clothing and design stores, beauty clinics, pavement cafés and restaurants. It's the cruising strip of choice for nouveau-riche Istanbul.

Haydarpaşa

Across the bay from Kadıköy stands the imposing edifice of **Haydarpaşa station**, which would look more at home in the Rhineland – not surprising, given that it was a gift from Kaiser Wilhelm of Germany and was designed by German architects. It's the terminus of the Anatolian railway system, the end of the line for trains from as far east as Tehran (serviced by the weekly TransAsya Express). On the waterfront piazza in front of the station is a small but perfectly formed ferry terminal, another Vedat Tek design.

Reliving the story of modern nursing at the **Florence Nightingale Müzesi**. *See p109.*

Sightseeing

Arriving at **Üsküdar** – welcome to Asia.

The area north of Haydarpaşa is thinly developed, largely because it belongs to the military and Marmara University, who each own one of the two imposing buildings that dominate the area.

The **Selimiye Barracks** were originally constructed in 1799, during the reign of Selim III, as part of his plan to create a 'new army' to challenge the hegemony of the Janissaries. His plan backfired: he was murdered and his barracks were burnt down. Thirty years later, Mahmut II finally succeeded in defeating the Janissaries and he was responsible for putting up the present building, now part of a restricted military zone. During the Crimean War (1853-6) the barracks served as a hospital run by Florence Nightingale; the north-west corner is preserved as the **Florence Nightingale Museum**.

The other grand building is the former **Haydarpaşa High School**, now Marmara University medical faculty. It's the largest of the many commissions completed by Raimondo D'Aronco. Close by the High School, just off Burhan Felek Caddesi, is the **British Crimean War Cemetery**, containing the graves of Crimean War and World War I dead. As far-flung corners of foreign fields go, it's rather pleasant, with manicured lawns tended by the Commonwealth War Graves Commission. Access is through the gate lodge.

Largest of the area's cemeteries is the **Karaca Ahmet cemetery**, named after a warrior companion of the second Ottoman sultan, Orhan. The cemetery was probably founded back in the mid 14th century; estimates put the number of interments at over a million – by far the biggest boneyard in Turkey.

and Sebastopol. The overcrowded, unsanitary conditions meant that a hospital stay increased the likelihood of death, rather than recovery, and many of the hospital's former patients are buried in nearby Haydarpaşa Cemetery.

It was here that Florence Nightingale and her team of nurses developed modern hospital and nursing practice. The museum in her honour is housed in a corner tower. The lower floor contains life-sized statues of Turkish soldiers from the Crimean War to the War of Independence, a well as a waxwork of Florence Nightingale with a wounded patient. On the table is her famous lamp. And up a winding, wooden staircase is the room where she stayed. **Photo** *p107*.

Göztepe

This suburb, to the south of Haydarpaşa, is home to the new **Toy Museum**.

Istanbul Toy Museum

Istanbul Oyuncak Müzesi
*Dr. Zeki Zeren Sokak, off Ömerpaşa Caddesi 17,
Göztepe (0216 359 4550/www.sunayakin.info). Bus
GZ1, GZ2.* **Open** 9.30am-6pm Tue-Fri; 9.30am-7pm
Fri, Sat. **Admission** YTL6; YTL4 concessions.
Credit MC, V.
Founded by poet Sunay Akın in 2005 in an old wooden mansion in Göztepe, the collection here contains some 4,000 toys from around the world. Highlights include a French violin made in 1817, an American doll from 1820, hundred-year-old porcelain dolls from Germany and lots of collectable tin toys.

Üsküdar

Stepping ashore from the ferry you are pitched straight into a frenzy of buses, dolmuş and taxis tearing round the central square. All this activity is rather misleading because, in contrast to lively Kadıköy, Üsküdar is a highly conservative area, populated largely by migrants from rural Anatolia. During the Muslim holy month of Ramazan, Üsküdar is the site of one of the city's largest *iftar* (literally 'break-fast') tents, with masses of food donated by local businesses for the poor. The main point of interest for shoppers are the antique shops on **Büyük Hamam Sokak**, which is one block south of the **Mimar Sinan Çarşısı**, a 16th-century hamam converted into a small market.

Otherwise, the district's attractions are its mosques. Üsküdar was a favourite place to build these, because the Asian side lies closer to Mecca. The **İskele Mosque** (1548) opposite the ferry terminal, and the **Şemsi Ahmet Paşa Mosque** (1580), down on the shore, are both the work of Sinan. The Şemsi is particularly attractive; you can find it

To get to the barracks and cemeteries take any Üsküdar-bound dolmuş (YTL1.50) from the ranks south of Haydarpaşa Station.

Florence Nightingale Müzesi

*Birinci Ordu Komutanlığı, Selimiye Kışlası, Harem
(0216 343 7310).* **Open** by appointment 9am-5pm,
preferably weekdays. **Admission** free.
A visit to the city's least known museum requires forward planning: to gain access to the heavily guarded Selimiye army barracks, you must fax your passport details, expected time of arrival and phone number. The army will call back to issue permission. Be sure to take your passport.

Visitors enter through a series of guard posts at which the military rank and level of English improves progressively. During the Crimean War, the vast corridors of the barracks were crowded with wounded British, French and Turkish soldiers, shipped in from the battlefields of Balaclava

by walking south along the waterfront promenade past a string of floating fish restaurants. Inland on Şemsi Paşa Caddesi stands the earliest of Üsküdar's mosques, the **Rumi Mehmet Paşa Mosque**, built in 1471 for the grand vizier. He was of Greek origin, which may explain the strong Byzantine influence in the design, which incorporates a cylindrical drum under the dome.

The **Yeni Valide Mosque** back on Uncular Caddesi also has a Greek connection. It was constructed for Sultan Ahmet III, whose Greek mother was captured at the age of three and grew up in the harem, where she graduated from mistress to wife to mother of the sultan (*valide sultana*). The building is a late example of classical Ottoman style, with an attractive façade but a disappointing interior.

On a small island off the southern shore of Üsküdar is the stubby white **Maiden's Tower**, which for some reason is one of the city's best-loved landmarks.

Maiden's Tower

Kız Kulesi
0216 342 4747. **Open** *Tower* noon-7pm Mon-Sat.
Restaurant noon-1am Mon-Sat. **Credit** AmEx, MC, V. **Map** p296 U3.
Although this little island was occupied by a fortress in Byzantine times, the tower dates from the last century. In Turkish it's known as Kız Kulesi, or Maiden's Tower – supposedly after a princess who was confined here after a prophet predicted she would die from a snakebite. The fatal bite was duly delivered by a serpent that arrived in a basket of fruit. In English it's even more randomly known as Leander's Tower, after the Greek hero who swam the Hellespont. The tower has been variously used as a quarantine centre, a lighthouse, a customs control point and a hideout for the villainous Elektra (Sophie Marceau) in the 1999 James Bond movie, *The World is Not Enough*. These days, the tower is a café-restaurant decked out like an Ottoman banquet hall, which is very popular with wedding parties. It's a scenic spot for an average lunch, but dinner is an over-priced, reservations-only affair. To get here, walk along the promenade to Salacak (about 15-minutes from central Üsküdar), where boats leave every 15 minutes from noon to 1am. The return trip costs YTL4.

The Asian Bosphorus

Just beyond the first Bosphorus Bridge stands **Beylerbeyi Palace**, the last of the great, ugly Ottoman palaces. The eponymous village has a pretty harbour with several tea houses and pleasant restaurants lining the shore. Nearby **Hamidievvel Mosque** is unusual in having a rose garden. At weekends, the area by the ferry jetty is taken over by craft stalls.

Further north, the landscape gets much greener. In the 1990s, property prices here soared as rich commuters from the European shore moved in. The most exclusive properties are the *yalıs*, vast wooden mansions that hug the strip between the road and the sea. As they're mostly invisible behind high security walls, you'll need to take a Bosphorus cruise (*see p206*) to catch a glimpse of them.

Çengelköy, the next town up, was a humble village until it featured in a long-running TV soap, *Süper Baba*, precipitating an influx of money and car showrooms. The harbour is still pleasant, and there are a couple of waterside fish restaurants with great views.

The wide valley to the north of **Kandilli** is split by two narrow rivers, Küçüksu and Göksu Deresi, once collectively known as the 'Sweet Waters of Asia'. In Ottoman times, the meadows between them were a popular picnic ground for the rich. Even Sultan Abdül Mecit got in on the act, erecting the modest **Küçüksu Palace** on the shore.

Beylerbeyi Palace

Beylerbeyi Sarayı
Abdullah Ağa Caddesi 12 (0216 321 9320). Bus 15 from Üsküdar. **Open** 9.30am-5pm Tue, Wed, Fri-Sun (closes 1hr earlier Nov-Mar). **Admission** YTL8.
No credit cards.
After being deposed in 1908, Sultan Abdül Hamit II spent the last years of his life here. Facing north-west, the palace gets little direct sunlight – it was intended as a summer annexe to the main palace at Dolmabahçe. Beylerbeyi didn't even have its own kitchen: food was brought over from the European shore by boat. Tours only take 15 to 20 minutes, racing through the sumptuous palace dripping with crystal chandeliers and some of its five adjoining pavilions.

Küçüksu Palace

Küçüksu Sarayı
Küçüksu Caddesi, Beykoz (0216 332 3303). Bus 15 from Üsküdar/101 from Beşiktaş. **Open** 9.30am-4pm Tue, Wed, Fri-Sun. **Admission** YTL4.
Completed in 1857, this relatively small palace was used by Ottoman sultans for short stays during country excursions and hunting trips. Unlike other imperial buildings, Küçüksu was not surrounded by high walls but by cast iron railings. The ornate façade and twin staircases sweeping around the ornamental pool and fountain create a grand impression, which is echoed inside. the ceilings are richly decorated with plaster motifs and painted designs. And there are so many marble fireplaces that Küçüksu is like a museum dedicated to 19th century fireplace design.

The pavilion was extensively restored in 1994 and the surrounding gardens, fountain and quay are being transformed into a park where the public can enjoy picnics as in centuries past.

Eat, Drink, Shop

çokçok
by kaya on coast

thai kitchen of istanbul

Tepebaşı Meşrutiyet Caddesi 51
Beyoğlu İstanbul

T:90 212 292 6496 E : info@cokcok.com.tr
F:90 212 292 6497 W: www.cokcok.com.tr

tha

Restaurants

Global fusion creates competition for Ottoman feasts and Turkish taverns.

A taste of the high life: **Seasons**. *See p116.*

If your idea of a Turkish meal is a greasy kebab to sponge up several pints of beer, be prepared for a shock. Real Turkish cuisine is a heady mix of cultural and historical influences absorbed from the Ottoman Empire's former territories, which stretched through the Balkans, the Caucasus, the Levant and the Mediterranean.

In addition to restaurants that showcase this culinary heritage, Istanbul has a growing fleet of eateries serving modern European food, often with a Turkish twist. Global fusion is also increasingly popular with the young and hip, giving rise to a steady stream of new openings.

DINING OUT

Like so many other things in Istanbul, eating out has changed dramatically in recent years. Gone are the days when a bite to eat meant *meze* (a shared feast of small dishes) washed down with plenty of *rakı* (the anise-flavoured national spirit) at a smoky male dominated *meyhane* (taverna), or canteen-style service at a *lokanta,* where workers eat *hazır yemek* (ready-made dishes) served from bains-marie.

Fine dining is no longer the preserve of five-star hotels. Istanbul has enjoyed an influx of top chefs from abroad, including Mike Norman, head chef at the excellent **360** (*see p119*). In addition, many of the city's younger chefs now train overseas, picking up influences from other countries. These innovative newcomers and returnees have broadened the cooking in the city's restaurants. In fact, eating out in Istanbul has never been so exciting. Whether you're after a YTL3 *döner* from a street vendor in Taksim, or a romantic dinner for two with a Bosphorus view, you'll find it in Istanbul.

WHERE TO EAT

The quintessential Istanbul eating experience remains the *meyhane*. These places are cheap and frequently boisterous. Filling the table with myriad *meze* to share keeps everyone happy, even vegetarians. *Meyhanes* are found city-wide, but there's a heavy concentration around **Nevizade Sokak** (*see p120*) in Beyoğlu. Other top *meyhanes* include **Refik** (*see p125*), **Sofyalı 9** (*see p125*) and **Zarifi** (*see p123*).

Fish is another local speciality. Most visitors are directed to **Kumkapı** (*see p116*), which has the greatest concentration of seafood restaurants and is close to the hotel district of Sultanahmet. But there are plenty of other enticing options away from the hordes. A city staple is **Doğa Balık** (*see p125*) in Cihangir, just downhill from Taksim, or **Balıkçı Sabahattin** (*see p114*) in Sultanahmet. For the day's catch in refined surroundings, head up the Bosphorus to the village of **Arnavutköy**, which is packed with fish restaurants and has a scenic walkway by the water. A little further up is **Poseidon** (*see p127*) in Bebek, **Rumeli İskele** (*see p128*) up at Rumeli Hisarı or **Körfez** (*see p130*) on the Asian shore.

Taste a real kebab at a *kebapçı* or *ocakbaşı*. There are more varieties than you can shake a skewer at, and you may come to appreciate

❶ Purple numbers given correspond to each restaurant's location, marked on the street maps. *See pp242-251.*

Eat, Drink, Shop

that a *döner* is to a properly prepared kebab what a hamburger is to a T-bone steak.

For the kind of food that pleasured the palates of sultans, such as *imambayıldı* ('the imam fainted', slow-roast aubergines with onions and tomatoes), *dilberdudağı* ('lady's lips', pastry soaked in syrup), *karnıyarık* ('slit stomach', aubergine stuffed with minced meat) and *kadınbudu köfte* ('ladies' thighs', battered, fried meatballs), visit a restaurant serving traditional Ottoman cuisine, using recipes directly from the kitchens of Topkapı. Expect elaborate dishes mixing rice, fruit and vegetables with meat and fish. Try **Asitane** (*see p119*), for the real Ottoman deal, or **Rumeli** (*see p115*) and **Sarnıç** (*see p116*) for updated twists on the same theme.

If you're more in the mood for modernity, the latest restaurants beloved of the glamour brigade include **360**, **Mikla** (*see p121*), **Vogue** (*see p129*), **Banlieue6080** (*see p120*) and **Ulus 29** (*see p130*).

TIPPING AND RESERVATIONS
Tipping is expected at restaurants in Istanbul; ten per cent is sufficient. Service charges are rarely included except at high-end places, where tips are expected anyway. Reservations are a must on Friday and Saturday, and advisable during the week at the most popular restaurants.

Sultanahmet

Big on sights it may be, but Sultanahmet is woefully underserved by decent restaurants. It would be unfair say that all the eateries are tourist traps, but it wouldn't be far off the mark. Although new cafés and restaurants seem to open daily among the hotels on **Akbıyık Caddesi**, their standards remain mediocre. Below are a few exceptions.

Amedros
Hoca Rüstem Sokak 7, off Divan Yolu (0212 522 8356). Tram Sultanahmet. **Open** 11am-1am daily. **Starters** YTL8-YTL14. **Main courses** YTL16-YTL30. **Credit** DC, MC, V. **Map** p243 M10 **❶**
Though it's a European-style bistro, Amedros also does good Ottoman dishes. The house special is *testi kebabı*, lamb roasted with vegetables in a sealed clay pot that is cracked open at the table. In summer, candlelit tables are lined up in the cobbled alley; in winter, diners are warmed by a crackling fire.

Balıkçı Sabahattin
Seyit Hasan Kuyu Sokak 1, off Cankurtaran Caddesi (0212 458 1824). Tram Sultanahmet. **Open** 11am-1.30am daily. **Starters** from YTL7. **Main courses** YTL25-YTL40. **Credit** AmEx, MC, V. **Map** p244 N11 **❷**
Most visitors staying around Sultanahmet head to Kumkapı for fish, unaware that there's a far better option on their doorstep. In fact, Balıkçı Sabahattin is one of the few restaurants that will tempt

Pandeli. *See p117.*

Istanbullus down from Beyoğlu and over the Golden Horn. It benefits from a gorgeous setting: a street of picturesque old wooden houses, periodically rattled to their foundations by the commuter trains passing in and out of Sirkeci. There's no menu: instead, bow-tied waiters present you with a tray of various *meze* and, later, a huge iced platter of seasonal fish and seafood from which to choose. Entertainment comes in the form of skittering cats skilled at doleful looks and pleading meows. Reservations essential.

Dubb Indian Restaurant

İncili Çavuş Sokak 10 (0212 513 7308). Tram Sultanahmet. **Open** noon-11pm daily. **Starters** YTL5-YTL12. **Main courses** YTL11-YTL24. **Credit** AmEx, DC, MC, V. **Map** p243 N10 ❸

Istanbul is not exactly brimming with Indian restaurants, and this little gem in the heart of Sultanahmet might be the closest you'll get to eating authentic dishes from the subcontinent. There's a wide variety of curries, thalis and dishes from the tandoor, plus Indian bevvies like salty or sweet lassi. The roof terrace – up seemingly endless flights of stairs – is worth the climb, and often patronised by happy diners from the subcontinent.

Mozaik

İncili Çavuş Sokak 1 (0212 512 4177). Tram Sultanahmet. **Open** 9am-midnight daily (bar 2am). **Starters** YTL5-YTL14. **Main courses** YTL12-YTL22. **Credit** AmEx, DC, MC, V. **Map** p244 N10 ❹

A cut above many of Sultanahmet's more slapdash establishments. With wooden floors carpeted with old kilims, copper platters and creaking stairs between the restaurant's three floors, a night at Mozaik feels like a trip back in time. The quaint 'Ottoman' room drips with romantic potential for dinner *à deux*. The international menu covers a worrying amount of ground – everything from chicken mandarin to T-bone steak – but chef Aydın Fidan's special is *abant kebap*, a spectacular West Anatolian dish. After dinner, head for the basement bar, one of the best in Sultanahmet.

Pudding Shop

Divanyolu Caddesi 6 (0212 522 2970). Tram Sultanahmet. **Open** 7am-11pm daily. **Starters** YTL6. **Main courses** YTL12. **Credit** AmEx, MC, V, **Map** p245 N10 ❺

A landmark in hippie history. In the pre-Lonely Planet days of the late '60s and early '70s, the Pudding Shop (founded 1957) was a bottleneck for all the overland traffic passing through on its tie-dyed, spliff-addled way east to Kathmandu. In addition to the food, the place served up travel information, courtesy of the two brothers who owned it, a busy bulletin board, and the like-minded company. It even crops up in the movie *Midnight Express*. Smartened up for the 21st-century tourist – plate-glass windows, gleaming display cabinets and slick staff – the restaurant still doles out basic canteen-style fare, no better or worse than half a dozen similar restaurants along this strip.

For Bosphorus views
Poseidon (*see p127*); **Rumeli Iskele** (*see p127*); **Sunset Bar & Grill** (*see p130*); **Ulus 29** (*see p130*).

For a taste of Ottoman culture
Asitane (*see p117*); **Hacı Abdullah** (*see p121*); **Rumeli** (*see below*); **Sarnıç** (*see below*); **Zarifi** (*see p122*).

For live fasıl music
Akvaryum (*see p116*); **Boncuk** (*see p123*). For other *meyhanes* with live fasıl, *see p189*.

For reliving the days of the Orient Express
Orient Express Restaurant (*see p117*).

For meat 'a la Turca'
Çiya (*see p128*); **Hamdi Et Lokantası** (*see p116*); **Zarifi** (*see p122*).

For high style
360 (*see p119*); **Banlieue6080** (*see p119*); **Wan-na** (*see p121*); **A'jia** (*see p128*).

For unusual style
Galata House (*see p125*); **Cahide Sayfiye & Cahide Variete** (*see p120*).

For fish
Many locals love **Körfez** (*see p129*).

Rumeli

Ticarethane Sokak 8, off Divanyolu Caddesi (0212 512 00 08). Tram Sultanahmet. **Open** 9am-midnight daily. **Starters** YTL9-YTL12. **Main courses** YTL15-YTL20. **Credit** AmEx, DC, MC, V. **Map** p246 N10 ❻

Rumeli's food is far superior to the tourist fodder served at the the cluster of establishments at the bottom of Divan Yolu. A former printworks with a cavernous interior of exposed brick, stone and stained floorboards, it spans several floors from the cobbled side-street up to the roof terrace. Traditional Ottoman dishes are given a Mediterranean twist, along with excellent salads, pasta, and a very decent wine list. Staff are charming, too. *See also p122* **Summer loving, winter warming**.

Sarnıç

Soğukçeşme Sokağı (0212 512 42 91). Tram Gülhane/Sultanahmet. **Open** 7.30-10.30pm daily. **Starters** YTL18-YTL40. **Main courses** YTL20-YTL45. **Credit** AmEx, DC, MC, V. **Map** p243 N10 ❼

Eat, Drink, Shop

Sarnıç means 'cistern' in Turkish, and the trump card here is the setting. Housed in one of the area's Roman cisterns, the subterranean space is adorned with pillars, coats of arms and a huge stone fireplace. Candles are dotted around the walls and tables and glimmer on the wrought-iron chandelier, lending the place a medieval, almost Masonic feel. The food does not quite measure up to this decorative grandeur. The Ottoman-French cuisine is average in every aspect but the price, which is hiked well above the quality of the dishes.

Seasons Restaurant

Four Seasons Hotel, Tevfikhane Sokak 1 (0212 638 8200). Tram Sultanahmet. **Open** noon-3pm, 7-11pm. **Starters** YTL18-YTL26. **Main courses** YTL29-YTL50. **Credit** AmEx, DC, MC, V. **Map** p244 N10 ❽
Formerly the subject of rave reviews, Seasons has begun falling short of its reputation. Still a high-end Sultanahmet establishment with an international menu, it can't compare with the flair of newer restaurants like Ulus 29, Vogue and Tuus. Set in a glass enclosure in the gardens of the Four Seasons Hotel, the restaurant aims at elegance – but the look is still very hotel-like, and diners are mainly tourists or hotel guests. **Photo** *p113.*

Kumkapı

Situated inside the city walls on the Sea of Marmara coast, this former fishing port is now an inner-city neighbourhood of cobbled lanes lined with seafood restaurants, where persistent hawkers attempt to waylay passers-by. A shortish taxi ride from Sultanahme, **Kumkapı** is not a bad choice for fresh fish, although the restaurants along **Çapari Sokak** have long been eclipsed by the *meyhanes* at Nevizade and fancy fish places up the Bosphorus.

In total, there are around 50 restaurants in Kumkapı. There are a few that locals rate highly, including **Akvaryum Fish Restaurant**, which has live *fasıl* music (*see p189*), as does **Çapari**, one of the district's oldest establishments. **Kartallar Balıkçı** is famous for its *balık çorbası* (fish chowder) and *buğulama* (steamed fish casserole) – and boasts a large celeb quotient among its clientele. In business since 1938, **Kör Agop** is known for its top quality fish and *fasıl*.

As at the Grand Bazaar, prices are conspicuously absent from menus, so make sure to agree on the bill in advance. Most places offer fixed meal deals, kicking off with *meze* followed by fish of the day and dessert. Expect to pay around YTL45 per person with booze (*rakı*, local wine or beer).

Gypsy musicians roam between the restaurants serenading outdoor diners, while an odd assortment of street vendors flog anything from fresh almonds to Cuban cigars.

Akvaryum Fish Restaurant

Çapari Sokak 39 (0212 517 2273). Kumkapı station. **Open** 10:30am-1am daily. **Credit** MC, V. **Map** p242 K11 ❾

Çapari

Çapari Sokak 22 (0212 517 7530). Kumkapı station. **Open** 10am-2am daily. **Credit** MC, V. **Map** p242 K11 ❿

Kartallar Balıkçı

Ördekli Bakkal Sokak 32 (0212 517 2254). Kumkapı station. **Open** 10am-midnight daily. **Credit** MC, V. **Map** p242 K11 ⓫

Kör Agop

Ördekli Bakkal Sokak 7 (0212 517 2334). Kumkapı station. **Open** noon-2am daily. **Credit** MC, V. **Map** p242 K11 ⓬

The Bazaar Quarter

Eating options are on the increase at the Grand Bazaar, but as yet these are confined to cafés and *lokanta*-style joints.

Darüzziyafe

Şifahane Sokak 6, Süleymaniye (0212 511 8414). Tram Beyazıt, Eminönü or Laleli. **Open** noon-11pm daily. **Starters** YTL5-YTL15. **Main courses** YTL25. **Credit** AmEx, MC, V. **Map** p242 K8 ⓭
The former soup kitchens of the Süleymaniye Mosque complex now turn out more varied fare. But if the present menu runs to several pages, the food is still canteen cooking – great for lunch (a favourite with tour buses) but too prosaic for dinner. The setting, a large courtyard filled with rose bushes and trees, is potentially lovely but rendered institutional by cheap furniture and neglect. Vegetarians beware: the lentil soup contains submerged mini meatballs. The restaurant is located to the north of the mosque, separate from the row of small eateries which line its west side. No alcohol.

Eminönü & the Golden Horn

Two blocks south of Sirkeci Station, narrow **Ibni Kemal Caddesi** is a street full of cheap eateries serving the local working population. The presence of neighbouring Hoca Paşa Mosque means no alcohol is served, but a meal costs less than YTL8 per person. The underslung section of the **Galata Bridge** is also crammed with budget fish restaurants, with menus in English and beer by the flagon.

Hamdi Et Lokantası

Kalçın Sokak 17, Tahmis Caddesi, Eminönü (0212 528 0390). Tram Eminönü. **Open** 11am-midnight daily. **Starters** YTL5-YTL10. **Main courses** YTL9-YTL15. **Credit** AmEx, DC, MC, V. **Map** p242 L7 ⓮
Right on Eminönü square, Hamdi is a hot favourite among Istanbul natives, particularly business lunchers and carniverous fans of south-eastern

Turkish food. Hamdi serves meat 'alaturca' at its very best, grilled to succulent perfection on the *mangal*. The restaurant occupies four floors, but the top one is the most memorable. Situated in an enclosed glass terrace, it offers sweeping views of the Golden Horn and Beyoğlu. It's particularly lovely in the summer, when the windows are opened completely. Otherwise, opt for the curious Oriental Saloon on the first floor, kitted out with cuckoo clocks and startled nymphs.

Orient Express Restaurant

Sirkeci Station, Istasyon Caddesi (0212 522 2280). Tram Sirkeci. **Open** 11.30am-midnight daily. **Starters** YTL3-YTL8. **Main courses** YTL8-YTL17.50. **Credit** MC, V. **Map** p243 N8 ⓯
An essential stop for fans of the Orient Express and Agatha Christie, this time-warp is bang in the centre of Sirkeci station, the final stop of the world's most famous train. In warmer weather, tables are set outside on the station platform, providing people-watching opportunities as commuters spill on and off the suburban trains. The only obvious change in the dining room since the restaurant's launch in 1890 is the incongruous concrete fishpond in the centre, which jars with the Oriental backdrop. The walls are adorned with black and white stills of Sean Connery, Lauren Bacall, Vanessa Redgrave and Ingrid Bergman in the 1974 movie *Murder on the Orient Express*. Food is standard Turkish fare, reasonably priced. It's a shame the restaurant is usually empty.

Pandeli

Mısır Çarşısı 1, Eminönü Square (0212 527 3909). Tram Eminönü. **Open** 11.30am-4pm Mon-Sat. **Starters** YTL6-YTL25. **Main courses** YTL13-YTL28. **Credit** AmEx, DC, MC, V. **Map** p242 L8 ⓰
Not a bad place for lunch if you're shopping in the Egyptian Bazaar. Occupying a wonderful set of domed rooms above the bazaar entrance, Pandeli is very much the essence of genteel old Stamboul. Decorated throughout in blue and white tiling, it's worth a visit for the interior alone. The food, by contrast, is run of the mill Turkish and grossly over-priced, while waiters have a tendency towards brusqueness. Ask for a table in the front room with views of the Golden Horn. Open for lunch only. **Photo** *p114*.

The Western Districts

These relatively poor, religiously conservative parts of town get few visitors, so there's little call for restaurants. But things are beginning to change, with **Balat** being tipped as the hot new neighbourhood in which to invest.

Asitane

Kariye Hotel, Kariye Camii Sokak 18, Edirnekapı (0212 534 8414). Bus 28, 77MT, 87. **Open** 11.30am-11pm daily. **Starters** YTL8-YTL15. **Main courses** YTL20-YTL30. **Credit** AmEx, DC, MC, V. **Map** p244 D4 ⓱

Ottoman inspiration: dine like a Sultan at **Asitane**.

Nu Teras. *See p136.*

It may be a trek to Edirnekapı, but it's worth it for this one-of-a-kind restaurant, in the eponymous hotel next door, specialising in authentic Ottoman food. Authentic means just that: the same dishes as those served at the circumcision feasts of Sultan Süleyman's sons, Beyazıd and Cihangir, in 1539. Expect lots of sweet and sour fruit and meat combos: *kavun dolması* is melon stuffed with mincemeat, rice, almonds, currants and pistachios; *nirbaç* is a stew made with diced lamb, meatballs and carrots, spiced with coriander, ginger, cinnamon, pomegranate and crushed walnuts. The leafy garden is lovely in summer. **Photos** *p117*.

Halat

Kumbarhane Caddesi 2, Hasköy (0212 297 6644). Bus 47E, 54HT. **Open** 10am-midnight Tue-Sun. **Starters** YTL7-YTL15. **Main courses** $10-$14. **Credit** AmEx, DC, MC, V

In addition to being a world-class museum (*see p98*), the Rahmi Koç boasts a couple of excellent restaurants in the Café du Levant, a fancy French bistro, and Halat, with quayside dining under canvas awnings. The menu ranges from a 'tea-time' selection of sandwiches and tarts to breaded crab claws and heavenly desserts. Black-waistcoated staff and classical music suggest formality, but the vibe is laid back. The views –across the Golden Horn to the tumbling orange roofs of Balat– are stunning.

Beyoğlu

Istanbul's 'West End' or 'Downtown', Beyoğlu has the biggest and best selection of dining options. Its narrow backstreets are loaded with traditional restaurants and *meyhanes*, with the heaviest concentration around **Çiçek Pasajı** and **Nevizade Sokak** (*see p120*). The main drag, **Istiklal Caddesi**, is lined with *lokantas,* serving wholesome fast-food Turkish style.

360

Mısır Apartmani 32/309, Istiklal Caddesi (0212 251 1042/www.360istanbul.com). **Open** noon-4pm Mon-Fri; 6pm-2.30am Fri; 6pm-4am Sat; 6pm-2.30am Sun. **Starters** YTL9-YTL15. **Main courses** YTL16-YTL39. **Set menu** YTL55. **Credit** DC, MC, V. **Map** p248 N3 ⓭

As the name suggests, this restaurant on the roof of the historic Mısır apartment block on Istiklal has magnificent 360-degree views of the city. The spacious dining area is a high-tech fusion of steel and glass with brick walls. Popular with posh Turks and foreigners, the place is geared towards English speakers, from the toilet signs to the billboard above the bar. International dishes such as squid ink papardelle with salmon and artichokes in cream sauce don't taste quite as good as they sound. Instead, go for simpler starters like grilled sardines wrapped in vine leaves, sushi or steak. Reservations are essential on Fridays and Saturdays, with two sittings per night. If you stick around, 360 turns into a fairly boisterous club after midnight. *See also p122* **Summer loving, winter warming**.

Banlieue6080

Takşıla Caddesi 13, Maçka Demokrası Parkı, Maçka (0212 231 0356). **Open** 7pm-2am daily. **Starters** YTL15-YTL40. **Main courses** YTL40-YTL95. **Credit** AmEx, V, MC.

360.

Çiçek Pasajı and Nevizade Sokak

Everyone needs a place to let loose. The British down pints in pubs, the French guzzle wine in brasseries, and the Greeks smash plates in tavernas. The Turks? They make merry in the *meyhane*, the age-old Istanbul version of a tapas bar. This is where locals meet, eat *meze*, drink *rakı* and are cajoled by house musicians into belting out folk songs.

The city's most famous *meyhane* district is the **Çiçek Pasajı** (Flower Passage), an elegant 19th-century arcade off Istiklal Caddesi. With its neo-classical façade, barrelled glass roof, old-fashioned street lamps and cascading plastic flora, the atmosphere is not what it once was. Many joints work on waiters' recommendations rather than menus, so try to confirm prices in advance to avoid confrontations with unscrupulous staff.

Locals prefer neighbouring **Nevizade Sokak**, an alley lined with restaurants leading off Balık Pazarı (Fish Market). Though home to some of the city's best *meyhanes*, the area is being swamped by cheap beer joints with giant screens for football matches. Rows of tables are set outside as if for one giant street party, which is what the place looks like most evenings: every seat is filled by garrulous diners, attended by dashing waiters, wandering minstrels and hopeful street vendors. If you have just one night in Istanbul, spend it on Nevizade Sokak.

Most *meyhanes* also have two or three floors of indoor dining, sometimes with a roof terrace. They don't differ much in terms of food and prices, but everyone has their favourites. We like **Boncuk**, which specialises in Armenian dishes and features live *fasıl* music. **Krependeki Imroz**, one of the oldest *meyhanes*, deserves a mention. Imroz is the Greek name for Gökçeada, one of the Aegean islands, and home to the Greek owners. **Cumhuriyet Meyhanesi**, once frequented by Atatürk, is notable for its *fasıl* musicians.

When ordering from the heaped tray of *meze*, the more dishes the merrier, since sharing is what it's all about. Cold dishes cost about YTL3-4, hot ones YTL4-YTL7, and seafood appetisers YTL9-YTL12. For two people, six dishes are usually enough; you can order main courses later if you have room. Or go for a set menu of *meze*, fish, meat and dessert, with unlimited *rakı*, beer or wine, which costs about YTL35-YTL60 a head.

Owned by impresario Izzet Çapa of Cahide Sayfiye fame (*see below*), this relatively new venture illustrates the trend du jour in Istanbul restaurants: it joins the increasing number of designer eateries with 360-degree views. The interior's not bad either. Banlieue6080's ice-cool clientele is offset by its dark leather interior, with sliding glass skylights that open up on summer nights. The menu is the usual fusion theme, though this time, it's a rather bizarre combination of sushi, South American, Italian and Argentine dishes. The house special consists of a giant steak served on a wooden board, slathered in various sauces of your choice. Try to bag one of the coveted tables near the glass-walled front of the restaurant; these have fabulous views across the city and receive marginally more attention from the unashamedly louche staff. Reservations are recommended. *See also p122* **Summer loving, winter warming**.

Cahide Sayfiye & Cahide Variete

Kadırgalar Caddesi, Demokrasi Parkı içi Yanı, Maçka (0212 219 6530). **Open** 6pm-2am Mon-Sat. **Starters** YTL20-YTL25. **Main courses** YTL30-YTL50. **Credit** MC, V.

A cabaret, theatre and restaurant rolled into one, Cahide Sayfiye is a curious spot. The summer venue (in winter it moves to Beyoğlu) is an alfresco extravaganza with four-poster divans covered by canopies set in a garden. Seafood is served on Marilyn Monroe plates, while drag queens perform farcical shows. Gay fashionistas, paparazzi-dodging celebrities and boisterous hen parties lap it up.

Gani Gani

Kuyu Sokak 13, Taksim (0212 244 8401).
Open 10am-midnight Mon-Thur, Sun; 10am-1am
Fri, Sat. **Starters** YTL3-YTL6. **Main courses**
YTL7-YTL10. **Credit** AmEx, MC, V.
Map p249 O3 ⑲
Popular with locals, this unusual eaterie buried in
the backstreets near Taksim Square offers
Anatolian eating at its best. Set on six floors, the
place feels like a showcase for rural artefacts. Most
of the seating – either in private dining rooms or
cosy communal spaces – is traditional Anatolian
style, with low tables surrounded by kilims and
cushions on the floor. Authentic eastern Turkish
specialities include *çiğ köfte* (a la turca steak tartare
made with cracked wheat and chili), *mantı* (ravioli
with yoghurt sauce), *pide* or *lahmacun* (Turkish-
style pizzas), plus a range of kebabs. *Narghiles*
(waterpipes) are available. No alcohol. *See also p122*
Summer loving, winter warming.

Hacı Abdullah

*Sakızağacı Caddesi 17, off Istiklal Caddesi, Beyoğlu
(0212 293 8561).* **Open** 11am-10.30pm daily.
Starters YTL5-YTL6. **Main courses** YTL9-
YTL15; set menu YTL40. **Credit** AmEx, V, MC.
Map p248 N3 ⑳
One of the oldest restaurants in Istanbul, Hacı
Abdullah is deservedly famous for traditional
Ottoman fare. Three old-school dining rooms are
brightened by a few contemporary flourishes. Opt
for the pale pink room at the rear, complete with
skylight and chandelier. The restaurant is renowned
for its pickles, stored in colourful jars , and bizarrely
described in the English menu as 'the symbols of
pooped politicians'. An array of pre-cooked dishes
is on display in the front room. No alcohol is served.

Leb-i Derya Richmond

*Sixth Floor, Richmond Hotel, Istiklal Caddesi 445
(0212 243 4375).* **Open** 11am-2am Mon-Thur,
Sun; 11am-4am Fri, Sat. **Starters** YTL11-YTL22.
Main courses YTL15-YTL26. **Credit** AmEx, DC,
MC, V. **Map** p248 M4 ㉑
A more sophisticated alternative to its popular
predecessor around the corner on Kumbaracı Sokak.
The new premises, on the sixth floor of the
Richmond Hotel on Istiklal Caddesi, boast
breathtaking views, even by Istanbul standards. Try
the extraordinary Forty-Spice Steak, Tike kebab
with aubergine caviar, or *mahmudiye* – chicken
curry with honey, almonds, apricot and cinnamon.
Stifado, a tough steak and mushroom stew, is less
successful. The restaurant stops serving lunch in
July and August due to the greenhouse effect of its
glass panelling. Reservation recommended. *See also
p137* **Up on the roofs.**

Lokanta

*Meşrutiyet Caddesi 145-147, Beyoğlu (0212
245 5810).* **Open** noon-3pm, 6.30pm-2am
Mon-Thur; noon-3pm, 6.30pm-5am Fri, Sat.
Closed July-Oct. **Main courses** YTL15-YTL33.
Credit DC, MC, V. **Map** p248 M4 ㉒

Lokanta roughly translates into English as 'canteen',
appropriate given the plain decorative style. No
matter, it's all about the food, notable for top-
quality ingredients and an unfussy approach. The
atmosphere is low-key and casual, and the place is
usually busy, with a constant hum of conversation
– just like a *lokanta*. This is a very enjoyable place
to spend time at winter weekends; in summer
the same menu and staff move upstairs to their
fashionable terrace venue, which has a panoramic
view (*see p137* **Up on the roofs**).

Mikla

*The Marmara Pera, Meşrutiyet Caddesi 167-185,
(0212 293 5656).* **Open** noon-3.30pm, 6.30pm-2am
Mon-Sat. **Starters** YTL6-YTL12. **Main courses**
YTL15-YTL22. **Credit** AmEx, DC, MC, V
Map p248 M4 ㉓
On the roof garden of the 18-storey Marmara Pera
hotel, Mikla is the latest project of Turco-Finnish
chef Mehmet Gürs (formerly of Lokanta) and is
already one Istanbul's most exclusive eateries. The
European menu is brief but inventive. Starters are
big enough to share (just as well, as prices are steep).
Lamb escalope is a fantastic main course. The place
doesn't fill up until 10.30pm, so don't book too early
or you'll miss the buzz. *See also p122* **Summer
loving, winter warming.**

Nature and Peace

Büyükparmakkapı Sokak 21-23 (0212 252 8609).
Open 11am-11.30pm Mon-Thur, Sun; 1-11.30pm
Fri, Sat. **Set lunch** YTL11-YTL22. **Main courses**
YTL15-YTL26. **Credit** AmEx, DC, MC, V.
Map p249 O3 ㉔
Vegetarian restaurants are rare in Istanbul, and even
this pretender serves several chicken dishes. The set
lunch is great value and the dinner menu includes a
soup and salad with any main course; pasta and
falafel are reliable choices. The small, unpretentious
café is cosy, if slightly musty.

Rejans

*Emir Nevrus Sokak 17, Galatasaray (0212 244
1610).* **Open** noon-3pm, 7pm-midnight Mon-Sat.
Starters YTL4-YTL30. **Main courses** YTL12-
YTL30. **Credit** AmEx, MC, V. **Map** p248 N3 ㉕
Founded by White Russians who relocated to
Istanbul in the wake of the Soviet revolution,
Rejans was reputedly one of Atatürk's favourite
restaurants. Left-wing Turkish intellectuals would
come here to gripe over borscht and vodka. Since the
red star was spurned in favour of the gold card,
Rejans is now frequented by visiting Russians with
deep pockets, who knock back flavoured vodkas as
they gorge on 'tsar's zakuski'. Caviar costs anything
from YTL25 to an astonishing YTL173 for
100 grammes. If the Slavic food is so-so, Rejans still
oozes charm, with its polished wood, high ceilings,
musicians' gallery and a drunken doorman to hang
customers' coats on hooks personalised with
the names of long-dead regulars. *See also* **Summer
loving, winter warming.**

Eat, Drink, Shop

Tokyo Restaurant

Meşelik Sokak 24, off Istiklal Caddesi (0212 293 5858). **Open** 11am-11pm daily. **Starters** YTL5-YTL20. **Main courses** YTL19-YTL30. **Credit** AmEx, DC, MC, V. **Map** p247 O2 **㉖**

With its modern-traditional scarlet decor and tatami rooms, Tokyo is a hit with the local Japanese. The menu includes dozens of noodle, rice and teriyaki dishes, plus good sushi and sashimi (though they often run out of tuna). The sushi chefs show off their skills behind an open counter, dopey waiters perform remarkable feats of forgetfulness.

Wan-na

Meşrutiyet Caddesi 151, Tepebaşı (0212 243 1794/ 244 5922). **Open** noon-4am Tue-Sat. Closed May-Sept. **Starters** YTL14-YTL24. **Main courses** YTL23-YTL40. **Credit** AmEx, DC, MC, V. **Map** p246 M3-4/N3 **㉗**

Among the clutch of fashionable spots on Meşrutiyet Caddesi, Wan-na is the latest dining venture from Istanbul's Doors group, the entrepreneurs behind some of the city's trendiest joints, including Vogue, Anjelique and A'jia. Wan-na's high-style interior provides a cool backdrop for modern renditions of classic Vietnamese, Thai, Japanese and Chinese dishes. Expect a steep bill if you sample the innovative cocktails. *See also p122* **Summer loving, winter warming**.

Zarifi

Çukurlu Çeşme Sokak 13 (0212 293 5480). **Summer venue** *Muallim Naci Caddesi 44, Kuruçeşme (0212 293 54 80)*. **Open** 8pm-4am daily. **Starters** YTL5-YTL10. **Main courses** YTL15-YTL22. **Credit** AmEx, MC, V. **Map** (winter venue) p249 O3 **㉘**

An update on the *meyhane* that's very popular with fashionable young Turks. Zarifi's extensive menu covers all the classic *meze* and grilled meats, as well as Ottoman dishes and recipes inherited from the former Greek residents of the Pera neighbourhood, like shrimp *saganaki* and octopus stew. The soundtrack is equally eclectic --a mix of Turkish folk,

Summer loving, winter warming

It's true of virtually every city in the world that visits are best made during the summer, when the architectural gems – and residents – are basking in photogenic sunshine.

Istanbul is more or less guaranteed three straight months of warm, rainless days and nights during the summer season. The city undergoes an extraordinary transformation during the mid-year period, when restaurant tables sneak out on to streets, balconies, terraces and rooftops. In Istanbul it's considered a crime to waste the warm summer nights, so every inch of available outdoor eating space is sure to be filled with happy, sun-kissed diners.

Banlieue6080 (*see p120*), **Ulus 29** (*see p130*, **Mikla** (*see p121*), **Vogue** (*see p130*) and **360** (*see p119*) are just some of the many top-end dining establishments that throw open their doors, windows and terraces during the summer, boasting fine views and making a breezy alternative to air-conditioned or stuffy interiors.

Some venues without the capacity for seasonal transformations may move their premises altogether during the summer months, locking up enclosed winter locations in favour of a temporary home on a rooftop, or a garden overlooking the Bosphorus.

For example, between June and September, you'll find **Wan-na** (*see p122*) at the Anjelique club in Ortaköy (*see p194*). Next door, ground-floor restaurant **Lokanta** (*see p121*) is only open for lunch in summer, as the focus moves up to the lively, rooftop **NuTeras** (*see p137* **Up on the roofs**), which transforms itself from a restaurant into a bar and club at around midnight.

Upmarket *meyhane* **Zarifi** (*see p122*) also shuts its Beyoğlu doors and relocates to summer quarters near the Bosphorus, on the same site as the New Yorker, on Muallim Naci Caddesi in Kuruçeme.

Then there are establishments such as Nişantaşı's **Salomanje** (*see p127*) and **Çapari** (Sahilyolu 104, Küçükyalı, 0216 366 9371), a fish restaurant on the Asian side, which both open in the balmy Sortie club (*see p194* **Bosphorus bling**) on the Bosphorus at Kuruçeşme, as does the excellent and perennially popular **Supper Club**, which is one of Istanbul's few summer-only restaurants.

But winter visitors shouldn't despair, as Istanbul has more than its fair share of cosy indoor restaurants, ideal for warm nights out of the chill winter air. **5.Kat** (*see p123*) in Cihangir has a fiery and inviting interior, as does cosy vegetarian **Zencefil** (*see p123*), while **Rumeli** in Sultanahmet (*see p115*) has a big fireplace to thaw out cold bones.

Alternatively, you can heat up from within, Russian style, with an assortment of vodkas to accompany your meal at **Rejans** (*see p121*), or snuggle up among the floor cushions and kilims in authentic Anatolian style at **Gani Gani** (*see p121*), tucked away near Taksim.

Eat, Drink, Shop

chill-out tunes and mainstream pop. Once the *rakı* is flowing freely, the spirit of the *meyhane* usually takes over and spontaneous table-top dancing breaks out. This winning formula is duplicated every summer at Zarifi's supper club at the New Yorker in Kuruçeşme. *See also p122* **Summer loving, winter warming**.

Zencefil
Kurabiye Sokak 8 (0212 244 8234). **Open** 11am-midnight Mon-Sat. **Starters** YTL4-YTL8. **Main courses** YTL5-YTL12. **Credit** AmEx, MC, V. **Map** p249 O2 ㉙
Probably the best vegetarian restaurant in Istanbul (though purists may be infuriated by the fact that chicken makes an occasional appearance on the menu). The setting is urban café meets country kitchen, with shelves lined with jars of produce and giant blackboards listing the daily specials, from soups to spicy stews and freshly baked breads. The home-style food is unfalteringly delicious, likewise the homemade lemonade. *See also p122* **Summer loving, winter warming**.

Cihangir

Rehabilitated from its dirty days as a shady part of town, Cihangir is now one of Istanbul's most coveted neighbourhoods, just down **Sıraselviler Caddesi** from Taksim Square. This transformation has been accompanied by the long overdue arrival of a decent selection of cafés and bars catering to the area's predominantly arty and foreign residents. The area's culinary options are increasingly cosmopolitan, too. In warm weather, restaurants and cafés spread their tables out on to **Akarsu Caddesi** and stay open well into the small hours.

Beşinci Kat (5.Kat)
5th floor, Soğancı Sokak 7, off Sıraselviler Caddesi (0212 293 3774/www.5kat.com). **Open** 10am-2am Mon-Thur, Sun; 10am-3am Fri, Sat. **Starters** YTL8-YTL22. **Main courses** YTL22-YTL30. **Credit** AmEx, DC, MC, V. **Map** p249 O3 ㉚
With its bright colours, velvet furnishings and an eye-catching floor piece of a nude young Norma Jean Baker, 5.Kat boasts one of the city's most striking interiors. As its name implies (*kat* means floor), it occupies the fifth floor of a back-street building in Cihangir. A giant neon angel shines at street level, and a rooftop terrace lit with red lanterns opens during the summer. The menu is a culinary jack-of-all-trades (Turkish, French, Italian, Oriental); everything is acceptable, although nothing stands out. 5.Kat's actress proprietor, Yasemin Alkaya, keeps a close watch, even after hours when the dance music is cranked up and a clubby atmosphere takes over. There are occasional live events and regular singles nights. *See also p137* **Up on the roofs** and *p122* **Summer loving, winter warming**.

Lokal. *See p125.*

Doğa Balık
Akarsu Yokuşu Caddesi 46 (0212 293 9143). **Open** noon-midnight daily. **Starters** YTL5-YTL15. **Main courses** YTL15-YTL50. **Credit** AmEx, MC, V. **Map** p249 O4 ㉛
Don't let the entrance via the dismal lobby of the Villa Zurich Hotel put you off: Doğa Balık is a splendid neighbourhood fish restaurant. The dining rooms on the seventh floor are notable for their rooftop terrace, which boasts stunning views across to Sultanahmet and the back of Beyoğlu. The cooking is equally impressive. The kitchen specialises in lightly cooked greens (up to 18 varieties) and perfectly grilled seasonal fish drizzled with garlicky olive oil. This is the quintessential Aegean comfort food – and it's good for you, too.

Miss Pizza
Haynar Sokak 7, off Akarsu Caddesi (0212 251 3278). **Open** noon-midnight daily (last orders 10.30pm). **Pizza** YTL9-YTL28; **Side orders** YTL14-YTL20. **Credit** AmEx, MC, V. **Map** p249 O4 ㉜
Arguably the best pizzeria in town, this cosy eatery in the heart of Cihangir is a big hit with resident foreigners. Selen and Elif, who both have backgrounds in textiles, were inspired to create Miss Pizza by trips to Europe. An Italian chef created the menu and taught them to make pizza dough, which they perfected through endless practice at home. Pizza funghi, made with gorgonzola and porcini mushrooms marinated in truffle oil, is a real treat.

Nevizade Sokak. *See p120*.

Besides pizza, there are good cheese and chacuterie platters and salads. There are only six tables, but you can also order home delivery. Reservations are essential on Fridays and Saturdays.

Tünel/Galata/Nevizade Sokak

Property prices are booming in the warren of narrow, atmospheric streets stretching from **Tünel Square** down to the **Galata Tower**. Filled with an interesting mix of restaurants, cafés and bars frequented by locals, it's a trendy but low-key area. **Nevizade Sokak**, Çiçek Pasajı and a few neighbouring streets form the city's most famous *meyhane* district.

Boncuk

Nevizade Sokak 19 (0212 243 1219). **Open** 11.30am-2am daily. **Credit** MC, V. **Map** p248 N3 ③
See p120 **Çiçek Pasajı & Nevizade Sokak**.

Cumhuriyet Meyhanesi

Sahne Sokak 47, Balık Pazarı (0212 293 1977).
Open 9.30am-2am daily. **Credit** MC, V.
Map p248 N3 ③
See p120 **Çiçek Pasajı & Nevizade Sokak**.

Krependeki Imroz

Nevizade Sokak 24 (0212 249 9073). Open 11.30am-2am daily. Credit MC, V. Map p248 N3 ③
See p120 **Çiçek Pasajı & Nevizade Sokak**.

Galata House

Galata Kulesi Sokak 61, Galata (0212 245 1861/ www.thegalatahouse.com). **Open** noon-midnight Tue-Sun. **Starters** YTL8-YTL16. **Main courses** YTL13-YTL16. **Credit** MC, V. **Map** p246 M5 ③
Down the hill from the Galata Tower, this hideaway is also known as the 'Old British Jail' (Eski Ingiliz Karakolu), owing to its former incarnation as a prison of the British Empire at the turn of the 20th century. Lovingly restored by architects Mete and Nadire Göktuğ, who run the place, the four characterful dining rooms are littered with junk-shop finds. Look for inscriptions of former inmates on the rough walls. Nadire also gives a nightly piano performance. The menu is a well-executed mix of Georgian, Russian and Tartar dishes.

Lokal

Müeyyet Sokak 5/A, off Istiklal Caddesi (0212 245 5744). Open 10am-midnight daily. **Starters** YTL7-YTL15. **Main courses** YTL15-YTL25.
Credit AmEx, MC, V. **Map** p248 M4 ③
Once one of the hippest eateries in town, Lokal has graduated to classic status. On a tiny side-street off Asmalımescit, Lokal is easy to locate thanks to the films projected on the wall opposite, ranging from footage of skateboarders to spaghetti westerns. Menus bound by kitsch LP covers read like an encyclopedia of global fusion: pesto linguine, chicken tikka, pad Thai, salmon teriyaki and chicken wings. All are surpisingly good, but service can be slow. **Photo** *p123*.

Refik

Sofyalı Sokak 10-12 (0212 243 2834). **Open** noon-3pm, 7-11.30pm Mon-Fri; 7pm-midnight Sat. **Set menu** YTL50. **Credit** MC, V. **Map** p248 M4 ③
Established in 1954, this upmarket *meyhane* is a great starting point to immerse yourself in *meze* culture and acquire a taste for *rakı*. Gravel voiced Refik Arslan still meets patrons at the door, including a devoted clientele of leftie hacks and intellectuals. Most regulars smoke and drink more than they eat, but the place is renowned for seafood dishes from the Black Sea. If in doubt, point to your choice in the glass-fronted fridge. There's no music, as it would interfere with the animated conversation.

Sofyalı 9

Sofyalı Sokak 9, Tünel (0212 245 0362/ www.sofyali.com.tr/eng). **Open** noon-1am Mon-Sat. **Starters** YTL4-YTL10. **Main courses** YTL10-YTL20. **Credit** AmEx, MC, V. **Map** p248 M4 ③
A *meyhane* maybe, but *très* genteel. This cosy local haunt feels like someone's front room – someone with money, taste and a fine old house. There are mustard walls, exposed brickwork, wooden floors, and hanging lanterns. The ground floor space is small, but tables spill on to the alley and there are two floors upstairs. Even so, reservations are a must, as the city's literati and gay crowd love this place. The food is a cut above – superior *meze*, followed by meat and fish dishes prepared with the freshest ingredients and a lightness of touch. Highly recommended.

Teşvikiye & Nişantaşı

Few visitors make it up the hill to these upmarket neighbourhoods, with their impressive selection of designer boutiques and equally swanky eateries, particularly on and around **Abdi Ipekçi Caddesi** and **Teşvikiye Caddesi**. Most of them, like **Loft** and **Brasserie Nişantaşı**, offer a credible, if imitative, spin on European cuisine; others, like **Hünkar**, take Turkish dining to new heights.

Brasserie Nişantaşı

Abdi Ipekçi Caddesi 23/1, Nişantaşı (0212 343 0443). Metro Osmanbey. **Open** 10am-1am daily. **Starters** YTL10-YTL20. **Main courses** YTL15-YTL50. **Credit** AmEx, DC, MC, V.
This brasserie succeeds in recreating the French bohemian vibe with its dark, mirrored interior, high ceilings offset by a huge chandelier, and posters for local events casually pinned on the walls. The menu sticks to brasserie classics like salmon and beef carpaccio, 'le steak' and fine French desserts. There's outdoor seating in summer.

Hünkar

Mim Kemal Öke Caddesi 21, Nişantaşı (0212 225 4665). Metro Osmanbey. **Open** noon-midnight daily. **Starters** YTL7-YTL15. **Main courses** YTL12-YTL20. **Credit** AmEx, MC, V.

Eat, Drink, Shop

The original Hünkar opened in 1950 in the far-flung, working-class Fatih neighbourhood. This new offshoot in Nişantaşı has taken the old-school Ottoman brand upmarket. Diners include Chanel-suited ladies who lunch and deal-clinching businessmen who schmooze over homely dishes like sheep's trotter soup, stuffed cabbage, anchovy pilaf, or the signature dish *hünkar beğendi* – 'the sultan's delight' – a rich lamb stew with aubergine purée. Decorative touches (jars of preserves, copper artefacts) maintain one foot in the past; street-side seating allows clients to keep an eye on the present.

Loft

Lütfi Kırdar Kongre Merkezi, Darülbedai Caddesi 6, Harbiye (0212 219 6384). Bus 43, 46Ç, 46ÇY, 46H, 46KY. **Open** 11am-2am Mon-Sat; 4pm-2am Sun. **Starters** YTL10-YTL25. **Main courses** YTL30-YTL80. **Credit** AmEx, DC, MC, V.

It's located in the distinctly unglamorous Istanbul Convention and Exhibition Centre, but the plush interior is a world apart: geometric leather banquettes, low-slung Japanese lanterns and a long marble bar. And there's the added bonus of a rooftop terrace. French-trained chef Ümit Özkanca dishes up

The House Café. *See p127.*

ambitious international fare – think Moroccan shrimp salad, grilled quail, and Peking duck with porcini and bok choy.

Salomanje

Belkıs Apartmanı 4/1-2, Atiye Sokak, Nişantaşı (0212 327 3577). Metro Osmanbey. **Open** 11.30am-2am Mon-Sat. **Starters** YTL9-YTL14. **Main courses** YTL22-YTL30. **Credit** MC, V.
This new café-restaurant is an instant hit with Nişantaşı's most stylish residents, although entering the undersized venue on Atiye Sokak you might wonder why. With a bar, a handful of tables and a small terrace out the back, the decor is unremarkable but cosy. The menu combines Turkish and international standards. In summer, Salomanje moves to Sortie nightclub in Kuruçeşme.

Tuus

Sofa Hotel, Teşvikiye Caddesi 123, Nişantaşı (0212 224 8181/www.tuus.com.tr). Metro Osmanbey. **Open** noon-2am Mon-Sat. **Starters** YTL17-YTL32. **Main courses** YTL26-YTL49. **Credit** AmEx, DC, MC, V.
On the first floor of the new Sofa Hotel in Nişantaşı, Tuus is in many ways a typical hotel restaurant: classic decor, exclusive clientele, intuitive service, very high prices. In this case, we have to add 'very good food'. Complimentary appetisers get things started (if you're lucky, you'll get a shot of amazing lobster soup). Starters and mains are classic European (spicy steak tartare, wood-roasted lamb), with the odd twist – braised oxtail and parmesan cream worked well. The drawbacks: imported Italian branded water at YTL8 a bottle, and staff who tend to take things a bit too fast. Gripes aside, Tuus is one of the city's outstanding restaurants.

The Bosphorus Villages

This string of waterfront settlements starts at **Beşiktaş** and runs north through **Ortaköy**, **Arnavutköy** and **Bebek**, as far as **Rumeli Hisarı**. Restaurants in this district tend to be pricey, cashing in on their seaside setting, but remain popular.

Banyan Ortaköy

Muallim Naci Caddesi Salhane Sokak 3, Ortaköy (0212 259 9060). Bus 40, 40T, 42T. **Open** noon-2am daily. **Starters** YTL12-YTL20. **Main courses** YTL25-YTL40. **Credit** AmEx, DC, MC, V.
With spectacular views of the original Bosphorus bridge and floodlit Ortaköy mosque, Banyan comes into its own on summer nights, and enjoys a far superior location to its sister in Nişantaşı. Bonsai trees scattered around the tables lend an exotic twist to the refined interior. Living up to the slogan 'Food for the Soul', all ingredients are organic and ethically sourced. The menu is a melange of Asian influences. Chinese, Japanese, Vietnamese and Indian delicacies are all beautifully presented and prepared. This is fusion food at its best – good for the soul, but hard on the wallet.

The House Café

Salhane Sokak 1, off Muallim Naci Caddesi, Ortaköy. (0212 227 2699). Bus 40, 40T, 42T. **Open** 9am-2am Mon-Thur, Sun; 8am-2am Fri, Sat. **Starters** YTL8-YTL22. **Main courses** YTL15-YTL30. **Credit** AmEx, DC, MC, V.
With its industrial-chic interior and blissful terrace right on the Bosphorus, the Ortaköy branch is by far the most popular of The House Café's three venues (the other two outposts are in Nişantaşı and Tünel). Weekend brunch is a fixture for the young and well-heeled. The menu is a mishmash of global comfort food using gourmet ingredients. Try the superlative House burger, thin-crust pizzas, imaginative bruschetta and salads. Pint-sized fresh fruit cocktails are a joy to behold and delicious to boot. **Photos** *p126.*

Mangerie

Cevdetpaşa Caddesi 69, Bebek. (0212 263 5199). Bus 40, 40T, 42T. **Open** 8am-midnight daily. **Starters** YTL3-YTL12. **Main courses** YTL18-YTL26. **Credit** MC, V.
Tucked away behind the fancy waterside eateries in Bebek, this delightful eaterie is worth seeking out. (Head for the Küçük Bebek end of the high street and follow the steps leading up past a hairdresser.) The airy interior is all white wood, with a balcony overlooking the rooftops of Bebek to the Bosphorus. The relaxed atmosphere makes this an ideal lunch spot, with simple salads and sandwiches served on a great breads, all baked on the premises. The house special *zeytinyağlı*, seasonal vegetables and fruits stewed in olive oil, is recommended.

Poseidon

Küçük Bebek, Cevdet Paşa Caddesi 58, Bebek (0212 263 3823). Bus 40, 40T, 42T. **Open** noon-midnight daily. **Starters** YTL4-YTL15. **Main courses** YTL22-YTL36. **Credit** AmEx, MC, V.
A supremely stylish affair, Poseidon serves superior seafood at vertiginous prices. Sampling the *meze* menu will hike up the bill, but specalities like stuffed calamari, marinated sea bass and fish croquettes are worth it. The catch of the day is priced by the kilo. Your dining companions will be well-bred, well-manicured big spenders. The large deck is virtually suspended above the Bosphorus and has gorgeous views of Bebek bay, but the view from indoors is almost as magical. **Photo** *p130.*

Rumeli Iskele

Yahya Kemal Caddesi 1, Rumeli Hisarı (0212 263 2997). Bus 40, 40T, 42T. **Open** noon-2am daily. **Starters** YTL3-YTL10. **Main courses** YTL7-YTL44. **Credit** AmEx, MC, V.
Despite competition from newer, shinier seafood restaurants, this place is always packed. The best tables are on the waterfront deck, with a view of the hilltop castle of Anadolu Hisarı across the strait. The menu holds few surprises – *meze* and Mediterranean fish – but the food is good. Service is unobtrusive and efficient.

Menu & glossary

Useful phrases

Can I see a menu? **Menüye bakabilir miyim?**
Do you have a table for (number) people?
(Number) kişilik masanız var mı?
I want to book a table for (time) o'clock.
Saat (time) için bir masa ayırmak istiyorum.
I'll have (name of food). **Ben (name of food) istiyorum.**
I'll have (name of food) without salt.
Ben tuzsuz (name of food) istiyorum.
I'll have (name of food) without oil.
Ben yagsiz (name of food) istiyorum.
I'm a vegetarian. **Et yemiyorum.**
Can I have an ashtray? **Kültablası alabilir miyim?**
Can I have the bill please? **Hesap, lütfen.**

Basics

breakfast **kahvaltı**
lunch **öğle yemeği**
dinner **akşam yemeği**
dessert **tatlı**
menu **menü**
service charge **servis**
cup **fincan**
glass **bardak**
fork **çatal**
knife **biçak**
spoon **kaşık**
napkin **peçete**
plate **tabak**
baked **fırında pişmiş**
boiled **kaynamiş**
fried **kizarmiş**
grilled **ızgara**
roast **kavrulmuş**
bread **ekmek**

thin flat bread **pide** or **lavaş**
brown bread **kepekli ekmek**
pasta **makarna**
rice **pilav**
soup **çorba**
cheese **peynir**
hardboiled/softboiled egg **katı yumurta/ rafadan yumurta**
yoghurt **yoğurt**
garlic **sarımsak**
salt **tuz**
red/black/hot pepper **pul/kara/acı biber**

Meat

beef **dana**
chicken **tavuk**
lamb **kuzu**

Fish

fish **balık**
anchovy **hamsi**
bluefish **lüfer**
bonito **palamut**
crab **yengeç**
lobster **istakoz**
mackerel **uskumra**
monkfish **fener**
sardines **sardalya**
sea bass **levrek**
sea bream **sarıgöz/sinarit**
shrimp **karides**
sole **dil**
swordfish **kılıç**
tuna **torik**

Vegetables

aubergine **patlıcan**
carrots **havuç**

The Asian Shore

Head to the Asian side to eat where the locals do. **Çiya** and **Kanaat** offer a fantastic array of classic, and more unusual, Turkish dishes at bargain prices, while exclusive **A'jia** and **Körfez** are worth crossing a continent to visit.

A'jia

A'jia Hotel, Ahmet Rasim Paşa Yalısı, Çubuklu Caddesi 27, Kanlıca (0216 336 3013). Ferry from Beşiktaş or Eminönü to Üsküdar then taxi. **Open** 7am-midnight daily. **Main courses** YTL20-YTL50. **Credit** AmEx, MC, V.
A'jia's remote location – a boutique hotel in a converted *yalı* on the shores of the Bosphorus – is actually an advantage. Far from the hustle of the city centre, the waterfront terrace has sweeping views of European Istanbul, while the sleek interior marries Ottoman elegance with contemporary designer pieces. Highlights of the international menu include fresh pasta and octopus carpaccio.

Çiya

Güneşlibahçe Sokak 43-44, Kadıköy (0216 418 5115). Ferry from Eminönü or Karaköy to Kadıköy. **Open** 11am-10pm daily. **Starters** YTL4-YTL8. **Main courses** YTL7-YTL12. **Credit** AmEx, MC, V. **Map** p251 W7 ④⓪
Most of the little local eateries on Güneşlibahçe are indistinguishable, but Çiya is so good – and so successful – that it is taking over most of them. Çiya Sofrası specialises in traditional dishes from around Turkey. Opposite is Çiya Kebapçı, heaven

cucumber **salatalık**
lentils **mercimek**
lettuce **marul**
okra **bamya**
onions **soğan**
peas **bezelye**
peppers **biber**
potatoes **patates**
spinach **ıspanak**
tomatoes **domates**
courgette **kabak**

Fruit & nuts

fruit **meyve**
apples **elma**
banana **muz**
cherries **kiraz**
grapes **üzüm**
hazelnuts **fındık**
honeydew melon **kavun**
lemon **llmon**
peanuts **fıstık**
pistachio nuts **şam fıstığı**
oranges **portakal**
walnuts **ceviz**
watermelon **karpuz**

Meze

börek flaky savoury pastry with parsley
and/or whIte cheese, minced meat, spinach
or other vegetables
çerkez tavuğu shredded chicken served
cold in a walnut cream sauce
çoban salata 'shepherd's salad' of tomatoes,
cucumbers, hot peppers and onions with
lemon and olive oil
dolma cabbage, grape leaves, pepper or
squash, served cold and stuffed with rice,

pine nuts, currants and spices. When served
hot, dolma are usually also stuffed with
minced meat
imambayıldı aubergines cooked with onion,
tomato and olive oil, served cold
karnıyarık baked aubergines stuffed with
minced meat, onion, tomato, and spices
kısır Turkish style tabouleh salad with
parsley, bulgar, lemon, tomato, onion, olive
oil, pomegranate, and mint
lahmacun spiced minced meat on a thin
crust pizza-like bread called *pide*
mücver deep-fried patties made with grated
courgette in a batter of egg and flour
zeytinyağli cold dishes with olive oil

Mains

güveç casserole cooked in a clay pot
karides güveç shrimps cooked with onions
in a peppery tomato sauce
köfte meatballs
pirzola lamb chops

Drinks

apple juice **elma suyu**
beer **bira**
cherry juice **vişne suyu**
coffee **kahve**
Turkish coffee **Türk kahvesi**; without sugar
sade; a little sugar **az şekerli**; medium sweet
orta şekerli; sweet **şekerli**
milk **süt**
orange juice **taze portakal suyu**
peach juice **şeftali suyu**
red wine **kırmızı şarap**
tea **çay**
water **su**
white wine **beyaz şarap**

for kebab aficionados, where chefs in white hats
conjure up a mind-boggling selection of skewered
meats and freshly made flat breads in the open
kitchen. Both venues are smart and clean, with tiled
white floors, pine furniture, and sepia photos of
pastoral scenes. Friendly staff are the picture of
brisk efficiency.

Kanaat

Selmanipak Caddesi 25, Üsküdar (0216 341 5444).
Ferry from Eminönü or Beşiktaş to Üsküdar.
Öpen 6am-11pm daily. **Starters** YTL3-YTL6.
Main courses YTL4-YTL8. **No credit cards.**
Map p250 W2 ④
Kannat is a perfect example of a historical *lokanta*
that appears to have changed little since it was
founded in 1933. Equally popular at both lunch and

dinner, the vast menu of traditional but
increasingly hard-to-find Turkish dishes represents
excellent value. Choose from dozens of stuffed,
stewed, and spiced vegetables and a mouthwatering
array of grilled, baked, and roastmed dishes, from
rich lamb stew to spicy meatballs. There's a
separate section dedicated to desserts. Baked quince
with clotted cream and delicate milk puddings with
various combinations of dried fruit and nuts are
especially memorable.

Körfez

Körfez Caddesi 78, Kanlıca (0216 413 4314/
www.korfez.com). Bus 40, 40T, 42T to Rumeli
Hisarı, where a special shuttle departs from opposite
Edwards of Hisar; or ferry from Eminönü or
Beşiktaş to Üsküdar, then 15min taxi ride.

Open noon-4pm, 7pm-midnight daily.
Starters YTL6-YTL13. **Main courses**
YTL30-YTL79. **Credit** AmEx, MC, V.

Gourmands from all over Istanbul regularly make the pilgrimage to Kanlıca, midway up the Bosphorus, for what many locals swear is the finest fish in Istanbul. As with most seafood restaurants, the emphasis is on whatever is freshest, but try not to miss the signature dish, *tuzda balık* or 'fish in salt'– a whole fish baked in a crust of sea salt, a method which preserves all the flavour and succulence. Booking is essential.

Vogue
Spor Caddesi 92, BJK Plaza A Blok 13, Akaretler, Beşiktaş (0212 227 2545). **Open** noon-3pm, 7pm-2am daily. **Starters** YTL20-YTL35. **Main courses** YTL30-YTL55. **Credit** AmEx, DC, MC, V

Despite being eclipsed by newer, trendier joints, Vogue has managed to retain its stylish clientele and high standards. Though curiously situated on the top floor of an office block, the restaurant serves sophisticated Californian-fusion and freshly prepared sushi. Afterwards, dip into the excellent cocktail menu at the adjacent bar. Reservations are still essential at weekends. *See also p122* **Summer loving, winter warming**.

Levent & Etiler

A couple of Istanbul's wealthier districts – comprising glass skyscrapers, monolithic malls, and bumper-to-bumper SUVs – Levent and Etiler are home to a handful of fine restaurants.

Sunset Grill & Bar
Yol Sokak 2, off Adnan Saygun Caddesi, Ulus Parkı, Ulus (0212 287 0357). Metro Levent. **Open** noon-3pm, 7pm-2am daily. **Starters** YTL15-YTL40. **Main courses** YTL35-YTL80. **Credit** AmEx, DC, MC, V.

A gorgeous setting for a romantic tryst – a tree-lined terrace set on a hilltop high above the Bosphorus. The menu is an unlikely but well-executed mix of Californian fusion, meat-heavy modern Turkish dishes, and superior sushi. The restaurant is a five- or ten-minute walk from Levent metro station. Predictably, it's hugely popular at sunset, when you are advised to book ahead.

Ulus 29
Kireçhane Sokak 1, Adnan Saygun Caddesi, Ulus Parkı, Ulus (0212 265 6181/www.club29.com). Metro Levent. **Open** noon-3pm, 7pm-midnight daily. **Starters** YTL18-YTL30. **Main courses** YTL22-YTL88. **Credit** AmEx, DC, MC, V.

Someone to impress? Something to celebrate? Or simply feel like living out a Sinatra song? Ulus 29 fits the bill. Thanks to yet another spectacular hillside setting (just above the Sunset Grill & Bar, *see above*), the views from the semi-circular verandah are unbeatable. Models make eyes with moguls against an opulent Oriental backdrop, decked with muslin drapes and lit by oil lamps. The restaurant is immaculately designed by local nightlife impressario Metin Fadıllıoğlu and his interior designer wife, Zeynep, who make gracious hosts. The surly service is less impressive than the food, which focuses on the eastern Mediterranean. *See also p122* **Summer loving, winter warming**.

Where better to eat fish? **Poseidon** in Bebek. *See p127*.

Bars & Cafés

Cocktails with stunning views or a *narghile* and a glass of tea.

Bar culture, as understood in the West, has come late to Turkey. Atatürk was allegedly partial to *rakı*, but for the common folk coffee was as strong as it got (although a Turkish *kahve* has the kick of a double espresso).

All that is now changing - and fast. Once confined to seedy taverns frequented by older men, alcohol consumption has come out of the closet, while multinational café chains have moved in, adding milk and froth to the local 'black mud'. Since the mid 1990s, the bar business has boomed. Initially, the favoured style was Parisian Left Bank meets student squat – bare brick, wooden floors and flea-market furnishings – but interiors have increasingly got the *Wallpaper** factor. Style bars are often enhanced by killer locations, either beside the Bosphorus or up on the rooftops (*see p137* **Up on the roofs**). You can even get fancy cocktails at these places. Inevitably, prices have risen accordingly.

WHERE TO DRINK
There is now a new take on the traditional men-only coffee- or teahouse, the *kıraathane*, thanks to the current popularity of the *narghile* (hookah pipe) with young people of both sexes: *see p132* **Hava narghile**. These joints don't serve alcohol. Otherwise, most places blur the boundaries between bar and café, serving coffee and food throughout the day, becoming increasingly smoky and boozy after night falls.

Heaven for bar-hoppers, **Beyoğlu** has a density of drinking venues that would do any German city proud. There's not much worthwhile on the main drag, Istiklal Caddesi, but the surrounding side streets are packed with watering holes, ranging from the good, the bad to the ugly. An evening in Ortaköy or Arnavutköy is pleasant, but quality options are limited. The same is true in swanky Nişantaşı and Teşvikye. A night on **Kadife Sokak** in Kadıköy, on the Asian Shore, has the potential to turn into something enjoyably regrettable, but getting home could be troublesome.

WHAT TO DRINK
There are now countless places where you can order a cocktail with confidence (try **Cezayir**, **Leb-i Derya**, or **Zoe**). Local vintners are also producing and marketing a greater variety of wine (*şarap*) of steadily improving quality, although ordering an unspecified glass of house red or white will still generally result in remorse. There are some reliable labels, though: you won't go wrong with Kavaklıdere's Angora (red and white), Çankaya (white) and Yakut (red), or Doluca's Villa Doluca (red and white). Wine isn't particularly cheap, and there's a very high tax on imported booze. Turks consume twice as much *rakı* – the anise-flavoured spirit similar to the Greek ouzo or French *pastis* – as all other alcohol combined; it's generally drunk with *meze*.

Eat, Drink, Shop

The best Cafés and bars

For a drink beside the Bosphorus
Aşşk Café (*see p141*); **Garga** (*see p141*).

For drinks right on the water
Any of the cheap and cheerful bars strung underneath the **Galata Bridge**.

For beer and live music
Badehane (*see p135*); **Enginar** (*see p135*); **James Joyce** (*see p139*).

For soaking up the Asian scene
Karga (*see p142*); and any of the bars lining **Kadife Sokak** on the Asian Shore.

For old-style elegance
Büyük Londra (*see p135*).

For cocktails
Rıız (*see p140*); **Leb-i Derya Richmond** (*see p136*); **Lucca** (*see p142*); **Zoe** (*see p138*). .

For stunning interiors
Ceyazir (*see p136*); **Müzedechanga** (*see p142*).

For coffee and contemplation
Kaffeehaus (*see p135*); **Sedir** (*see p142*), **Smyrna** (*see p135*).

Hava *narghile*

Waterpipe, hookah, or 'hubbly-bubbly'. Call it what you will, Turks have been smoking the *narghile* since the early 17th century, despite religious authorities periodically denouncing the practice and calling for it to be banned. The tyrannical Murat IV (1623-40) decreed that anyone caught having so much as a quick puff should be sentenced to death.

In the late 19th and early 20th century, *narghile* smoking was all the rage in high society, particularly among women. That fad passed and in republican Istanbul the *narghile* was relegated to a pastime of the peasantry. Why it should suddenly be making a comeback in the 21st century is anybody's guess. But in the last couple of years a slew of cafés devoted to the waterpipe have opened. A few are aimed squarely at tourists, but most custom comes from students.

Narghile tobacco is typically soaked in molasses or apple juice, giving it a slightly sweet flavour; but you can get it straight and strong by asking for *tömbeki*.

Narghile cafés serve tea and coffee, but no alcohol. Prices are around YTL4-YTL6 a pipe, which lasts a good hour or more. Contrary to popular misconception, hashish is not an option, nor, sadly, is the traditional Ottoman blend of opium, perfume and crushed pearls.

The best place to sample a *narghile* is on the nameless pedestrian strip by the American Pazarı, below the old cannon foundry at Tophane. Until recently there was just a row of small shops; now it's lined with nothing but *narghile* cafés. At any time of day or night, there might be 300 to 400 people here, an extraordinary mix of students, couples and families, all belching forth great clouds of grey smoke. Certain cafés at the north end of the strip have drawn fire in the press for providing cushion-strewn banquettes, which apparently encourage al fresco canoodling. With or without the bodily contact, this is a fine place to wind down after a night out in Beyoğlu. Otherwise, try one of the following:

Enjoyer Café

The most touristy of the many *narghile* cafés on the pedestrianised street north of Divan Yolu. Avoid the fruity tobaccos.
For listings *see p133*.

Erenler Çay Bahçesi

In the idyllic courtyard of an Ottoman seminary, Erenler's low tables and benches are shaded with ivy-hung trellises. Despite signs advertising 'Magic Waterpipe Garden', few tourists visit; it's filled with students from nearby Istanbul University in Beyazit.
For listings, *see p133*.

Meşale

This sunken café beside an arcade of tourist shops is very pleasant when the shops close and locals descend. There are nightly performances of Turkish classical music and dervish dancing shows on Friday, Saturday and Sunday between 7pm and 10pm.
For listings, *see p134*.

Fes Café.

South of the Golden Horn

With the exception of **Mozaik** restaurant's basement bar (*see p115*), there's a shortage of decent bars in Sultanahmet. Options are limited to a row of nondescript tourist cafés east of the Hippodrome, the odd rowdy backpacker joint on **Akbıyık Caddesi** and one or two somnolent hotel bars. You're better off walking downhill to **Eminönü** to check out the many cafés beneath the **Galata Bridge**. Or forgo the booze and give your lungs a workout at one of the local *narghile* cafés.

Cheers

Akbıyık Caddesi 20 (no phone), Sultanahmet. Tram Sultanahmet. **Open** 10am-2am daily. **Licensed. No credit cards. Map** p243 N11 ❶
Akbıyık Caddesi is backpacker boulevard, all cut-rate travel agencies, hostels and last-ditch diners. Bars are as transient as their clientele, but Cheers has been around longer than most. It's small, cramped, and crowded most nights with an international throng with no qualms about meeting strangers. On the right night, it's like a house party; on the wrong night, you may find yourself trading tales of bad bowels with a blotto backpacker.

Divan

Kapalıçarşı Cevahir Bedesten 143-151 (0212 520 2250). Tram Beyazıt Kapalıçarşı. **Not licensed. Open** 8.30am-7pm Mon-Sat. **Credit** MC, V. **Map** p242 L9 ❷
The Grand Bazaar has a few little places to stop for a *çay*, but there's one place in the Old Bazaar, or Cevahir Bedesten, that stands out. Divan is a

simulated slice of the suave old days of the Republic, with burgundy walls, red leather couches, a huge Turkish flag draped from the ceiling, and a crystal chandelier beside a giant portrait of Atatürk. The extensive coffee menu features the likes of frappuccinos, plus decent sandwiches and sweets.

Enjoyer Café

İncili Çavuş Sokak 25, Sultanahmet (0212 512 8759). Tram Sultanahmet. **Open** 9am-2am daily. **Not licensed. Credit** MC, V. **Map** p243 N10 ❸
For review, *see p132* **Hava *narghile*.**

Erenler Çay Bahçesi

Çorlulu Ali Paşa Medresesi, Yeniçeriler Caddesi 36/28, Beyazıt (0212 528 3785). Tram Beyazıt. **Open** *Summer* 7am-3am daily. *Winter* 7am-midnight daily. **Not licensed. No credit cards. Map** p242 L10 ❹
For review, *see p132* **Hava *narghile*.**

Fes Café

Ali Baba Türbe Sokak 25-27, Sultanahmet (0212 526 3071). Tram Çemberlitaş. **Not licensed. Open** 9am-10pm daily. **Credit** MC, V. **Map** p242 M9 ❺
On a quiet back street near Nuruosmaniye Mosque, just off Nuruosmaniye Caddesi, this café's modern design blends surprisingly well with its antiquated surroundings. With a sister establishment smack in the centre of the Grand Bazaar, Fes Café is something of a local institution. The fresh-pressed lemonade and mint tea are refreshing after a heavy shopping session. Be sure to check out Abdullah, a little shop in the café that sells gorgeous natural textiles, plus an assortment of olive oil-based soaps. There's another branch inside the Grand Bazaar.

Leyla: a great place for whiling away a lazy afternoon.

Meşale

Arasta Bazaar 45, Sultanahmet (0212 518 9562).
Open 24 hours daily. *Tram Sultanahmet.* **Not licensed. Credit** MC, V. **Map** p242 N11 ⑥
For review, *see p132* **Hava** *narghile.*

Pierre Loti

Balmumcu Sokak 5, off Gümüşsuyu Caddesi, Eyüp(0212 581 2696). Bus 55ET. **Open** 8am-midnight daily. **Not licensed. No credit cards.**
On a hilltop with a stunning vantage point over the Golden Horn, this café is dedicated to French naval officer Pierre Loti, who was so obsessed with Istanbul that he took to masquerading as a Turk and remodelled his house as a 'Sultan's palace'. Legend has it Loti would sit at this spot for hours, gazing over the city and gathering inspiration for his literary masterpiece, *Aziyade*. To get to this modest teahouse, climb up through the scenic cemetery near Eyüp Mosque or take a cable car, which is signposted from the mosque.

Yeşil Ev Beer Garden

Kabasakal Caddesi 5, Sultanahmet (0212 517 6785). Tram Sultanahmet. **Open** 10.30am-11pm daily.
Licensed. Credit AmEx, MC, V. **Map** p243 N10 ⑦
This idyllic garden of towering laurel, linden and horse chestnut trees belongs to the quaint Yeşil Ev guesthouse. It's the finest place for an aperitif this side of the Golden Horn. In winter, guests are sheltered in a large conservatory amid hanging plants. Pricey, but worth it.

Beyoğlu

Cihangir

This bohemian enclave boasts countless style-conscious cafés and bars. Most are concentrated along and around **Akarsu Sokak.** Things really liven up after dark and at weekends, when a lesiurely brunch can easily last all day.

Cuppa

Yeni Yuva Sokak 26 (0212 249 5723/www.cuppa juice.com). **Open** 9am-10pm Mon-Sat; 9am-9pm Sun. **Credit** MC, V. **Map** p249 O4 ⑧
On one of the smaller streets behind Cihangir's main drag, this juice bar is the perfect antidote to Beyoğlu's boozy bars. Choose from around 40 fruit and veggie cocktails, plus nutritious extras like wheatgrass, guarana or Echinacea. The healthy menu extends to salads, wraps and sandwiches.

Leyla

Akarsu Caddesi 46 (0212 244 5350). **Open** 9am-4am daily. **Licensed. Credit** MC, V.
Map p249 O4 ⑨
Currently the place in Cihangir where you're most likely to have to queue for a table, Leyla is wildly popular at peak times. The café is unpretentiously cool, with a relaxed, airy interior whose large windows open on to street tables in good weather. Menu highlights include the all-day themed breakfasts,

which run from Istanbul to Oslo, Madrid and London. The English breakfast is a generous plate of bacon and eggs, with orange juice, tea and a selection of rolls. The bar stays open late.

Smyrna

Akarsu Caddesi 29 (0212 244 2466). **Open** 9am-2am daily. **Licensed**. **Credit** MC, V. **Map** p249 O4 ⑩
Traditionally, Cihangir's favourite hangout has been the cluster of teahouses by the mosque, where local loafers can spend a whole day or evening ensconced beneath the plane trees, nursing a dirt-cheap glass of tea. Nearby Smyrna is where the teahouse regulars come when they're feeling flush, to rub shoulders with the actors and artists who live in the area. Laid-back enough for daytime lounging and lunching, Smyrna shifts up a few gears after dark.

Galata and Tünel

The cobbled streets found around **Galata**, **Asmalımescit** and **Tünel** are home to some of the city's most exciting and distinctive venues. Residents come from all over the city to catch live Turkish music at **Badehane** or jazz and pop bands at **Babylon** (*see p183*).

Badehane

General Yazgan Sokak 5, Tünel (0212 249 0550). **Open** 9am-2am daily. **Licensed**. **Credit** MC, V. **Map** p248 M4 ⑪
A modest, single-room venue just off Tünel Square, Badehane began as an eaterie, but quickly evolved into one of the most popular bars in town. Smarter after a recent renovation, it's still a big hit with students and slackers. On Wednesdays, live gypsy music (including local legend Selim Sesler) gets the crowd dancing around the tiny, packed tables. In summer, the café spills out on to the street, where backgammon tournaments take place. **Photo** *p136*.

Enginar

Şah Kapısı Sokak 4A, Kuledibi, Galata (0212 251 7321). **Open** noon-2am daily. **Licensed**. **Credit** AmEx, MC, V. **Map** p246 M5 ⑫
The neighbourhood around the Galata Tower is getting a major facelift: streets have been repaved and cafés have spread their tables across the spruced up square surrounding the tower. Enginar, one of the area's popular bars, has a claim to fame as a set for a local soap opera, and with its stained-glass windows and rustic interior, it is a perfect pit stop after a tour of the tower or midway on the steep climb from Karaköy to Tünel. There's a varied programme of live music several times a week.

Kaffeehaus

Tünel Square 4 (0212 245 4028). **Open** 8am-1am daily. **Licensed**. **Credit** MC, V. **Map** p248 M4 ⑬
The tiny façade facing Tünel Square is deceptive: inside is a long, lofty space with Wedgwood blue walls. Famous for its selection of coffees and

resident grey cat, Kaffeehaus is a local favourite for brunch. Try the traditional Turkish breakfast or spicy scrambled eggs. Solitary customers are catered for with plenty of magazines and newspapers. The tables in the window provide unrivalled people-watching opportunities – try upstairs if those on the ground floor are taken.

KV Café

Tünel Geçidi 10, Tünel (0212 251 4338). **Open** 8am-2am daily. **Licensed**. **Credit** MC, V. **Map** p248 M4 ⑭
Opposite Tünel station, an elaborate iron gate leads to an enchanting 19th-century arcade overgrown with potted plants. Of the handful of cafés lucky enough to share this secret passageway, KV is the most atmospheric. Couples cosy up on wrought-iron furniture, snacking on cakes or lingering over cheese and wine. Inside, the café occupies three beautiful bare-brick rooms with tiled floors, arched windows, and unusual antiques. At dusk, the setting is even more romantic, lit by candles and Victorian lamps, with live piano music wafting throgh the arcade.

Şimdi

Asmalımescit Sokak 9, Tünel (0212 252 5443). **Open** 9am-midnight daily. **Licensed**. **Credit** MC, V. **Map** p246 M4 ⑮
This relaxed refuge off Istiklal is one of the most stylish all-day café-bars anywhere in Istanbul. Hipsters hang out in the retro front room, where low seating and low lighting encourage lounging. And there's free wireless internet; you can bring your own laptop or use the Mac provided. There's an above-average selection of wine by the glass, accompanied by addictive balls of spiced cheese. Simple but delicious Mediterranean dishes are served in the dining area at the rear.

Galatasaray

Discerning drinkers head to the stylish cafés and bars around the **Galatasaray Lycée**, where Istanbul's intellectuals, designers, and media types congregate. Photographers favour **Kafe Ara**, named after Magnum snapper Ara Güler, who lives upstairs.

Büyük Londra

Meşrutiyet Caddesi 117, Tepebaşı (0212 293 1619). **Open** 4pm-2am daily. **Licensed**. **Credit** MC, V. **Map** p248 M3 ⑯
Fans of colonial watering holes tend to head for the bar at the Pera Palas Hotel (currently closed for renovations); that's because they don't know about the Büyük Londra. Another late 19th-century time warp, it may be a little less grand than the Pera Palas, but it's way more eccentric. The two gilded salons are plushly carpeted and decked with giant chandeliers. The immaculate barman occasionally sallies forth from the tiny bar at the back to change the 78 on the wind-up gramophone. Otherwise, the soundtrack is provided by caged songbirds on the windowsills.

Locals love to let loose at **Badehane**. *See p135.*

Open late and rarely crowded, Büyük Londra is an open secret that's good to know. **Photo** *p.139.*

Cezayir
Hayriye Caddesi 16, Galatasaray (0212 245 9981/ www.cezayir-istanbul.com). **Open** 9am-2am Mon-Thur, Sun; 9am-4am Fri, Sat. **Licensed**. **Credit** MC, V. **Map** p248 N3 ⓱
Behind the Galatasaray Lycée, this fabulous 19th-century building was originally a school for the Italian Workers' Association. Beautifully converted into a glamorous bar and restaurant, Cezayir throngs with the city's literati and glitterati. The baroque silver and white dining room is stunning. The back room, with original floor tiles, soaring ceilings and a long wooden bar, is a stylish place for sharing some of the most inventive *meze* in Istanbul. There's a louche lounge with large mirrors and sofas, and a garden at the back that opens on to the twee restaurants of French Street. **Photo** *p141.*

Kafe Ara
Tosbağa Sokak 8/A, off Yeniçarşı Caddesi, Galatasaray (0212 245 4105). **Open** 8am-midnight Mon-Thur, Sun; 10am-midnight Fri, Sat. **Not licensed**. **Credit** AmEx, MC, V. **Map** p248 N3 ⓲
A continental-style café owned by local Magnum photographer Ara Güler, whose evocative black and white shots of Istanbul adorn the walls and place mats. In fine weather, tables in the little alley opposite the Galatasaray Lycée fill up fast. In

winter, the smart, split-level interior buzzes with cultured patrons armed with portfolios, notebooks, or laptops. No alcohol is served, but the fresh-pressed lemonade and milkshakes are great. Snack on sandwiches, pasta, and desserts. **Photo** *p.142.*

Leb-i Derya Richmond
Richmond Hotel, Istiklal Caddesi 445 (0212 243 4375/www.lebiderya.com). **Open** 11am-2am Mon-Thur, Sun; 11am-4am Fri, Sat. **Licensed**. **Credit** MC, V. **Map** p248 M4 ⓳
On the top floor of the Richmond Hotel, right on Istiklal Caddesi, this bright and airy new branch of the original Leb-i Derya down the road is very chic. The food is excellent, but avoid lunch in summer as the glassed-in terrace creates a greenhouse effect. Instead, go for sundowners, with breathtaking views of the Bosphorus and the Sea of Marmara.
Other locations: Kumbaracı İş Hani 115, Kumbaracı Yokuşu, Tünel (0212 293 4989).

Nu Teras
Meşrutiyet Caddesi 145-147 (0212 245 5810). **Open** *June-Oct* 6.30pm-2am Mon-Thur, Sun; 6.30pm-5am Fri, Sat. **Credit** DC, MC, V. **Map** p248 M4 ⓴
On the rooftop of the Nu Pera building, Nu Teras is the epitome of hip Istanbul – with the backdrop of a stunning view of the Golden Horn. The area behind the bar is given over to long tables for diners, who tuck into the same nouvelle Turkish cuisine as at Lokanta, the winter venue on the ground floor (*see*

Up on the roofs

Yesterday I watched you from a noble hill,
Noble Istanbul
I know every street, every alleyway,
I love you Istanbul
Yahya Kemal Batah (1884-1958)

Now, as then, the best way to see Istanbul is from above, as Istanbul's nightlife impresarios have discovered – a revelation that has revolutionised dining and drinking in recent years. Rooftop bars and restaurants are springing up everywhere, desperately trying to outdo each other with the most sweeping skyline and exotic cocktail list.

The frontrunner of this trend is **5.Kat** (*see p123*), owned by actress Yasemin Alkaya: it's a heady mix of art deco and kitsch, starlit romance and late-night shenanigans. Another pioneer of the roof terrace scene is **Leb-i Derya Richmond** (*see p136*). Four years ago, owner Cem Sancer was bowled over by the view from what was then a dilapidated building down a narrow side street off Istiklal

Caddesi. Sancer transformed the sea of rubble into a vertiginous oasis for Istanbul's international elite. **Nu Teras** (pictured, *see p136*) is another stunner: up on the seventh floor, and with amazing views over the Golden Horn, this is a place to be seen – summer central for hip Istanbullus.

In the last year, scores more bars, restaurants, cafés and cake shops have launched open-air outposts offering fabulous cityscapes. The talk of the town is **360** (*see p119*): a restaurant, bar and club rolled into one, this glass-walled pleasure palace sits atop one of Beyoğlu's most famous apartment blocks, smack in the middle of Istiklal Caddesi. As its name suggests, it boasts 360-degree views, with sky-high prices to match.

Rooftop revelry is not confined to the rich. Many of Beyoğlu's *meyhanes* and humble coffee shops have also opened up their top floors to the elements – though they can't all boast the same views.

Eat, Drink, Shop

p121). Dancing is tolerated, but swaying is considered cooler. This was the first Beyoğlu venue to lure posh Turks from their usual haunts in Etiler. Unlike other new venues that were crowded out then swiftly abandoned, Nu Teras is a survivor that can be considered a classic. *See p137* **Up on the roofs**.

Sefahathane

Atlas Pasajı, İstiklal Caddesi 209 (0212 251 2245). **Open** 11.30am-2pm. Closed Mon. **Licensed**. **Credit** MC, V. **Map** p248 N3 **㉑**

Sefahathane's obscure location in Atlas Pasajı, does not stop it being perennially popular. During the day, customers grab a coffee before shopping or catching a movie next door. In the evenings, a wilder bunch of students and musicians spill out into the arcade, milling among the marble columns and swaying to '90s pop and rock. Cult movies are projected on to the video screen by the bar.

Zoe

Tomtom Mahallesi, Yeniçarşı Caddesi 58/5, Galatasaray (0212 251 7491). **Open** noon-2am daily. **Licensed**. **Credit** MC, V. **Map** p246 N3 **㉒**

Despite the gruff bouncers manning the red velvet entrance, Zoe is actually a relatively laid-back bar/restaurant that puts equal emphasis on food and drink. It's one of many venues that makes the most of its rooftop; in the summer, lively groups of customers party under the stars.

Nevizade

Nevizade Sokak is a safe bet for a lively night out. Young Turks down *rakı* in packed *meyhanes* or huddle around tankards of beer in the nearby pubs.

Gizli Bahçe

Nevizade Sokak 27 (0212 249 2192). **Open** noon-3am daily. **Licensed**. **Credit** MC, V. **Map** p248 N3 **㉓**

The only way to tell this place apart from the dozens of other establishments on Nevizade Sokak is by the '27' crudely painted on the wall. There's a mellow bar on the ground floor and a livelier space up two flights of stairs, littered with low tables and armchairs. The name means 'Secret Garden' – and that's

Turkey's own brands

Coke may be widely consumed and American café chains may be booming, but for most locals these offer an alternative, rather than a replacement to traditional tipples.

Turkish tea, made from black tea leaves grown in the Black Sea region, brewed in a teapot and sipped from elegant little tulip-shaped glasses, is as ubiquitous as it ever was. And making and drinking traditional Turkish coffee is still a familiar ritual: boiled in a miniature copper or brass beaker known as a *cezve*, it is served in miniature porcelain cups. After draining your cup, turn the remaining sludge upside down to have your fortune read from the dregs. As the Turkish saying goes: *Bir fincan kahvenin kırk yıllık hatrı vardır* (One cup of coffee brings 40 years of gratitude).

Certain towns, such as Susurluk and Çine, are famous for their *ayran*, a cold drink made from yoghurt and water. More refreshing than it sounds, it is a great foil to Turkish dishes such as *gözleme* (thin pancakes) or *pide*. Some restaurants are renowned for their home-made *ayran*; of the packaged brands, those sold in glass bottles are generally the best.

Fruit juice is rarely drunk in Turkish homes, but the syrup from home-made fruit compotes, especially sour cherries, plums and apricots, is a popular refreshment in summer. In winter, a comforting and popular hot drink is *sahlep*, a thick brew of orchid roots mixed with milk and water, topped with cinnamon and ginger. The enduring appeal of *boza* is less understandable. This cold blend of crushed millet and water, traditionally sold from wooden barrels by street vendors, and served with roasted chickpeas, is thick, bittersweet, and frankly unpalatable. The most famous brand is Vefa, which has a stall near the Süleymaniye Mosque; you can also find it in supermarkets and the odd café.

When it comes to alcohol, Turkey is best known for *rakı* – the anise spirit that turns milky when mixed with water, hence its nickname 'lion's milk' (*aslan sütü*). Careful drinkers fill a third of their glass with *rakı* and top up with water and ice. Unlike beer, *rakı* contains no malt, which allegedly saves drinkers from killer hangovers. Even so, you can have a very bad *rakı* experience unless you wash it down with plenty of water and soak it up wth copious *meze*. The old Anatolian habit of drinking *şalgam* – a sour and spicy drink made from turnips, carrots and vinegar – alongside rakı is making a comeback in Istanbul; it is said to relieve an upset stomach. With or without *şalgam*, *rakı* should never be drunk without an edible accompaniment. Try white Turkish cheese and melon.

The endearingly eccentric **Büyük Londra**. *See p135.*

upstairs, too. The music is an odd medley of modern electro and obscure '80s tracks. The door policy can be uncharacteristically picky for the area.

James Joyce

Balo Sokak 26, off Istiklal Caddesi (0212 244 7970/ www.theirishcentre.com). **Open** noon-2am Mon-Thur, Sun; noon-4am Fri, Sat. **Licensed. Credit** AmEx, MC,V. **Map** p249 O2
The first and only Irish pub in Istanbul. The decor is predictably clichéd, but the punters are a mixed bag of worldly Turks, expats and tourists who come for the decent range of fairly pricy beers (Guinness included). Irish breakfast is served all day and there's often live music. The place gets packed for international football matches, when the atmosphere can be electric. The interior could do with a facelift, given that most of its neighbours have recently smartened up their acts.

Şahika

Nevizade Sokak 17 (0212 249 6196). **Open** noon-4am daily. **Licensed. Credit** MC, V. **Map** p248 N3
Another lively but laidback venue with dozens of stools and tiny tables packed into the small space outside, from where a predominantly younger crowd watches the world go by. Inside, wooden stairs lead to five levels of dining rooms and a summer roof terrace where the good times roll to a mix of '80s, electronica and alternative rock. The simple menu is good value for money.

Taksim

Almost every side-street off mile-and-a-half long Istiklal Caddesi is riddled with bars and cafés. The greatest concentration are near **Taksim Square**, with venues for every tribe: Africans, Anatolians, goths, bikers, students, intellectuals, gays and transvestites. Those in search of a cheap beer or a puff on a *narghile* loiter around **Mis Sokak** and **Büyük Parmakkapı Sokak**.

Kaktüs

Imam Adnan Sokak 4, off Istiklal Caddesi (0212 249 5979). **Open** 9am-2am Mon-Sat; 11am-2am Sun. **Licensed. Credit** MC, V. **Map** p249 O2
Kaktüs' elegant dark-wood interior owes a great deal to the classic French café. Its patrons do their best to recreate the ambience of a Godard movie by chain-smoking and sipping blonde beers or black coffee. Stand-offish staff process the short-order menu that changes daily. Since opening in the early 1990s, Kaktüs has spawned countless imitators, but it remains the coolest hang-out with some of the

highest prices. Cadde-i Kebir across the street is similar in style, but sells beer for about half the price.

Klub Karaoke

Zambak Sokak 15 (0212 293 7639/www.klub-karaoke.com). **Open** 8pm-3am Mon-Thur, Sun; 8pm-5am Fri, Sat. **Licensed**. **Credit** MC, V. **Map** p249 O2 **㉗**

This karaoke club near Taksim Square consists of a small bar and two private rooms that are available for hire – the intimate, red-leather Tokyo Room and the larger, darker Fetish Room. Look out for theme nights dedicated to ladies, men, Turkish tunes or disco hits. Things don't really get going until around 11pm, then everyone wants a turn on the mike.

Limonlu Bahçe

Yeniçarşı Caddesi 98, Galatasaray (0212 252 1094). **Open** *Nov-Mar* noon-11pm daily. *Apr-Oct* 9.30am-2am daily. **Licensed**. **Credit** MC, V. **Map** 248 N3 **㉘**

Part-way down the precipitous slope of Yeniçarşı, Limonlu Bahçe is set in a big, bucolic bar-garden. This pretty setting draws a self-conscious young crowd who loll on cushions, flop in hammocks or gather around chunky wooden tables. There are plenty of tight T-shirts, cute tattoos and bare midriffs on display. And if there aren't enough staff, nobody seems to mind.

The North Shield

AFM Fitaş Building, Istiklal Caddesi 24-26 (0212 245 2162/www.thenorthshield.com). **Open** noon-1am Mon-Thur, Sun; noon-4am Fri, Sat. **Licensed**. **Credit** MC, V. **Map** p249 O2 **㉙**

The North Shield transports its regulars to suburban middle England, circa 1975. Think tartan carpets, Famous Grouse mirrors, etched glass screens, wooden benches and a dark, polished bar. There's even Abba, Elton John and Santana on the sound system. Homesick Brits get together here and at five other North Shields around town, including the newest outpost in Gülhane, near Sultanahmet.

Old City

Turnacı Başı Sokak 5/5, off Istiklal Caddesi (0212 244 28 96). **Open** 8pm-4am daily. **Licensed**. **Credit** MC, V. **Map** p249 O3 **㉚**

Old City has been a late-night haunt of nocturnal Istanbullus for years. It remains to be seen whether the recent renovation from its former dark and pokey state has stripped away some of its unmistakeable atmosphere. The place is a bit of a hit or miss affair. But on the right night, you're guaranteed shot-fuelled dancing to live cover bands until all hours. The best way to avoid the wrong night (and the occasional entrance fee) is to peek through the windows on Istiklal Caddesi: there's no mistaking if the joint is jumping.

Pano

Hamalbaşı Caddesi 26, Galatasaray (0212 292 6664). **Open** 11am-2am daily. **Licensed**. **Credit** AmEx, MC, V. **Map** p248 N3 **㉛**

Over a century old, Pano is an Istanbul institution. This atmospheric wine bar is like an updated take on a typical Greek taverna, with wood-panelled interior and rows of giant barrels above the bar. The later it gets, the more people pile in, and there's often standing room only. Then customers squeeze around the narrow counters, sampling Turkish and imported wines by the glass or bottle. Beer is also plentiful and cheap. Tasty finger food includes a generous cheese platter. Only the lucky few will find a table for a proper *meze* dinner.

Pia

Bekar Sokak 6, off Istiklal Caddesi (0212 252 7100). **Open** 10am-2am daily. **Licensed**. **Credit** MC, V. **Map** p249 O2 **㉜**

The uncluttered decor and gallery-style mezzanine create a sense of space where there isn't much at all. Ornate mirrors and a single George Grosz print set the tone. This is a hang-out for writers, film-makers and other creative types. It's also the kind of place where single women will feel comfortable – in fact, some of the city's most beautiful women have been seen to drop into Pia. Dishes inspired by the owners' travels are served all day. The daily specials are usually worth a gamble.

For a different take on Istanbul's bar life, head up to **Nişantaşı** or **Teşvikiye**, a pair of upper-class neighbourhoods north of Taksim with a lively bar scene.

Buz

Abdi Ipekci Caddesi 42/2, Teşvikiye (0212 291 0065). Metro Osmanbey. **Open** 4pm-midnight Mon-Thur, 4pm-2am Fri-Sat. **Licensed**. **Credit** MC, V.

The decor at Buz, a decadent chain of nightspots frequented by Istanbul's bohemians, is nothing if not eccentric: there is almost as much furniture and glassware stuck to the ceiling as on the floor and tables. The cocktails are punchy, but pricey. PR professionals come here to do lunch, grazing on a decent selection of international dishes.

Corridor

Milli Reasürans Carşışı 47/48, Abdi Ipekci Caddesi, Teşvikiye (0212 343 0241). Metro Osmanbey. **Open** 2pm-2am Mon-Sat. **Licensed**. **Credit** MC, V.

A shopping mall may seem like a strange place for a bar, but Nişantaşı's Milli Reasürans Carşışı is full of them. Corridor has a lively but laid-back atmosphere, without the snob factor and dismissive doormen of so many Nişantaşı locations. The hipsters don't seem to mind taking their drinks out to the closed shopping centre.

Taps

Atiye Sokak 5, off Teşvikiye Caddesi, Teşvikiye (0212 296 2020/www.tapsistanbul.com). Metro Osmanbey. **Open** noon-1am Mon-Thur, Sun; noon-2am Fri, Sat. **Licensed**. **Credit** MC, V.

Turkey's first microbrewery, Taps arrived on the scene in 2002. It's still the only bar in Istanbul that serves a decent pint. In fact, you wouldn't know you were in Turkey: with its exposed pipes, ferocious air-conditioning and burble of Beyonce, Britney and Christina courtesy of multi-screen MTV, it could be in any North American city. Prices are positively Western, too. The place is hugely popular, particularly with loud-tied professionals.

Touchdown

Milli Reasürans Çarşışı 61/11, Abdi Ipekci Caddesi, Teşvikiye (0212 231 3671/www.touchdown.com.tr). *Metro Osmanbey.* **Open** 11am-midnight Mon-Thur; 11am-2am Fri, Sat. **Licensed. Credit** (minimum YTL40) MC, V.

Touchdown manages to successfully recreate the atmosphere of an American corner bar, despite the fact that it's in a shopping small. It's a popular spot for drinks after work; on busy nights, customers trickle down the stairway of the Reasürans Centre. Although a favourite with media and advertising executives, it's not flashy. In fact, it feels more like a student union bar. Prices are pretty reasonable, too.

The Bosphorus Villages

On the shores of the Bosphorus, picturesque, well-to-do **Ortaköy**, **Arnavutköy** and **Bebek** are made for indolent afternoons measured out in coffee cups and moonlit evenings fuelled by Martinis. The most successful venues owe as much to their waterfront settings as their designer decor and fancy drinks.

Aşşk Café

Muallim Naci Caddesi 64/B, Kuruçeşme (0212 265 4734). Bus 25T, 40. **Open** 9am-10pm Tue-Sun. **Licensed. Credit** MC, V.

Once you get past that name – the Turkish word for 'love' drawn out into a lisping 'aşşk' – this place has a lot to recommend it. To find it, follow the unmarked staircase down to the Bosphorus from the Macrocenter in Kuruçeşme. The setting is gorgeous: a clubhouse beside the Bosphorus with a lovely garden. The lavish breakfasts and organic salads are deservedly renowned, but rather overpriced.

Dali

Iskele Caddesi, Salhane Sokak 2, Ortaköy (0212 260 2332). **Licensed. Credit** MC, V.

Drolly named after the café's designer, Ali, this relatively new addition to Ortaköy's nightlife absorbs the overflow from its noisier neighbour, the House Café, especially for weekend brunches and early evening drinks. Spread over two floors, the bright brasserie offers an extensive (and gaudily illustrated) menu of breakfast options, salads, and wraps. Dali was closed at the time of writing; phone to check opening times.

Garga

Arnavutköy Caddesi 50/1, Arnavutköy (0212 263 6221). Bus 22, 22R, 25E, 30D, 40, 42T. **Open** 8.30am-4am daily. **Licensed. Credit** MC, V.

Arnavutköy's coolest new venue is housed in a converted Ottoman *yalı*, which stands out from the throng of nearby fish restaurants with its burgundy façade. If you can't grab one of the cushioned

Cezayir. *See p136.*

Kafe Ara. *See p136.*

benches at the outdoor bar, head for the second-floor counter around the open kitchen, or the fourth-floor terrace with superb Bosphorus views. An equally good spot for coffee, drinks, or a seafood supper.

Lucca

Cevdetpaşa Caddesi 51/B, Bebek (0212 257 1255). Bus 22, 22R, 25E, 30D, 40, 42T. **Open** noon-2am Mon; 10am-2am Tue-Sun. **Licensed. Credit** MC, V.
If you're caught in a traffic jam in Bebek, the likely cause is the string of SUVs double-parked outside this neighbourhood hotspot. Sleek society girls pick at plates of sashimi and check each other out from the sidewalk seating or through the floor-to-ceiling windows. At night, DJs hit the decks and party people kick off the night with exotic cocktails.

Müzedechanga

Sakıp Sabancı Caddesi 22, Emirgan (0212 323 0901/www.changa-istanbul.com). Metro Levent, then Bus EL1, EL2. **Open** 10.30am-1am Tue-Sun. **Credit** MC, V.
In the Sakıp Sabancı Museum in Emirgan, Müzedechanga is much more than a museum café. Try to come here for lunch if you're anywhere in the area. A spin-off from the acclaimed Changa restaurant in Taksim, it's housed in a mansion remodelled with a modern mixture of glass, wood and steel, with custom-made furniture by renowned local designers, Autoban. The terrace has amazing views across the manicured museum gardens to the Bosphorus. The Turkish-Med menu, supervised by consutant chef Peter Gordon of Sugar Club fame, is faultless

and well-priced for this quality (about YTL30 per person for lunch). Highly recommended.

Sedir

Mecidiye Köprüsü Sokak 16-18, Ortaköy (0212 327 9870). Bus DT1, DT2. **Open** 9.30am-midnight daily. **Not licensed. Credit** MC, V.
In a converted house next door to Ortaköy mosque, Sedir is a laid-back choice for all-day dining or a coffee break, although conversation is punctuated by the wail of the muezzin. The decor is deliberately designed to feel like home, with sofas, old books, and hand-painted patterns on the walls. The split-level conservatory, with its creeping ivy and stained glass windows, is especially inviting.

Asian Shore

Savvy residents of the Asian side turn their noses up at the prospect of crossing the Bosphorus for a night out. Kadıköy's **Kadife Sokak** (also know as 'Barlar Sokak', in recognition of its plethora of boozers) is packed with bars and cafés offering cheap beer and live music. It's also worth checking out the lively nightlife at bars such as **İçr** and **Moda Terrace** in **Moda**, near Kadıköy.

İçr

Moda Cadessi 239, Kadıköy (0216 414 7291). Ferry from Karaköy or Beşiktaş to Kadıköy. **Open** 3pm-2am daily. **Licensed. Credit** MC, V.
This no-nonsense bar is a big hit with the young locals of Moda, many of whom are expats. The red-brick interior features a random assortment of brightly coloured furniture, a dartboard, and a gaping devil looming above the bar. Beers are cheap, but so are the spirits used in the house cocktails.

Isis

Kadife Sokak 26, Kadıköy (0216 349 7381). Ferry from Karaköy or Beşiktaş to Kadıköy. **Open** 11am-2am daily. **Licensed. Credit** MC, V. **Map** p251 W8 ③③
This Egyptian-themed bar, with wall paintings and statues, is incongruously located in a converted three-storey townhouse. The top-floor wine bar holds regular tastings accompanied by live music. The large garden gets crammed on summer nights.

Karga

*Kadife Sokak 16, Kadıköy (0216 449 1725/ www.kargart.com). Ferry from Karaköy or Beşiktaş to Kadıköy.***Open** 11am-2am daily. **Licensed. Credit** AmEx, DC, MC, V. **Map** p251 W8 ③④
This much-loved haunt in the heart of Kadıköy's bar strip is known for three things: alternative music, cheap beer and fine art. The music policy can only be described as eclectic. Themed nights range from Belgian pop to Bill Laswell. These usually take place in the ground-floor bar, which is like a pub with lower lighting and louder music. Changing art exhibitions are held in the quieter space upstairs.

Shops & Services

Something old, something new.

Istanbul's image as a blend of ancient and modern may be a cliché, but that doesn't mean it isn't true, and the old-new fusion is as apparent in the city's shops as anywhere else. The oriental shopping experience, with a visit to the **Grand Bazaar** (*see p76*) or the **Egyptian Bazaar** (*see p82*), is an integral part of a visit to Istanbul. At the same time, shopping mall culture has come to the city – and stayed (*see p144* **Mall life**). There are enough aspirational, sophisticated consumers to support local fashion designers and retailers, and enough with sufficient cash to spend on big international labels, too.

Popular buys for visitors include oriental antiques, exotic jewellery, knock-off designer copies, traditional ceramics, carpets and kilims. Turkish people love to haggle, and they're renowned for it. Be careful that you choose the right time and place, though; it is appropriate at the bazaars, but not in stores where prices are clearly marked. (*See p78* **Shopping the bazaar** and *p154* **The rug trade** for more on bazaar shopping and bargaining.)

Istanbul is not as cheap as it used to be, but prices are still reasonable compared with Europe, if you buy local goods. Imports suffer from high taxes and are therefore expensive. On the other hand, services – from shoeshining to knife sharpening – are a steal, provided you can bridge the language gap.

SHOPPING AREAS

Sultanahmet is prime tourist territory, and is well supplied with tacky souvenir stores and pushy carpet sellers. Prices are marked up accordingly. That said, some of the handicraft places and rug stores, particularly off the main drag, can turn up some interesting stuff – just don't expect bargains. Things get spicier as you head west towards the **Grand Bazaar** area, which may have lost its lustre to locals now attuned to the mall, but remains the oriental shopping experience par excellence (*see p78* **Shopping the bazaar**).

By comparison, **Beyoğlu** offers an altogether more western shopping experience. The street that is the backbone of the area, **Istiklal Caddesi**, is fast becoming bland anywhere-in-the-world high-street territory. The current line-up includes Top Shop, the Body Shop, Mango, Nike and multiple Starbucks, with at least one massive mall under construction at

the time of writing. But dive into the side streets, be enticed by the Paris-style passages, and things start to get more interesting. That's also the case as you head away from the mainstream Taksim, past Galatasaray to the more off-beat Tünel end.

For committed shoppers in search of sophistication, head to **Nişantaşı** and neighbouring **Teşvikiye**, two districts about a mile north of Taksim Square. This is serious label territory. On **Abdi Ipekçi Caddesi** the likes of Armani, Louis Vuitton and Tiffany sit alongside sophisticated Turkish jeweller **Urart** (*see p159*), while one block north is MaxMara rival **Mudo Collection** (Teşvikiye Caddesi 143, 0212 225 2941).

TAXES AND REFUNDS

VAT (KDV) on goods and services is a standard 18 per cent. Non-residents are eligible for refunds on purchases of goods (not services) over YTL118 from stores displaying the tax-free sticker, and reclaiming the money is not the tedious process it used to be. The retailer fills out a special receipt in quadruplicate and gives you three copies, which you then present to customs – along with your purchases – upon departure; this must be within three months of the purchase. You can then get a cash refund in the currency of your choosing on the other side of passport control.

One-stop shopping

Department stores

Turkey doesn't have the same department store culture that exists in the west. The few that do exist tend to cater to the high end of the market.

Beymen

Akmerkez Mall 107, Nispetiye Caddesi, Etiler (0212 282 0380/www.beymen.com.tr). Metro Levent. Bus 59R, 59UL, 559C, U1, U2, UL57. **Open** 10am-10pm daily. **Credit** AmEx, MC, V.
Beymen started life as a men's clothing store, but is now synonymous with designer clothing and accessories for men and women, combining own-label products with select international brands. You'll also find cosmetics and home accessories.
Other locations: Abdi Ipekçi Caddesi 23/1, Nişantaşı (0212 343 0404); Bağdat Caddesi 493, Suadiye, Asian Shore (0216 467 1845).

Mall life

Cruise Harvey Nichols with a personal shopper, stop off for some noodles at Wagamama, then stock up on Häagen-Dazs: just a regular day out in Istanbul if you spend it at **Kanyon** (*pictured*), the new and massively hyped 'alternative urban life centre' – aka shopping mall – in Levent.

Kanyon is one of more than 40 malls that have opened in Istanbul in the last two decades, helped along by the city's burgeoning population, the emergence of a new middle class and increasing access to Western culture, not to mention a buoyant economy and phenomenal credit boom.

Boyner

Metro City Mall, Büyükdere Caddesi 171, Levent (0212 344 0575/www.boyner.com.tr). Metro Levent. **Open** 10am-10pm daily. **Credit** MC, V.

Part of the eponymous Boyner Group, which also owns Beymen, Boyner is a less label-conscious version of its sister store. It stocks a comprehensive selection of clothes, shoes, sportswear, cosmetics, fabrics, china, glass and home accessories.

Vakko

Kanyon Mall, Büyükdere Caddesi 185, Levent (0212 353 1080/www.vakko.com.tr). Metro Levent. **Open** 10am-10pm daily. **Credit** AmEx, DC, MC, V.

Vakko was once Turkey's authority on fashion and still has huge cachet locally. Aside from some eye-catching window displays, the store has lost much of its originality today. The exceptions are own-label scarves and ties (worth checking out in the duty free store at Atatürk Airport) and some lavish Ottoman-design furnishings and fabrics. Besides the inevitable perfumery and cosmetics hall, there's also a bridal department that does brisk business with the city's eligible elite.

Other locations: Akmerkez Mall 212, Nispetiye Caddesi, Etiler (0212 282 0695); Bağdat Caddesi 422, Suadiye, Asian Shore (0216 416 4204).

YKM

Halaskargazi Caddesi 368, Şişli (0212 232 7728/ www.ykm.com.tr). Metro Şişli. **Open** 10am-9pm Mon-Sat; noon-10pm Sun. **Credit** MC, V.

Turkey's oldest department store started life as a humble shop behind the Spice Bazaar in 1950. Today, it's the closest thing Istanbul has to a real department store. Unlike its more exclusive rivals, it caters to a broad market, selling everything from unisex clothing to sports gear, toys, home accessories and electronics.

Other locations: Cevahir Mall, Büyükdere Caddesi, Şişli (0212 382 0342).

Malls

Mall mania has seized the city since the arrival of the first one in 1988. Since then, Istanbullus have eagerly embraced the whole lifestyle package from across the pond. Yet even for a city inured to inflation, the explosion in choice

While Istanbul has been a trade centre for centuries, its modern-day residents only really discovered consumerism after the military coup in 1980. The following decade changed Turkey economically, politically and culturally. Money and individualism were glorified, giving rise to an aspirational, depoliticised generation; in the new free market economy, making money was key and the ability to consume was the measure of success. Social status became increasingly dependent on material success. Imports – from luxury clothing labels to MTV – started to flood in to meet rising demand.

Mass immigration from the provinces added to the mix. New arrivals may not have had much money to spend, but they had absorbed the new consumerist values. And if they couldn't buy, they could look. So when American-style shopping malls came to town, a new style of recreation was born, one that put shanty-town residents under the same roof as the city's elite: Istanbullus of all classes started to spend time at the mall.

Every year, Istanbul buzzes with the opening of another shopping mall – bigger, better, more sophisticated than the last. Istanbul's first mall, **Galleria** (Sahil Yolu, Ataköy) – the pet project of then prime minister Özal – opened in 1988. Five years later, **Akmerkez**

(see p145) arrived. Located between the upmarket Etiler and Ulus neighbourhoods, it remains one of the city's elite shopping centres, and attracts around 1.5 million visitors each month.

A five-minute taxi ride from Akmerkez are **Metrocity** (see p145) and **Kanyon** (see p145). Though adjacent, they draw crowds from different parts of Istanbul. Designed – you've guessed it – like a canyon, Kanyon's marketing has concentrated on its 'alternative urban life centre' tag. This mall was to be more than a mere collection of shops. And with unique brands, sophisticated places to eat, a cinema, state-of-the-art gym, innovative store design and large public spaces, it does stand out from its competitors.

The most popular mall of them all is **Cevahir** (see p145). Branded as the biggest mall not only in Turkey, but all of Europe, and the second biggest in the world. Cevahir is always crowded, attracting mostly middle- and lower-class residents.

Whatever criticism the malls may deserve, there's no denying their popularity with people from disparate social and economic backgrounds, and the phenomenon of these groups being brought together – even though many of those visiting are just window shopping.

over the last few years has been bewildering. **Kanyon** is the latest addition to Istanbul's mall roster. *See above* **Mall life**.

Akmerkez
Nişpetiye Caddesi, Etiler (0212 282 0170). Metro Levent. Bus 59R, 59UL, 559C, U1, U2, UL57. **Open** 10am-10pm daily.
An upmarket mall with 250 shops, a food court, cinema and one of the city's better Italian restaurants, Paper Moon. But its infuriating design means it's hard to find your way out. Once Istanbul's slickest mall, Akmerkez is now eclipsed by the competition and suffers from an inconvenient location a good 15 minutes from the metro.

Cevahir
Büyükdere Caddesi 22, Şişli (0212 380 0893/4). Metro Şişli. **Open** 10am-10pm daily.
Europe's biggest mall, and the second largest in the world; its six storeys can seem confusing, especially in the absence of floor plans – there seems to be just one on each floor. Besides direct access from the metro, the mall's greatest asset is Koç Taş, one of the city's only DIY stores reachable by public transport.

Kanyon
Büyükdere Caddesi 185, Levent (0212 353 5300/ www.kanyon.com.tr). Metro Levent. **Open** 10am-10pm daily.
The latest addition to Istanbul's mall society, this is a mall with a difference. Open to, yet sheltered from, the elements, its canyon-inspired design houses 170 boutique-style shops, a plethora of restaurants including Wagamama and Le Pain Quotidien and the plushest cinema in town. Shopping-wise, the accent is on prestige fashion and lifestyle labels, both local and foreign: the likes of Harvey Nichols, Georg Jenson, Vakko and Swarovski. There's also a new Apple flagship store.

Metrocity
Büyükdere Caddesi 171, Levent (212 344 0660). Metro Levent. **Open** 10am-10pm daily.
Like Kanyon across the road, this four-storey mall is served by a direct link to the metro. What's different is that it pitches to a far more middle-of-the-road clientele. Among the 140 stores, you'll find Marks & Spencer vying for business with Benetton, Zara, Mavi Jeans and the like. There's also a food court offering standard mall fare.

Eat, Drink, Shop

Eski Fener.

Antiques

One of the best places for browsing is
Çukurcuma, a quiet Beyoğlu backwater
behind the Galatasaray Lycée. Its roller-coaster
streets harbour a plethora of small shops with
a wealth of antiquaria from rural Anatolia –
anything from oil lamps and painted trunks
to carved doors. There's also a fair amount of
sophisticated glass and porcelain ware, Ottoman
screens and chandeliers, as well as shops
specialising in single items such as tin toys.

Items over a century old must be cleared by
the Museums Directorate before being taken
overseas. Dealers should know the procedure.

Artrium

*Tünel Gecidi İş Hanı, A Blok 3, 5, & 7, Tünel (0212
251 4302).* **Open** 9am-7pm Mon-Sat. **Credit** AmEx,
MC, V. **Map** p248 M4.
A shop attracting a more sophisticated breed of anti-
quarian, with three spacious display rooms and a
prime location in the passage just across from
KV Café. It has a fine selection of miniatures, maps,
prints and calligraphy, along with Kütahya ceramics and the odd film and advertising poster.

Can Shop

*Avrupa Pasajı 7, Meşrutiyet Caddesi 16, Galatasaray,
Beyoğlu (0212 249 3280).* **Open** 10am-7pm Mon-Sat.
No credit cards. Map p248 N3.
Tins, pins, coins and toys, from clanky cars to planes
and tanks. There's a surprising amount of Turkish
stuff, dating mostly from Ottoman and early republic times, including dossiers crammed with old share
certificates, some of which date back 70 years.

Eski Fener

*Aga Hamam Sokak 25-27, Çukurcuma, Beyoğlu
(0212 251 6278).* **Open** 11am-7pm Mon-Sat.
No credit cards. Map p249 O3.

A select assortment of furniture, doors, oil lamps and
copperware, mostly picked up in rural Anatolia.
You'll find things like low-legged dough-rolling
tables, wooden butter churns and storm lamps. All
items have been painstakingly restored.

Leyla

*Altıpatlar Sokak 6, Çukurcuma, Beyoğlu (0212 293
7410).* **Open** 10am-7pm Mon-Sat. **Credit** AmEx,
MC, V. **Map** p249 O3.
A massive selection of antique clothes, costumes,
hats, embroidered linens, wall hangings and tapes-
tries collected by Leyla Seyhanlı, an old hand in
the business. Prices are quite high, but it's all top
quality stuff.

Popcorn

*Turnacıbaşı Caddesi, Faik Paşa Sokak 2, Çukurcuma,
Beyoğlu (0212 249 5859/www.popcornistanbul.com).*
Open 10am-7pm Mon-Sat. **No credit cards.**
A favourite with visiting artists and locals alike, this
eclectic shop specialises in rare books, furniture and
knick-knacks from the 1950s.

Books

Ranging from American-style chains with the
obligatory coffee bar to tiny specialists in pulp
fiction, the book shops are varied and delightful.
And don't forget the **Booksellers' Bazaar** (*see
p76*), an adjunct to the Grand Bazaar, where you
can pick up new and used English books among
the textbooks and Turkish literature.

Galeri Kayseri

*Divan Yolu 58, Sultanahmet (0212 512 0456).
Tram Sultanahmet.* **Open** 9am-8.30pm daily.
Credit AmEx, MC, V. **Map** p243 M10.
This shop is devoted exclusively to books about
Istanbul and Turkey. Whatever the genre, you'll find
it here: fiction, non-fiction, guidebooks and coffee-
table volumes.

Yargıcı. *See p149.*

Eat, Drink, Shop

Homer Kitapevi

*Yeniçarşi Caddesi 12A, Galatasaray, Beyoğlu
(0212 249 5902).* **Open** 10am-7.30pm Mon-Sat;
12.30-5.30pm Sun. **Credit** MC, V. **Map** p248 N3.
Alongside the Galatasaray Lycée, this smart, air-
conditioned shop has what is widely considered to
be the best collection of foreign non-fiction in town.
It's particularly strong on art and academic subjects.

Pandora

*Büyükparmakkapı Sokak 3, Beyoğlu (0212 243 3503/
www.pandora.com.tr).* **Open** 10am-8pm Mon-Thur;
10am-9pm Fri, Sat; 1-8pm Sun. **Credit** AmEx, MC,
V. **Map** p249 O3.
A fine little bookshop squeezed into three tight
floors. The top one is filled with English-language
titles, including fiction, poetry, art, local interest and
a decent history section. Flyers and posters downstairs advertise events around town.

Robinson Crusoe

Istiklal Caddesi 389, Beyoğlu (0212 293 6968).
Open 9am-9.30pm Mon-Sat; 10am-9.30pm Sun.
Credit AmEx, DC, MC, V. **Map** p248 M4.
A good-looking but cramped space saved by its tall
ceilings, the store has an especially well-chosen
selection of English-language fiction, international
music and art mags, plus an array of titles on
Istanbul and Turkey.

Antiquarian

Denizler Kitapevi

Istiklal Caddesi 395, Beyoğlu (0212 243 3174). **Open**
10am-7.30pm Mon-Sat. **Credit** MC, V. **Map** p248 M4.
The 130-year-old premises once housed the Dutch
Consulate. This shop specialises in books on a maritime theme (*deniz* means 'sea'), but is also strong on
travel guides, especially on Turkey.

Librairie de Pera

*Galipdede Caddesi 22, Tünel, Beyoğlu (0212 252
3078).* **Open** 9am-7pm daily. **Credit** AmEx, MC, V.
Map p248 M5.
Situated just downhill from Tünel Square, this shop
carries old and rare books in numerous languages,
many concerned with travel and Turkey.

Second-hand

There are about half a dozen shops packed with
second-hand books, many in English, in the
Aslıhan Pasajı, an inconspicuous passage
just off the Balık Pazarı halfway down Istiklal
Caddesi. Some shops also deal in vinyl,
magazines and old film posters.

Natural Foreign Book Exchange

*Akbıyık Caddesi 31, Sultanahmet (0212 517 0383).
Tram Sultanahmet.* **Open** 9am-9pm daily. **Credit**
AmEx, DC, MC, V. **Map** p243 N11.
Slap in the middle of the backpacker enclave, NFBE
has a predictably huge stock of airport fiction and
used travel guides. Prices are a bit ridiculous, but the
stock, shelved in a gloomy basement, is extensive.

Selim Mumcu Sahaf

*Yeniçarşi Caddesi 33/C, Galatasaray, Beyoğlu
(0212 245 4496).* **Open** 10am-8pm Mon-Sat.
Credit AmEx, MC, V. **Map** p248 N3.
What the stock lacks in depth it more than makes
up for in eclecticism. There are also hundreds of
old movie posters, photos, postcards and other memorabilia for sale.

Cosmetics

Toiletries and a limited range of cosmetics
are available in most supermarkets. Some
pharmacies also stock imported brands like
Vichy and RoC. For upmarket labels, go to a
specialist *parfümeri*, but note that prices are
pushed up by stiff import taxes. Better to stock
up in duty free before your trip.

Erkul Cosmetics

Istiklal Caddesi 311, Beyoğlu (0212 251 7662).
Open 10.30am-9pm Mon-Sat. **Credit** AmEx, MC, V.
Map p248 N3.
A one-stop cosmetics store where you can find every
grooming product imaginable. In addition to its own
range, Erkul stocks reasonably priced perfumes and
cosmetics from around the world.

Fashion

See also *p159* **Leather**.

Damat Tween

*Akmerkez Mall 214, Nispetiye Caddesi, Etiler
(0212 282 0112/www.damat.com.tr).* **Bus** 59R,
59UL, 559C, U1, U2, UL57. **Open** 10am-10pm
daily. **Credit** AmEx, MC, V.

A local boy made good, Damat has branches in a dozen countries in addition to his mini-empire in Turkey. His stock-in-trade is classic menswear, ranging from suits to knitwear. The Tween label features casual collections in bold styles that are distinctive both for design and quality.

Gönül Paksoy

Atiye Sokak 6A, Teşvikiye (0212 261 9081). Metro Osmanbey. **Open** 1-7pm Mon; 10am-7pm Tue-Sat. **Credit** AmEx, MC, V.

Ms Paksoy claims her designs are unique, not just in Turkey but worldwide. She's probably right. Her collections reinterpret Ottoman designs, using original fabrics and the finest natural weaves hand-dyed in subtle shades. She also does a great line in Ottoman-style slippers, handbags and shoes.

Mavi Jeans

İstiklal Caddesi 195, Beyoğlu (0212 244 6255/ www.mavijeans.com). **Open** 10am-10pm Mon-Sat; 11am-10pm Sun. **Credit** AmEx, DC, MC, V. **Map** p249 O3.

Since making it big in the US, Mavi's prices have rocketed, but compared with imported brands, prices are still reasonable. Designs aren't cutting edge, but they are very wearable. T-shirts, sweatshirts and casual co-ordinates complete the look. **Other locations**: Akmerkez Mall 235-238, Nispetiye Caddesi, Etiler (0212 282 0423); Metrocity Mall 134-135, Büyükdere Caddesi 171, Levent.

Ümit Ünal

Ensiz Sokak 3, Tünel, Beyoğlu (0212 245 7886/ www.umitunal.com). **Open** 10am-7.30pm Mon-Fri; 10am-noon Sat. **No credit cards**. **Map** p248 M5.

Ümit Ünal is the best example of an Istanbul-based designer who is plugged into the international fashion scene. His avant-garde fashion shows are more like performances, and his multi-layered, complex creations are art installations as much as garments. Ünal's influences are diverse – Celtic banshees, Himalayan mountain tribes, gypsies. He travels the globe in search of unusual fabrics and accessories.

Yargıcı

Valikonağı Caddesi 30, Nişantaşı (0212 225 2912/ www.yargici.com.tr). Metro Osmanbey. **Open** 9.30am-7.30pm Mon-Sat; 1-6pm Sun. **Credit** AmEx, DC, MC, V.

This popular shop sells middle-of-the-road fashion for men and women. You're talking dependable quality rather than cutting-edge design. Beware the sizing, which can be baffling. (You thought you were a 36? Well, here you're a 32.) **Photo** p148. **Other locations**: Akmerkez Mall 208, Nispetiye Caddesi, Etiler (0212 282 0501).

Second-hand

Roll

Turnacıbaşı Sokak 23-25, Galatasaray, Beyoğlu (0212 244 9656). **Open** 10am-9.30pm Mon-Sat; noon-9.30pm Sun. **Credit** MC, V. **Map** p248 N3.

If you're after retro fashion, this is the place. Most stock is shipped from Europe and dates from the 1960s and '70s – loud nylon shirts, suede and velvet jackets, and vintage Adidas tracksuit tops.

Fashion accessories

See also *p158* **Jewellery**.

Antique Objet

Zenneciler Caddesi 48-50, Grand Bazaar (0212 526 7451/antiqueobjet.com). Tram Beyazıt. **Open** 9am-7pm Mon-Sat. **Credit** AmEx, MC, V. **Map** p79.

Crammed into an awkward space by the entrance to the market's İç Bedesten, this den of delights stocks own-label boots, Cinderella slippers and jackets in velvet Suzani cloth, sleek short coats of rich Ottoman fabric and a line of bags in Suzani and *ikat*. Workmanship is top notch.

İpek

İstiklal Caddesi 230, Beyoğlu (0212 249 8207). **Open** 10am-8pm Mon-Sat. **Credit** AmEx, DC, MC, V. **Map** p248 M4.

If it's neckwear you're after, this is the place to head. Along with charmingly persuasive service, you'll find an exhaustive range of scarves, shawls and ties in an exhaustive range of fabrics.

Matraş

Akmerkez Mall, Nispetiye Caddesi, Etiler (0212 282 0215/www.matras.com). Bus 59R, 59UL, 559C, U1, U2, UL57. **Open** 10am-10pm daily. **Credit** AmEx, DC, MC, V.

Classic, high quality designs from Turkey's leading leather accessories label. As well as handbags, wallets and belts, products include briefcases, luggage and smaller items such as purses and cardholders. **Other locations**: Bağdat Caddesi 273, Erenköy, Kadıköy (0216 385 0622).

Seyitağaoğulları Carpet Kilim Hand Crafts

Avrupa Pasajı 15 (off Balık Pazarı), Meşrutiyet Caddesi 16, Galatasaray, Beyoğlu (0212 249 2903). **Open** 9.30am-9pm daily. **Credit** MC, V. **Map** p248 N3.

Kilim accessories are everywhere these days, but what you'll find here – from belts and footwear to bags, purses and stationery – is a cut above the rest. The products are all handmade, the kilims are kosher and the leather trim really is leather. **Other locations**: Küçükayasofya Caddesi 35, Sultanahmet (0212 518 1295); Arasta Çarşısı, Sultanahmet (0212 516 9351).

Haberdashery

Celal Akagün Tuhafiye

Marpuççular Alacahamam Caddesi 53, Eminönü (0212 526 5828). Tram Eminönü. **Open** 8.30am-6pm Mon-Fri; 8.30am-4pm Sat. **Credit** MC, V. **Map** p243 M8.

Beyoğlu's fashion *pasajs*

Atlas Pasajı.

In the last few decades, Turkey has become one of the world's most prolific producers of clothing, with over 40,000 factories nationwide. Many leading American and European brands now manufacture their clothing in Turkey.

Savvy local shoppers can reap the benefits by visiting factory outlets, where seconds and overruns can be bought for a fraction of the retail price. In Istanbul, you don't even have to trek to the suburbs to find a factory outlet: you can find seconds at unofficial outlets right in the city centre, if you know where to look.

Off Beyoğlu's Istiklal Caddesi are a number of *pasajs* (covered arcades) tucked away in backstreets, bursting with cheap clothing, stacked in bins or hung on rails, at knock-down prices. A pair of jeans, say, might be YTL35 or YTL40. Be prepared to rummage, as clothes are often crammed indiscriminately on to racks and it's up to you to find the right size.

As part of the trade agreement between the fashion companies and factories, extras usually have their labels removed. Part of the fun is trying to figure out whether you've got your hands on the latest style from H&M or Miss Sixty. Some companies don't allow their factory cast-offs to be resold, although you may well find faithful rip-offs of well-known brands anyway.

Below is a selection of the best factory 'outlets' in Beyoğlu.

Atlas Pasajı

Atlas Pasajı, off Istiklal Caddesi, Beyoğlu. **Map** p248 N3.

Popular with the grungy and black-clad, the layout of this arcade (*pictured*) behind the Atlas cinema is more structured than most, and its stock is of a higher quality, with a better claim to street cred than the Beyoğlu *pasaj* norm. Atlas is also home to an interesting selection of jewellery, second-hand clothes, kitsch collectibles, records, posters and comics. Its vaguely gothic vibe is reminiscent of London's Camden Market.

Beyoğlu Iş Merkezi

Beyoğlu Iş Merkezi 365, off Istiklal Caddesi, Beyoğlu. **Map** p248 N3.

Opposite the Odakule building (286 Istiklal Caddesi), this vast *pasaj* has three underground floors packed with real bargains. Most of the clothes are casual and sporty, with the emphasis on denim.

Terkoz Çıkmazı Karaaslan Iş Merkezi

Terkoz Çıkmazı Karaaslan Iş Merkezi 8, off Istiklal Caddesi, Beyoğlu. **Map** p248 N3.

With a rather hard-to-find entrance across from the Dutch consulate at 393 Istiklal Caddesi, this *pasaj* has piles and piles of clothing at rock-bottom prices, as well as some small boutiques with more discriminating selections.

After 58 years in the business, Mr Akagün is the oldest haberdasher in town, and still works from his original store. His stock, 90 per cent of which is Turkish-made, includes a bewildering array of buttons, lace, embroidered trimmings and ribbons.

Lingerie & swimwear

TEN
Cevahir Mall, Büyükdere Caddesi 22, Mecidiyeköy (0212 380 1018/www.ten.com.tr). Metro Şişli. **Open** 10am-10pm. **Credit** AmEx, MC, V.
A favourite with Turkish young professionals looking for quality lingerie at affordable prices.
Other locations: Huzur Sokak 23, off Sıra Cevizler Caddesi, Bomonti, Şişli (0212 233 8958).

Zeki
Akkavak Sokak 47/9, Tunaman Çarşısı, Nişantaşı (0212 233 8279/www.zekitriko.com.tr). Metro Osmanbey. **Open** 9.30am-7.30pm Mon-Sat. **Credit** AmEx, MC, V.
Not only is Zeki the premier swimwear label at home, it's also one of Turkey's most successful exports. Prices are high, but so is the quality. Check out the own-label lingerie.
Other locations: Akmerkez Mall 366, Nispetiye Caddesi, Etiler (0212 282 0591); Cevahir Mall, Büyükdere Caddesi 22, No.146, Şişli (0212 380 0807).

Sunglasses

Emgen Optik
Istiklal Caddesi 65, Beyoğlu (0212 292 3577). **Open** 9am-8pm Mon-Sat. **Credit** AmEx, MC, V. **Map** p249 O2.
Emgen Optik does a roaring trade in fashion-conscious frames and shades. Around since 1925, this local institution carries a huge selection of big brands like Ray-Ban, Police, Gucci and Armani. It also deals in prescription lenses and repairs.

Florists

Freshly cut flowers abound at the gypsy stands at the top of **Tarlabaşı Bulvarı**, off Taksim Square, and by the jetties at Kadıköy, Üsküdar, Karaköy and Beşiktaş. Prices drop as the day wears on, but you should still try and haggle to avoid paying over the odds. Otherwise, most neighbourhoods are well served by flower shops.

Fotis Çiçek Evi
Istiklal Caddesi 382, Tünel, Beyoğlu (0212 244 0606). **Open** 8am-8pm daily. **Credit** MC, V. **Map** p248 M4.
The only florist to have glided through the glory days of Old Pera intact. It's been at the same premises at the Tünel end of Istiklal Caddesi since 1899. The shop is strictly no frills, but the flowers are wonderful. It does Interflora, too.

Food & drink

For the freshest, best-quality produce, visit the **Halk Pazarı**, situated opposite the jetty in Beşiktaş, and the more upmarket **Balık Pazarı**, located off Istiklal Caddesi, with delicacies from quail's eggs to fresh clotted cream. For regional specialities, head for the stalls lining the west side of the **Egyptian Bazaar** or the many delicatessens in the backstreets of **Kadıköy** on the Asian shore.

Ali Muhiddin Hacı Bekir
Istiklal Caddesi 129, Beyoğlu (0212 244 2804). **Open** 8am-9pm Mon-Sat; 9am-9pm Sun. **Credit** MC, V. **Map** p248 N3.
You can't come to Turkey without trying Turkish delight. This place – which has been in the confection business since 1777 – is where to try and buy it. You should also suck on some *akide*, colourful boiled sweets which come in every conceivable flavour. Other tasty gifts include halva, baklava and marzipan (*badem ezmesi*) which all come in beautiful gift-wrapped boxes.
Other locations: Hamidiye Caddesi 83, Sirkeci (0212 522 0666).

Antre Gourmet Shop
Akarsu Caddesi 52, Cihangir, Beyoğlu (0212 292 8972/www.antregourmet.com). **Open** 9am-9pm Mon-Sat; 9am-8pm Sun. **Credit** AmEx, MC, V. **Map** p249 O4.
Antre stocks around 40 regional cheeses, all bought from local producers and free from additives. There's also a fair selection of cold meats, Austrian wholegrain breads, home-made *mezedes* and jams, olive oil, honeycomb (in season) and natural yoghurt.

Asri Turşucu
Ağa Hamamı Sokak, opposite Firüzağa Mosque, off Sıraselviler Caddesi, Cihangir, Beyoğlu (0212 244 4724). **Open** 9am-9pm Mon-Sat; noon-9pm Sun. Closed Aug. **No credit cards. Map** p249 O4.
You name it, this place pickles it. Going strong since 1938, the artistic displays of colourful jars are a sight to behold. In addition to old-fashioned pickles, you can down tankards of *şalgam suyu* (pickle juice) here, as well as *boza* (a fermented millet drink) and *şıra* (grape juice).

Güllüoğlu
Mumhane Caddesi 171, Karaköy (0212 293 0910). Tram Karaköy. **Open** 7am-9.30pm Mon-Sat. **Credit** MC, V.
Güllüoğlu is the king of baklava and *su böreği* (baked layers of cheese, fresh herbs and filo pastry). A must for sweet-toothed travellers, the syrup-soaked cakes make great gifts, too.

Kurukahveci Mehmet Efendi
Tahmis Sokak 66, Eminönü (0212 511 4262/ www.mehmetefendi.com). Tram Eminönü. **Open** 8.30am-7pm Mon-Fri; 9am-6.30pm Sat. **No credit cards. Map** p242 L8.

Eat, Drink, Shop

Ortaköy. *See p103.*

Derviş. *See p157.*

Reputedly the first shop to sell bagged Turkish coffee, Mehmet Efendi has been doing roaring business since 1871. It's opposite the west entrance to the Egyptian Market – just follow your nose. Besides the traditional Turkish variety, there's filter and espresso coffee, whole roasted beans, cocoa and *sahlep*, a winter drink made from ground orchid root.

La Cave

Sıraselviler Caddesi 109A, Cihangir, Beyoğlu (0212 243 2405/www.lacavesarap.com). **Open** 9am-9pm Mon-Sat; 9am-8pm Sun. **Credit** MC, V. **Map** p249 O4.

One of the city's first speciality wine shops and certainly the most serious. Owner Esat Ayhan, a connoisseur, keeps a comprehensive cellar filled with wines from all over Turkey, Europe and the New World. He also stocks imported spirits, bar accessories and a limited range of Havana cigars.

Namlı Pastırmacı

Hasırcılar Caddesi 14-16, Eminönü (0212 511 6393/ www.namlipastirma.com.tr). Tram Eminönü. **Open** 8.30am-8pm Mon-Sat. **Credit** MC, V. **Map** p242 L8.

A hugely popular deli just along from the west end of the Egyptian Market. It specialises in *pastırma* (Turkish pastrami) but also has a tantalising selection of cold cuts, cheeses, halva, honeycomb, *pekmez* (fruit-based molasses), olives and pickles.

Saray

İstiklal Caddesi 102, Beyoğlu (0212 292 3434). **Open** 6am-2am daily. **Credit** MC, V. **Map** p248 N3.

Delectable Turkish desserts, from milk puddings to *aşure*, popularly known as Noah's pudding. Since 1949, Saray has served as a sugar-fuelled pit stop during or after a night out in the bars and cafés of Beyoğlu. There are smoking and non-smoking sections, and a takeaway service.
Other locations: 105/1 Teşvikiye Caddesi, Teşvikiye (0212 236 1617).

Savoy Pastanesi

Sıraselviler Caddesi 91A, Taksim, Beyoğlu (0212 249 1818). **Open** 7am-10.30pm daily. **Credit** AmEx, MC, V. **Map** p249 O3.

One of Istanbul's best cake shops, and now something of an institution. There's a reasonably sized café up on the first floor, which gets especially busy at breakfast.

Şütte

Dudu Odaları Sokak 21, Balık Pazarı, Galatasaray, Beyoğlu (0212 293 9292). **Open** 9am-8pm Mon-Sat **Credit** AmEx, MC, V. **Map** p248 N3.

This long-running deli, owned by Macedonians, is one of the few places in Istanbul that stocks pork products other than bacon. It also carries pricey but wonderful imported cheeses, plus cheaper local cheeses, ready-made *meze* and condiments.

Supermarkets

Ten years ago there were barely any supermarkets in Istanbul. These days they are commonplace. Chains vary from the classy

The rug trade

Buying a carpet in Istanbul has unfortunate associations with hassle, hustle and hoodwinking. It doesn't have to be that way. With a bit of homework and common sense, you can enjoy the buying process *and* go home with a beautiful carpet at the right price.

To be a confident and successful bargainer and buyer, first you need to determine how much you are prepared to spend. If you're interested in hand-made carpets or kilims made of natural fibres, expect to spend YTL450 and above. Unless you're an expert, don't bother paying a premium for vintage;

modern carpets are just as high quality and are usually made with natural dyes (*kök boya*). Under no circumstances should you tell the dealer your budget. Instead, ask the prices, get a feel for what's on offer, and be prepared to shop around. Look at carpets that are double your price range, then offer what you have.

Carpet dealers have all the time in the world. It is their job to answer your questions, explain details of origin and design, and unroll hundreds of kilims, all the while keeping you fortified with miniature glasses of strong tea.

(Mackro) to no-frills bargain basement (Dia, BIM). Thankfully, they have yet to kill off the local corner store (*bakkal*).

Gima

Sıraselviler Caddesi 74A, Cihangir, Beyoğlu (0212 293 5158/355 8080/www.gima.com.tr). **Open** 9am-10pm daily. **Credit** MC, V. **Map** p249 O3.
Gima has an excellent but somewhat overpriced in-house bakery and also offers a home delivery and online ordering service.
Other locations: Eski Büyükdere Caddesi 5/7, Şişli (0212 219 6439).

Mackro

Abdi Ipekçi Caddesi 24-26, Nişantaşı (0212 231 3999/www.tansas.com.tr). Metro Osmanbey.
Open 8.30am-9pm daily. **Credit** AmEx, MC, V.

Caters for the upper end of the market, with a wide selection of imported foods and prices to match. Prices may be slightly above average, but the deli, fresh fish and meat counters are especially good and there's a wide, fairly priced selection of local wines, in this case at very reasonable prices.
Other locations: Akmerkez Mall 325, Nispetiye Caddesi, Etiler (0212 282 0310); Muallim Naci Caddesi 170, Kuruçeşme (0212 257 1381).

Handicrafts

Besides carpets, Turkey offers a wealth of lesser-known – and equally traditional – handicrafts. The ceramics trade dates back to the Selçuk Empire of the 11th century. Original tiles, vases and plates with the traditional tulip

Ultimately, the final price depends a great deal on your rapport with the dealer and your determination to buy a carpet. It all comes down to one thing: how much do you want it? If you have the slightest hesitation concerning patterns or colours, keep looking.

Nearly all shops, including those listed below, have English-speaking staff, can be trusted to handle overseas shipping, and allow exchanges if you are unhappy with your purchase. If you find the Grand Bazaar too bewildering, try browsing at the comparatively peaceful **Arasta Bazaar** (**Map** *p243 N11*).

Ahmet Hazım

Takkeciler Caddesi 61-63, Grand Bazaar (0212 52 9886/www.ahmethazim.com). Tram Beyazıt. **Open** 8.30am-7pm Mon-Sat. **Credit** MC, V. **Map** p79.
One of the oldest rug merchants in the bazaar, specialising in kilims and carpets from Turkey, Iran and the Caucasus and Suzanis from Uzbekistan. What you get is quality service and none of the hard sell.

Ethnicon

Kapalıçarşı Takkeciler Sokak 58-60, Grand Bazaar (0212 527 6841/www.ethnicon.com). Tram Beyazıt. **Open** 8.30am-7pm Mon-Sat. **Credit** MC, V. **Map** p79.
Ethnicon (short for 'ethnic contemporary') creates kilims with a modern twist. They are made without child labour and using environmentally friendly processes, so colours tend to be muted. Browsing in Ethnicon is a very different – and more peaceful – experience compared to the rest of the bazaar. Prices are fixed.

Kalender Carpets

Tekkeciler Caddesi 24-26, Grand Bazaar (0212 527 5518). Tram Beyazıt. **Open** 8.30am-7pm Mon-Sat. **Credit** AmEx, MC, V. **Map** p79.
Kalender stocks a great collection of full-size, deep pile Anatolian carpets, which start from as little as YTL1,500. A good place to start your mission in 'carpet row', in the heart of the bazaar.

Şişko Osman

Zincirli Han 15, Grand Bazaar (0212 528 3548/www.siskoosman.com). Tram Beyazıt. **Open** 8.30am-6.30pm Mon-Sat. **Credit** AmEx, MC, V. **Map** p79.
Şişko 'Fat Man' Osman is acknowledged around the Grand Bazaar as the leading authority on carpets and kilims. His well-stocked shop fills most of the historic Zincirli Han, and his international clientele includes many well-known people. So while you can be sure of quality, don't expect a bargain.

Yörük

Kürkçüler Çarşısı 16, Grand Bazaar (0212 527 3211). Çar Beyazıt. **Open** 8.30am-7pm Mon-Sat. **Credit** AmEx, DC, MC, V. **Map** p79.
The shop (*pictured*) may be tiny, but it's the front to some of the finest treasures of the bazaar. You'll find lots of kilims here, although the real emphasis is on old ethnic rugs of all sizes, mostly from the Caucasus. Guide yourself towards Gürsel, one of the dashing young partners, and you're promised entertainment, little pressure to buy and, quite probably, the rug of your dreams.

motif are now displayed in museums worldwide. The tradition lives on in Kütahya, western Anatolia, where artists hand-craft reproductions and more contemporary designs. Then there's *ebru*, a Central Asian variation of paper marbling, which took off during calligraphy's heyday. Today, the technique is also applied to fabrics. Other handicrafts include carved meerschaum pipes, prayer beads, backgammon sets, and silks. Most of these crafts can be found at the **Grand Bazaar** (*see p78* **Shopping the bazaar**).

Abdulla

Halıcılar Caddesi 53, Grand Bazaar (0212 522 9078/www.abdulla.com). Tram Beyazıt. **Open** 9am-7pm Mon-Sat. **Credit** MC, V. **Map** p79.

Abdulla is all about a contemporary take on traditional crafts. The bywords are 'natural' and 'hand-made', the main product line hamam accessories, so you will find towels, *peştemals* and olive oil soaps in scents from cinnamon and tea to sesame. Other good buys include sheepskin throws and hand-spun silk-and-wool cloth.

Deli Kızın Yeri

Halıcılar Caddesi 82, Grand Bazaar (0212 526 1251/www.delikiz.com). Tram Beyazıt. **Open** 8.30am-7pm Mon-Sat. **Credit** AmEx, MC, V. **Map** p79.
Linda Caldwell, a retired American and self-styled crazy lady (*deli kız*) turns traditional Turkish handicrafts, motifs and fabrics into something more offbeat. Her unique designs include hand-made clothes, tablecloths, placemats and dolls.

Eat, Drink, Shop

Hasırcılar Caddesi. *See p82.*

Derviş

Keseciler Caddesi 33-35, Grand Bazaar (0212 514 4525). Tram Beyazıt. **Open** 9am-7pm Mon-Sat. **Credit** MC, V. **Map** p79.

Derviş nestles behind the narrowest of shop fronts like a hidden temple to Anatolian handicrafts. But like at Abdulla, where owner Tayfun Utkan was a former partner, the point is that traditions are reinvented. Again, bathroom accessories are big, including handmade soaps in a host of natural flavours, super-soft unbleached cotton towels, and *peştemals* in linen, cotton and silk. But there are also shimmering scarves of hand-spun silk, felt slippers, rugs and throws, and mohair and patchwork fur blankets; plus brimming shelves of original dowry items, trawled from the depths of Anatolia by Utkan himself. Look out for the hand-stitched bolero jackets, ethnic coats and dresses in fabulous colours and fabrics, and exquisitely embroidered linens. This is the kind of place where you just have to touch everything. **Photo** *p153*.

Istanbul Handicrafts Centre

Kabasakal Caddesi 5, Sultanahmet (0212 517 6784/8). Tram Sultanahmet. **Open** 9am-7pm daily. **Credit** AmEx, MC, V. **Map** p243 N10.

The Istanbul Handicrafts Centre is located in a restored *medrese* (religious school), opposite the Baths of Roxelana. It now houses a warren of workshops, each with its own specialisation. The most accomplished handicrafts are the illuminated manuscripts, miniatures and calligraphy. Other highlights include cloth-painting, dolls, ceramics, glassware and hand-bound books. The artists work on site, so you can watch them at their trade.

Health & herbals

As mainstream brands tap into the healthy eating trend, it's relatively easy to find wholewheat products these days – usually referred to as '*diyet*'. The organic concept is catching on quickly too, with many supermarkets opening dedicated sections, including fresh fruit and vegetables. But, as in other countries, organic produce doesn't come cheap – and it's hard to authenticate.

Ambar

Kallavi Sokak 12, off Istiklal Caddesi, Beyoğlu (0212 292 9272/www.nuhunambari.com). **Open** 8am-8pm Mon-Fri; 9.30am-8pm Sat; noon-8pm Sun. **Credit** AmEx, MC, V. **Map** p248 M3.

One of the few places in Istanbul that sells fresh tofu. Other worthwhile buys include wholegrain bread, organic grains and pulses, hulled pumpkin and sunflower seeds and a range of organic fruit and veg.

Bünsa

Dudu Odaları Sokak 26, Balık Pazarı, Galatasaray, Beyoğlu (0212 243 6265). **Open** 9am-8pm Mon-Sat; noon-8pm Sun. **Credit** MC, V. **Map** p248 N3.

Herbal remedies and healing tonics, from medicinal teas to ginseng, karakovan honey and rare varieties of *pekmez* (fruit molasses). Tell them your ailment,

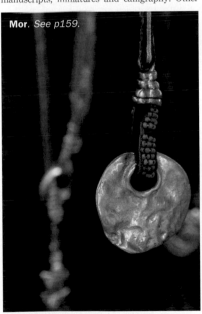

Mor. *See p159.*

Market day

Once a week, in most Istanbul neighbourhoods, a few streets are taken over by the *mahalle pazarı*, or local market. The awnings go up, wooden stalls jam the streets, and stallholders compete for custom at high volume.

Stalls are heaped with everything from jumbo olives and village cheese (*köy peyniri*) to cheap clothing, cooking pots and tools. Apples, melons and all manner of seasonal fruit and vegetables are stacked in colourful pyramids.

Bargain hunters can sometimes find well-known European and American clothing brands at knock-down prices. Turkey's factories produce garments for the likes of Gap and Calvin Klein, and manufacturers sometimes sell surplus stock to market traders. But be sure to check items for faults. (For more on picking up surplus fashion stock, *see* p150 **Beğoğlu's fashion pasajs**.)

As a general rule, trading kicks off around 9am and winds down around 5pm (later during the summer), when prices are slashed for the small pickings that remain. Below we list Istanbul's biggest and best-known market, but most neighbourhoods have one. Ask around for your nearest.

Salı Pazarı

Kuşdili Sokak, Kadıköy. **Open** Tue, Fri, Sun. **Map** p251 X7.
Be prepared to mingle with middle-class matrons and Anatolian mamas in search of bargain bras and the freshest figs. On Sunday, the same site metamorphoses into a European-style flea market with stallholders touting antiques, furniture and jewellery.

and they'll prescribe a potion. The most popular panacea is a concoction of honey, royal jelly, nettle and ginseng, guaranteed to beat fatigue.

Kalmaz Baharat

Mısır Çarşısı 41/1, Eminönü (0212 522 6604).
Tram Eminönü. **Open** 8am-7pm Mon-Sat. **No credit cards. Map** p243 L8.
One of the oldest stores in the Egyptian Bazaar, this atmospheric place – just east of the main intersection – still has its original drawers and tea caddies. Specialities include spices, medicinal herbs, healing teas and aromatic oils.

Household

Turkey has a strong textile industry, so towels, linens, curtains and fabrics make excellent buys. For a dazzling choice of furnishing fabrics, go to blocks one and two of the **IMÇ** (Istanbul Manifaturacılar Çarşısı), located on the west side of Unkapanı between the Golden Horn and the Aqueduct of Valens. Quality towels and linens are found in Sultanhamam, around the back of the Egyptian Bazaar (*see p82*) – look out for the Taç label.

Özgül Çeyiz

Mısır Çarşısı 83, Sultanhamam, Eminönü (0212 522 7068). *Tram Eminönü.* **Open** 9am-7pm Mon-Sat. **Credit** MC, V. **Map** p243 L8.
The east end of the Egyptian Bazaar was once crammed with stores in the trousseau (*çeyiz*) business. In days of yore, young ladies were wheeled along by their female relatives to make wholesale purchases that would improve their prospects. Özgül is one of the few survivors from those days. It's a minimal store packed with fancy embroidered sheets, quilts, towels, and robes. Trousseau-hunting or not, there's some great stuff at very reasonable prices – like the fluffy Begonville towels.

Paşabahçe

İstiklal Caddesi 314, Beyoğlu (0212 244 0544/ www.pasabahce.com.tr). **Open** 10am-8pm Mon-Thur; 10am-8.30pm Fri, Sat; 11am-7pm Sun. **Credit** AmEx, MC, V. **Map** p248 M4.
This stylish shop on three floors, a favourite with Istanbul's upwardly mobile, is Turkey's answer to Habitat. Head to the basement for kitchenware, basic china and glass, the ground floor for vases and ornaments, and the first floor for special collections. The latter includes some impressive hand-blown glass, using traditional motifs – a conscious revival of time-honoured techniques.
Other locations: Teşvikiye Caddesi 117, Teşvikiye (0212 233 5005).

Jewellery

The **Grand Bazaar** (*see p76*) houses the largest selection of jewellery and gold under one roof, and where designs once stopped at the classic, a new tide of creativity has been creeping in over the last few years. Still, for definitively modern pieces, try **Teşvikye**, home to several small, creative showrooms.

Mor

Turnacıbaşı Sokak 16/1, Beyoğlu (0212 292 8817). **Open** 10am-7.30pm Mon-Sat. **Credit** AmEx, MC, V. **Map** p248 N3.

A stylish, glass-fronted studio just down from the Galatasaray Hamam, selling inspired originals designed by an in-house team. Most pieces are fashioned from silver and bronze, often combining scraps of ethnic jewellery from eastern Turkey, Turkmenistan and Afghanistan. **Photo** *p157*.

Nelia

Valikona 35 Caddesi, Halil Bey Pasajı 40/19, Nişantaşı (0212 291 1123/www.nelia.com.tr). *Metro Osmanbey.* **Open** 10am-7.30pm Mon-Sat. **Credit** AmEx, DC, MC, V.

A newly opened space at the back of a Nişantaşı passage, Nelia produces funky, chunky jewellery with a tribal twist. In-house designer Banu Kosifoğlu works with a multitude of materials – from semiprecious stones and sterling silver to ribbon, silk tassels and snippets of ethnic cloth – crafting weird and wonderful combinations to produce pieces that are all unique.

Urart

Abdi İpekçi Caddesi 18/1, Nişantaşı (0212 246 7194). *Metro Osmanbey.* **Open** 9am-7pm Mon-Sat. **Credit** AmEx, DC, MC, V.

Sophisticated jewellery with an Anatolian slant. Designs are drawn from the countless civilisations that have peopled Anatolia from palaeolithic to Ottoman times, using a combination of silver, gold and semi-precious stones. Pricey, but beautiful. **Concessions**: Topkapı Museum, Swissôtel.

Leather

For the best selection of leather (*deri*) head to the **Grand Bazaar** (*see p76*). Be careful though, because quality can often be poor: 'antelope skin', for example, is unlikely to be genuine. You'll have to work hard to get a fair price. If it all seems like too much hassle, there are stores that specialise in quality leather at fixed prices – albeit prices that aren't much cheaper than you'd find at home.

Derimod

Akmerkez Mall 362, Nispetiye Caddesi, Etiler (0212 282 0668). Bus 59R, 59UL, 559C, U1, U2, UL57. **Open** 10am-10pm daily. **Credit** AmEx, DC, MC, V.

Classic and contemporary designs in top quality leather for both men and women. There are coats, jackets and waistcoats by the dozen, as well as an extensive range of leather accessories. **Other locations**: Valikonağı Caddesi 103/16, Nişantaşı (0212 247 7481).

Music

International CDs are no cheaper here than in Europe, though the equivalent for local artists offer better value for money.

Ada Müzike

Orhan Adli Apaydin Sokak 20, off İstiklal Caddesi, Tünel, Beyoğlu (0212 251 3878). **Open** 9am-10pm Mon-Thur, Sun; 9am-11pm Fri, Sat. **Credit** AmEx, V, MC. **Map** p248 M4.

Owned by local record company Ada, this is the first shop to specialise in Turkish rock and protest music. The setting is surprisingly smart, and there's a small café and Biletix ticket booth attached. There's also a decent range of foreign CDs, newspapers and magazines.

Lale Plak

Galipdede 1, Tünel, Beyoğlu (0212 293 7739). **Open** 9am-7.30pm Mon-Sat; 11.30am-7pm Sun. **Credit** MC, V. **Map** p248 M5.

In business for 45 years, the city's top jazz, ethnic and classical music retailer is the favourite hangout of visiting jazz musicians. There is also a comprehensive selection of traditional Turkish music. Staff are knowledgeable and helpful.

Mimplak

Aslıhan Sahaflar Çarşısı 49, Beyoğlu (0212 252 6877). **Open** noon-8pm daily. **Credit** MC, V. **Map** p248 M3.

In a passageway crammed with second-hand book and record shops, this tiny shop is the best of the lot. Look for bargain deals on old disco and soundtrack albums, plus rare Turkish releases.

Services

Barbers

Cihangir Erkek Kuaförü

Akarsu Yokuşu Caddesi 49/1, Cihangir, Beyoğlu (0212 251 1660). **Open** 8am-8.30pm Mon-Sat; 10am-5pm Sun. **No credit cards. Map** p249 O4.

All the usual services, delivered with a smile and some English. The Cihangir neighbourhood is popular with expats, so the staff are used to dealing with foreigners.

Computer repairs

Bilgisayar Hastanesi

İnönü Caddesi 72/3, Gümüşsuyu, Taksim, Beyoğlu (0212 252 1575/www.bilgisayarhastanesi.com). **Open** 9am-6pm Mon-Fri. **Credit** MC, V. **Map** p247 P2.

An authorised service provider for Compaq, Hewlett Packard and Epson. Staff will clean, maintain and repair computers and order spare parts. Bilgisayar Hastanesi also operates an emergency service, but you pay a 50 per cent premium for any work done outside office hours. Otherwise, expect a long wait. You can also buy second-hand laptops here.

Hair & beauty salons

Grooming is next to godliness for Turkish girls, which means that the beauty salon (*güzellik salonu*) is a second home and the city is brimming with them. For the face, it's tweezers and expertly teased thread; for the body it's waxing (*ağda* – Turkey is the home of the all-over wax), plus manicures (*manikür*), pedicures (*pedikür*), and all manner of hair treatments. Dyeing is a favourite, and the blow-dry (*fön*) – involving at least two attendants and an army of brushes – essential.

Hüseyin Günday

Sıraselviler Caddesi 80, Cihangir, Beyoğlu (0212 251 0005/252 0947). **Open** 8am-8pm Mon-Sat. **Credit** MC, V. **Map** p249 O3.
Hüseyin Günday is a typical neighbourhood *kuaför* offering the full range of beauty services. Bright young things attend to your every whim. Prices are very reasonable.

MOS

Bronz Sokak 65/7, off Abdi İpekçi Caddesi, Maçka, Teşvikiye (0212 240 1970/246 3222). *Metro Osmanbey*. **Open** 9am-7pm Mon-Sat. **Credit** MC, V.
MOS equates with class on the Istanbul hairdressing scene. Despite being production-line stuff, it's a great favourite with the well-heeled of both sexes, who book in for all manner of treatments (services are unisex). But beauty doesn't come cheap: prices are high by Turkish standards.
Other locations: Akmerkez Mall 122, Nispetiye Caddesi, Etiler (0212 282 0554).

Laundry & dry-cleaning

There may be no such thing as a coin-operated laundromat in Istanbul, but there are still some laundries, though these are a dying breed now that most people have washing machines at home. Dry-cleaners are plentiful and reasonably priced.

Can Laundry

Bakraç Sokak 32/A, off Sıraselviler Caddesi, Cihangir, Beyoğlu (0212 252 9360). **Open** 8.30am-7.30pm Mon-Fri; 8.30am-4pm Sat. **No credit cards**. **Map** p249 O4.
Neighbourhood laundry services with a smile. You can either pay per load or by individual item. Ironing is optional and is charged per item.

Çınar

Sıraselviler Caddesi 152/A, Cihangir, Beyoğlu (0212 251 4204/252 1938). **Open** 8am-7.30pm Mon-Sat. **Credit** MC, V. **Map** p249 O3.

A dry-cleaner and conventional laundry running a pick-up and delivery service in the Taksim area (hotels included). A same-day service is available, while mending/alteration jobs are outsourced to the local tailor.

Photography

Photographic studios can be found on almost every high street. Many will do portrait and passport-size (*vesikalık*) photos, as well as selling and developing film.

Stüdyo Mor İpek

Selvi Han, Sıraselviler Caddesi 61, Taksim, Beyoğlu (0212 249 5877/251 9253/www.moripek.com). **Open** 8.30am-8pm Mon-Sat. **Credit** MC, V. **Map** p249 O3.
This basement photographic studio caters to both professionals and amateurs. They can also do colour passport photographs.

Yalçınlar

Ankara Caddesi 159, Sirkeci (0212 514 3009/ www.yalcinlar.com.tr). *Tram Sirkeci*. **Open** 8.30am-8pm Mon-Sat. **Credit** AmEx, MC, V. **Map** p243 M10.
One of 30 branches offering developing and printing services for professionals and amateurs.
Other locations: Cevahir Shopping Mall, Büyükdere Caddesi 22, Şişli (0212 380 0292).

Shoe repairs

Most neighbourhoods have a resident cobbler, who will re-heel, re-sole or repair your shoes at rock-bottom prices.

Havai Lostra Salonu

Ağa Camii Sokak 15, Beyoğlu (0212 245 1652). **Open** 8.30am-8.30pm Mon-Sat; 10am-8pm Sun. **No credit cards**. **Map** p249 O2.
One of Beyoğlu's original shoe-shine salons, complete with customer thrones, Havai also does repairs and sells an array of shoelaces. A standard shoeshine will set you back around YTL3.

Tailors

Gone are the days when a single tailor would clothe an entire neighbourhood. But if the bespoke business is foundering, there's still a living to be made from mending and alterations. Tailors (*terzi*) are found throughout the city and will take on the simplest of jobs (*tadilat*) for a snip.

Acar Terzihane

Yeni Yuva Sokak 30, Cihangir, Taksim (0212 251 3745/0535 762 7320). **Open** 8am-8pm Mon-Sat. **No credit cards**. **Map** p249 O4.
A long-running outfit, competent at all kinds of stitching and mending, as well as more ambitious custom-made outfits for ladies and gents.

Eat, Drink, Shop

Arts & Entertainment

Festivals & Events

Jazz jams, movie premieres and starry nights.

Taking music to the streets at the **International Istanbul Jazz Festival**. *See p163.*

Back in the golden days of the Ottoman Empire, extravagant celebrations were held on every possible occasion, with the sultan providing most of the excuses. For the circumcision of three of Süleyman's sons in 1530, tents sewn with tulips were raised on gold-plated poles at the Hippodrome, where crowds were entertained by tightrope walkers on a cord stretched from the Egyptian Obelisk at its centre. The public was fed on roast oxen, from which fled live foxes as the feast was served. During the annual tulip festivals, small armies of tortoises were released to roam the imperial gardens with candles fixed to their shells.

When the republic was founded in 1923, it was just this sort of foppish excess that set the country's new rulers on their move to the austere Anatolian flatlands. Decrees from the new, party-pooping capital of Ankara put an end both to imperial traditions and to overt religious celebrations. In their place came a dour bunch of annual excuses for flag-waving, such as Republic Day (29 October) and Victory Day (30 August). The late 20th century brought another depressing development: the infiltration

of a slew of heavily marketed imports like Sevgililer Günü (Valentine's Day), Mothers' Day and even Christmas, which naturally tends to get confused with New Year's Day, given that more than 95 per cent of the population is Muslim.

Thankfully, in recent years, the full-blown festive spirit has returned. Nowadays, winter apart, every month sees a festival of some kind, with the city's youthful population giving these events a dynamism that more than makes up for any lack of experience. Many of these events are superbly managed and promoted by the Istanbul Foundation for Arts and Cultures (Istanbul Kültür ve Sanat Vakfı; www.iksv.org), which consistently attracts a roster of international big names. Now all they need to do is bring back the tortoises.

Information & tickets

For information about festivals and events, try the English-language *Time Out Istanbul*, or www.istanbul.com, which lists that particular day's events. To buy tickets for various festivals, try the following outlets:

Atatürk Cultural Centre (AKM)

Taksim Square (0212 251 5600). **Open** 10am-noon, 1-7pm daily. **No credit cards**. **Map** p247 P2.
This ugly 1970s building looms over Taksim Square. Tickets for several major festivals are sold here. Students receive discounts.

Biletix

www.biletix.com/0216 556 9800. **Open** *Call centre* 8.30am-11pm Mon-Fri; 10am-9pm Sat, Sun. **Credit** DC, MC, V.
Tickets can be booked on the phone or the website (in English and Turkish), or at one of the many desks in selected outlets of Vakkorama, Ada, and supermarket Migros, and at music retailer Raksotek (Istiklal Caddesi 162, Beyoğlu). There's a booking charge of YTL3 per transaction if you buy online or on the phone (irrespective of the number of tickets purchased), while an extra YTL2 will buy delivery to your home address.

Spring

International Istanbul Film Festival

Various venues (0212 334 0700/www.iksv.org). **Date** April. **Tickets** venues, Biletix. **Admission** 2.50YTL-15YTL.
An annual highlight, eagerly anticipated for the glamour factor of visiting movie stars. Be warned: this is the city's most popular cultural jamboree, and tickets sell out in advance. For more information on this and other film festivals, *see p172*.

Orthodox Easter

Patrikhane (Orthodox Patriarchate Building), Sadrazam Ali Paşa Caddesi 35, Fener (0212 531 9674). **Date** Apr/May. **Admission** free. **Map** p245 G4.
The city's last remaining Greek residents – as well as hundreds of pilgrims from Greece – flock to Easter Sunday mass in the venerable Patriarchate in Fener on the Golden Horn. In a church illuminated by hundreds of candles, the aura of ancient ritual is powerful enough to move even the most ardent of atheists.

International Istanbul Theatre Festival

Various venues (0212 334 0700/334 0777/www.iksv.org). **Date** May (even years only). **Tickets** venues, AKM, Biletix. **Admission** varies.
One of the few opportunities to see international theatre in Istanbul. In the past, big draws have included the likes of Robert Wilson, Pina Bausch, the Berliner Ensemble, the Piccolo Teatro di Milano and Britain's Royal Shakespeare Company. The programme also features a selection of the year's best Turkish plays. Most performances are held at city theatres including the Atatürk Cultural Centre, the Kenter Theatre and the Aksanat Cultural Centre (for venues, *see p198*). A few events take place at more unusual venues, such as the Rumeli Hisarı fortress on the Bosphorus.

International Istanbul Puppet Festival

Akkarga Sokak 22, Elmadağ (0212 232 0224). **Date** 2nd week of May. **Tickets** venues, Biletix. **Admission** varies. **Credit** MC, V
Puppet, marionette and shadow theatre was big in Ottoman times, but is rarely performed today. This festival is an opportunity to witness this almost forgotten art, with around a dozen shows by Turkish and international companies at the Kenter Theatre (*see p198*) and various other venues. Most plays are silent and suitable for children and adults.

Conquest Week Celebrations

Various venues (0212 449 4000/www.ibb.gov.tr). **Date** late May. **Admission** free.
A lively celebration of the Turkish conquest of Constantinople (29 May, 1453), featuring exhibitions of traditional Turkish arts and parades by the 'Ottoman' Mehter band, plus concerts, conferences, lectures, screenings, fireworks and some rabble-rousing by the nationalist and Islamist parties.

Summer

International Istanbul Music Festival

Various venues (0212 334 0700/334 0736/www.iksv.org). **Date** June-July. **Tickets** AKM, Biletix. **Admission** YTL10-YTL200.
Inaugurated in 1973 on the occasion of the 50th anniversary of the republic, the IMF is the most prestigious event on the city's cultural calendar. It comprises about 30 performances of orchestra and chamber music, dance and ballet. Big hitters at past festivals have included Kiri Te Kanawa, Philip Glass, the Michael Nyman Ensemble, Cecilia Bartoli and the Kronos Quartet. It's worth attending just to get a rare peek inside Haghia Irene church (*see p68*), normally closed to the public.

International Istanbul Jazz Festival

Various venues (0212 334 0700/334 0708/www.iksv.org). **Date** July. **Tickets** venues, Biletix. **Admission** varies.
This two-week festival pushes the boundaries of what defines modern jazz. Keith Jarrett, Wynton Marsalis and Dizzy Gillespie have all performed in the 4,000-seat Harbiye open-air theatre, as have less likely musicians like Björk, Nick Cave, Lou Reed and Paul Smith. Consistently the best programme of any Turkish music festival. **Photo** *p162*.

Traditional Istanbul Açıkhava (Open-Air) Concerts

Harbiye Cemil Topuzlu, Açıkhava Tiyatrosu (0212 257 6200/www.mostproduction.com). **Date** mid July/early Aug. **Tickets** Açıkhava Tiyatrosu (box office 0212 232 1652), Biletix. **Admission** varies.
Launched in the mid 1980s, this season of open-air concerts in Harbiye is worth checking out. The line-up mixes mainstream names from Turkish pop, rock

Arts & Entertainment

and folk with a variety of alternative genres. It's a good opportunity to see the more innovative end of the local music scene. Past performers include the Mercan Dede Fusion Project, with its blend of Turkish folk, trance and whirling Dervishes, alongside Balkan stars such as Goran Bregovic.

Electronica Festival Istanbul
Burc Beach (0212 283 5050/www.future generation.net). **Date** mid July-late Aug. **Tickets** Biletix **Admission** varies.
The second EFI in 2005 brought a heavyweight roster headlined by three of the best DJs in the world, Sasha and John Digweed playing back to back, followed by Armin Van Buuren; it pulled 10,000 people to Burç Beach on the Black Sea coast. Over 100 DJs are expected to perform this year.

Rock 'n' Coke
Hezarfen Airfield (0212 334 0100/www.pozitif-ist.com/www.rockncoke.com). **Date** Early Sept. **Tickets** Biletix. **Admission** YTL65 (one day), YTL125 (camping, two days).
Since it began in 2003, Rock 'n' Coke has become Istanbul's biggest (late) summer opportunity to stand in a beer queue with 50,000 of your closest friends. In 2004, 50 Cent headlined, along with Iggy & the Stooges, while Muse and Placebo shared top billing in 2006. DJs run the second stage. Echo and the Bunnymen, the Dead Kennedys, the Cure, and NYC's Gogol Bordello have also played at Turkey's largest open-air festival.

Autumn

International Istanbul Biennial
Various venues (0212 334 0700, 334 0763/ www.iksv.org). **Date** Sept-Nov, odd yrs only. **Tickets** venues. **Admission** YTL7-YTL15; Festival Pass YTL25. **Credit** MC, V.
Alternating with the Istanbul Theatre Festival (*see p163*), every other year more than 50 artists from around 50 countries exhibit around a theme set by a guest curator. In 2005, to explore the theme of 'Istanbul', the lucky artists were invited to live in Istanbul for six months. Expect to find paintings, installations, screenings, walkabouts, films, panel discussions, lectures and daily guided tours (in English). The next Biennal will be held in 2007.

Akbank Jazz Festival
Various venues (0212 334 0100/www.pozitif-ist.com). **Date** Oct. **Tickets** venues, Biletix. **Admission** 5-40YTL.
Unlike July's international jamboree, this festival is less about big names and more about jazz. Some ten bands perform every day over a two-week period, with jam sessions at venues including Babylon (*see p183*) and Nardis (*see p186*). Max Roach, the Art Ensemble of Chicago, Archie Shepp and Cecil Taylor have all participated in recent years. In addition to great music, there are film screenings and workshops.

Phonem/Electronic Music Plateau
Various venues (0212 334 0700/www.iksv.org). **Date** Late Oct-early Nov. **Tickets** venues, Biletix. **Admission** varies.
An international platform for exploring electronic music, with discussions, technology exhibitions and performances. Expect a string of parties featuring local and international DJs, plus concerts, video art, film and video screenings, and workshops.

Istanbul Arts Fair
Tüyap Centre, E5 Hwy (Karayolu), Gürpınar Jcn (Kavşağı, Beylikdüzü (0212 886 6843/www. tuyap.com.tr). **Date** Oct/Nov. **Admission** YTL5; students free. **No credit cards**.
Recently relocated from its city centre home to the less accessible Tüyap Centre near the airport, this vast, week-long sales fair has retained its massive appeal. Some 50 Istanbul galleries plus a handful of international art dealers come to offload paintings, sculpture and ceramics on an increasingly receptive local market. Don't let the remote location put you off: free shuttle services depart from AKM on Taksim Square, Atatürk airport, the Bakırköy ferry stop and the Esenler bus terminal.

Anniversary of Atatürk's Death
Date 10 Nov.
Every 10 November at 9.05am, the death of Mustafa Kemal Atatürk is commemorated with a minute's silence. Sirens howl mournfully and the Bosphorus ferries sound their foghorns, while buses, cars, and people everywhere come to a sudden standstill. The experience is both moving and eerie – a testament to the great leader's lasting grip on the Turkish public's imagination.

Istanbul Book Fair
Tüyap Centre, E5 Hwy (Karayolu), Gürpınar Jcn (Kavşağı, Beylikdüzü (0212 886 6843/www.tuyap. com.tr). **Date** Nov. **Tickets** at the door. **Admission** YTL5; students free. **No credit cards**.
Over 200 of Turkey's publishing houses, as well as several publishers from abroad, gather for ten days in the city to trade their wares. Leading writers, academics and intellectuals participate in non-stop conferences and round-table discussions. Attendees get discounts on new publications. Free shuttle services run from AKM on Taksim Square, Atatürk airport, the Bakırköy ferry stop and Esenler bus terminal.

Winter

Efes Pilsen Blues Festival
Lütfü Kırdar Convention Centre, Harbiye (0212 334 0100/www.pozitif-ist.com). **Date** Nov/Dec. **Tickets** Biletix. **Admission** varies. **No credit cards**.
This hugely popular festival, running since 1990, is a showcase for new talent, with three bands performing every night. This doesn't stop the occasional star (such as Bobby Rush or Long John Hunter) from showing up.

The new cosmopolitans

When it comes to cultural life, all that 'bridge between east and west' stuff has generally been viewed with scepticism by modern Istanbul residents: until recently, the idea that the city was still a cultural melting pot, as it had been in the Ottoman era, simply wasn't credible. But Istanbul has begun to regain its pre-Kemalist reputation with a new wave of cultural dynamism. As a *Newsweek* cover story put it in 2005, Istanbul has become 'cool'.

The loosening grip of rigid Kemalism helped the process. Kemalism involved adopting Western high culture, while ruthlessly bashing 'inferior' local art forms. Arabesque and gypsy music were typical victims – declared 'low class' by the state, they were banned from TV. Meanwhile other genres, like rock, remained derivative. That has all changed these days.

Istanbul's new cosmopolitanism is less to do with hosting many different cultures, as was the case in the Ottoman days; rather, it is about rediscovering origins and unearthing an older, more open spirit. There aren't many Jews, Greeks, Armenians or Italians left in Istanbul any more; but their cultural heritage endures, and Turks are starting to reflect this in their own arts and culture. Balkan, Kurdish, Greek and Armenian music can be heard in many bars, and CD sales are healthy. Turkish pop or rock has also started to draw on these influences – and gained popularity, creativity and credibility in the process. As the rock band Duman put it: 'It happened when we stopped fighting our origins and decided to respect what we couldn't defeat.'

Cruising Istiklal Caddesi.

Istanbul's openness to influences and ideas, both local and foreign, is also reflected in events staged in and around the city. Summer 2006's Biennial was the biggest ever in terms of international contributions and visitor numbers. Unlike previous years, it appealed to more than just an arty minority; it seemed as if the whole city was infected with enthusiasm for the event. The Istanbul Film Festival in April 2006 marked its 25th anniversary with the kind of programme that had students skipping classes to attend cheap daytime screenings. The big summer music festivals are pulling bigger names and bigger crowds; while throughout winter you can catch well known bands on weekends.

These days, big business and banks often sponsor art events, keen to be identified with cultural happenings that appeal to their high-spending target market (and to enjoy some new tax breaks at the same time). Two high-profile museums, Istanbul Modern and Pera Museum, have opened in the last couple of years. The Pera Museum was hosting a Rembrandt exhibition at the time of writing, and the city has also seen exhibitions of work by the likes of Picasso and Rodin (both at the Sakıp Sabancı). Even the theatre scene, routinely dismissed by most young Turks for being old-fashioned and pretentious, is getting more experimental and contemporary.

The city's new cultural dynamism – and its growing grassroots support – was acknowledged recently when Istanbul successfully bid to be one of three European Cities of Culture in 2010.

Arts & Entertainment

Children

Turkish delights for mites.

Is Istanbul a good city for kids? The answer depends partly on the length of your visit. For a short stay, the allure of the bazaars, large carpeted mosques with lots of space to run around, and boat trips on the Bosphorus will keep the kids happy and entertained. Turks are physically affectionate towards kids – sometimes in ways that can seem unusual to the uninitiated. Gestures can vary from a gentle kiss or cuddle to vigorous pinches and even bites on the cheeks or thighs. Foreign kids are generally spared, but not always.

There are down sides to spending time in Istanbul with children – these tend to become more obvious the longer you spend in the city. There are no centrally located amusement parks, zoos or even large playgrounds. And there's too much traffic and too little urban planning with children in mind. On the other hand, you can take children almost everywhere, though it's not always physically easy to do so: pushing a pram through Istanbul traffic is a battle involving encounters with steep hills, high kerbs and narrow passes – which is why most Turks transport their children in their arms.

Childhood is quite a different experience here. Kids are the centre of attention, as in the rest of the world, but rather than parents accompanying children into their children's world, kids accompany their parents in the adult world. They enjoy being part of almost all aspects of adult life, from smoky restaurants to gossip sessions with the neighbours.

Parks & playgrounds

There are two nice playgrounds in Cihangir (Güneşli Caddesi) and and Bebek (Cevdetpaşa Caddesi). The downside is that on sunny weekends they attract families from other districts and may get overcrowded.

There are also some lovely parks further from the centre, which may require a bit of a struggle through traffic at the weekends. Just north of the city centre, in Beşiktaş, **Yıldız Park** is beautiful and leafy and a fine place to let kids run free. The small fairground **Maçka Luna Park** is in a park north of Taksim. A little further north of Bebek is the large **Emirgan Park**, located just beside the Bosphorus, with an ornamental lake, playground and some of the nicest landscaping

to be found in Istanbul. Be aware that the coast road is heavy with traffic at the weekends; go early and leave early to beat it.

Park Orman (parkorman.com.tr) is a lovely woodland area in Maslak, north of the city, with sports facilities including a swimming pool, picnic areas, playground and fast-food outlets. It also hosts organised parties and activities for children. The Istanbul Culture and Arts Foundation organises a festival, Manifest, here in the last weekend of September, where kids are introduced to the arts through entertaining workshops.

Trips out of town

Kilyos and **Demirciköy** (for both, see p210), the villages on the Black Sea coast north of Kemerburgaz on the European side, have beaches that are popular in summer, with food, umbrellas and loungers available. The Black Sea has some strong currents, so be sure not to let children to swim outside the designated areas. Still, wave-surfing and the beach itself are fun enough for the kids. Just make sure you leave home early so you can have a decent time at the beach and leave before the early evening rush. The convoy in late morning and early evening can make the journey as long as two hours each way, instead of the usual 30 minutes.

Polonezköy, the old Polish village on the way to Şile on the Asian side, is also a 30-minute drive (traffic permitting). For many Istanbullus, a visit here is a rare opportunity to see large patches of grass you're actually allowed to walk on. It's a great place for children to run around, kick a ball and ride horses. There are several restaurants. **Leonardo's** (Köyiçi 32, 216 432 3082) in the centre is among the best. Brunch, served 11am-5pm daily, costs YTL45 per person (and there's a 50 per cent discount for children between three and seven). A swimming pool (and a small pool for kids) and a large playground are major assets.

Theatre & music

Atatürk Cultural Centre (see p196) and **Taksim Stage** (Taksim Sahnesi, see p198) both show plays for Turkish-speaking children every Sunday at 1pm. Admission is only YTL2. They also hold international children's theatre

Emirgan Park. *See p166.*

festivals throughout the year. For information, www.devtiyatro.gov.tr/web/cocuk.htm.

Atatürk Kültür Merkezi also stages opera and ballet for kids throughout the year on Saturdays at 11am. Admission is YTL4. For more information, go to www.idobale.com.

Museums

The museum with the most direct appeal to kids is probably the **Toy Museum** (*see p109*), with displays of toys dating from the beginning of the 20th century to the 1960s. As well as old Anatolian toys and *karagoz* puppets, there is a Wild West section highlighting the lives of native Americans, and puppets of American presidents from George Washington to Nixon. At weekends there are puppet shows, magic shows and plenty of other activities. The puppet theatre starts at 1.30pm.

Several other museums make some special provision for children. The **Archaeology Museum** (*see p71*) has a small area set aside for children, with displays at youngsters' eye level. The **Military Museum** (*see p98*) has tanks and soldiers' uniforms. The **Ural Ataman Classical Car museum** (Nuripşa Caddesi, 41, Tarabya, 212 299 4539) displays cars, trucks, motorbikes and war vehicles dating back more than 100 years. Best of the lot is the **Rahmi M Koç Museum** (*see p98*), which has a heaps of interactive displays and working models, and a submarine to clamber around.

Sakıp Sabancı Museum (*see p105*) and **Istanbul Modern** (*see p100*) both arrange free programmes to make the visual arts fun for kids. At the time of writing they take place in summer only.

Activities

For babies under two, the free mother-and-baby group, at the British International School (Fulyalı Sokak 24, Levent, 0212 270 7801) is pretty good; the International Women of Istanbul (IWI, www.iwi-tr.org) organises similar free groups.

Bab Bowling Café

Yeşilçam Sokak, 24, Beyoğlu (212 251 1595). **Open** 10am-midnight daily. **Games** YTL4.5 daytime, YTL6 evening Mon-Fri; YTL7.5 Sat, Sun. **Credit** MC, V. **Map** p246 N3.
This bowling café is one of the most popular among young people in Istanbul. There are also pool tables, and a café serving fast food and snacks.

Bosphorus Zoo

Tuzla Caddesi 15, Bayramoğlu, Izmit (0262 653 8315). **Open** *May-Oct* 8.30am-8pm daily. *Nov-Apr* 8.30am-5pm daily. **Admission** YTL15; free under-6s. **Credit** MC, V.
Located way out in Darıca, 45km (30 miles) from the city centre, but worth the trip for its wide range of exotic birds and animals, gardens and playground.

Dance Akademik

Tepecik Yolu, Cevher Sokak 6, Etiler (0212 352 7046/www.dansakademik.com). Metro Levent. **Credit** MC, V (not for beginners' classes).
Ballet and jazz classes start at YTL180 for a course.

Enka Sports Centre

Sadi Gülçelik Spor Sitesi, Istinye (0212 276 5084). Bus 40, 40T/Metro 4 Levent then dolmuş. **Open** 7am-10pm daily. **Credit** MC, V.
Facilities for swimming, tennis, basketball, football, volleyball and athletics, with nine-week courses for children in swimming and tennis (YTL295).

In the Kitchen with the Kids

Çocuğumla Mutfaktayız
Tepecik Yolu 28/2, Etiler (0212 358 1825/ www.mutfaktayiz.com). Metro Levent. **Open** 9am-6pm Mon-Fri; weekend hrs vary according to course times. **Credit** AmEx, MC, V.
Organises cooking courses for parents and their children. Cooking activities for kids take place once a month on Saturday or Sunday. Call ahead for the date and reservation. One course is YTL89 (plus VAT) for the parent and the child.

Galleria Ice Skating

Galleria Shopping Mall, Sahilyolu, Ataköy (212 560 8550). Bus 71T, 72T, E-50. **Open** 10am-10pm daily. **Admission** YTL9 children, YTL12 adults, 40mins Mon-Fri; YTL14 30mins all Sat, 1-10pm Sun. **Credit** MC, V.

Galleria, the first shopping mall in Istanbul, still offers the most entertaining shopping experience for families with kids, thanks to its skating rink. Private lessons are also available for YTL25 a session.

Miniaturk

Imrahor Caddesi, Sütlüce (0212 222 2882/www. miniaturk.com). Bus 47E, 54H. **Open** Nov-Apr 9am-5pm daily. May-Oct 9am-7pm Mon-Fri; 9am-9pm Sat, Sun. **Admission** YTL10; free under-9s. **Credit** MC, V.

An absolutely magical attraction, which recreates 105 of Turkey's most famous sights in miniature. The models range from a palm-sized Leander's Tower to a Sultanahmet Mosque the size of a small car and an Atatürk airport complete with taxiing jumbos; the level of detail is incredible. Card-operated speakers deliver commentary in English and Turkish. It's one of our favourite things in Istanbul. There is also a train going around the sights, a playground and a maze for the kids.

Play 'n' Learn

Havyar Sokak, 46, Cihangir, Beyoğlu (212 244 9151/ www.playnlearn-tr.com). **Open** 8.30am-6pm Mon-Sat. **Admission** YTL22.5/hr. **Credit** MC, V. **Map** p247 O4.

Activities for children up to six. There are workshops on arts and crafts, drama, experiments and games. Arrangements are flexible: you can join in with your child, or drop him off for a few hours.

Play Barn

Kirazlıbağ Sokak 4, Yeniköy (0212 299 4803). **Open** 9am-7pm daily. **Admission** YTL25/hr. **Credit** MC, V.

This indoor playground has three different rooms – all supervised – and a great outdoor playground, featuring mazes and tube slides. There's also a half- or full-day crèche for three days a week for children between one-and-a-half and four (YTL475 per month half-day, YTL575 full day), a twice-weekly mother and baby group (YTL25 for three hours), plus a couple of child-friendly cafés.

Tatilya

Beylikdüzü Mevkii, Avcılar (0212 852 0505/ www.tatilya.com).

A large, covered entertainment complex with fairground rides, restaurants and shops. There is also a small theatre with hourly shows at weekends. It was under reconstruction at the time of writing.

Restaurants

Although most Istanbul restaurants welcome children, few offer amenities such as high chairs or children's menus. If asked, many will serve children's portions and cook special requests. In fact, having a child often ensures that you

receive better service. The restaurants we list here go out of their way to cater for children.

Mezzaluna

Abdi Ipekçi Caddesi 38/1, Nişantaşı (0212 231 3142). Metro Osmanbey. **Open** noon-11.30pm daily. **Main courses** YTL15-YTL30. **Credit** AmEx, DC, MC, V.

This famous Italian chain is always crammed with children. Staff are down-to-earth and the atmosphere's casual. It's noisy, but kids love it. The restaurant also offers highchairs.

Secret Garden

Kalender Üstü, Atadan Sokak, Yeniköy (0212 299 0077). **Open** 10am-1am daily. **Main courses** YTL10-YTL15. **Credit** MC, V.

In summer, tables are laid out in this big hilly garden overlooking the Bosphorus, which also has a play area with swings, slides and a big lawn. The restaurant serves decent food: pancakes and sausages, barbecued meatballs and lamb chops.

TGI Fridays

Nispetiye Caddesi 19, Etiler (0212 257 7078). Metro Levent. **Open** 11.30am-midnight daily. **Kids courses** YTL10-YTL15. **Credit** AmEx, MC, V.

Burgers, hot dogs and fancy ice-cream desserts. There is a dedicated kids' menu.

Shopping

Kids' clothing and toy stores are at all the large malls (*see p144*). Pharmacists (*eczane*) are found in most neighbourhoods. Almost all supermarkets sell a good selection of Milupa baby food and Turkish brands like Ülker. Nappies and wipes can be found at most grocery stores, including Migros and Makro. For supermarkets, *see p153*.

Gelar

Nispetiye Caddesi, Petrol Sitesi 1, Blok 4, Levent (0212 351 9515). Metro Levent. **Open** 9am-6pm Mon-Fri. **Credit** MC, V.

Imported educational tools, wooden toys and playground equipment of excellent quality. Prices are high but the range is unique in Turkey.

Toys 'R' Us

Migros Building Ground Floor, Büyükdere Caddesi, Maslak (0212 286 0016/www.toyrus.com.tr). Metro 4 Levent then dolmuş. **Open** 10am-10pm daily. **Credit** AmEx, DC, MC, V.

The largest selection of toys in the city. It also has kids' clothing, shoes, baby food and nappies.

Babysitting

Deluxe hotels provide babysitting services for guests. Smaller hotels will usually make every effort to find someone. Beyond that, you could try Anglo Nannies London (0212 287 6898/ www.anglonannies.com), which provides live-in nannies from England.

Film

Call it kismet, but Turkish cinema is looking stronger every year.

A mixed bag of programming at the once-imposing **Atlas** *See p171*.

2005 was a mixed year for world cinema, but for the Turks it brought sunshine and roses: local films grabbed an unprecedented 42 per cent of annual admissions, the number of cinema-goers increased one and a half times, and the top grossing titles were all Turkish. There's more good news ahead: at least 30 new Turkish films are due to hit screens by the end of 2006, compared with only a dozen new films annually in the mid 1990s. And around 60 more projects are currently in production.

Increased quantity has brought improved quality, keener attention to production values, and a wider diversity of genres: horror, action and sci-fi now vie with comedy and drama for audiences. The rise in output reflects a more benevolent funding environment. The state has finally launched its first film fund; though far from perfect, it's a start. A stronger national economy also helps. Flush corporate sponsors are starting to realise the potential exposure offered by box office success, as well as the appeal of tax breaks. Beyond its borders, Turkey suffers from being neither officially 'European' nor a 'developing' country; but there are plenty of cinema funds that producers can and do tap, notably the Council of Europe's co-production fund, Eurimages.

The film industry is not, of course, without its problems, and still lacks a coherent infrastructure. But Turkish cineastes have every reason to be optimistic.

TITLES

Commercial success usually calls for a star-studded cast borrowed from TV soaps, pop bands and the catwalk, with a celebrity director to boot. Comedy is the most popular genre. Slapstick abounds, such as the never ending *Hababam* (*Class of Chaos*) series. Inspired by a cult 1970s movie, the sequels still pull audiences of more than two million. But there's more intelligent fare, too. Ömer Faruk Sorak's *G.O.R.A.*, a sci-fi parody written by comedian Cem Yılmaz, in which a carpet seller is abducted by aliens, racked up over four million admissions. Crammed with cultural references, it takes a subtle swipe at Turkey's deference to the US and Europe. Another recent smash hit was actor-director Yılmaz Erdoğan's latest comedy *Organize İşler* (*Magic Carpet Ride*), a spoof on Istanbul's organised crime racket.

But box office bounty is not confined to comedy. A case in point is Çağan Irmak's drama *Babam ve Oğlum* (*My Father and Son*), a rural tale of father and son relationships, set against the backdrop of Turkey's troubled political past. It drips with melodrama – but that usually works with the Turks. As budgets rise, action thrillers are entering the fray. The prime example is *Kurtlar Vadisi – Irak* (*Valley of the Wolves: Iraq*), a spin-off of a popular TV series that raised hackles across the Atlantic early in 2006 and earned record box office takings at home. Built around a real-life event in 2003, when US troops arrested and 'hooded' a group of Turkish officers in northern Iraq, the film sets the scene for hero Polat Alemdar to avenge the incident. Despite the token Hollywood talent (Billy Zane and Gary Busey), it would be hard to make a more ham-fisted or crudely nationalistic movie.

DIRECTORS

For all its domestic success, Turkish cinema rarely gets released or recognised beyond the five million homesick Turks resident in Europe. This is less true of lower-budget art-house productions, which have sparked growing interest in Turkish cinema abroad through the festival circuit. The best known director is probably Nuri Bilge Ceylan, creator of the acclaimed *Uzak* (*Distant*), whose latest feature *İklimler* (*Climates*) also won an award at the Cannes Film Festival, securing sales to several international markets. While Ceylan's cinema is a simple but subtle reflection on the human condition, director Zeki Demirkubuz has made waves with his ruthless realism. In 2002, two of Demirkubuz' films were simultaneously selected for Cannes. His latest feature *Kader* (*Destiny*), a grim love triangle and prequel to *Masumiyet* (*Innocence*), merits similar attention.

A crop of new directors is also commanding international recognition. Özer Kızıltan's debut feature *Takva* (*Takva – A Man's Fear of God*), an ironic look at the inner workings of an Islamic sect, won the Swarovski Cultural Innovation Award at the Toronto Film Festival. Yüksel Aksu's debut *Dondurmam Gaymak* (*Ice Cream, I Scream*) took the comic and colourful tale of a small trader struggling hopelessly against globalisation to the Oscars as Turkey's official entry for best foreign language film. However, in most cases such plaudits are the preserve of festivals, rather than the box office.

Cinemas

Istanbul's movie-goers are well served with over 200 screens, an annual world-class film festival and several smaller cinematic events. The dominance of Hollywood blockbusters still prevails, but an increasingly diverse programme is on offer, with a handful of theatres now specialising in independent and art-house films.

Feriye. *See p172.*

All films, except animation and the biggest blockbusters, are shown in the original language with Turkish subtitles, but don't expect English subtitles for Turkish films. Contrary to expectations, the once over-zealous censors have retreated into virtual oblivion under the current Islamic government.

Catching a movie isn't as cheap as it once was, but theatre standards have improved. Tickets cost an average of YTL9-YTL14. Most cinemas have a 'People's Day' once or twice a week, when all seats are reduced. The first screening of the day is often cheaper, and students and OAPs generally qualify for a discount at all times with proof of identity.

Phone and online reservations are accepted at some cinemas, and a growing number, particularly the multiplexes, take credit cards. Seating is assigned. In the older cinemas, ushers often expect a tip; the going rate is around YTL1. Be prepared for an intermission – basically a fag break – during all screenings.

To find out what's on where, check the *Turkish Daily News* for cinema listings or the ad pages in one of the Turkish dailies.

Sultanahmet

Şafak Movieplex

Darüşşafaka Sitesi Pasajı, Yeniçeriler Caddesi, Çemberlitaş (0212 516 2660/www.ozenfilm.com.tr). Tram Çemberlitaş. **Tickets** YTL9; YTL7 Mon. **Credit** MC, V. **Map** p242 L10.
Get past the grim clothing arcade and head downstairs to this granite-floored, seven-screen multiplex. All screens have Dolby Digital sound and offer a range of current US, European and local releases. Sultanahmet's only cinema couldn't be better positioned, right by a tram stop.

Beyoğlu

AFM Fitaş

Fitaş Pasajı, Istiklal Caddesi 24-26 (0212 251 2020/www.afm.com.tr). **Tickets** YTL10. **Credit** MC, V. **Map** p249 O2.
Just below Taksim Square, this US-style multiplex is at the back of a blaring arcade selling CDs. The 11 screens show a mix of Hollywood hits, indie and Turkish film. The IF Festival (*see p172*) takes place here early in the year.

Alkazar

Istiklal Caddesi 179 (0212 293 2466). **Tickets** YTL9; YTL7 Wed. **No credit cards. Map** p248 N3.
Behind an improbably narrow facade, the Alkazar was a porn theatre until its makeover in 1994. It's now throughly respectable – the only bare breasts belong to the art nouveau caryatids in the foyer. The three screens show an eclectic mix of art-house and Hollywood fare.

Atlas

Atlas Pasajı, Istiklal Caddesi 209 (0212 252 8576). **Tickets** YTL10; YTL7 Mon, Wed. **No credit cards. Map** p248 N3.
Above a muddled arcade selling anything from kitsch accessories to second-hand clothes, this once imposing cinema has been carved into three smaller screens. The largest still boasts the city's most steeply raked auditorium. The programme is a typically mixed bag. **Photo** *p169.*

Emek

Yeşilçam Sokak 5, off Istiklal Caddesi (0212 293 8439). **Tickets** YTL10; YTL7 Wed. **No credit cards. Map** p248 N3.
During the golden age of Turkish cinema, Yeşilçam Sokak was Turkey's answer to Hollywood. No more. But the Emek still stands as a relic of former glories, built in the 1920s with an impressively ornate 875-seat hall. Forgive the newer lino flooring and sagging upholstery and catch a film here if you can.

Sinepop

Yeşilçam Sokak 22, off Istiklal Caddesi (0212 251 1176/www.ozenfilm.com.tr). **Tickets** YTL10; YTL8 Mon, Thur. **Credit** MC, V. **Map** p248 N3.
It's hard to imagine that this modern theatre was used as a club by the Germans during World War I, before the French converted it into a cinema. It now houses two screens with a varied programme of local and international fare.

Taksim-Beyoğlu

Halep Pasajı, Istiklal Caddesi 140 (0212 251 3240/www.beyoglusinemasi.com.tr). **Tickets** YTL10; YTL7 Wed. **No credit cards. Map** p248 N3.
Directly across from the Atlas Pasajı, the Beyoğlu has an authentic art-house feel with a programme to match. From July to September, there's a daily programme of critics' picks from the past year, but this one slides into anything from the past decade. Across from the foyer/café is the small-screen Pera, with the same management and similar screenings.

Yeşilçam

Imam Adnan Sokak 10, off Istiklal Caddesi (0212 293 6800/www.yesilcamsinemasi.com). **Tickets** YTL6; YTL5 Wed. **No credit cards. Map** p249 O2.
At this small, basement art-house cinema, the programming leans towards local and European independent film. The charming foyer is full of old projection machines and fading film posters.

Levent

Kanyon Mars

Kanyon Mall, Büyükdere Caddesi 185, Levent (0212 353 0853). Metro Levent. **Tickets** YTL12.50; YTL8 Thur. **Credit** MC, V.
The ultimate cinema experience. Step into the cutting-edge complex and you're in a world of plush design and smooth service, from the ticket booths to the conveniences. Worth every penny.

Arts & Entertainment

Levent Kültür Merkezi Sinema

Çalıkuşu Sokak 2, Levent (0212 325 7228). Metro Levent. **Tickets** YTL5. **No credit cards.**
Run by TÜRSAK (the Turkish Foundation of Cinema and Audiovisual Culture), this art-house venue shows almost exclusively indie fare, as well as hosting various festivals. There's a pleasant café with seats outside in summer.

Karaköy

Istanbul Modern

Liman İşletmeleri Sahası, Antrepo 4, off Meclis-i Mebusan Caddesi, Karaköy (0212 334 7300/ www.istanbulmodern.org). Tram Karaköy. **Tickets** YTL10. **No credit cards.**
A state-of-the-art theatre within the new museum (*see p101*), which runs a monthly programme dedicated to home-grown and international art-house movies, including retrospectives, documentaries, animation and shorts.

Ortaköy

Feriye

Çırağan Caddesi 124 (0212 236 2864/www.umut sanat.com.tr). Bus 40, 40T, 42T. **Tickets** YTL10; YTL12.50 Sat, Sun. **Credit** MC, V.
Formerly part of the Feriye police station, this cinema is now part of a classy cultural complex on the shores of the Bosphorus. There are three screens with a varied programme. The Living Room Café makes a pleasant pit-stop before or after screenings. It's just a short stroll from the lively waterfront bars and cafés of Ortaköy. **Photo** *p170.*

Asian Shore

Rexx

Sakız Gülü Sokak 20-22, off Bahariye Caddesi, Kadıköy (0216 336 0112/www.rexx-online.com). Ferry from Karaköy or Eminönü. **Tickets** YTL8.50; YTL6.50 Wed. **No credit cards. Map** p251 W8.
One of the city's oldest cinemas, Rexx prides itself on being big: 'big screen, big sound, big seating, big difference'. The main screen and three smaller ones dish up standard Hollywood fare, leavened with the odd independent European or local film. It's the only Asian venue for the International Istanbul Film Festival.

Festivals

Istanbul hosts a film event almost every week of the year. Needless to say, some are more worthwhile than others.

IF AFM Independent Film Festival

IF AFM Bağımsız Filmler Festivali
AFM Fitaş, Fitaş Pasajı, Istiklal Caddesi 24-6 (0212 251 2020/www.ifistanbul.com). **Date** Feb.

Launched in 2002, this slick, hugely popular event is run by the cinema chain AFM. The programming is distinctly right-on, with strands dedicated to digital, political, and gay/lesbian cinema, plus hardcore sex and violence. Try to book tickets in advance, either online or at the AFM Fitaş cinema, where all screenings are held.

International Istanbul Film Festival

Uluslararası Istanbul Film Festivali
Various venues (0212 334 0723/www.iksv.org). **Date** Apr. **Tickets** Biletix, participating cinemas.
A highlight of the Turkish cultural calendar, this glamorous festival brings a real buzz to Beyoğlu. Some 200 films from around the world, plus all the latest Turkish productions, are crammed into a two-week programme. Alongside national and international competitions, themes include tributes, documentaries, animation, adaptation and world cinema. Festival season is also a chance to stargaze, with an impressive contingent of heavyweight directors and actors in attendance most years. Buy tickets in advance to guarantee seats and qualify for a discount.

International 1001 Documentary Film Festival

Uluslararası 1001 Belgesel Film Festivali
Various venues (0212 249 2317/www.bsb.org.tr). **Date** late Sept.
Refreshingly, this one-week festival run by the Association of Documentary Film Makers (BSB) does not focus on any particular theme. As well as unusual factual films, there are panel discussions, master classes and Q&A sessions. Screenings are mostly in Beyoğlu. Admission is free.

International Meeting of Cinema and History Film Festival

Uluslararası Sinema ve Tarih Buluşması
Film Festivali
Various venues (0212 244 5251/www.tursak.org.tr). **Date** mid Dec.
One of a string of festivals run by TÜRSAK (the foundation for cinema and audiovisual culture), this is a showcase for over 50 features and documentaries from around the world with a political or human rights dimension. Most screenings are held around Beyoğlu and at the TÜRSAK cinema in Levent. Admission fees are nominal.

Istanbul International Short Film Festival

Uluslararası Istanbul Kısa Film Festivali
Various venues (0212 252 5700/www.istanbul filmfestival.com). **Date** late March.
A long-running event masterminded by short film aficionado Hilmi Etikan, this week-long festival is based at various cultural centres in Beyoğlu and the Istanbul Modern. The programme includes short fiction, experimental fare and animation from all over the world. All films have English subtitles and all screenings are free.

Galleries

Private collectors and corporate sponsors put Istanbul's artists on the map.

Platform Garanti. *See p175.*

Over the last two decades, Istanbul's contemporary art scene has gained international recognition and respect. However, it was specific artists that first attracted attention, rather than the city's art institutions, museum collections or commercial galleries. For many years, the **International Istanbul Biennial** was the only specialist art event that invited international artists to exhibit in Istanbul, but also gave selected local artists the opportunity to present their work in professionally curated, large-scale exhibitions. With the Biennial taking place only every two years, the city lacked a more permanent support structure for ongoing artistic production and presentation.

Over the last few years, the situation has shifted to the opposite extreme. Although there is almost no state funding for contemporary culture in Turkey, wealthy patrons and banks, which have a history of providing charitable financial support to the arts, have taken it upon themselves to create their own 'branded', non-commercial galleries, cultural centres and museums. It is now so fashionable to own an art institution that Istanbul – or rather the relatively small area around Beyoğlu, Karaköy

and the Golden Horn – is bursting with new developments and prospective projects.

In 2004, Istanbul acquired its very own version of London's Tate Modern. The similarly styled and named **Istanbul Modern** (*see p100*) is housed in an old customs warehouse on the Bosphorus, a great space previously used for the fourth and eighth Biennials. Alongside a fairly standard collection of modern Turkish painting, the museum showcases some interesting recent acquisitions and stages several temporary exhibitions each year.

Hot on the heels of Istanbul Modern came the **Pera Museum** (*see p94*), with an historical collection displayed alongside work by young contemporary artists. High-profile exhibitions of Picasso and Rodin followed at the **Sakip Sabanci Museum** (*see p105*). Next on the horizon is the eagerly anticipated **Santral Cultural Centre** at Bilgi University, a complex of permanent collections, temporary galleries, residencies and workshops due to open on the Golden Horn in late 2006.

Galerist, the city's most prestigious commercial gallery, has raised the stakes by moving from suburban Nişantaşi to an impressive white cube in the new art hub of

Arts & Entertainment

Istiklal Caddesi. In its wake, the new space to watch in Nişantaşi is **Galeri X-ist**, home to a roster of strong painters and photographers. Of the many bank-owned galleries on Istiklal, the rising stars are **Platform Garanti** and **GG** (both owned by Garanti Bank), **Yapi Kredi** and **Akbank Sanat**. Platform showcases contemporary and international art in the gallery; upstairs, there's an archive of work by Turkish artists that is open to the public, as well as a residency programme for foreign artists. Its sister space GG is the only gallery in Istanbul dedicated to architecture and design. Yapi Kredi has a distinctly modern approach, while Akbank Sanat often features work by Turkey's younger artists.

On the face of things, these developments suggest a sudden wave of artistic movement and production; but Istanbul continues to lack artist-led initiatives and independent spaces. Without such grassroots activities to feed into the more grandiose gestures, there is little to fuel their expansion.

The effects of privatisation and urban gentrification is a hot topic among Istanbul's artists and cultural producers, as a number of initiatives have recently lost their spaces as a result of urban development. Two spaces that will hopefully last longer are **Pist** and **BAS**. Located in off-piste Pangaltı, Pist has already attracted international attention; it is set to host the prestigious e-flux art video collection in late 2006 (see www.e-flux.com). BAS specialises in presenting and producing art publications, filling another gap in Istanbul's art scene.

Akbank Kültür Sanat Merkezi

Istiklal Caddesi 14-18, Beyoğlu (0212 252 3500/ www.akbanksanat.com). **Open** 10.30am-7.30pm Tue-Sat. **Map** p249 O2.

Of the many galleries affiliated to a bank, this one has perhaps the most interesting programme . Close to Taksim Square, the first-floor space is accessible via the main entrance on the side of the building. The exhibition programme fluctuates between externally curated shows of international artists, including big names like Martha Rosler and Walid Sadek, and exhibitions by Turkish art students.

BAS

Meşrutiyet Caddesi 166, Beyoğlu (0212 245 9024/www.b-a-s.info). **Open** 2-7pm Tue-Sat. **Map** p248 M4.

Launched by artist Banu Cennetoğlu to display and produce art books and publications, BAS has already published several books by Turkish artists, which can be purchased here. The rest of the collection is a useful reference resource.

Galeri Apel

Hayriye Caddesi 7, Galatasaray (212 292 7236/ www.galeriapel.com). **Open** 11.30am-6.30pm Tue-Sat. **No credit cards. Map** p248 N3.

Apel hosts exhibitions in a variety of media that verge on craft and design. Expect weird and wonderful works from Turkey's avant-garde, as well as

Breaking the mould at **Galerist**. *See p175.*

surreal paintings by international artists. As you might expect for an underground space, it's a little hard to find: up a few steps at the corner of the street right behind the Galatasaray Lycée.

Galeri Nev

Maçka Caddesi 33, Maçka (0212 231 6763/ www.galerinev.com). Bus 30A, 30M. **Open** 11am-6.30pm Tue-Sat.

Founded in 1984 by architects Ali Artun and Haldun Dostoğlu, Galeri Nev has a sister gallery in Ankara. Essentially a commercial space, it represents Turkish artists such as Hale Tenger and Inci Eviner, as well as exhibiting work by artists from abroad.

Galerist

Mısır Apartment 311/4, Istiklal Caddesi, Beyoğlu (0212 244 8230/www.galerist.com.tr). **Open** 10am-6pm Mon-Fri; noon-6pm Sat. **No credit cards.** **Map** p248 N3.

Galerist has the strongest international reputation of any contemporary art gallery in Istanbul. Its roster of illutrious local artists include the likes of Huseyin Chalayan, Ayşe Erkmen and Haluk Akakce. The gallery stages about eight temporary exhibitions a year.

Galeri X-Ist

Açıkhava Appartment 15, Eytam Caddesi, Nişantaşi (0212 291 7784/www.artxist.com). Metro Osmanbey. **Open** 11am-7pm Tue-Sat. **No credit cards.**

One of the newest commercial galleries in town, Galeri X-Ist is committed to working with young Turkish artists, giving them the opportunity to show and develop their work from an early stage in their career. Photography and painting are high on the agenda. Cutting-edge work by artists such as Ahmet Polat, who won the New York International Center of Photography's Infinity award in 2006, are definitely worth checking out.

Garanti Galeri (GG)

Istiklal Cadessi 187, Beyoğlu (0212 293 6371). **Open** 11am-8pm daily. **Map** p248 N3.

The only gallery in Istanbul dedicated exclusively to architecture and design, GG is corporate in feel and intellectual in concept. Recently, it has shown work by internationally renowned architects such as Zaha Hadid, but also works with local talents specialised in diverse areas as diverse ranging from graphic design to orchestral composition.

Kargart

Kadife Sokak 16, Kadıköy (0216 330 3151/www. kargart.org). Ferry from Karaköy or Eminönü. **Open** 12.30-8pm Tue-Sat. **No credit cards.** **Map** p251 W8.

Located above a popular student hang-out in Kadıköy, Kargart is easily the most experimental and interesting gallery on the Asian side. The exhibitions often feature works by young artists from the area, which attract a loyal local following. This is a good place to grab a beer and find out what's happening beyond Beyoğlu.

Karşı Sanat

Elhamra Han, Istiklal Caddesi 258, Beyoğlu (0212 245 1508, 245 4657/www.karsi.com). **Open** 11am-7.30pm Mon-Sat. **Credit** MC, V. **Map** p248 N3.

A well-hidden location adds to the exclusive air of this gallery. The unusual space – a U-shaped corridor – hosts group and solo exhibitions, which focus mainly on young local and international artists. To find it, go up to the third floor of the Elhamra Han and ring the bell by the door on the left of the landing.

Platform Garanti Contemporary Art Centre

Istiklal Caddesi 276, Beyoğlu (0212 293 2361/ www.platform.garanti.com.tr). **Open** 1-8pm Tue-Thur; 1-10pm Fri, Sat. **Map** p248 M4.

Right on Istiklal Caddesi, Platform Garanti is home to an exhibition space, archive centre, and an international artist-in-residence. The emphasis is on video art, performance and installations. In 2004, the gallery hosted Tracey Emin's first solo exhibition in Turkey. More recently, Phil Collins, Mark Leckey and Roman Ondak have shown work here. If you're interested in researching the local art scene, check out the extensive archives on the first floor.

Pist

Pangaltı Dere Sokak 12-16, Şişli (No phone/www.pist. org.tr). Metro Şişli. **Open** check website for details.

A very new independent space – so new that it didn't yet have a phone or fixed opening hours at the time of writing – located in the unlikely, off-centre district of Pangaltı. In a large, street level space previously occupied by three shops – a *bakkal* (corner shop), an electrician and a restaurant – Pist offers a lively interdisciplinary programme that includes solo installations displayed in the window, performances and collaborations with international artists' collectives.

Projeşl Elgiz Museum

Harmancı-Giz Plaza, Harman Sokak, Levent (0212 281 5150). Metro Levent. **Open** 10am-7pm Wed-Fri; 10am-4pm Sat; by appointment Tue.

Originally created as a museum for temporary exhibitions, ProjeşL is now devoted to the private collection of art aficionado Can Elgiz. The Artvarium gallery hosts exhibitions by Turkish artists that change every month.

Yapı Kredi Kultur Merkezi Kazım Taşkent Galerisi

Istiklal Caddesi 285, Galatasaray (0212 252 4700/ www.ykykultur.com.tr). **Open** 10am-7pm Mon-Fri; 10am-6pm Sat; 1-6pm Sun. **Map** p248 M4.

This spacious gallery is situated on the first floor of the Yapı Kredi Bank (just south of the Galatasaray Lycée). It specialises in retrospectives of important Turkish artists such as sculptor Ilhan Koman, as well as hosting an eclectic mix of international artists ranging from figurative and abstract painting to exhibitions on Anatolian culture.

Arts & Entertainment

Gay & Lesbian

Forget your preconceptions.

Enjoying the sounds at **Love Point**. *See p178.*

In Istanbul, where nothing is ever quite what it seems, sexuality is no exception. And when it comes to homosexuality, it's that much more complicated. No, those moustachioed men in tight jeans and bomber jackets, checking out their blow-dried reflections in shop windows as they saunter down the street hand in hand, are not the local Greenwich Village clones. They're just a couple of traditional guys in a country where public displays of male affection have been assumed to mean just that – and only that. And no, that doesn't mean you and your boyfriend can walk down the street hand in hand. Urban Turks are savvy enough to sense when male affection means more, and you'd draw the same reactions in the streets of Istanbul as in a small city in the American deep south, or in 1950s London.

While Turkey's strictly secular nature means the gay community is not subjected to the ranting of religious figures, the traditional family structure is still firmly in place, and there is enormous pressure to marry. A high premium is placed on knuckle-dragging masculinity, which is one reason why so many bisexual and gay men present themselves in public as straight. Even for those few gay men with the financial means and firmness of character to strike out on their own, the downside of strong neighbourly ties is that liberated anonymity, even in large cities, is very difficult to achieve.

The whole concept of a gay rights movement complete with full social acceptance is a foreign import. The same is not true of gay sex. Oscar Wilde's 'love that dare not speak its name' had been expressed in loving detail in Ottoman court literature centuries earlier. It didn't need a name. It was just love, and nothing at all to be afraid of.

Ironically, it is in comparison to European norms that Turkey is now found wanting. And the legal codification of gay rights is among the criteria Turkey must fulfil in order to join the EU. As is the case in terms of geography and culture, Turkey lies somewhere between Europe and the Middle East, but Istanbul still boasts the most vibrant gay nightlife scene between Prague and Cape Town.

Bars and clubs abound, Turkish baths are as steamy as ever, cyber hook-ups are an increasingly favoured sexual and social outlet for the closeted majority, and secluded public parks are wildly cruisy. While home-grown transsexual diva Bülent Ersoy has been revered for nearly two decades, and fellow singer Zeki Muren's gold lamé boots and thigh-baring tunics did his career no harm, until very recently even the campest celebrities have not been subjected to the 'outing' campaigns of the West, or pressured to 'admit' to their sexual orientations. Homosexuality is not illegal, and hasn't been since the mid-1800s, when it was decriminalised after a short-lived ban instigated mainly in response to European influences.

When it comes to gay culture, Turkey is neither permissive nor repressive, and the long, slow march to full acceptance will be won the same way it will (eventually) be won in the West: a family member, a friend, a colleague, a neighbour at a time. In the meantime, momentum continues in the form of a gay presence at the annual 1 May parade, and positive publicity in the form of the Istanbul Gay and Lesbian Film Festival, not to mention the unstoppable determination of a small but swelling crowd of queers, dykes and trannies determined to meet, party, have sex and settle down, whether society likes it or not.

Advice & information

LAMBDA Istanbul

0212 233 4966/www.lambdaistanbul.org.
This umbrella group has links to international organisations, including the International Gay and Lesbian Association. LAMBDA is involved in a wide range of legal, social, cultural, health and political issues of concern to the gay community.

Websites

Begin at **www.trgi.info**, a comprehensive portal in Turkish and English. Although littered with ads, the site has useful links to all things gay in Istanbul and Turkey. Smooth and slick, **www.absolutesultans.com** peddles Istanbul as a sophisticated and cultured gay travel destination and offers exclusive package deals. It also provides ungrudging free information via the website or phone. The oldest gay website, **www.eshcinsel.net**, has been in business since 1998. Reviews in Turkish of Madonna's latest album are unlikely to appeal to an international crowd, but visit the chat room to strike up pre-travel friendships.

Venues

If you come to Istanbul expecting to find a gay nightlife scene comparable to that of major cities in the US and Europe, you will be disappointed – although incredible strides have been made, from just one bar in the 1980s to over a dozen by the turn of the 20th century. In the last few years, however, the scene has grown decidedly less diverse.

While there have never been 'niche bars' catering exclusively to a mature crowd, leather queens or other subsets, there used to be a wider selection of more upmarket 'Western-style' venues. Gone is the open-air Douche Club on the shores of the Golden Horn, the rooftop G-Launch, cutting-edge 'new Pera' Academy 14 and high-energy Neo – all of them a Turkish take on clubs you may have visited back home. Of the three Western clubs that remain open, **Privé** has gone downmarket, and **Bar Bahçe** and **Love Point** have become the victims of their own success, unless well-heeled suburban PR ladies and their banker boyfriends are elements you'd like in your social mix.

That said, if you're in search of a truly Turkish experience, you're still in luck. There are at least half a dozen clubs and bars within walking distance of each other in Beyoğlu, tucked into side streets on both sides of Istiklal Caddesi. Expect a mix of scratchy techno dance tunes and Turkish pop, an average age barely over 20, minimal decor at best, a ventilation system unable to cope with the summer heat and clouds of cigarette smoke, drinks costing YTL10, and fellow revellers running the gamut from post-op girl about town to self-professed straight offering his services only if the price is right. What you won't see much of are lesbians, who are faced with the same nightlife choices men had until about 15 years ago: none.

On the other hand, even if all of that's not your thing, on the right night, in the right mood, after the right number of overpriced cocktails, you just might find yourself appreciating the sheer energy, lack of pretension and a realisation that you have indeed strayed far from home.

Most places fill up only on Wednesday nights and weekends, if then. Don't bother turning up before midnight unless you're particularly enamoured of your own company, and be prepared to pay a nominal admission, usually in exchange for a drink ticket.

Western

Not places in which chaps with chaps and cowboy hats hang out; by Western we mean the sort of bar where monied, liberated and largely moustache-free Turks tend to congregate. While still distinctly local in flavour, they're the kind of places that straights and women – lesbian or otherwise – will feel comfortable.

Bar Bahçe

1st floor, Soğancı Sokak 7, off Sıraselviler Caddesi, Cihangir (0212 245 1718). **Open** 10pm-4am daily. **Admission** YTL10 Mon-Thur; YTL20 Fri, Sat. **Credit** MC, V. **Map** p249 O3.

Bar Bahçe has been a fixture on the gay nightlife scene for over a decade, but it stays fresh by reinventing itself every couple of years. In its latest incarnation, you have to walk across the dancefloor to reach the main bar against the far wall under a DJ booth. Fortunately, the former chill-out room in the back now also sports a bar, as well as an enormous aquarium. BB is a well-designed if smallish venue packed to the rafters with young clubbers of all sexes and persuasions into house tunes and each other.

Love Point

Cumhuriyet Caddesi 349/1, Harbiye (0212 296 3357). **Open** 11.30pm-4am Tue-Thur; 11.30pm-5am Fri, Sat. **Admission** free Tue-Thur; YTL20 Fri, Sat. **Credit** MC, V. **Map** p247 P1.

The only gay venue worthy of the title 'club', Love Point has a full-size dancefloor, a no riff-raff door policy, professional sound system and groovy DJs. It draws a mixed crowd, most of whom are too focused on dancing and preening to notice anyone else but themselves. **Photo** *p176*.

Other Side

Lamartin Caddesi 11/4, Beyoğlu (0212 235 7914). **Open** 8pm-3am daily. **Admission** free. **Credit** MC, V. **Map** p247 O1.

What used to be Istanbul's first gay restaurant is now a club complete with house music, go-go boys and a tiny dancefloor. It's on the fourth floor of an apartment building; the main bar is in the former living room and the back room is the place to discreetly make bedroom eyes at your new friend.

Privé

Tarlabaşı Bulvarı 28A, Taksim (0212 235 7999). **Open** 11pm-5am daily. **Admission** free Mon-Thur, Sun; YTL20 Fri, Sat. **Credit** MC, V. **Map** p247 O2.

An after-hours club that used to mix the slightly sordid with the upmarket, Privé was the place where minor celebrities and socialites could slum in safety. Lately, the more unsavoury elements appear to have taken over, with thuggish hustlers scaring off the more well-heeled. Be thankful for the hulking bodyguards at the door – you may well need their help.

A la Turca

Be warned: some of these venues are minefields for anyone not sufficiently attuned to the local social dynamics. That tall, dark number cruising you from his dim corner could well be more of a homophobe than the most redneck straight. Our list includes only the safer venues, but even so, brace yourself for the unexpected.

Alternative

Şehit Muhtar Mahallesi, Taksim Caddesi, Kargın Apt. **Open** 10pm-5am daily. **Admission** free. **Credit** MC, V. **Map** p247 O1.

Up a narrow, creaking staircase is this fantasy land inspired by a New Orleans bordello – all dim lighting, red velvet, purple lights, tassels and beads. In a separate area, away from the crowded bar, is a sitting room with faded armchairs. Alternatively, take the spiral staircase to the even more secluded second floor, where there's occasional live music.

Deja Vu

Sadri Alışık Sokak 26/1, Beyoğlu (0212 252 6131). **Open** 10pm-4am daily. **Admission** varies. No credit cards. **Map** p249 O3.

One of the few clubs with room to wander and a crowd midweek, Déjà vu is inconspicuously tucked into a side street across from a 24-hour men's health club (and, handily for uniform queens, just around the corner from the local police station). Most of the ground floor is taken up by a dance floor filled with 18-year-olds who look as though they've pilfered their mother's purses for the admission money. Head downstairs for the dungeon-like 'chat room' and relief from the thumping Eurotrash music.

Mon Key

Eski Yeşilcam Sokak 9/1, Beyoğlu (0536 983 6476). **Open** 10pm-4am daily. **Admission** free. **No credit cards.**

The latest addition to the club scene, Mon Key is housed in a three-storey building just across from a back street lined with tranny brothels. It's unusually roomy and well-designed for a club of its kind – a pity the management didn't spend more on speakers. A second floor affords a welcome haven from the distorted thumping and a bird's-eye view of the dancers below. A sofa for two is helpfully positioned just outside the men's toilets on the third floor.

Queen

Zambak Sokak 23/A, Beyoğlu (0212 249 2397). **Open** 9.30pm-5am daily. **Admission** free. **Credit** MC, V. **Map** p249 O2.

This is one of the few à la Turca venues to really make an effort. The freshly painted, tiny main bar area is cheery enough, while the new 'chat room' upstairs shows the owner's heart is in the right place, even if it is smaller than your average closet.

Tek Yön

Meşrutiyet Caddesi 54/1, Galatasaray (0212 249 7036). **Open** 10pm-5am daily. **Admission** free. **No credit cards. Map** p248 M3.

This is currently the most happening place in town, able to retain a few bears even as its new sound system, video screen and club tunes have begun packing in the clubbers, middle classes and foreigners. For a Turkish night on the tiles in an unthreatening environment, this is your best bet.

Transgender

There are an estimated 3,000 transsexuals in Istanbul, nearly all of whom survive through prostitution. Tranny admirers are drawn primarily from the ranks of the straight, and the bars and clubs they frequent are pick-up scenes dominated by moustachioed men in badly cut

Sugar Café.

European guests. The cafe's handy location and evening crowds make it a good starting point for a night of carousing.

Hamams & saunas

None of Istanbul's hamams and saunas is officially gay, but the ones listed below cater almost exclusively to men unabashedly seeking a bit more than a good exfoliation. Their sheer numbers, and the decline in the popularity of public bathing, have resulted in the small local hamams listed below becoming gay by default, simply because they've been swamped by an almost exclusively queer clientele. No matter how zealous the management's efforts to stamp out any monkey business, boys will be boys: clingy cloths are hitched up or allowed to slip down, groins are repeatedly lathered and rinsed. One notoriously busy hamam in the Sultanahmet district responded by adopting a women-only policy; others have helplessly thrown in the towel and sexual activity is tolerated as long it is not seen. Pointing out that a couple in the next room were moments ago having sex won't necessarily save you from a rapid ejection if you're spotted doing the same.

Ağa Hamam

Turnacıbaşı Sokak 66, Çukurcuma, Beyoğlu (0212 249 5027). **Open** *men* 5pm-9am daily; *women* 9am-5pm daily. **Admission** YTL15; YTL25 with massage. **No credit cards. Map** p249 O3.

A beautifully restored historical hamam where the management do their best to prevent any unseemly behaviour. But when your business is located at the bottom of a street of tranny bars and the place is full of drunken men in skimpy wraps, all congregated in a steamy communal space in the early hours of the morning, what can you expect?

Çeşme Hamam

Yeni Çeşme Sokak 9, off Perşembe Pazarı Caddesi, Karaköy (0212 252 3441). **Open** 8am-7pm daily. **Admission** YTL15. **No credit cards. Map** p246 L6.

A makeover several years ago did little to improve the forbidding appearance of this hard-to-find hamam, hidden among the backstreet hardware stores. The staff are apathetic enough to take a relaxed approach to the eight of great tubby things flirting and more in the underground bathing area.

Yeşildirek Hamam

Tersane Caddesi 74, Azapkapı (0212 297 7223). **Open** 6am-9pm daily. **Admission** YTL15; YTL25 with massage. **No credit cards. Map** p246 L5.

A neighbourhood hamam across from the Azapkapı Mosque at the base of the Atatürk Bridge. As good an introduction to the bathing scene as you'll get anywhere, with the added bonus of being relatively clean. The large, jam-packed sauna reeks of sweat and testosterone, if that's your thing.

suits. Go take a look if you dare, but don't come crying to us afterwards. You're bound to catch a glimpse of scantily clad 'girls' flocking towards Sahra, the only tranny club where a gay presence is tolerated, if not necessarily appreciated.

Sahra

Sadri Alışık Sokak 42/A, off Istiklal Caddesi, Beyoğlu (0212 244 3306). **Open** 10pm-4am daily. **Admission** varies. **No credit cards. Map** p247 O3.

Chamber of horrors or fun house? Sahra is three floors of get-it-here trannies basking in the tongue-lolling attention of young greasers, drooling hicks and aged toughs. Meanwhile, the few gay boys present dance, preen and vie for the attention of a 'real man' reckless, adventurous, or drunk enough to be stolen away from the 'ladies'.

Restaurants & cafés

Sugar Cafe

Sakasalim Çıkmazı, off Istiklal Caddesi, Galatasaray, Beyoğlu (0212 244 1275). **Open** 11am-midnight daily. **No credit cards. Map** p248 N3.

Under new management, Istanbul's first gay café not only offers smart decor, strong espresso and homemade Turkish sweets, but the chance for gay travellers to get an update on the local scene from proprietor Murat, who speaks fluent English and whose stint as an art student in Holland gives him rare insight into the tastes and expectations of his

Arts & Entertainment

Hamams

Scrub up on history.

Paying a burly, near-naked stranger to scrape, knead and pummel your flesh, while you're laid flat out on a steamy slab of marble, is one of Istanbul's hedonistic highlights. As British novelist Maggie O'Farrell put it when she visited the city in 2003: 'If heaven exists, I hope it's a hamam.'

Hamams were always intended to purify. Part of Islamic tradition is that followers should adhere to a strict set of rules for ablutions, washing hands, arms, face and feet with running water before praying. This was not necessarily carried out in a hamam, but the link between the mosque and hamam was always close, and the precincts of all major mosques incorporated a public bathhouse.

In the earliest times, the hamam was for men only, but the privilege was later extended to women. No mixing, of course: either the hamam would have two sections, one for each sex, or it would admit men and women at separate times of day. This is still the case. In male-dominated Ottoman times, women particularly valued their visits as a rare freedom: far more than just somewhere to get clean, the hamam was a rare opportunity to be away from the home unchaperoned. Hamams were the favoured places for arranging marriages, somewhere a mother could get a good eyeful of any prospective daughter-in-law. When the wedding came along, the equivalent of an Ottoman stag or hen night was spent getting steamed, lathered, hennaed and

depilated. For a husband to deny his wife access to the hamam was grounds for divorce.

Newborn babies would be taken out of the family home for the first time 40 days after birth for a visit to a hamam, an event that also marked the end of housebound confinement for the mother. And after a lifetime of hamam-going came to its inevitable end, a person's body would be carried in one last time to be washed, before being laid out at the mosque. Thankfully, this tradition has passed away; these days, there's no chance that you might have to share your steam room with a corpse.

Hamam-going itself has been on the verge of extinction since the advent of affordable internal plumbing. Whereas 80 years ago there were more than 2,500 bathhouses in Istanbul, now there are only about a hundred. Many of these struggle to survive. The few that flourish do so largely by courting the tourist dollar – hence some exorbitant admission prices.

BARE ESSENTIALS

For the uninitiated, entering a hamam for the first time can be a daunting experience.

Lengthy menus offer such treats as massage, depilation and pedicures (also soap and shampoo, although you may prefer to bring your own – and don't forget a hairbrush or comb). Outside tourist-frequented hamams such as **Çemberlitaş**, **Cağaloğlu** and **Galatasaray**, this will all be in Turkish. It all boils down to whether you just want to look after yourself, or whether you want to pay extra fo the services of a masseur (who'll also give you a good soaping and scrub).

Once you've paid, you enter the *camekan*, a kind of reception area. Some of these are splendid affairs with several storeys of wooden cubicles, like boxes at an opera house, and a gurgling central fountain. This is where you get changed. You will be given a colourful checked cloth, known as a *peştemal*, to be tied around the waist for modesty. Keep this on at all times – it's bad form to flash. Women are less concerned and often ditch the peştemal in the steam room, though many keep on their knickers. Both sexes also get *takunya*, wooden clogs that can be lethal on wet marble floors. Plastic slippers are often substituted nowadays.

Gedikpaşa Hamamı. *See p182*.

A door from the *camekan* leads through to the *soğukluk*, which is for cooling off and has showers and toilets; another gives into the *hararet*, or steam room. These can be plain or ornate, but are nearly always covered in marble and feature a great dome inset with star-shaped coloured glass admitting a soft, diffuse light. Billowing clouds of steam fog the air.

There are no pools, as Muslims traditionally considered still water to be unclean. Instead, the hararet is dominated by a great marble slab known as the *göbektaşı* or 'navel stone'. Here, customers lie and sizzle like eggs on a skillet.

The hamams

For anyone who is interested in the unique architecture of hamams but doesn't fancy the heat, a few hamams have been converted to other uses. Built in the mid 16th century by Sinan, and named in honour of Süleyman the Magnificent's wife, the **Baths of Roxelana** on Sultanahmet Square now serve as an exhibition centre and carpet store.

Be warned that many hamams are run-down to the point of being downright filthy. For instance, the Park Hamam in Sultanahmet should be avoided. We recommend sticking to the places reviewed below. For gay-friendly hamams, *see p180*.

Büyük Hamam

Potinciler Sokak 22, Kasımpaşa, Beyoğlu (men 0212 238 9800/women 0212 256 9835). **Open** *Men* 5.30am-10.30pm daily. *Women* 9am-7pm daily. **Admission** *Men* YTL14; YTL18.50 with massage. *Women* YTL12.50; YTL16.50 with massage. **No credit cards. Map** p246 L3.
This no-frills hamam is favoured by locals. The name means 'the big bathhouse' – indeed, this is Istanbul's largest. The huge *hararet* has 60 wash stations, compared to the usual dozen or so. The beautiful details are courtesy of the Ottoman architect Sinan (also responsible for the mosque next door). An open-air swimming pool has been added to the men's section. The Büyük is a ten-minute walk from central Beyoğlu. Cross six-lane Tarlabaşı Bulvarı beside the Pera Palas Hotel and head west along Tepebaşı Caddesi, looking out for the minaret of Kasımpaşa Mosque.

Cağaloğlu Hamamı

Prof Kazım Ismail Gürkan Caddesi 34, Cağaloğlu, Sultanahmet (0212 522 2424/www.cagaloglu hamami.com.tr). Tram Gülhane or Sultanahmet. **Open** *Men* 8am-10pm daily. *Women* 8am-8pm daily. **Admission** YTL19; YTL38 with massage. **No credit cards. Map** p243 M9.
More or less unchanged since it was built in 1741, Cağaloğlu – pronounced 'jaah-lo-loo' – is Istanbul's most famous hamam. It is often used as a backdrop for soap ads and pop videos. The two-storey-

camekan has a baroque fountain, while the grand *hararet* seems inspired by the domed chamber of an imperial mosque. Illustrious bathers include Franz Liszt, Florence Nightingale and Tony Curtis. Unfortunately, Cağaloğlu is starting to rest on its laurels: on a recent visit, the steam room was so under-heated we shivered instead of sweating.

Çemberlitaş Hamamı

Vezirhan Caddesi 8, Çemberlitaş (0212 522 7974/ www.cemberlitashamami.com.tr). Tram Çemberlitaş. **Open** 6am-midnight daily. **Admission** YTL24; YTL36 with massage. **Credit** AmEx, MC, V. **Map** p243 M10.
Possibly the cleanest and most atmospheric hamam in town. Built in 1584 by Sinan, it was commissioned by Nurbanu, wife of Sultan Selim the Sot, as a charitable foundation for the poor. The hamam has been in continual use ever since. There are sections for both sexes, but part of the ladies' wing was torn down in the 19th century. Women now change in a corridor rather than a proper *camekan*, although the main *hararet* is lovely. Close to the Grand Bazaar, the hamam is frequented by foreigners; as a result, the masseurs are perfunctory and more interested in hassling for tips. But there's usually someone at reception who speaks English, and if you're a hamam virgin, this is a good place to begin.

Galatasaray Hamamı

Turnacıbaşı Sokak 24, Galatasaray, Beyoğlu (men 0212 252 4242/women 0212 249 4342). **Open** *Men* 7am-10pm daily. *Women* 8.30am-8pm daily. **Admission** YTL58 with massage. **Credit** MC, V. **Map** p248 N3.
Built in 1481, for almost 500 years this hamam was for men only. A small women's section was finally added in 1963. Little else has been altered. The *camekan* is particularly fine, and there's some beautiful tilework at the entrance to the men's steam room. Unlike other hamams, the Galatasaray has marble slabs in the *soğukluk* where you can have a massage in semi-privacy. Because it's used largely by locals, the steam room is hot, hot, hot – towels have to be laid on the *göbektaşı* before anyone can lie on it. Staff are shameless about hustling for tips, but at least they give a good massage. To find the place, take the side-street off Istiklal Caddesi immediately north of the Galatasaray Lycée.

Gedikpaşa Hamamı

Hamam Caddesi 65-7, off Gedikpaşa Caddesi, Beyazıt (0212 517 8956). Tram Beyazıt. **Open** *Men* 6am-11pm daily. *Women* 9am-9pm daily. **Admission** YTL20; YTL30 with massage. **No credit cards. Map** p242 L10.
One of Istanbul's oldest hamams, Gedikpaşa was built in 1457 by one of Mehmet the Conqueror's viziers, next door to the mosque that also bears his name. Although not in the same architectural league as the Çemberlitaş or Cağaloğlu, the interior remains largely intact. Both men's and women's sections are a little run-down but clean. The men's area includes a small pool and sauna. **Photo** *p181*.

Music

Istanbul finds its voice.

Turkey is a nation in love with music. Not always the best music, mind you, but you'll hear music of some kind everywhere you go. Pop, rock and arabesque, which dominate the city's high streets and airwaves, are a lot easier to sample live these days, thanks to new venues like **Balans** and **Parkorman**. A a series of large-scale, predominantly pop concerts take place at the open-air theatres in Rumeli Hısarı each summer (*see p105*).

Being filmed looking wistful beside the Bosphorus and getting snapped by paparazzi outside nightclubs seem to be the primary goals of today's pop stars. Crossing over into the international market may become another, now that **Tarkan**, the undisputed prince of Turkish pop, has released an album sung in English – although at the time of writing only the Germans had caught on **Sertab Erener** has also recorded in English.

In fact, there's a new generation of musicians looking outside Turkey for their influences, and more venues where they can perform are opening all the time. The internet is also starting to have a positive effect, as bands can now be widely heard without having to rely on cash-strapped local record labels. For the first time since the golden age of Turkish rock in the 1970s, Istanbul is developing its own credible contemporary music scene (*see p188* **Bosphorus beats**).

The new breed of fusionists, whose spiritual and commercial home is the Pozitif organisation's Doublemoon label, are also reaching out to an expanding global market. Many of these artists are featured in Fatih Akın's *Crossing the Bridge* documentary (*see p185*). Look out, too, for performances by **Burhan Öçal**, a prolific percussionist who's recently hit a purple patch.

TICKETS AND INFORMATION

To find current information on live music events, visit the venues or pick up flyers in cafés and bookshops around Istiklal Caddesi. The monthly *Time Out Istanbul* (in English) has listings and previews, as does the fortnightly *Zip* (distributed free in bars and cafés around Beyoğlu, but only in Turkish). For online listings try: www.pozitif-ist.com, www.istfest.org, www.echoesproduction.com, www.biletex.com and www.ticketturk.com.

Biletix sells tickets online and at ticket booths around town, including downstairs at the Ada bookshop at 330 Istiklal Caddesi.

Rock & world music

Most of Istanbul's music venues are located on the side-streets off Istiklal Caddesi, making it easy to keep up with what's going on – though it helps if you're prepared to tolerate cramped and smoky conditions. At many venues, the bouncers are in charge of the door policy, which means that men may have trouble entering if not accompanied by women, although foreigners usually get the nod. Many places include a drink in the price of admission. In addition to venues listed below, Parkorman in Maslak (Büyükdere Caddesi, 0212 328 2000) hosts some big names.

Beyoğlu

Babylon
Şehbender Sokak 3, Asmalımescit (0212 292 7368/ www.babylon-ist.com). **Open** 9.30pm-2am Tue-Thur; 10pm-3am Fri, Sat. Closed mid July-mid Sept. **Admission** varies. **Credit** AmEx, DC, MC, V. **Map** p248 M4.
Far and away Istanbul's finest live music venue, this modestly sized brick vault with a mezzanine is located in the backstreets near Tünel. There's a lot of jazz, but Babylon is also the place for world music, electronica and anything avant-garde. The management, which also runs the Doublemoon record label and the city's best music festivals, consistently attracts the best local and international names.

Balans
Balo Sokak 22, off Istiklal Caddesi, Beyoğlu (0212 251 7020/www.balansmusichall.com). **Open** 9pm-3am Mon-Thur; 10pm-4am Fri, Sat. **Admission** YTL10-YTL30. **Credit** AmEx, DC, MC, V. **Map** p248 N3.
The new home of 'pop-rock' in Istanbul, Balans started out a couple of years ago with huge ambitions and attracted huge international bands to its well-appointed stage. It's still a smart venue that occasionally pulls in global guests, but today you're more likely to find local stars like pop rocker Teoman and Eurovision Song Contest winner Sertab Erener.

Indigo
Akarsu Sokak 1-5, off Istiklal Caddesi, Beyoğlu (0212 244 8567/www.livingindigo.com). **Open** 10pm-4am

Up close and personal at **Nardis jazz club**. *See p186.*

Mon-Thur, Sun; 11pm-5am Fri, Sat. **Admission** YTL25. **Credit** AmEx, MC, V. **Map** p248 N3.
Better known as a nightclub, Indigo is also at the cutting edge for electronic live acts. As one of very few venues with an interest in new music, it has built up a loyal audience of electro-rockers who are prepared to queues for hours to get in, so it's best to arrive early or buy tickets in advance.

Mojo
Büyükparmakkapı Sokak 26, off Istiklal Caddesi (0212 243 2927, 243 2991/www.mojomusic.org). **Open** 10pm-4am daily. **Admission** YTL7 Mon-Thur, Sun; YTL15 Fri; YTL20 Sat. **No credit cards**. **Map** p249 O3.
A basement decorated with giant posters of rock 'n' roll legends, Mojo is the type of bar where long hair and leather jackets never go out of fashion. Istanbul has dozens of similar joints, including many more on this very street. Cover bands have struck chords and poses here every night of the week for almost a decade. Concerts usually begin around midnight.

Peyote
Kalyoncu Kulluğu Caddesi 42, off Nevizade Sokak, Beyoğlu (0212 251 4398/www.peyote.com.tr). **Open** midnight-4am daily. **Admission** varies. **Credit** MC, V. **Map** p248 N3.
Spread over several floors, this joint is a favourite of the city's alternative crowd. Peyote recently added a small performance space on the second floor, where various local bands play original mate-

rial. With capacity limited to one hundred, it's the place to discover some of Istanbul's finest new talent. The beer is cheap, too. **Photo** *p188.*

Riddim
Sıraselviler Caddesi 69/1, Taksim (0212 251 2723). **Open** 9pm-4am daily. **Admission** Free Mon-Thur, Sun; YTL15 Fri; YTL20 Sat. **Credit** MC, V. **Map** p248 N3.
Formerly the long-running Kemancı rock bar, this new venue is an odd mixture of musical genres, with one floor devoted to rock, and another to hip hop and R&B. Locals seem to be lapping it up.

Roxy
Arslan Yatağı Sokak 3, off Sıraselviler Caddesi, Taksim (0212 2491283, 245 6539/www.roxy. com.tr). **Open** 9pm-3am Wed, Thur; 10pm-5am Fri, Sat. Closed July-Sept. **Admission** YTL30. **Credit** MC, V. **Map** p249 O3.
Roxy used to be one a major live venue, but its weekend club nights became so successful that live music has been relegated to the odd midweeker or an addendum to city-wide festivals. These live events are eclectic, with artists ranging from Luke Haines to Chumbawumba via Japanese 'acid mothers' Afrirampo.

Studio Live
Büyük Bayram Sokak 31-33/2-3, off Sakızağacı Caddesi, Beyoğlu (0212 244 7712/www.studio-live.org). **Open** 10pm-4am Fri, Sat. **Admission** varies. **Credit** MC, V. **Map** p248 N2.

Along with Balans, Studio Live is one of a new breed of venues that caters for both international acts and local cover bands, with the occasional DJ party thrown into the mix.

Asian shore

Buddha
Kadife Sokak 14/1, Kadıköy (0216 345 8798). Ferry from Karaköy or Eminönü to Kadıköy. **Open** 9pm-2am Mon-Thur, Sun; 9pm-4am Fri, Sat. **Admission** free Mon-Thur, Sun; YTL10 Fri, Sat. **Credit** MC, V. **Map** p251 W8.
This popular student hangout on two floors is supplemented with a pleasant garden in summer. It gets busy early, with crowds turning up for

passable Britpop and rock cover bands. The beer is cheap, the atmosphere convivial and relaxed.

Shaft
Osmancık Sokak 13, off Serasker Caddesi, Kadıköy (0216 349 9956/www.shaftclub.com.tr). Ferry from Karaköy or Eminönü to Kadıköy. **Open** 2pm-4am daily. **Admission** free Mon-Thur, Sun; YTL10 Fri, Sat. **Credit** MC, V. **Map** p251 W7.
The most established live venue on the Asian side, Shaft has a varied programme of rock, blues and jazz concerts, featuring original artists, cover bands and an open stage on Monday nights. There's not very much to lure anyone over from Beyoğlu, but this is one of the few late-night options on this side of the water. Be warned: the last dolmuş back to Taksim leaves the bus station about 2am.

Crossing the Bridge

'I don't believe the East starts in Istanbul and goes to China or wherever, and the West starts in Greece and goes to LA,' says Richard Hamer, an American member of local 'beats'n' fusion' band Orient Expressions. It's probably the only categorical statement in the 2005 film *Crossing the Bridge*, selected for the Cannes Film Festival and a hit with critics around the world. The rest of the film lets the music do the talking.

The film is directed by Fatih Akın, Turkish-German winner of the Golden Bear at the Berlin Film Festival for his previous film, *Head On*, and presented by Alexander Hacke, bass player for experimental band Einstürzende Neubauten, and producer of the music for *Head On*.

Using the simple device of following Hacke around as he interviews and records different musicians against photogenic backgrounds, Akın navigates the city's many musical styles. There's little attempt to analyse or explain, but the sheer range of performers – as well as what they express through their music – adds up to an insight into many aspects of contemporary Istanbul. The result is not only a colourful tour of Istanbul's aural landscape, but an inspired portrait of a city in transition that sidesteps the stereotypes and tourist traps. If you see the film after your visit to Istanbul, you'll recognise many places and sounds; see it before your trip and you'll be aware of some of the undercurrents that run through modern city life.

Jumping across ethnic, social and age groups, *Crossing the Bridge* suggests that music is the best way for visitors to experience the varied elements of Istanbul's

cultural fabric. The rest of the arts are stuck on the sidelines: Istanbul has a few prominent writers; its best film-makers – like Akın – were raised in Germany; and theatre is the preserve of out-of-work TV actors. Music, on the other hand, is ubiquitous. As people from all regions of the country relocate to Istanbul, music and food are the ties that bind them to their homelands. Hang out with the fishermen on the Galata Bridge and you'll be surprised by how many people sing to themselves as they cross it.

Alexander Hacke.

Jazz

In Istanbul, jazz has a revered status, with a hardcore of devotees and musicians who keep the scene varied and vibrant. Jazz is the focus of the prestigious **International Jazz Festival** (*see p163*), the **Akbank Jazz Festival** (*see p164*), and a wonderful jazz bar called Nardis. Both festivals draw a glittering array of global stars (partly because of a very broad definition of jazz); thanks to Nardis, the line-ups feature strong local players, too.

In the past, many of Istanbul's great jazz musicians found recognition abroad before they made it big back home: **Maffy Falay** (discovered by Dizzy Gillespie), percussionist **Okay Temiz** and guitarist **Önder Focan** all emigrated to Scandinavia; percussionist **Burhan Öçal** moved to Switzerland; drummer **Selahattin Can Kozlu** went to Africa; and tenor saxophonist **Ilhan Erşahin** moved to New York, where he has a bar, a record label and high-profile friends like Norah Jones.

Today, many Turkish musical talents are returning to their roots, encouraged by the fresh group of musicians making a name for themselves in Istanbul. New names to watch are pianists **Kerem Görsev** and **Aydın Esen**, who has worked with Pat Metheny, and trumpeter **Imer Demirer**. Of the old school, Öçal now records for the Doublemoon label, Erşahin makes regular visits, while percussionist Temiz now runs a 'rhythm school' in Galata (www.okaytemiz.com).

Jazz Café

Hasnün Galip Sokak 20, off Büyükparmakkapi Sokak, Beyoğlu (0212 245 0516/www.jazzcafe istanbul.com). **Open** 6pm-4am Mon-Sat. Closed July-mid Sept. **Credit** MC, V. **Map** p251 O3.

A dimly lit and cosy little venue allied to the 24-hour Jazz Café FM. Downstairs is a standard bar; upstairs is where the musicians perform to respectful silence. The main draw is veteran guitarist Bülent Ortaçgil, whose Wednesday night sessions have been going strong for ten years. His highly talented backing band includes fretless guitar maestro Erkan Oğur.

KV

Tünel Geçidi 10, off Tünel Square, Beyoğlu (0212 251 4338). **Open** 8am-2am daily. **Admission** free. **Credit** MC, V. **Map** p251 O3.

This laid-back café, (pronounced 'Kahve') situated in a gorgeous, old-fashioned arcade off Tünel Square, hosts low-key jazz every evening in winter, including regular appearances by former Mingus sideman and Istanbul resident Ricky Ford.

Nardis Jazz Club

Galata Kulesi Sokak 14, Galata (0212 244 6327/ www.nardisjazz.com). **Open** 8.30pm-2am Mon-Sat. **Admission** YTL20. **Credit** MC, V. **Map** p246 M5.

Nardis is a dedicated jazz venue, just a few steps downhill from the Galata Tower, whose patrons certainly know their jazz. Small and sparsely decorated – bare floorboards and brick walls – Nardis benefits from an intimate atmosphere. The place is run by guitarist and regular performer Önder Focan and his wife, who also edit *Jazz* magazine. Food is served, if you want it. Reservations are essential for tables near the stage. The music usually kicks off around 9.30pm or 10pm. **Photo** *p184*.

Turkish music

Turkish music – blasting from taxis, echoing out of kebab joints, wafting through markets – is one of the more startling sensory surprises for the visitor to Istanbul. The market may be inundated with mainstream pop and rock, but locals haven't lost their taste for indigenous sounds. Turkey boasts a local music scene as diverse as world music centres like Brazil, Cuba or West Africa.

Some of the music you'll hear is what's known as 'arabesque'. Much maligned by serious musical commentators – often with good reason – arabesque is a melancholic fusion of Turkish folk with borrowed 'oriental' frills.

In the days before electrified arabesque conquered Istanbul with its incessant *dum-shikka-shikka*, traditional Turkish music was one of the most influential in the world. The Ottomans understood a thing or two about melting pots. Instruments and musical styles from Central Asia and Persia were mixed with elements of Byzantine music, which has encouraged many new sounds to flourish. Echoes of Ottoman music are still audible today in genres ranging from Jewish *klezmer* to Greek *bouzouki* to Romanian *lautar*. Today, Turkey's musical roots are still expanding and spreading in different directions.

SONGS OF OLD STAMBOUL

To get a sense of how this music flows through the city, spend an evening in a *meyhane*, one of the boozy backstreet restaurants. As you nibble on *meze*, a quartet of musicians (usually Roma) warms up the crowd with nostalgic songs from 'old Stamboul'. By the time the main courses arrive – several hours and shots of rakı later – the rhythm has stepped up and the diners are dancing around, or on the tables.

One striking feature of this music is the wide variety of rhythms. If you can't keep time clapping, that could be because it's in 9/8, 10/16, or some other bizarre signature. Also, Turkish scales often employ notes between the notes, sometimes referred to as quarter-tones.

Although crossovers abound, traditional Turkish music can be divided into four basic

Strut your stuff and shake your hanky with the regulars at **Eylül**.

styles: folk, which generally has a regional or rural flavour; *fasıl*, the boisterous music found most often in *meyhanes*; Turkish classical (or Ottoman) music, the refined soundtrack of the court; and Sufi music, the ethereal sounds that inspire the dervishes to whirl.

Folk music

Halk müziği (folk music) is an important part of the local music scene. Usually what gets labelled as folk are the slightly modernised, *bağlama*-heavy songs played in bars. The *bağlama*, a long-necked lute also called a *saz*, was adopted by Atatürk's reformers as a national folk symbol because of its rural Anatolian connotations.

It's also the instrument favoured by the Alevi and Bektaşi, sects of Islam that stress inter-sectarian tolerance and equality between men and women, and are frowned upon by the orthodox majority. Their folk poets, known as *aşıks*, have been wandering the Anatolian plains since the tenth century or earlier.

Istanbul is also home to many immigrants from the Black Sea coast, whose characteristic instrument is the *kemençe*. The wonderfully chaotic music that comes out of this pear-shaped

fiddle accompanies improvised musical 'duels' between the singers and players.

Bağlama bars, identified by signs announcing *halk müziği*, are especially prevalent in **Hasnün Galip Sokak** off Istiklal Caddesi and in **Kadıköy** on the Asian shore. With low seating, folk art and cosy kilims, these cosy venues exude Anatolian nostalgia. It's not unusual to see family groups late at night, and men and women mingling more freely than is the norm in Turkey. Most venues offer two live sets a day, providing non-stop music from mid-afternoon until after midnight. Booze is served, tables are shared, and in addition to singing along, there's bound to be dancing. There is usually no admission charge, but patrons are, of course, expected to drink.

For a more sober experience, and probably more polished performances, head for the **Atatürk Cultural Centre (AKM)** in Taksim Square (*see p190*), which hosts recitals by state ensembles such as the Modern Folk Music and Turkish Music Groups.

Eylül
Erol Dernek Sokak 16, off Istiklal Caddesi, Beyoğlu (0212 245 2415). **Open** noon-2am daily. **Credit** MC, V. **Map** p249.

Bosphorus beats

Not so long ago, it seemed that the lot of Turkish musicians – outside the confines of pop and arabesque, and with the exception of a few iconic rockers of the '70s – was to endlessly rework traditional songs. It could be old folk songs or Eagles cover versions, but whatever it was, it was very unlikely to be an original composition.

One or two labels and bands tried to buck the trend, with occasional success, but anyone looking for an 'alternative music scene' would have been disappointed. When John Peel visited Istanbul in 1994, all he could find was a fanzine editor who made audio collages of old Turkish films. **Serhat Köksal** kept at it until eventually he recorded a Peel session in 2003. Since then, he has played festivals all over Europe and even released a record (see www.2-5bz.com).

It's still not easy for new bands to get noticed, but things are looking up for a handful of groups. The heavy metal label **Hammer Müzik** (www.hammermuzik.com) has scored a surprising hit with its hip hop offshoot – notably **Ceza's** *Rapstar* album. Avant rockers **Replikas** have been given some proper promotion by the Doublemoon label (www.doublemoon.com.tr); punk rockers **Rashit** had one of Iggy's Stooges guest starring on their latest album, released by Sony; indie rockers **Mor ve Ötesi** are riding high in the charts; and hard rockers **Duman** are already stars.

Record labels **Doublemoon** and **Ada Müzik** deserve the most credit for promoting local talent. After a few false starts, **Elec-Trip** (www.electrip.com) is getting its acts together, especially with new signing **Portecho**, one of whose members edits Turkey's alternative music magazine *Bant* (www.bantdergi.com). And if

it's great house music you're after, there's always the **Red Flag Collective**.

Even more exciting is the underground scene. **Peyote** (*see p184*) has a stage for unsigned bands with ambitions beyond cover versions, and Turkish musicians have started to use the internet to promote themselves. You can listen to tracks from a few recommended bands on these sites: www.homegrownss.com, www.ayyuka.com, www.cindugunu.com, www.dandadadan.com, www.theneighbors.co.uk, www.remoov.com. Many more bands have music online on MySpace. Good starting points include www.myspace.com/12m3 and www.my space.com/deafvoiceless.

Peyote.

Eylül means September, but this bar engenders a kind of balmy, best-years-of-our-lives vibe all year round. A long-established venue with reliably good musicians and an all-singing, all-dancing crowd of regulars, it's a great place in which to while away the afternoons. The music kicks off around 3pm, so you don't have to eat. Evenings get much busier and tables are at more of a premium.

Havar
Hasnün Galip Sokak 29, off Istiklal Caddesi, Beyoğlu (0212 251 3359). **Open** noon-1.30am daily. **Credit** MC, V. **Map** p249 O3.

Among the cluster of *bağlama* bars that run parallel to Istiklal Caddesi, Havar is one of the best. It's a large room, but there's precious little space for dancing: most nights, it's packed with a young

Arts & Entertainment

crowd that often includes groups of girls out on the town. From early evening onwards, there's a heady atmosphere fuelled by loud, energetic music.

Munzur

Hasnün Galip Sokak 21A, Beyoğlu (0212 245 4669). **Open** 6pm-4am daily. **Credit** MC, V. **Map** p249 O3.
From the outside, Munzur doesn't look that special. The inside is pretty nondescript too, but when the live music starts this little bar suddenly becomes extraordinary. The outstanding quality of the musicians, who have a wicked way with a *bağlama*, is inspirational. Highly recommended.

Türkü Bar

Imam Adnan Sokak 9, off Istiklal Caddesi, Beyoğlu (0212 292 9281). **Open** 10am-4am daily. **Credit** MC, V. **Map** p249 O2.
A boisterous, open-fronted establishment with low stools scattered outside on one of the busiest bar streets in Beyoğlu. The dancers regularly spill on to the street too, dancing around the potted trees on the pavement before snaking back inside. The cool customers at Kaktüs, opposite, look on with barely disguised disdain. Live music kicks off at 3pm on weekends, 6pm during the week.

Fasıl

Defining *fasıl* is one for the musicologists. At times it sounds like gypsy music, but it's also quite classical; or maybe it's just folk. In fact, it's all three – and more.

The word *fasıl* comes from Ottoman classical music. It refers to a suite involving different types of vocal and instrumental works strung together on the basis of their *makam* (mode and melodic shape). Today, *fasıl* bears very little resemblance to this style, except for the tendency of musicians to organise their compositions in a *makam*.

Unlike folk, which is basically bar music, *fasıl* is most commonly encountered in *meyhanes*. The musicians tend to appear later in the evening, by which time most of the diners are already warmed up by a few drinks. The vast majority of *fasıl* musicians touring the restaurants are Roma, skilled at working their audience into a state of *keyif* – or ecstasy. Not that anyone needs much encouragement to lose their inhibitions: most Turks don't have any. Every song is belted out by everyone in the room and tables are often pushed aside to create an impromptu dance floor. Nostalgia is an essential element of *fasıl*, and most *meyhanes* are decorated with photos and prints that evoke the good old days of Beyoğlu.

Most *fasıl* venues offer set menus with drinks and music included, although it is customary to tip the musicians a few lira per person at the end of each set. Bring an appetite and try to go

with a group of Turkish friends, and don't forget that a *fasıl* night is a participatory event.

A word of warning that applies to every venue on this list: if it's a slow night and the *meyhane* isn't filling up, the musicians may not play or the management may send them home early. This is more likely to occur early in the week and during the summer.

Andon

Sıraselviler Caddesi 89, Taksim (0212 251 0222/ www.andon.com.tr). **Open** 7pm-5am daily. **Credit** MC, V. **Map** p249 O3.
A four-storey multi-purpose venue close to Taksim. As well as being a *meyhane*, it's equipped with a wine bar, terrace restaurant and disco bar, not to mention Bosphorus views, accomplished musicians and smart service. The dimly lit interior creates a flattering backdrop for the dressed-up diners. A good place to start exploring *fasıl* if you're not ready to jump in at the deep end.

Despina

Açıkyol Sokak 9, Kurtuluş (0212 232 6720). Bus 70KE, 70KY. **Open** noon-midnight daily. **Credit** MC, V.
Located in the far-from-glamorous district of Kurtuluş, an area once home to a sizeable Greek community, Despina doesn't look promising at first. Its fluorescent lights and plastic flowers are a far cry from the snug *meyhanes* of Beyoğlu. But some fine musicians frequent the place, drawing an appreciative and demonstrative audience, who submit requests for their favourite *oyun havaları* (dance songs). On the right night, this can be the best party in town. The easiest way to find it is by taxi.

Ehli Keyif

Kallavi Sokak 20, off Istiklal Caddesi, Beyoğlu (0212 251 1010). **Open** noon-2am Mon-Sat. **Credit** MC, V. **Map** p248 M3.
Tucked away on its own little street off Istiklal, this classic little *meyhane* has decent food and, most weekend nights, an exhilarating atmosphere. It has one of the best reputations for *fasıl*, which makes reservations essential. Dancing in the street is not uncommon. Highly recommended.

Süheyla

Balık Pazarı, Galatasaray, Beyoğlu (0212 251 8347). **Open** 7pm-2am daily. **No credit cards**. **Map** p248 N3.
Another prime *fasıl* venue, nestled among the many restaurants in the Nevizade Sokak area, with two large rooms and above-average musicians. The set menu includes unlimited rakı for YTL60 per head. The place gets packed at weekends.

Turkish classical

Real Turkish classical music is not something that most visitors to Istanbul will have the opportunity to hear, because it's rarely performed in public these days. In the new Turkish Republic of the 1920s, Ottoman music was considered elitist and backward, so the state did its best to bury it. There has been a slow revival over the last couple of decades; percussionist **Burhan Öçal** is the latest to pay his respects, with his classically inspired *Yeni Rüya* album. To hear other faithful renditions, look in music shops for Turkish classical music on the Kalan label.

Also known as Ottoman, Osmanlı or Court-Enderun music, Turkish classical music is based on the principle of *makam*. Like the Indian *ragas,* the *makams* are modal. The melodies are subtle, the rhythms gentle and sometimes quite slow, although towards the end of a programme you'll often hear lively numbers as the pace picks up.

No single venue in Istanbul devotes itself exclusively to performances of Turkish classical music, although it does feature in the annual **International Istanbul Music Festival** (*see p163*).

Atatürk Cultural Centre

Atatürk Kültür Merkezi/AKM, Taksim Square (0212 251 5600/251 1023). **Open** 10am-noon, 1-7pm daily. **No credit cards. Map** p247 P2.

This hall on Taksim Square is the most likely place to find Turkish classical music. The Türk Müziği chorus performs in the lower auditorium most Sundays from autumn to late spring.

Cemal Reşit Rey Konser Salonu

Cemal Reşit Rey Konser Salonu Darülbedai Caddesi 1, Harbiye (0212 232 9830). **Open** Box office 10am-8pm daily. **Admission** YTL8-21 **Credit** MC, V.

This large, comfortable and under-appreciated auditorium with excellent acoustics is not far north of Taksim Square. Run by the Istanbul Municipality, the venue hosts occasional concerts of Turkish classical music.

Sufi music

They may be promoted as one of the enduring symbols of Turkey abroad, but the Whirling Dervishes, better known locally as the Mevlevi

Doing the *Oryantal*

The pelvis plays a prominent role in Turkish life. Belly-dancing shows are a staple of the package-holiday circuit, gyrations are a required movement for Turkish pop stars, while hip-swaying *dansöz* are celebrities.

Funny, then, that belly-dancing isn't even a Turkish tradition. Sure, there were dancing girls in the harems, but the belly-dancing familiar to most – long-haired female *dansöz* in gauzy, sequined garments, undulating rhythmically – is actually an Egyptian import, which only caught on here during the 20th century. Turks acknowledge the dance's Arab heritage in their name for it: *Oryantal.*

Whatever its origin, the Turks have embraced hip-swivelling with gusto. Ordinary Turks can perform similar moves to the professionals, but they don't call it *Oryantal*: when civilians gyrate it's referred to as *gobek atmak*, which literally means 'to fling one's belly'.

Belly-flinging wasn't always so acceptable. Once upon a time, the *dansöz* was considered a fallen woman, whose spangles and lamé were confined to entertaining men in seedy nightclubs.

That changed in the late 1970s, when a *dansöz* appeared on Turkish television for the first time. Nesrin

Topkapı's five-minute spot on national television transfixed the country: she became an overnight celebrity, dragging belly-dancing out of the backroom and on to the front page. In the 1990s, it was the turn of Sibel Can to make the leap from seedy belly-dancing clubs to the pop charts. And in the 2003 Eurovision Song Contest, winner Sertap Erener brought belly dancing into millions of living rooms across the world.

But traces of the demi-monde vibe remain. These famous names aside, the world of professional dancing is still pretty much wedded to its image of greasy banknotes stuffed into skimpy costumes.

Andon.

order of Sufis, are quite rare in Istanbul –
not least because the sect is still technically
outlawed in Turkey. You can catch a *sema*
(performance) in designated tourist spots, but
this is promoted as a colourful historical oddity,
rather than an ecstatic connection with God
through music, dance and *zikr* (a form of
rhythmic breathing).

The **Galata Mevlevihanesi** in Tünel
(Galip Dede Caddesi 15), a centre for whirling
dervishes sanitised as a Museum for Classical
Literature (Divan Edebiyat Müzesi), stages two
performances a month exclusively for tourists.
The same dervishes also perform three times a
week in a waiting room in Sirkeci train station,
but the lousy acoustics and noisy surroundings
disturb the atmosphere of enchantment.

Genuine dervish ceremonies are not always
accessible to the outsider. One place to catch
one is in **Fatih**, where the Cerrahi brotherhood
operates the **Museum for the Study and
Preservation of Tasavvuf Music** (Nurettin
Tekkesi Sokak, Karagümrük), actually a fully
functioning mosque. Visitors are not
necessarily welcome, as the place is obliged
to keep a low profile, but if you go with a
respectful attitude and an open mind, you
may be able to witness a ceremony on Monday
nights starting from 10pm. On Thursday
evenings, the brotherhood holds *zikr* ceremonies
– a rousing chorus of Sufis locked together in
concentric dancing circles around a solo singer
and a drummer. More an act of worship than a
concert, it's an unforgettable experience.

Another opportunity to hear Sufi music in
Istanbul is during the **Mystic Music Festival**
held at Cemal Resit Rey Concert Hall every
November. Check www.biletix.com for details.

Festivals

The number of music festivals is multiplying
every year. Events range from one night of
performances in a touring show to a month of
citywide activities. The Istanbul Culture and
Art Foundation (www.iksv.org) organises an
ambitious two-week **Jazz Festival** every July
and the **Phonem Advanced & Electronic
Contemporary Music Festival** staged in
November (together with Kod Müzik). Another
key player on the festival scene is Pozitif
(www.pozitif-ist.com), the organisation behind
October's **Akbank Jazz Festival**, the **Efes
Pilsen Blues Festival**, which tours Turkey
and much of Russia, the **One Love Festival**,
two days of eclectic bands in a park north of
the city, and the **Rock 'n' Coke Festival**, a
three day event that hosts international and
local acts at an airstrip, complete with a
Glastonbury-style camp site.

Local stars of pop and arabesque perform
series of concerts each summer at the open air
theatres in Rumeli Hisarı and Harbiye. Look
out for details on www.biletix.com.

The summer festivals held at beach clubs on
the Black Sea coast usually include some kind
of shuttle service from Taksim Square, but
standards of organisation vary widely.

Arts & Entertainment

Nightlife

Istanbul knows how to party.

The Istanbul club scene has boomed in a relatively short period of time. Given that Turks are obsessive followers of fads, club promoters tend to stick to tried and tested formulas. So although smaller clubs cater to most musical tastes, from rock and jazz to Latin or electronica, the majority of big clubs play house and techno. This is offset by the frequency and variety of guest DJs like Tiesto, Kruder & Dorfmeister, John Digweed and Paul Oakenfold. But Istanbul also has plenty of talented local DJs: look out for Yunus Güvenen, Barış Türker and Murat Uncuoğlu.

Although new venues crop up every month, it's safest to stick with big names like **Crystal** (electronic, after hours), **Roxy** (rock, pop, theme parties), **NuPera** (electronic, dance, disco), or **Babylon** (excellent live acts and a monthly Oldies But Goldies party).

Istanbul's lively party scene has its idiosyncrasies. Turks definitely like to dress up, so make an effort not to look too casual. You won't find any rowdy, alcohol-induced behaviour at clubs or on the streets. Although disturbances are rare, belligerent bouncers can be a hassle. Drinks are generally expensive, due to heavy taxes on alcohol. Be warned that police sometimes raid clubs and crack down hard on anyone caught in possession of illegal substances.

The party doesn't really get started until after midnight, with clubs peaking between 1am and 4am. Fridays and Saturdays are the busiest nights. There are sometimes special events on Wednesdays. Bars are busy on Thursdays, but it's usually dead in clubs. From July to September, the party shifts to the shores of the Bosphorus (see *p195* **Bosphorus bling**). When it comes to getting around, taxis are cheap, reliable, and generally safe.

Finding up-to-date nightlife listings is a challenge. Check out www.x-ist.com or *Time Out Istanbul* (in English) and its online edition www.timeout.com.tr.

Festivals & events

Despite drawbacks like heavy-handed security and expensive taxi rides home, one-off raves and annual festivals in far-flung locales are a growth industry. Many events are held at **The Venue** (better known as Maslak Venue), with its huge indoor and outdoor arenas on the outskirts of Maslak business district. Just beyond Maslak is **Park Orman**, a huge bar/restaurant complex with a pool. A new addition is **Yeni Melek**, a giant space that hosts parties and concerts in the heart of Beyoğlu. During summer, the action moves to **Solar Beach** or **Burç Beach** in Kilyos on the Black Sea coast (*see p210*).

Big events are advertised around town, and clubs distribute flyers at bars, cafés and bookshops in Beyoğlu. You can buy tickets online at Biletix. Websites that list upcoming events include www.pozitif-ist.com, www.hippro.com, www.fabrikainternational. com and www.kodmuzik.com.

Venues

Babylon
Şehbender Sokak 3, Tünel, Beyoğlu (0212 292 7368/ www.babylon.com.tr). **Open** 9.30pm-4am Tue-Sat. **Admission** varies. **Credit** AmEx, DC, MC, V. **Map** p248 M4.
More of a live music venue (*see p183*) than a club, the intimate Babylon hosts some of the best parties in town. Run by the prolific Pozitif group, it's one of the few places that offers more than techno. Nights range from funk to Oldies But Goldies parties, where cheesy ballads and dirty dancing are *de rigueur*.

Cahide On5
193 Meşrutiyet Caddesi, Beyoğlu (0212 292 2425). **Open** 7pm-2am Mon-Sat. **Admission** YTL35. **Credit** V, MC. **Map** p248 M3.
A kitsch fantasy, complete with surreal decor and transvestite staff. Surprisingly popular with trend-setting socialites, though the cocktails cost a fortune. The soundtrack is cheesy pop – past and present – and camp, carnival atmosphere is infectious.

Crystal
Muallim Naci Caddesi 65, Ortaköy (0212 229 7152/www.clubcrystal.org). Bus DT1, DT2. **Open** midnight-5.30am Fri, Sat. **Admission** YTL35. **Credit** MC, V.
One of the few late clubs that is open all year. Cosmopolitan thirty-somethings get down to hardcore techno, then chill out in the enclosed garden bar. Besides a roster of resident DJs, Crystal is a destination for techno luminaries from abroad. Weekends are packed, fun and messy. Thursday nights are relaxed, with fresh progressive house sounds. Gets going after 1am. **Photo** *193*.

Crystal. *See p193.*

Bosphorus bling

If you like your nightlife flashy, you'll love the clubs along the Bosphorus between Ortaköy and Kuruçeşme. So-called superclubs like **Reina** and **Sortie** are a gaudy swirl of swaggering playboys, C-list celebrities and anorexic gold-diggers sipping exorbitant cocktails as they sway to trashy Turkish and European pop. Patrons roll up in sports cars or even speedboats. They might be barely dressed girls desperate to get into local gossip mags like *Alem* or *Şamdan*, soap stars eager to flash their cash; or nouveau-riche upstarts trying to scramble up the social ladder. Whatever the case, the name of the game is see and be seen.

These clubs – particularly Reina – are notoriously elitist. A beer can cost YTL17, a cocktail YTL35, and a meal around YTL150

per person. You have to pay YTL45 just to get in – if, that is, you're lucky enough to make it past the bouncers.

These venues are at the peak of their popularity in summer, when the fine moonlit views offer cool respite for those stuck in the city. Some venues close in winter, others keep their indoor dancefloors open and close the outdoor spaces. Some, like chic Anjelique, more relaxed than the others.

Anjelique

Salhane Sokak 10/2,off Muallim Naci Caddesi, Ortaköy (0212 287 5641). Bus DT1, DT2. **Open** 6pm-4am Mon-Sat. **Admission** varies. **Credit** MC, V.
The most tasteful of the Bosphorus bunch. Anjelique's assets include stunning views,

above average food at the refined Da Mario restaurant, and delicious apple martinis. There are resident and guest DJs, but Western and Turkish sing-along pap predominates.

Blackk

Muallim Naci Caddesi 119, Ortaköy (0212 236 7256/ www.blackk.net). Bus DT1, DT2. **Open** 8pm-late daily. **Admission** varies. **Credit** AmEx, MC, V.
This relative newcomer is giving its upmarket neighbours a run for their money. Dinner will set you back about YTL90-YTL120.

Dogzstar

Tosboğa Sokkak 22, Galatasaray, Beyoğlu (0212 244 1081). **Open** 10.30am-10.30pm Mon-Thur, Sun; 2pm-4am Fri, Sat. **Admission** free. **Credit** MC, V. **Map** p248 N3.
It may be small, but Dogzstar proves that size doesn't matter: this diminutive club in Beyoğlu has garnered quite a reputation. Although owners Koray and Kutayare planning to relocate to a bigger venue, but we're glad they didn't: the laid-back, let-loose, neo-punk vibe here packs a punch. It can get a little cramped, but it's a good place to boogie, thanks to resident DJ Ari.

Dulcinea

Meşelik Sokak 20, Beyoğlu (0212 245 1071/ www.dulcinea.org). **Open** 11pm-2am Mon-Wed; 11pm-4am Thur-Sat. **Admission** YTL20. **Credit** MC, V. **Map** p249 O2.

It may be in the heart of Beyoğlu, but the decor at Dulcinea is straight out of SoHo. So it's no surprise that the downstairs space at this bar/restaurant is a good place for a dance. A roster of guest DJs keeps the floor filled with a blend of cutting-edge electro and nu-jazz. The upstairs bar and dining area is more mellow.

Gossip Bar

Hyatt Regency Hotel, Takışla Sokak 1, Taksim (0212 368 1234/www.mundolatinodance.com). **Open** 9pm-2am Wed-Sat. **Admission** free. **Credit** AmEx, MC, V. **Map** p247 P1.
Gossip Bar has taken over from Alegria as Istanbul's leading Latin venue. The Latin nights on Thursdays and Saturdays are legendary, and there's also great live jazz from time to time. The crowd are older and mellower than most, but when it comes to salsa they are no less nimble on the dancefloor.

Try a frozen watermelon cocktail (YTL25) on the upper terrace, decked out with antiques and ceramics. Occasional live jazz.

Çubuklu Hayal Kahvesi

Çubuklu Ağaçlık Mesire Yeri, Burunbahçe (0216 413 6880). Ferry from Beşiktaş to Üsküdar, then bus 15. Or ferry from Karaköy or Eminönü to Kadıköy, then bus 15BK, 15F. **Open** 7pm-4am daily. **Admission** varies. **Credit** MC, V.
Right on the waterfront in a leafy Asian suburb. Free boats whisk you across the Bosphorus to the club's private jetty (departing from Istinye Motor Iskelesi every 30 minutes from 7pm until closing time, and from 10am on Sundays).

Reina

Muallim Naci Caddesi 44, Ortaköy (0212 259 5919/www.reina.com.tr). Bus DT1, DT2. **Open** 7pm-4am daily. **Admission** varies. **Credit** AmEx, MC, V.
The city's most famous nightclub, Reina is paparazzi heaven. It's a stunning waterfront venue, resembling a swanky food court with a big dancefloor in the middle, hosting rich brats, playboys, celebs and wannabes. The music is pure Euro Med trash, and loud.

Sortie

Muallim Naci Sokak 141-142, Kuruçeşme (0212 327 8585). Bus 25T, 40. **Open** *Summer only* 6pm-5am daily. **Admission** summer 2007 prices not available at time of writing. **Credit** MC, V.

Sortie has successfully replicated the Bosphorus bling formula. Like many of the area's neighbouring clubs, It's a nightspot that is well known for the collection of pricey restaurants that surround the central bar area. Though big and brash in the summer, Sortie is closed in winter.

Indigo

Akarsu Sokak 1-5, Beyoğlu (0212 244 8567). **Open** 10pm-4am Tue-Thur, Sun; 11pm-5am Fri, Sat. **Admission** YTL25. **Credit** AmEx, MC, V. **Map** p248 N3.
Attracting a mix of local and foreign bands and DJs, Indigo is the definitive venue for fans of electronic music. Smack in the centre of Beyoğlu, it is also jammed every weekend. So be warned: if you don't like people pushing you around, rubbing up against you and treading on your toes, it might be best to steer clear. In the summer, Indigo moves to its other venue, Blanco.

Nu Club

Meşrutiyet Caddesi 145-147, Beyoğlu (0212 245 5810). **Open** *Oct-May* 11pm-4am Fri, Sat. Closed June-Sept. **Admission** free. **Credit** MC, V. **Map** p248 M3.

The Nu Pera complex is known for great modern Turkish cuisine (Lokanta) and amazing views (Nu Teras). Come winter, the action moves downstairs to this intimate basement club, where everyone knows everyone, and anyone who doesn't soon will. Top-notch local DJs like Yunus Güvenen and Barış Türker are complemented with a guest DJ from Paris once a month. Unpretentious and great fun.

Roxy

Arslan Yatağı Sokak 7, off Sıraselviler Caddesi, Beyoğlu (0212 249 1283, 245 6539/www.roxy. com.tr). **Open** 10pm-5am Fri, Sat. **Admission** YTL35. **Credit** MC, V. **Map** p249 O3.
Not exactly cutting edge, this established venue is a showcase for mainstream rock and pop bands. The place is usually packed with sociable, easy-going regulars, swigging bottled Sex On The Beach. Look out for the regular theme parties.

Arts & Entertainment

Performing Arts

A small scene, but some great venues.

Despite the best efforts of the reformist Turkish state in the early years of the republic, Western performing arts generally appeal only to a minority of Turks, drawn almost entirely from the westernised upper classes. The rest of the population prefer homegrown folk and traditional art.

However, a new trend for international festivals, the success of local talent at home and abroad, and regular visits by some exceptional foreign theatre companies, dance troupes, and musicians from around the world seem to be making a difference.

Tickets for concerts, opera and theatre (as well as sports events) can be bought online from Biletex (www.biletix.com).

Classical Music, Opera & Ballet

Turkey doesn't have a long tradition of western classical music. The Ottomans had their own **courtly music** (*see p190*), but it was banned by Atatürk, who considered it regressive and elitist. He promoted western-style music instead, which in the early years of the republic was generally put in the service of Turkish nationalism.

Today Istanbul is home to a respectable – if small – classical music, opera and ballet scene. Although the choice is pretty limited, Istanbul boasts some decent symphonic and chamber music orchestras, and also hosts the major annual **International Istanbul Music Festival** (*see p163*). And there is one area in which Istanbul can compete with any major city in the world, and that's the unique venues where concerts and events are held; these include ancient underground cisterns, Byzantine churches and Ottoman palaces.

The standard modern venues are also very good, if few; chief among them is the **Atatürk Cultural Centre (AKM)**, where the Istanbul Symphony Orchestra and the Istanbul State Opera and Ballet company perform, along with foreign companies. Other leading local companies are the Akbank Chamber Orchestra,

► For Turkish, rock and world music, *see pp183-191*.

Borusan Istanbul Philharmonic Orchestra, and the Cemal Reşit Rey Symphony Orchestra. Most venues and ensembles are sponsored by corporations, universities and banks, and there is some very limited public funding.

The performance season runs from November to May; summer is usually dead. Check the classical music section in the monthly *Time Out Istanbul* magazine to keep track of what's on.

Concert halls

Akbank Culture and Arts Centre
Akbank Kültür ve Sanat Merkezi (better known as Akbank Sanat)
Istiklal Caddesi 14-18, Beyoğlu (0212 252 3500).
Performances 11am (children's plays), 8pm Mon-Sat. **Credit** DC, MC, V. **Map** p249 O2.
Opened in 1992 and fully renovated in 2001, this arts centre in the heart of Beyoğlu boasts its own chamber music orchestra and a cosy, 135-seat, multi-purpose concert hall. The six-storey building hosts all sorts of cultural activities, from theatre to exhibitions to workshops.

Atatürk Cultural Centre (AKM)
Atatürk Kültür Merkezi
Taksim Square (box office 0212 251 5600, opera & ballet enquiries 243 2011/251 1023/ www.idobale.com). **Box office** 10am-6pm daily.
Performances usually 3.30pm, 8pm Mon-Sat.
Credit MC, V. **Map** p247 P2.
Istanbul's premier performing arts venue. Behind the brutalist 1960s design, the AKM is surprisingly grand and vibrant inside. It has two main concert halls, with a capacity of 1,300 and 520 each. Ticket prices are kept low through state subsidies. **Photo** p197.

Bosphorus University Albert Long Hall Cultural Centre
Boğaziçi Üniversitesi Albert Long Hall Kültür Merkezi
Boğaziçi Üniversitesi, Bebek (0212 358 1540). Bus 22, 22R, 25E, 30D, 40, 42T. **Performances** vary.
No credit cards.
The Albert Long Hall building is an iconic symbol of Bosphorus University, one of Turkey's oldest and most renowned. The building dates from 1891, and the 479-seat hall was recently restored to provide an important venue for classical music concerts by leading local and foreign musicians, orchestras and companies. The Bosphorus University campus is in Rumeli Hisarı, near the Fatih Sultan Mehmet Bridge.

Arts & Entertainment

Cemal Reşit Rey Concert Hall

Cemal Reşit Rey Konser Salonu
*Darülbedai Caddesi 1, Harbiye (0212 232 9830/
www.crrks.org). Bus 43, 46Ç, 46ÇYm 46H, 46KY.*
Box office 10.30am-7.30pm daily. **Performances**
8pm daily. Closed June-Sept. **Credit** MC, V.
This venue, the 860-seat home of the municipal CRR
Symphony Orchestra has a diverse programme,
including Turkish religious and traditional music.
Itl is a key venue for several festivals, including
October's International Mystic Music Festival,
December's International CRR Piano Festival,
January's International Istanbul Baroque Days,
April's International Dance Festival and the
International Youth Festival in May.

Enka Auditorium

Enka Oditoryumu
*Sadi Gülçelik Spor Sitesi, Istinye (0212 276 2214/
www.enkasanat.org). Metro Şişli* **Performances**
8pm Mon-Sat; 11.15am Sun. **Credit** MC, V.
A 600-seat modern auditorium with perfect
acoustics. It hosts a variety of events, including
drama, concerts, folk dancing and ballet, and
regularly plays host to the local metropolitan and
state music and dance companies.

Iş Art and Culture Centre

Iş Sanat Kültür Merkezi
*Iş Towers (Iş Kuleleri), Kule 1 17, Levent (0212
316 1083/www.iskultursanat.com.tr). Metro Levent.*
Box office 9am-6pm daily. **Performances** 8pm
most Sat & twice during the week; 3pm Sun. Closed
June-Oct. **Credit** DC, MC, V.
An 800-seat concert hall with a prestigious programme and an unconventional location: in the basement of the highest skyscraper in Levent. Classical
music concerts are performed by Turkish and
foreign symphony and chamber orchestras. Other
draws include recitals, jazz and world music. The
centre also hosts art exhibitions and plays, and
boasts a large shopping centre.

Lütfi Kırdar Convention and Exhibition Centre

Lütfi Kırdar Kongre ve Sergi Sarayı
*Darülbedayi Caddesi 60, Harbiye (0212 296 3055/
www.icec.org/en). Bus 43, 46Ç, 46ÇYM, 46H, 46KY.*
The convention centre houses one of the city's
biggest auditoriums, seating up to 3,500 people.
Although it is not a dedicated music venue, it is
actually one of Istanbul's top venues for classical
music, along with the AKM.

Flying the cultural flag at the **Atatürk Cultural Centre (AKM)**. *See p196.*

Theatre

Theatre in Istanbul is far more vital and varied than the classical music, opera or ballet scenes. More than 30 stages are scattered across the city, even in the remotest districts.

The **Istanbul State Company** offers a broad programme of classic and contemporary productions, including Turkish works, which are performed regularly in four theatres around the city. About 15 to 20 different plays are staged every month, including plays for children and musicals, at the **Atatürk Cultural Centre**.

The city, meanwhile, owns six theatres in Harbiye, Fatih, Gaziosmanpaşa and the Asian districts of Üsküdar and Kadıköy. For a healthy mix of classic and contemporary productions, check out the City Players (Kent Oyuncuları), starring Yıldız Kenter, at the **Kenter Theatre**, or the **Theatre Studio** (Tiyatro Stüdyosu) directed by Ahmet Levendoğlu. These are considered Istanbul's leading theatre companies.

Otherwise, the best chance for seeing good theatre is during the **International Istanbul Theatre Festival** (*see p163*) organised by the Istanbul Foundation for Culture and Arts (2KSV), and the **Location Theatre Festival** (Mekan Tiyatro Festivali), organised by the Istanbul Metropolitan Municipality. Both festivals feature performances from dozens of foreign companies, with performances staged in their original languages.

In most cases, though, performances will be in Turkish. Also be aware that many theatres are closed from June to September.

Kenter Theatre

Kenter Tiyatrosu
35 Halaskargazi Caddesi, Harbiye (0212 246 3589/www.kentoyunculari.com). Bus 43, 46Ç, 46ÇY, 46H, 46KY. **Box office** 11am-6pm daily. **Performances** 8pm Wed-Sat; 3pm Sun. **Credit** MC, V.
A private 450-seat theatre, founded in 1968 by Yıldız Kenter, one of Turkish theatre's leading actresses. Here, the City Players (Kent Oyuncuları) perform two or three plays a year, usually classics by the likes of Shakespeare and Chekhov. Performances usually star Yıldız Kenter and tend towards the old-fashioned and earnest.

Maya Sahnesi

Halep İş Hanı, 140/20 İstiklal Caddesi, Beyoğlu (0212 252 7452/www.mayasanat.com). **Box office** 9am-7pm daily. **Performances** 8.30pm Wed, Sat, Sun. **No credit cards**. **Map** p248 N3.
In the heart of buzzing Beyoğlu, this 100-seat venue has attracted a loyal following of young theatre buffs since it opened in 2001. It hosts several young theatre companies. There is also a cosy café complete with a piano, library and snack bar. Music performances, film screenings and workshops take place here, too.

Muhsin Ertuğrul Stage

Muhsin Ertuğrul Sahnesi
3 Darülbedai Caddesi, Harbiye (0212 240 7720/ www.ibst.gov.tr). Bus 43, 46Ç, 46ÇY, 46H, 46KY. **Box office** 11am-6pm Mon; 11am-8.30pm Tue-Sat; 10am-6pm Sun. **Performances** 8.30pm Tue-Sat; 3pm Sun. Closed May-Sept. **Credit** MC,V.
Founded in 1914 as a conservatory, then renamed the Istanbul Municipal Theatre in 1931, this venue had significant influence on the development of Turkish theatre. Its golden period occurred under the directorship of Muhsin Ertuğrul, who is regarded as the founder of modern Turkish theatre. Of the classic and contemporary plays performed here, half are by Turkish writers and include musicals and children's plays. Low ticket prices ensure packed houses. Booking is recommended at weekends.

Ses-1885 Ortaoyuncular Theatre

Ses-1885 Ortaoyuncular Tiyatrosu
İstiklal Caddesi 140/90, Beyoğlu (0212 251 1865/ www.ortaoyuncular.com). **Box office** 11am-8.30pm daily. **Performances** 8pm Thur-Sat; 3pm Sun. Closed June-Sept. **Credit** MC, V. **Map** p248 N3.
Istanbul's oldest functioning theatre and one of its most beautiful. The wooden hall, with 554 seats on two floors, plus boxes and a balcony, is dripping in nostalgia. The Ses-1885 usually hosts performances by the Ortaoyuncular Company under Ferhan Şensoy, who trained in France in the famous Magic Circus band of Jérôme Savary. The company's productions are extremely popular. *Ferhangi Şeyler*, a solo act by Şensoy and the company's biggest hit, has been performed more than 1,500 times.

Taksim Stage

Taksim Sahnesi
Sıraselviler Caddesi 39, Taksim (0212 249 6944/ www.istdt.gov.tr). **Box office** 10am-8pm daily. **Performances** 8pm Mon-Fri; 3pm, 8pm Sat; 3pm Sun. **Credit** MC, V. **Map** p249 O3.
This intimate 520-seat hall owned by the Turkish Ministry of Cultural Affairs is home to the Istanbul State Theatre. Around four different plays are put on every month, each for one-week runs. Productions tend to be bit po-faced.

Tiyatro Pera

Pera Theatre
Billurcu Çıkmazı 14, Sıraselviler Caddesi, Taksim. (0212 245 4460). **Performances** 8pm Fri, Sat; 6.30pm Sun. **Credit** AmEx, MC, V.
The Pera Theatre is an ambitious project realised by Turkish actor/director/writer Nesrin Kazankaya. It's a theatre company and a drama school rolled into one. All the actors go through a six-year training programme before joining the company. Good news for foreigners: the company performs works in both English and Turkish.

Sport & Fitness

Football is a passion; everything else is a pastime.

Ask most Istanbullus about sport and they'll tell you about football. Turks are dedicated to the game, and Istanbul teams can rely on fervent support from armies of fans, whose fearsome reputation may have softened in recent years (*see p200* **Putting the boot in**). But reports that Turkish football had arrived as a force on the world stage following the national team's 2002 World Cup semi-final placing have proved to be exaggerated.

In other sports, Turks have only made their mark at world-class level in weightlifting and Greco-Roman wrestling, but in recent years, Turkish basketball teams have also begun making a name in the international arena.

Failed bids to host the Olympics in 2000, 2004, 2008 and 2012 haven't quite soured the city on the project. Being shortlisted a couple of times means Istanbul could still be in with a chance some day. In any case, revenue from state lotteries, horse racing and one per cent of the city budget has furnished the city with a spectacular 80,000-seat Olympic Stadium at Ikitelli, near the airport, designed by the architects of the Stade de France in Paris. And the authorities are investing billions of lira on other sports projects.

Spectator sports

All sporting events and fixtures are listed in the local press and at the online ticketing agency Biletix *(see above)*.

Football

The game has come a long way since the days when the only concern before international fixtures was the number of goals the Turkish team would concede. Istanbul is home to Turkey's three biggest clubs: Galatasaray, Beşiktaş and Fenerbahçe. The Black Sea side Trabzonspor supposedly completes the 'big four,' but has struggled to keep up in recent years. The domestic league runs from August to May and has a lopsided feel, as little clubs line up for a battering from the Istanbul heavyweights. For a really intense atmosphere, try to catch one of the Istanbul derbies.

To satisfy the TV companies, matches are staggered over the whole weekend, from Friday evening to Sunday evening. The fixture list is normally organised so that matches involving Istanbul teams don't coincide.

Tickets usually go on sale two or three days before a match, although for all but the biggest games it is surprisingly easy to pick them up at the stadium on the day. For matches involving the big three, tickets can also be bought in advance via booking agency Biletix (www.biletix.com).

Beşiktaş

İnönü Stadium, Dolmabahçe Caddesi, Beşiktaş (0212 236 7202/227 8780/www.bjk.com.tr). **Tickets** League games YTL25-YTL200. **No credit cards. Map** p247 R1/2.
National league champions in 2002-03 and Turkish Cup winners in 2006, the Beşiktaş 'Black Eagles' tend to play solid, unflamboyant football, though the team have led the trend for importing foreign coaches, including Gordon Milne, Christoph Daum and Mirceau Lucescu as well as the current coach, Jean Tigana. The club's İnönü Stadium is the city's most conveniently located, just uphill from Dolmabahçe Palace.

Fenerbahçe

Şükrü Saraçoğlu Stadium, Kadıköy (0216 449 5667/www.fenerbahce.org). Ferry from Eminönü or Karaköy to Kadıköy, then 10B bus. **Tickets** League games YTL27.50-YTL225. **No credit cards. Map** p251 Y8.
Despite winning a record number of Turkish league championships and having the deepest pockets of any Turkish team, Fener's European record is weak. Atatürk's favourite team, Fenerbahçe has historic links with the Turkish army, despite its decidedly unmilitary nickname –'the Canaries'. The home stadium is in the wealthy suburb of Fenerbahçe, on the Asian side.

Galatasaray

Atatürk Olimpiyat Stadium, Ikitelli (0212 413 3000/ www.galatasaray.org). **Tickets** League games YTL13-YTL160. **No credit cards.**
Easily Turkey's most famous club, Galatasaray boasts a string of European successes, crowned by victory over Arsenal in the UEFA Cup final in 2000. Known to fans as 'Cim Bom' for reasons no-one can explain, Galatasaray see themselves as the aristocracy of Turkish football. This superiority complex was somewhat undermined by their decrepit stadium, the hell pit that was the Ali Sami Yen, until the club moved to the new Olympic Stadium in Ikitelli in 2003. Shuttles transfer fans from Taksim Square and Eminönü and Topkapı bus stations.

Putting the boot in

Players and officials have overtaken fans in turning Turkish football grounds into 'hell' for visiting foreign teams.

What a difference a night makes. With everyone expecting outright warfare in Istanbul when England came to town for a crucial European Championship game against Turkey in October 2003, the only trouble was not on the terraces or in town, but on the pitch itself. A disciplined performance by the visitors in the face of severe provocation – some players were even punched in the tunnel at half-time – saw England earn a draw, and even the respect of the Turkish fans. The handful of English supporters who outsmarted a ticket ban and braved the hostile atmosphere, standing silent amid the usual 'Welcome to Hell' banners in the ground, spoke of being well treated when it became clear they were not Turkish turncoats.

Turkey's football grounds will always be intimidating, partly because of their relatively small size and intimacy, and partly because of supporters' traditions here. Fans turn up hours before kick-off to prepare an atmosphere with drums, smoke bombs and torches. During the warm-up, players will run towards the home fans, punch the air and leap while their names are chanted, a routine known as the *buraya*. That hasn't changed.

But if anything, Istanbul has become a lucky hunting ground for English teams. First, Liverpool won the European Cup in the most memorable of circumstances in 2005, at Istanbul's 80,000-seat Olympic stadium. True, that was against an Italian team, and far from the city centre, but Istanbul was filled with pissed, boisterous Scousers for days – and there were no incidents. In October 2006, Tottenham went to Beşiktaş, whose ground is within walking distance of Taksim Square – and not only won, but were applauded at the end. The European football authorities have just awarded Istanbul the right to stage another prestigious final, the UEFA Cup final, in 2009.

So where is the 'hell' of lore? Has Turkish football gone soft? Not as far as the players and officials are concerned. The national side may not have made a major final since that fateful night in 2003, but it has not been for want of trying – at all costs. The next crunch match came in 2005 for a place in the 2006 World Cup in Germany, home to millions of Turks. Qualification, against Switzerland, was essential – at any price. It never came. As the victorious Swiss players were leaving the pitch after another fiery night in Istanbul,

---

Basketball

While international soccer success has tended to eclipse Turkey's long-running love affair with basketball, the game still boasts a large fan base. A handful of Turkish-born players have moved on to the NBA, and lately Mehmet Okur, an Efes Pilsen alumnus, has emerged as a genuine star with the Utah Jazz. Though Okur and Hidayet Türkoğlu, the first Turk in the NBA, were both missing from the 2006 World Championships, Turkey's '12 Giant Men' (as the national team is fondly known) still managed a respectable sixth place showing.

Turkey's basketball season lasts roughly from October to June, with clubs playing at least twice a week, usually in the afternoon or early evening. Tickets for all but the biggest games are readily available on the day, or can be bought in advance. Information on games and fixtures is available on the Turkish Basketball Federation website (www.tbf.org.tr).

Beşiktaş ColaTurka

BJK Akatlar Spor ve Kültür Kompleksi
Gazeteciler Sitesi Mayadrom Arkası, Beşiktaş (0212 283 66 01/www.bjk.com.tr). Bus 105.
Tickets YTL6-YTL8. **No credit cards.**
Lagging behind their footballing colleagues, Beşiktaş haven't won the basketball championship since 1975.

Efes Pilsen

Abdi İpekçi Spor Salonu
Onuncu Y5l Caddesi, Zeytinburnu (0212 665 8647/ www.efesbasket.org). Bus 93C, 93M, 93T. **Tickets** YTL5-YTL17. **No credit cards.**
Founded in 1976, Efes Pilsen have won the Turkish title 12 times. In 1996, they scored their biggest success when they bagged the European Korac Cup.

Fenerbahçe-Ülker

Fenerbahçe Spor Kulübüğ Tesisleri
Dereağzı Tesisleri, Basketbol Şubesi, Kızıltoprak (0216 347 8438). Ferry from Eminönü or Karaköy to Kadıköy, and then 10B bus. **Tickets** YTL7.50-YTL15, from Biletex (*see p199*).

200 Time Out Istanbul

they were attacked by Turkish players and officials; fighting broke out; and one player, Stephane Grichting, was kicked so hard in the groin it severed his urinary canal.

Punishment from world body FIFA was swift and severe. Turkey were fined YTL90,000 and banned from playing at home for six matches, later reduced to three. Four Turkish players received serious individual bans. Swiss daily *Le Matin* later uncovered a meeting three days before the match between the Turkish team manager Fatih Terem, FA officials, police chiefs and leaders of hardcore fan groups. The topic of conversation? How to unnerve and intimidate the Swiss team upon their arrival in Istanbul.

Currently the Turks face old rivals Greece, among others, to qualify for the 2008 European Championships; until quite recently the two countries were deliberately kept apart when it came to group draws. The finals are due to take place in Switzerland.

Fenerbahçe last won the national championship way back in 1991. In 2006, they merged with Ülkerspor and pilfered the stronger squad's roster in a bid to unseat perennial champions Efes Pilsen. The address above is the training ground; games are played elsewhere, including the Abdi İpekçi Spor Salonu (*see p200*).

Galatasaray CafeCrown

Galatasaray Spor Kulübü
Metin Oktay Tesisleri, Basketbol Şubesi, Florya (0212 574 2901/www.galatasaray.org). Bus E-52. **Tickets** YTL5-YTL 15. **No credit cards.**
While both the men's and women's teams once topped their respective Istanbul leagues, neither is the team it once was. Games take place at Ahmet Cömert Spor Salonu in Ataköy (Ataköy 4. Kısım Sonu, Olimpiyatevi Yanı).

Active sports

With sparse facilities to choose from and precious little leisure time, few Turks actively participate in any sports other than the odd football match played on one of the city's many five-a-side pitches. The Kadıköy and Bakırköy municipalities have established bicycle paths along coastal roads, which are usually filled with joggers. Exercise in Istanbul is otherwise an expensive habit confined to the well-heeled.

Adventure sports

Recent Ministry of Tourism efforts to pitch Turkey as an ideal destination for adventure enthusiasts have not necessarily worked abroad, but have at least succeeded in getting more locals interested in sport. Clubs and companies catering to the recent demand for extreme sports have mushroomed.

Adrenalin

Büyük Beşiktaş Çarşısı 19, off Ortabahçe Caddesi, Beşiktaş (0212 260 6002/www.adrenalin.com.tr). Bus 22E, 28, 28T, 30A, 30M. **Open** 10am-8pm Mon-Sat. **Credit** MC, V.

Poolside pleasures at the **Cirağan Palace Hotel Kempinski**. *See p203.*

Adrenalin offers training in outdoor adventure sports, prefaced by classroom sessions on surviving the experience. Activities run the gamut from weekends camping in the Istanbul suburbs to mountain-climbing courses. Trainers all speak English, which is useful when scaling vertical cliffs.

Adre-X Extreme Organisation

Sahra Cedid Mahallesi, Mengi Sokak 17/3, Kozyatağı (0216 386 3335/www.adre-x.com). Bus 129T. **Open** 9am-8pm Mon-Fri; noon-6pm Sun. **Credit** V, MC.

This organisation provides outdoors training and adventure-sport weekends aimed principally at adrenaline-hungry business people. Activities include low- and high-rope systems, navigation and bungee jumping. English is spoken.
Other locations: Bağdat Caddesi 200-3, Selamiçeşme (0216 368 7864).

DSM Doğa

Kayışdağı Caddesi 17, second floor, Özplaza, İçerenköy (0216 469 4858/www.dsm.com.tr). Ferry from Eminönü or Karaköy to Kadıköy, then bus 10B. **Open** 9am-6pm Mon-Sat. **Credit** MC, V

Adventure sports centre organising group activities that include rafting, mountain climbing, caving, camping, trekking and paragliding, all under the guidance of expert trainers. English is spoken.

Gezici YAK

Selçuk Apt, Recep Paşa Caddesi 14/10, off Cumhuriyet Caddesi, Taksim (0212 238 5107/ www.geziciyak.com). **Open** 9am-7.30pm Mon-Sat. 11am-4pm Sun. **Credit** MC, V. **Map** p247 P1.

Organises day treks in the local area and river and rafting trips further afield. The company also organises scuba diving trips and training, for which a doctor's certificate is required. English is spoken.

Billiards

Sleazy snooker saloons, long a staple of the
Beyoğlu scene, have recently got competition
from smart, American-style pool halls. While
the former remain smoke-filled, men-only
affairs, the latter are popular with both male
and female students.

Ağa Bilardo Salonu

*Ağa Hamamı Caddesi 17/2, Cihangir, Beyoğlu
(0212 251 7469).* **Open** noon-midnight daily.
Rates YTL6.50/hr pool; YTL8/hr snooker.
No credit cards. Map p249 O3.
A spacious hall with two full-sized snooker tables,
three proper pool tables and another three that are
slightly undersized. For a change of pace, there are
also three table tennis tables. Under-18s must be
accompanied by a parent.

Omayra Billiards & Internet Café

*Aznavur Pasajı, İstiklal Caddesi 212, Galatasaray,
Beyoğlu (0212 244 3002).* **Open** 10am-midnight
daily. **Rates** YTL10/hr. **Credit** MC, V.
Map p248 N3.
On the third floor above the dippy hippy stalls of
Aznavur Pasajı, wannabe pool sharks circle six bil-
liard tables. There's also internet access and a café.

Swimming

The city's few Olympic-size pools are located in
university campuses or members-only sports
complexes, but you can get a day pass or
membership at several hotels. Call in advance,
as terms and conditions change frequently.

Çırağan Palace Hotel Kempinski

*Çırağan Caddesi 32, Beşiktaş (0212 258 3377/
www.ciraganpalace.com). Bus DT1, DT2.* **Open**
7am-11pm daily. **Rates** *Day pass* $95 Mon-Fri; $145
Sat, Sun. 40% discount under-12s; free under-6s.
Credit AmEx, DC, MC, V.
Right on the banks of the Bosphorus, the Çırağan's
33m-long (108ft) outdoor pool boasts the most spectacular setting in Istanbul. The indoor pool is a third
of the size, but additional features include a jacuzzi,
sauna, steam and fitness rooms. **Photo** *p202.*

Euro Plaza Health Club

*Turlubuşi Bulvarı 292, Tepebaşı (0212 254 5900/
www.hoteleuroplaza.com).* **Open** *Indoor pool* 10am-
10pm daily. *Outdoor pool* 10am-7pm daily. **Rates**
Day pass YTL20 Mon-Fri; YTL25 Sat, Sun. Half price
under 12s; free under 6s. **Credit** MC, V.
What the pool lacks in size – it's only 10m (33ft)
long– it makes up for with great views across the
water to Sultanahmet. It's also extremely cheap.

Hilton Istanbul

*Cumhuriyet Caddesi, Harbiye (0212 315 6000/
www.hilton.com).* **Open** *Outdoor pool* 7am-6pm
daily. *Indoor pool* 7am-10pm daily. **Rates** YTL60

Mon-Fri; YTL95 Sat, Sun. Half price under-12s; free
under-6s. **Credit** AmEx, MC, V. **Map** p247 P1.
The outdoor pool is approximately half Olympic
size, while the indoor pool is 18m (60ft) long. The
price includes use of all the health club facilities.
After 3pm, the price of a day pass drops to YTL30
on weekdays and YTL60 on weekends.

Beaches

Although Istanbul is surrounded by water and
the municipality has sponsored numerous high-
profile clean-up campaigns, swimming within
city limits is still a dodgy proposition. The
upper Bosphorus, near Sarıyer, is cleaner but
subject to treacherous currents.

Solar Beach & Party

*Eski Turban Yolu 4, Kilyos (0212 201 2139/
www.solarbeach.net).*
In addition to jet skiing, bungee jumping and tram-
polining during the day, Solar Beach hosts rave parties most summer weekends come nightfall. In past
years shuttle buses have transferred revellers from
Taksim Square to the beach; at the time of writing
it was uncertain who would be running the show for
summer 2007 or 2008.

Fitness

Weightlifting and bodybuilding are beloved of
Turkish men of all ages and income brackets.
Cheaper gyms and fitness centres tend to be
dominated by men, but women should find the
places listed below hassle-free, because they're
expensive enough to keep out the oglers. Most
big hotels also have fitness centres.

Flash Gym

*4th floor, Aznavur Pasajı, İstiklal Caddesi 212,
Beyoğlu (0212 249 5347).* **Open** 10am-10pm Mon-
Fri; 10am-9pm Sat; 1-7pm Sun. **Rates** *Day pass*
YTL15. *Monthly membership* YTL100 daily use;
YTL90 use 3 days/wk. **Credit** MC, V (YTL10
charge). **Map** p248 N3.
You get what you pay for and this is one of the
cheapest gyms in town. It's not exactly fragrant, due
to the lack of air-conditioning and sponge-effect carpet everywhere. Still, it's an economical place to get
in shape, and some of the staff speak English.

Marmara Gym

*The Marmara Hotel, Taksim Square (0212 251
4696/www.themarmarahotels.com).* **Open** 7am-
9.45pm daily. **Rates** *Day pass* YTL40 gym only,
YTL60 all facilities. *Monthly membership* YTL360
gym only, YTL480 all facilities. **Credit** AmEx, MC,
V. **Map** p249 P2.
This spacious, spotless gym has hi-tech equipment,
English-speaking trainers and panoramic views
over Taksim Square, which provide a welcome dis-
traction from the treadmill.

Arts & Entertainment

Clean water. It's the most basic human necessity. Yet one third of all poverty related deaths are caused by drinking dirty water. Saying *I'm in* means you're part of a growing movement that's fighting the injustice of poverty. Your £8 a month can help bring safe water to some of the world's poorest people. We can do this. We *can* end poverty. Are you in?

shouldn't everyone get clean water? I don't think that's too much to ask for

Let's end poverty together.
Text 'WATER' and your name to 87099 to give £8 a month.

Standard text rates apply. Registered charity No.202918

oxfam.org.uk

I'm in

Ⓧ **Oxfam**

Sarite Morales, Greenwich

Trips out of Town

The Princes' islands.

The Upper Bosphorus

Cruising between continents.

For centuries, the narrow waterway that separates Europe and Asia and snakes through the city's heart was Istanbul's *raison d'etre*. A bustling trade route for Vikings, Indians, Franks, Turkmens, Arabs, Romans, Greeks, Egyptians and Persians, the Bosphorus was essentially the city's main drag. Consequently, Istanbul has always presented its best face to the Bosphorus. The twisting shoreline is punctuated by imperial palaces, diplomatic hideaways and gorgeous old Ottoman *yalıs* (waterfront mansions), all ageing gracefully.

A cruise up the Bosphorus is as crucial to any Istanbul experience as a visit to Haghia Sophia or haggling in the Grand Bazaar.

The Bosphorus cruise

The standard Bosphorus cruise takes six hours and costs all of YTL7.50. Ferries depart daily all year round from Eminönü's Boğaz Hattı dock, 100 metres east of the Galata Bridge. Buy your tickets at the window labelled Eminönü-Kavaklar Boğaziçi Özel Gezi Seferleri (Eminönü-Kavaklar Bosphorus Special Tourist Excursions). Cruises depart at 10.30am and 1.30pm, with an extra service at noon from June to September. In summer and at weekends, board the boat at least 30 minutes before departure if you want to get a seat.

From Eminönü, the first stop is Beşiktaş near Dolmabahçe Palace. The ferry then tacks back and forth between the European and Asian shores, stopping at several Bosphorous villages along the way: notably Kanlıca, Yeniköy, Sarıyer, Rumeli Kavağı and Anadolu Kavağı. You can get off wherever you like, but you will have to make your own way onwards or back into town. Most first-timers stay on board until Anadolu Kavağı, where there's enough time for lunch at one of the fish restaurants before reboarding the ferry, which then makes a beeline back to Beşiktaş and Eminönü, with no other stops en route.

From June to September, a Moonlight Trip (YTL10) leaves Eminönü at 7.15pm or Ortaköy at 7.40pm. The ferry arrives at Anadolu Kavagi at 8.50pm, and departs at 10pm, returning to Beşiktaş at 11.05pm and Eminonu at 11.30pm. For further information call 0212 444 44 36 or check www.ido.com.tr and click on Special Bosphorus Trip in the timetable section.

Numerous private operators run shorter boat trips as well. These typically only go halfway up the Bosphorus, as far as Rumeli Hisarı, where passengers have an hour for lunch before the boat returns to Eminönü. There are no stops en route. Boats depart from Eminönü roughly every half hour between 10.30am and 6pm (4pm October to April). Touts who roam the wharfs sell tickets for YTL10-YTL15, but it's worth bargaining.

KANLICA

The first major sights – and, indeed, the last if you opt for the shorter cruise – are the twin fortresses of **Rumeli Hisarı** (*see p105*) and **Anadolu Hisarı**, looming on opposite shores of the Bosphorus.

Just before the second great suspension bridge, the 1,096-metre **Fatih Mehmet Bridge**, a battered, barn-like structure hangs over the water on the Asian side. This is the historic **Amcazade Hüseyin Paşa Yalısı**, Istanbul's oldest waterfront mansion. Built in 1699, its scandalous state of disrepair is nothing new: when French writer and long-time local resident Pierre Loti visited in 1910, he pleaded, 'Of all the *yalıs* on the Bosphorus, you must save the Amcazade Yalı'.

First stop on the standard Bosphorus cruise is **Kanlıca** on the Asian Shore, a lovely village dotted with picturesque mansions and backed by the lush Mihribad Forest Preserve. But Kanlıca's main claim to fame is bacterial: since the 17th century, it has been celebrated for its rich yoghurt, which hawkers bring on board to flog. It is worth the 20-minute walk uphill to visit **Khedive's Villa** (Hıdiv Kasrı), a former summer residence of the 19th-century rulers of Egypt. This architectural gem is beautifully restored and has a restaurant and tea garden with magnificent views. The restaurant serves Ottoman and Turkish cuisine – without alcohol. Weekend brunch will set you back YTL17; a buffet lunch or dinner costs YTL27.50. Kanlıca is linked by regular ferries to Arnavutköy and Bebek on the European shore.

On departing Kanlıca, the ferry noses back towards Europe. Shortly after Istinye Bay is the stunning **Ahmet Atıf Paşa Yalı**, a white neo-baroque fantasy of turrets and Ottoman roofs, created by Italian architect Alexandre Villaury for the original proprietor of the Pera Palas hotel (*see p40*).

Black Sea

Kumköy

Kilyos

Kısırkaya

Gümüşdere

Uskumruköy

Zekeriyaköy

Ottoman Fort ■
Rumeli Lighthouse ■
Rumeli Feneri

0
0   2 miles
© Copyright Time Out Group 2007

↑ To Şile

Anadolufeneri

Poyaz

E U R O P E

Altınkum

**Rumeli
Kavağı**

Bahçeköy

Belgrad
Forest

Sarıyer

■ Yoros Castle

**Anadolu
Kavağı**

Sadberk Hanım
Museum ■

Büyükdere

● Akbaba

Seyhan Deresi

British Summer Embassy ■
Tarabya   ■ Italian Summer Embassy
German Summer Embassy ■
Huber Mansion ■
Austrian Summer Embassy ■
Yeniköy

● Elmalı

Beykoz

Ayazağa

Ahmet Atıf Paşa Yalı ■

Sakıp Sabancı Museum ■
Emirgan   ● **Kanlıca**

Karıthane

Amcazade
Hüseyin Paşa
Yalı ■

● Çavuşbaşı

Rumeli Hisarı

Anadolu Hisarı

E 80

Bebek

Arnavutköy

A S I A

Küçüksu D.

E 80

Ortaköy
Beşiktaş   Dolmabahçe
Palace

Çengelköy

Cemke

Beyoğlu

Bosphorus (Boğaziçi)

Üsküdar

Yukarıdudullu

Eminönü
Sultanahmet

Ümraniye

Kurbağalı D.

Rumeli Feneri: a working fishing village, with a past steeped in mythology. *See p210.*

YENIKOY

The ferry then pulls in at **Yeniköy**. As the Ottoman Empire deteriorated in the early 19th century, increasingly desperate rulers used lavish gifts of land as a way of securing the support of foreign embassies in Istanbul. Yeniköy was considered choice real estate, and the waterfront is lined with the greatest concentration of restored Bosphorus mansions, several of which remain the summer residences of the city's consulates.

Just south of the landing is the boxy, white shuttered **Sait Halim Paşa**, also known as the Pink Lion Mansion because of the two stone lions on the quay. Sait Halim was grand vizier under Sultan Abdül Hamit in the dying days of the empire. The hapless Halim ended up taking much of the rap for the empire's disastrous decision to fight on Germany's side in World War I. Adding fatal injury to insult, he was shot dead by an Armenian extremist soon after the war. North of the landing is another Bosphorus landmark, the **Twin Yalı**, a symmetrical semi-detached, whose art nouveau scrollings mark it out as a work by Raimondo D'Aronco.

As the ferry departs Yeniköy it passes a string of rambling European summer embassies, including a vast pink edifice, partially screened by trees, belonging to Austria. About a mile north, spires and gables mark out the fantastic **Huber Mansion**, another D'Aronco design. The Hubers made

a vast fortune flogging Mauser rifles to the Ottoman government in the dying days of the empire. This residence was renowned for their lavish parties, earning them regular appearances in the late-19th-century versions of *Hello!* magazine. It is now the official Istanbul residence of the Turkish president. The forested slopes surrounding both these mansions give an idea of how most of the Bosphorus shoreline looked not so long ago.

Several more summer embassies follow in quick succession. With its distinctive bell tower, Germany's looks rather like a Black Forest town hall. Though dilapidated, the Italian Embassy remains supremely elegant. And the British ambassador's summer retreat is a small cottage set in luxuriant gardens.

SARIYER

The shoreline recedes to accommodate Büyükdere Bay, where the Bosphorus is at its widest (3.5 kilometres, or just under two miles). As the ferry approaches land, you will see a curious, flat-fronted building distinguished by bold yellow-and-white cross-hatching; this houses the **Sadberk Hanım Museum**, stuffed with Ottoman costumes, archaeological and ethnographic artefacts, and old tiles.

The ferry's next port of call is **Sarıyer**, beside the turreted **Naval Officers' Club**. Built in 1911, it bears the seal of Sultan Mehmet V Reşat. It is now a restaurant and social club for naval officers and their families.

Sarıyer, the largest village on the Upper Bosphorus, is one of Greater Istanbul's most conservative suburbs. As recently as 1995, a local woman was stoned to death here on suspicion of being a prostitute. For the morally unblemished, it is a lovely place to wander (if you disembark here, you can catch bus 25E back to Kabataş). There's a fine old fish market just north of the ferry landing, plus several good seafood restaurants.

On Sular Caddesi *dolmuş* depart for the next waterside village, Rumeli Kavağı. En route they pass the **burial place of Telli Baba**, a mystic Muslim saint revered by local singletons. Would-be brides come to pray at the saint's tomb and take away a charmed piece of golden wire, apparently guaranteed to secure them a husband. Newlyweds traditionally return on their wedding day to reattach the wire to the saint's tomb and pay homage to Telli Baba's matchmaking skills. On Saturday and Sunday afternoons, there are usually major traffic jams as convoys of husband-seekers pile up along the narrow road beside the Bosphorus.

RUMELI AND ANADOLU KAVAĞI

Rumeli Kavağı is a sleepy little place – no more than a string of houses and restaurants clustered around the ferry landing and the coastal road. From here, the road runs north up the Bosphorus, passing dozens of restaurants set into the cliffs and a few small, sandy private beaches, which usually charge entrance fees of around YTL3 YTL6.

Just before the coastal road ends abruptly at the gates of an army base is **Altınkum**, the best of the area's beaches, accessible via a narrow footpath between the trees. There is a restaurant serving meze and cold beer. The water is marked off by a line of buoys – stick within this line if you're swimming, as the Bosphorus is swept by strong currents further from the shore.

From Sarıyer, a couple of metres left of IDO harbour, boats depart between 8am and 1pm for Büyük Liman and Menekşe beaches, returning to Sarıyer between 5pm and 7pm. The round trip costs YTL6, including the entrance fee for the beaches. Menekşe beach is conservative: one day a week, it's ladies only.

The last stop for the ferry cruise is **Anadolu Kavağı** on the Asian Shore, which is almost opposite Rumeli Kavağı. Passengers have time to explore the village and eat in one of the many fish restaurants, which cater exclusively to passing tourist trade.

Alternatively, clamber up to **Yoros Castle**, which looms on the headland north of the village, offering commanding views of the Black Sea. Originally, the site of a temple to

Zeus, where ancient Greek sailors would make a sacrifice to ensure safe passage through the straits, the present fortress was built by the Byzantines, occupied by the Genoese in the mid 14th century, until it was seized by the Turks, who fortified the battlements. The castle lay abandoned until it was opened to the public in the 1980s. Descending from the castle, take the steep path across the heath, which leads to a tea house with half a dozen rickety tables and amazing views.

Khedive's Villa

Hıdiv Kasrı
Çubuklu Yolu 32, Kanlıca (0216 444 6644/ www.beltur.com.tr). **Open** 9am-10pm daily. **Admission** free.

Sadberk Hanım Museum

Sadberk Hanım Müzesi
Piyasa Caddesi 27-29, Büyükdere (0212 242 38 1 www.sadberkhanimmuzesi.org.tr). **Open** 10a 5pm Mon, Tue, Fri-Sun. **Admission** YTL5 **No credit cards.**

Belgrad Forest

Stretching over the hills and valleys north-east of the city, Belgrad Forest is popular with summer picnickers, cyclists and joggers. All leafy glades and oak, pine, plane and beech trees, the place has a distinctly Balkan feel. It is actually named after the Serbian residents entrusted by Süleyman the Magnificent with guarding the forest reservoirs that served as the city's water supply. Under the Byzantines and Ottomans, even today, you'll come across the remains of the reservoirs and aqueducts. The Serbs were booted out in the 1890s by the paranoid sultan Abdülhamit II, who suspected they were poisoning the water.

In centuries past, the wealthy European residents of Istanbul would retreat to Belgrad Village in summer to escape the heat and bouts of pestilence. In 1771, Lady Mary Wortley Montagu described the village as an Arcadian idyll, whose inhabitants would meet every night 'to sing and dance, the beauty and dress of the women exactly resembling the ancient nymphs'. All that's left of Belgrad village are a few bumps in the forest floor, hidden near one of the main picnic areas by **Büyük Bend** reservoir, one of the oldest parts of the Byzantine water system.

Following Mahmut II's purge of the Janissary corps in 1826 (*see p23*), those who escaped the massacre fled into the forest, where they took up traditional woodland pursuits such as shooting the sultan's deer and ambushing local traders. The sultan's radical response was to set the whole forest on fire.

Also worth visiting is the **Long Aqueduct**, on the road to Kısırmandıra, another work by Mimar Sinan (*see p21* **The mosque maker**), built for Süleyman the Magnificent in 1563. The stream it crosses is the Kağıthane Suyu, which eventually flows into the Golden Horn.

Getting there

From Kabataş take the 25E bus (or the 40 from Taksim) to Büyükdere. Take a *dolmuş* for Bahçeköy, on the east side of the forest, a one-mile (1.5 kilometre) walk to Büyük Bend.

The Black Sea coast

North of the twin landmarks of Rumeli Kavağı and Anadolu Kavağı, the mouth of the Bosphorus widens to meet the **Black Sea** (Karadeniz). Much of the coast is an off-limits military zone, but there are small enclaves of civilian life. On the European side, there's the fishing port of **Rumeli Feneri** and **Kilyos**, one of Istanbul's most popular beach resorts, mirrored on the Asian side by the resort of Şile.

Rumeli Feneri

Rumeli Feneri means 'European Lighthouse'. Perched atop sheer cliffs overlooking the entrance to the Bosphorus, the lighthouse was built by the British during the Crimean War. But the namesake village is most famous for the ancient Symplegades or 'clashing rocks' – two large humps at the end of the L-shaped harbour. In ancient mythology, these rocks were regarded as living creatures that would dash out to crash into passing boats. One such vessel was Jason's *Argo*, which managed to make it through the straits to the Black Sea, thanks to a neat trick with a pigeon and a helping hand from the goddess Athena.

These days, Rumeli Feneri is a working fishing village – a laid-back Sunday lunch venue for the few Istanbullus who have discovered it. On the Black Sea side of town is an **Ottoman fort**, once the area's main customs clearing house. Also of archaeological interest is the stone altar on top of the Symplegade closest to shore, which was used to make sacrifices to the sea god, Poseidon, and to light fires to warn passing ships. You can scale the rocks as long as you've got walking shoes and a head for heights.

One of the most exclusive spots on Istanbul's Black Sea coast, the **Golden Beach Club** at Rumeli Feneri, boasts an attractive beach and endless facilities including a restaurant, beach bar, beach volleyball, cycling tracks, climbing wall, mini golf, paintball, and sea-trampoline.

If you make a reservation one day in advance, you can be picked up from Sarıyer.

Golden Beach Club

Marmaracık Bay, Rumeli Feneri (0212 325 5583/ www.goldenbeachclub.net). **Admission** YTL15 Mon-Fri; YTL25 Sat, Sun, incl lounger & umbrella.

Kilyos and Demirciköy

Kilyos's long sandy beaches – **Nonstop Beach** (0212 201 2305,www.nonstopbeach.com, admission YTL10, YTL15 with lounger & umbrella) and **Solar Beach** (0212 201 2139, admission YTL15, including lounger & umbrella) – have been badly scarred by over-development. The glut of awfully tacky bars are full of disappointed-looking Russian package tourists. Tragically, this formula is being repeated all along the Black Sea coast, which isn't being damaged so much as devoured.

Both these beaches become party venues during the summer nights, when raves, concerts, and other special events draw crowds eager to escape the hot and sticky city. Solar beach is the more upmarket of the two, with lifeguards, a beachfront branch of Tommy Hilfiger, and a food court with a Köşebaşı Express serving upmarket kebabs.

People's Beach (admission YTL5) is the most downmarket of Kilyos's options. The cost of admission includes use of the shower and a locker, but you have to bring your own lounger and umbrella. **Dalia Beach** (0212 204 0368, www.clubdalia.com, admission YTL20, YL25 weekends, including lounger & umbrella) at Demirciköy, two kilometres from Kilyos, is much quieter and has a small fish restaurant. Access is by taxi (YTL3-YTL5); or you can take the 151 bus from Sarıyer.

Getting there

Kilyos is ten miles (15 km) north of Sarıyer, where regular dolmuş depart from Sular Caddesi (the dolmuş rank is just before you arrive at Sarıyer bus terminal, opposite the old municipality building). The journey takes half an hour and costs YTL1.50. The last dolmuş back to Sarıyer from Kilyos leaves about 8pm.

Rumeli Feneri can be reached by bus or taxi (around YTL15) from Sarıyer.

Buses 150 (Rumeli Feneri), 151 (Kilyos/ Demirciköy) and 152 (Kısırkaya) depart from Sarıyer every 15 minutes during summer weekends and every 20 minutes on weekdays. In winter, buses depart every 45 minutes, with the last bus returning around 10pm. Check www.iett.gov.tr/en/index.php for regularly updated timetables.

The Princes' Islands

Dissidents, minorities and horse-drawn carriages – island life, Istanbul style.

Set in the Marmara Sea off Istanbul's Asian Shore, the Princes' Islands (also known as the Kızıl Adalar or 'Red Islands') have come a long way since they were used as a place of exile and imprisonment. In the 19th century, they were 'discovered' as a luxury location for the summer houses and pleasure palaces of Istanbul's mainly non-Muslim elite. Today, they are one of the last places to offer a glimpse of the old ethnic mix of Istanbul. Greeks, Armenians and Jews still rub shoulders with Turks in the local squares, in a way that's no longer the case in the city itself, and churches are more numerous than mosques.

Almost all the houses are built of wood, fretted and carved into lacy designs to adorn fabulous mansions set in well-tended gardens. The streets are completely car-free and echo with the clip-clop of horse-drawn phaetons. The overall effect is of a 19th-century time capsule – strongest in winter when the hordes of summer day-trippers have vanished.

There are nine islands in total, of which four can be visited. Furthest from European Istanbul (20 kilometres, or 12 miles) is **Büyükada**, the largest and most popular island. It has traditionally been home to a large Jewish population. **Kınalıada** is predominantly Armenian, **Burgazada** is Greek and **Heybeliada** is mostly Turkish.

GETTING THERE

Regular ferries to the islands depart from Eminönü's Adalar Iskele, which is the dock nearest Sirkeci railway station. They stop at each of the islands in turn, taking an hour and a half to reach Büyükada (50 minutes to Kınalıada). The fare is YTL2. Departure times from Eminönü change with the season, but in summer there are at least a dozen sailings a day from 9.20am onwards. For ferry schedules and related information, call 0212 444 4436 or visit www.ido.com.tr. There is also a less frequent and more expensive fast catamaran service from Eminönü, but the time saved is not significant – and anyhow, the slow sail is a pleasure in itself.

Kınalıada

Kınalıada, the smallest of the four islands and the closest to Istanbul, is the least green of the islands. Its name (from *kına*, Turkish for 'dyed

with henna') comes from the reddish tinge of the shoreline cliffs, although the absence of greenery today is down to the fact that the island is almost completely scabbed over by modern housing. Historically, this was the place of exile of the Byzantine emperor Romanus IV, who suffered defeat by the Selçuks at the Battle of Manzikert in 1071.

The place comes to life during the summer months as the city's Armenian community descends en masse. The island is also a favoured spot for visiting Armenians from the global diaspora. On summer evenings the crowds along the seafront promenade are as dense as those on Istiklal Caddesi, but with one significant difference: in Beyoğlu everyone's looking in the shop windows, whereas here they're sizing each other up as eligible marriage partners. The older Armenian residents look on from the tables of the **Bahar Patisserie**, one of Istanbul's most famous cafés, which is on the corner of Kınalı Meydanı, the main square by the ferry landing.

On the waterfront at **Kınalıada**.

In Kınalıada there are no horse-drawn phaetons, but the island is small enough to walk round. There is also a boat from the harbour to Ayazma beach on the opposite side of the island. The cost is negotiable, but should be no more than YTL2.

If you don't mind climbing uphill, you can head up through the town over to the back of the island, past the heath where **Hristo Monastery** stands, before descending to Ayazma beach.

Sights in the town include a fine modernist mosque, the **Kınalıada Camii**, erected in 1964, with an angular roof and elegant minaret, and an Armenian church, the **Surp Krikor Lusavoria**, on Narciciyi Sokak, a ten-minute walk inland from the ferry landing. En route, pass by the grilled sheep's head vendors on **Akasya Caddesi**, which is also the place to hire bicycles (YTL3 an hour). Not that there are too many places to go to: south of the centre are a number of beaches, but they quickly become overcrowded at the first sign of balmy weather.

Where to eat

There is no accommodation on Kınalıada. In addition to the Bahar Patisserie, Kınalı Meydanı also has the **Bahar Pub**; both do cakes and snacks, the latter serves alcohol too. On Akasya Caddesi there are a number of *meyhanes* with little to choose between them. There's also a Greek taverna, the **Çınaraltı Plaka Restaurant** (6 Çınaraltı Köşk Sokak, 0216 381 5407) in Çınaraltı Meydanı, or square, which has been serving customers for 125 years in a former police station to the left of the ferry station. In summer, live Greek and Armenian music is thrown in; a classic *meze* and fish meal, with drinks, costs about YTL30 a head.

Another option is the **Mimoza** restaurant (12-14 Çerçi Caddesi, 0216 381 5267), also left of the ferry landing, but slightly pricier as it is closer to the waterfront. Expect to pay around YTL35-YTL45 a head.

Burgazada

Burgazada is best known for its connections with one of Turkey's most famous literary figures, the short-story writer Sait Faik (1906-54), who lived on the island from 1939 until his death. He was a specialist in brief vignettes of the lives of his neighbours. Gay, or at least bisexual, Faik probably enjoyed the freedom from the censorious mores of the city that island life could offer. His former home is now the modest **Sait Faik Museum**, which includes a musty collection of his works, translated into a dozen languages, and the author's death mask. If the place is locked, try the shed in the garden, where the caretaker lives with his family.

The other thing everybody knows about Burgazada is that it is strongly Greek in character. The dominant local landmark is the Greek Orthodox **Church of St John the Baptist**. The caretaker lives on the grounds, and will open the church for anyone interested.

Situated on the island's western shore, a 20-minute walk from the ferry landing, is the **Kalpazankaya Restaurant** (26 Kalpazankaya Yolu, 0216 381 1504, meal with drinks YTL23-YTL30), complete with statue of Sait Faik. From here you can look out over a flat Marmara Sea, with nothing to block your view as far as the horzion. A shoreline of pine woods and rocky coves adds to the pristine feel. This spot also has one of the scant stretches of coastline clean enough for swimming.

Burgazada.

Alternatively, catch a phaeton north of the ferry landing (a tour of the island costs YTL20 and takes 35-40 minutes; a trip to the restaurant is around YTL10) or rent a bicycle (YTL4 an hour) one street back from the waterfront.

Church of St John the Baptist

Takımağa Meydanı. **Services** 9am Sun.

Sait Faik Museum

15 Burgaz Çayırı Sokak (0216 381 2132). **Open** 10am-5pm Tue-Fri, Sun; 10am-1pm Sat. **Admission** free.

Where to stay & eat

The **Mehtap 45 Butik Otel** (45 Mehtap Caddesi, 0216 381 2660, doubles $85-$120) is set on top of a peaceful hill, but still close to town. All prices – quoted in dollars – include breakfast, and all rooms have air-conditioning, TV and bathroom. You can swim at the nearby (free) Çamakya beach. Open all year, discounts are often available during winter.

The area around the ferry landing is laden with fish restaurants, of which the Greek-owned **Barba Meyhane** (6B Yalı Caddesi, 0216 381 2404, meal with drinks YTL34-YTL37) is a popular choice, offering some 35 kinds of meze and live Greek music on Fridays and Saturdays.

Resources

Internet

Urfalım Café *9 Egemen Bahçe Caldesi (0216 381 2612)*. Set in a beautiful, quiet garden, the café offers internet access, billiards and narghiles.

Heybeliada

The name means 'saddlebag island' – a good description of how Heybeliada looks, with a low landmass between twin summits. A summer favourite with picnickers, it's also a source of international tension since Turkish authorities closed down the Greek Orthodox school of theology at the **Haghia Triada Monastery** in the 1970s, depriving the Greek community of its priesthood training centre. The justification? All religious instruction, whether Christian, Islamic or Jewish, is 'supervised by the state', but such hogwash sits badly with Turkey's EU ambitions, and a climb-down may not be far off.

Much of the rest of the island is occupied by the military, which maintains the **Turkish Naval Academy** to the left of the ferry landing. Within its grounds is the grave of Sir Edward Barton, ambassador of Queen Elizabeth I to the Ottoman court, but it's out of bounds to the public except by special request.

The best way of getting around the island is in a phaeton, picked up on Ayyıldız Caddesi, which runs parallel to the seafront. An island tour takes 45 minutes and costs YTL15; a trip to the monastery YTL15 (you can't get in, but the views are good). Bikes can be rented at the Trakya Gıda corner store on Işgüzar Sokak, which runs inland from the phaeton stop on Ayyıldız (YTL2 an hour, YTL5 at the weekend).

For a classic seaside break, try the **Green Beach Club** (Yeniskele Tarık Sokak, 0216 351 1600, www.clubgreenbeach.com). With free boat transport to the beach for customers from the harbour, the entry fee is YTL15 on weekdays, YTL20 at weekends; fee includes a sunlounger, umbrella, locker and water sports.

Where to stay

The budget option is the **Özdemir Pension** (41 Ayyıldız Caddesi, 0216 351 80 28, www.adalar-ozdemirpansiyon.com, doubles YTL50-YTL75), close to the ferry landing. Rooms come with TVs and en suite bathrooms, but breakfast isn't included.

Across the road, the **Prenset Pension** (40-42 Ayyıldız Caddesi, 0216 351 0042, www.halkiprenset.com, doubles YTL80-YTL100) has slightly better rooms.

The **Merit Halki Palace** (94 Refah Şehitleri Caddesi, 0216 351 0025, www.halkıpalacehotel.com, doubles YTL130) is set in a 19th-century Ottoman mansion. This grand hotel was refitted in period style following a fire in 1991. In summer its swimming pool is open to non-residents (YTL30 weekdays, YTL45 weekends).

Where to eat

The waterfront is brimming with restaurants. For value for money, hit **Gökşins Ambrosia** (30B Ayyıldız Caddesi, 0216 351 1388), where fish, *meze* and a drink comes to YTL30-YTL35 a head. At the other end of the scale, a meal at the restaurant at the **Merit Halki Palace** (*see above*), with wine, costs about YTL150 a head.

Serving seafood and *meze*, the **Halki Restaurant** (32 Ayyıldız Caddesi, 0216 351 8595, meal with drinks YTL35) is one of the oldest eateries on the island. The **Başak Restaurant** (26 Ayyıldız Cadessi, 0216 351 1289) serves meat dishes as well as *meze* and fish. Expect to pay around YTL45 a head for fish, *meze* and drinks.

Resources

Internet

Tuğçe Internet Café *1A Erkal Sokak (0216 351 0384)*.

Trips Out of Town

Büyükada

The largest Prince's island is suitably named: *büyük* means 'big', while *ada* is the word for 'island'. Previously, it was known as Prinkipo, Greek for 'prince', which may be a reference to the number of aristocrats who ended up here in hiding, in exile or imprisoned: in Byzantine times, there were an equal number of monasteries and jails on the island.

From 1929 to 1933, Büyükada was the home of Leon Trotsky, who bashed out his *History of the Russian Revolution* in exile at the **Izzet Paşa Köskü**, a recently restored wooden mansion at 55 Çankaya Caddesi. The island was probably the safest place for him, given that at the time Istanbul was also home to some 34,000 White Russians, living in exile after a crushing defeat by Trotsky's Red Army. Trotsky lived in the house surrounded by armed 'secretaries'. According to Turkish police reports, he did make one trip into Istanbul to see Charlie Chaplin's *City Lights*. The Izzet Paşa mansion is also where his daughter committed suicide in 1933.

The island is now a hugely popular but exclusive summer resort – a kind of Turkish take on the Hamptons. For the casual visitor, it's a gorgeous place for a long walk along leafy lanes scented heavily with blossom. The main settlement and ferry landing are on the northern tip of the island. A few steps south of the pier is the centre of town, Saat Meydanı, an open square with a conical clock tower. East is a corral of horse-drawn phaetons. Drivers offer big (YTL40) or small (YTL35) tours of the island, both of which end up at the foot of the hill, where you can climb up a cobbled path to **St George's Monastery** – or hire a donkey for YTL4. To walk to the monastery, head west from Saat Meydanı past the police station and then continue along main Çankaya Caddesi; it takes around 30 to 40 minutes. Bicycles can be hired from lots of places around Saat Meydanı for YTL3 an hour on weekdays and YTL4 at weekends.

As you climb the steep slope up to the monastery, note the hundreds of pieces of cloth tied to the branches of the trees: each represents a prayer, tied by the faithful of all religions, mostly women desperate for a child. Many infertile women still ascend to the monastery barefoot.

At the top are fine views and an excellent restaurant. The monastery's chapel is usually open to visitors, with icons depicting the old dragon-slayer, plus an assortment of saintly relics. From up here, the islands of **Yassıada** and **Sivriada** are visible, the former distinguished by a fort-like prison. Neither has a particularly wholesome history. It was in the Yassıada jail that former prime minister Adnan Menderes and two of his ministers were hanged in 1961 following a military coup, while Sivriada gained notoriety in 1911 when Istanbul's stray dogs were rounded up and left to starve on the island. Neither can be visited.

Up from the harbour on Çankaya Caddesi stands the Ottoman-era **Büyükada Kültürevi** Cultural Centre, with a garden restaurant where *köfte*, beer and chips will set you back around YTL18. The Centre also hosts the summer **International Islands Festival**, with worthy discussions on culture and the arts alongside concerts of classical Turkish, Greek and Armenian music.

Where to stay

The **Hotel Princess** (1 Iskele Caddesi, 0216 382 1628/2930, www.buyukadaprincess.com, doubles $110-$120) is right by the clock tower square. A little further west on the same street is the **Splendid Palas** (23 Nisan Caddesi 53, 0216 382 6950, www.splendidhotel.net, doubles from $90, closed Nov-Apr). Both hotels have lovely wooden façades disguising pleasant modern rooms. A cheaper, year-round option is the **Ideal Köşk Pension**, (16 Kadıyoran Caddesi, 0216 382 6857, doubles YTL33-YTL40 without breakfast).

Where to eat

Dozens of places will be touting for business the minute you step off the ferry, and there's not a lot of difference between them. We like **Ali Baba** (20 Gulistan Caddesi, 0216 382 3733,) where you can eat well for YTL45-YTL 50 a head without alcohol.

To sample more authentic island life, try the **Kıyı Restaurant** (2 Çiçekliyalı Sokak, 0216 382 5606), a run-down *meyhane* that plays Greek music and is famous for its *meze*. A meal costs around YTL25-YTL30.

The recent globalisation of Istanbul's eateries has spread to these islands, and the **Grille Brasserie & Sushi Bar** is a case in point. It's in the Büyükada Princess Hotel (2 Iskele Caddesi, 0216 382 1628, www.buyukada princess.com, meal with drinks YTL37). The brasserie has wi-fi access.

Resources

Internet

Apart from the Grille Brasserie (*see above*), the island's only other internet option is at 18 Çınar Caddesi (0216 382 2681).

Directory

Directory

Getting Around

Arriving by air

Istanbul's international **Atatürk Airport** is around 25km (15 miles) west of the city centre in Yeşilköy. The compact international terminal (Dış Hatlar) has several shops, restaurants, bars, a massage parlour, post office, 24-hour banking, exchange bureaux, car hire, a tourist office and hotel reservation desk. From landing to clearing customs usually takes 20 minutes. Security checks can delay check-in, so arrive at least 90 minutes before your flight.

A second international airport, **Sabiha Gökçen**, in Kurtköy on the Asian side was intended to handle three million travellers a year, but is woefully underused.

Atatürk International Airport
Atatürk Hava Limanı Yolu *(24-hr English flight info 0212 465 3000/www.ataturkairport.com).*

Major airlines

In addition to the following, Istanbul is served by many international carriers.

British Airways
Istanbul 0212 317 6600/UK 08708 509850/www.britishairways.com.

Turkish Airlines (THY)
Istanbul 0212 444 0849/UK 020 7766 9300/www.thy.com.

Connections to the city

There are three options for getting from the airport to the city centre: bus, light rail/underground or taxi.

The choice depends on where you're staying and how much time you've got.

Havaş operates the reliable **express airport bus** service, which leaves for four different destinations from a signposted stop outside the arrivals hall. The only one of use to visitors is the Taksim service – fine if you're staying in Beyoğlu or Taksim – which runs at 5am, 6am, then half-hourly until 11pm, stopping en route at the Bakırköy Sea Bus Terminal, Aksaray and Tepebaşı (just short of Taksim). The fare is around YTL8.50 (plus a 25 per cent surcharge between midnight and 6am), collected by a conductor on board.

The **underground**, or 'light metro', takes you to Aksaray in half an hour and costs just YTL1.30; from here, you can get a bus to Taksim or a tram to Sultanahmet. Services run 6.15am-midnight Mon-Sat, 6.30am-midnight Sun.

The simplest option is to take a **taxi** from the rank outside the arrivals hall. Fares are metered. Journeys to the centre of Sultanahmet should be around YTL15-YTL18 (half as much again at night). The ride takes about 20 minutes but can stretch to 45 minutes if the traffic's bad. To Taksim, it costs around YTL23 and takes anywhere between 20-50 minutes.

Arriving by train

The days of the Orient Express are long gone; rail travel from Europe to Istanbul is now the preserve of backpackers and the lower-income end of Turkey's Balkan diaspora.

The only direct route to Istanbul from Greece is from Thessaloniki, with a daily 7.25am departure taking around 15 hours to cover the 850km (510 miles). The other direct service from Europe is the daily Bosphorus Express, departing Bucharest at 2.05pm and pulling into Istanbul at 8.27am the following morning.

Trains from Europe arrive at **Sirkeci Station** (*gar*), beside the Golden Horn in Eminönü. From here, it's a short walk or tram ride up the hill to **Sultanahmet**. A taxi to Taksim costs YTL4-YTL5.

Trains from destinations to the south and east terminate at **Haydarpaşa Station** on the Asian Shore. International arrivals include the Trans-Asya, which departs from Tehran every Thursday at 8.15pm and limps into Istanbul some 69 hours later. From Syria, you could board the Toros Express in Damascus at 5.13am on Tuesday and be in Istanbul around 6pm the following evening.

Sirkeci and Haydarpaşa stations are connected by ferries, though there is also a tunnel link on the drawing board. Information lines serve Sirkeci (0212 527 0051) and Haydarpaşa (0216 348 8020 ext 336) between 7am-midnight daily, but are in Turkish only. Timetables for international and national services are posted on the state railway (TCDD) website (www.tcdd.gov.tr); the English-language version of the site is refreshingly good.

Sirkeci Station
Istasyon Caddesi, Eminönü (0212 520 6575 ext 417, for reservations 6am-6pm daily).

Haydarpaşa Station
Haydarpaşa Istasyon Caddesi, Kadıköy (0216 336 4470, for reservations 6am-6pm daily).

Arriving by coach

Turkish coach companies (such as Ulusoy and Varan) run regular services from many European cities. Be prepared for lengthy waits at border crossings – particularly with Bulgaria, where it can take up to three hours to clear customs.

Travellers arriving by coach disembark at the international and inter-city bus terminal (*otogar*) in Esenler, about ten kilometres (six miles) from the city centre. There are courtesy minibuses to Taksim and Sultanahmet. The underground 'light metro' connects the terminal to Aksaray, where you can trudge to the Taksim bus stop across the road, or take a tram to Sultanahmet.

Esenler bus terminal
Uluslararası Istanbul Otogarı
Büyük Istanbul Otogarı, Bayrampaşa (0212 658 0505/ www.otogaristanbul.com).
Open 24hrs daily.

Ulusoy
İnönü Caddesi 59, Gümüşsuyu (0212 244 6375/International journeys 0212 658 3006/ www.ulusoy.com.tr). **Open** 24hrs daily. **Credit** AmEx, MC, V.
Twice-weekly buses to and from Greece (Thessaloniki, 12hrs, YTL88; Athens, 21hrs, YTL135), Germany (Münich, 48hrs, YTL195; Frankfurt, 55hrs, YTL230) and Italy (Ancona via Munich YTL195). Bookings can be made through the website.

Varan
İnönü Caddesi 29/A, Gümüşsuyu (0212 251 7475-76/www.varan. com.tr). **Open** 24hrs daily. **Credit** MC, V.
Weekly buses to and from Greece (Thessaloniki, 12hrs, YTL88; Athens, 21hrs, YTL135) and Austria (Vienna, 33hrs, Salzburg, 37hrs, Linz, 39hrs, YTL190 flat fare).

Public transport

Public transport is cheap and improving all the time, thanks to a municipal campaign to defeat the city's chronic traffic problem. The result is reinforcement to the entire transport infrastructure: extensions to metro and tram lines, new bypasses and underpasses, new sea bus routes and funiculars are all under way or completed, and a trans-Bosphorus tunnel (Marmaray) is now under construction. But for the time being, Istanbul endures gridlock along major arteries.

Happily, the two areas where visitors are likely to spend most time – Beyoğlu and Sultanahmet – are easily explored on foot. However, buses are useful for heading up the Bosphorus coast to Ortaköy, Arnavutköy, Bebek and beyond, while trips to the districts of Üsküdar and Kadıköy on the Asian shore are best undertaken by ferry or sea bus. The easiest way to get to shopping and business districts in Nişantaşı, Teşvikye, Etiler and Levent is via the new metro line that runs north from Taksim.

The informative website of the IETT, the local transport authority, has an excellent English version that includes maps and timetables.

IETT
Istanbul Elektrik Tramway ve Tünel İşletmeleri Genel Müdürlüğü
Erkan-ı Harp Sokak 4, Tünel (0212 245 0720/free helpline 0800 211 6068/www.iett.gov.tr).

Akbil

Akbil, the 'smart card', is an electronic travel pass that can be used on all public transport except *dolmuş* and minibuses. You get a 10 per cent discount on fares. Akbils are available for a small refundable deposit (YTL6) from booths at all main bus, sea bus and metro stations. To use it, firmly press the circular metal stud into the socket on the orange machine located next to the driver on buses, or to the left of turnstiles at all metro, light rail, tram and ferry stations. Recharge at Akbil machines located at bus, metro and tram stations, ferry terminals or Akbil booths.

Particularly useful for visitors is the *mavi* (blue) travel pass valid for a day, a week, 15 days or a month.

Buses

Most city buses (*belediye otobüsü*) are operated by the municipality, but there are also private versions (*halk otobüsü*). Municipal buses are red and white or green; all have IETT written on the front. Private ones are pale blue and green.

Buy tickets (*bilet*) for municipal buses before boarding (they won't take money on the bus). On private buses, pay a conductor seated in the doorway (they won't take municipal tickets). Both IETT and private buses accept Akbil (*see above*) and charge the same fare (YTL1.30). Tickets for municipal buses are sold from booths at main stops and stations, or newsstands, nearby stalls and itinerant street vendors for a 30 per cent premium.

Newer buses have electronic signboards with route information. Bus stops also have route maps. Still, the sheer number of routes and the interminable traffic and roadworks can make bus travel a nightmare. Bus services run from 6am to 11pm. Kabataş and Taksim are the two main bus terminals north of the Golden Horn. These are useful bus routes:
Taksim – Topkapı 83
Taksim – Bahçeşehir 76E, 76D
Taksim – Sultanahmet T4
Taksim – Ortaköy DT1, DT2
Taksim – Edirnekapı 87
Taksim – Kadıköy 110

Directory

Taksim – Aksaray (metro) 83MT
Taksim – Sarıyer 25T, 40
Taksim – Otogar 83O
Otogar – Eminönü 91O
Otogar – Beşiktaş 28O
Kabataş – Beşiktaş 22E
Kabataş – Reşitpaşa 22RE, 58A
Kabataş - Sarıyer 25E
Topkapı – Beşiktaş 28T
Topkapı – Sarıyer 341T
Topkapı – Kadıköy 127
Sarıyer – Kilyos 151
Sarıyer – Beşiktaş 40B
Aksaray – Airport light metro
Edirnekapı – Beşiktaş 28

Dolmuş & minibuses

A *dolmuş* (which means 'full') is basically a shared taxi that sets off once every seat is taken. *Dolmuş* run fixed routes (starting points and final destinations are displayed in the front window) but with no set stops. Passengers flag the driver down to get on (if there's room) and holler out to be let off (*Inecek var!*). For local journeys, there's one fixed fare. Ask a fellow passenger how much it is or just watch what everyone else is paying. *Dolmuş* run later than buses, often as late as 2am.

Minibuses are more crowded than *dolmuş*, and less frequent. Minibus fares are lower, but chances are you'll make your journey standing while being blasted by tinny Turkish pop. Pay and get on/off as you would a *dolmuş*. The main routes are from Beşiktaş to the upper Bosphorus districts.

Metro & trams

The new metro and tram systems provide a comfortable and efficient alternative to clogged roads and crowded buses. However, coverage currently remains scant. At present, the metro runs from Taksim north to 4th Levent, stopping at Osmanbey, Şişli, Gayrettepe and Levent. Extensions slated for completion in 2008 will take the line south of Taksim to the sea bus jetty at Yenikapı and north as far as Maslak.

Another option is the 'light metro', which connects Aksaray (west of the Grand Bazaar) to the Esenler bus terminal and on to the airport.

The city's only modern tram runs from Zeytinburnu via Aksaray to Sultanahmet and terminates at Eminönü by the Galata Bridge. This is a useful service for visitors, linking the Grand Bazaar, Haghia Sophia, Sultanahmet, Topkapı, the Egyptian Bazaar and the Golden Horn. You can also use the tram to visit the city walls. Buy tokens in advance from kiosks at tram stops and feed them into the automatic barriers outside the platform. A single trip on the tram costs YTL1.30 irrespective of your destination. The service runs from around 6am-midnight.

An extension is being built between Eminönü and Beşiktaş, crossing the Galata Bridge. There'll be six stops in between, including Karaköy and Kabataş (which are already in service), the ferry and sea bus terminal.

A new funicular, which opened in 2006, connects Kabataş to Taksim Square, (connecting at the metro).

Tünel & tram

A 125-year-old funicular, known as the *tünel*, ascends from Karaköy to Tünel Square at the southern end of Istiklal Caddesi. It's a very short run, but saves a tiring climb up (or down) the sheer slope. The service runs 7am-10pm Mon-Sat and 7.30am-10pm Sun and costs around YTL0.90.

At Tünel, it connects with a century-old tram that shuttles up mile-and-a-half-long Istiklal Caddesi to Taksim Square and back. Akbil can be used for either, but not regular bus tickets. You need to buy a token for the funicular at the entrance, and a ticket for the tram from Tünel Square funicular station or a vendor

in Taksim Square. Tickets for either the tram or funicular cost YTL0.90.

Ferries & sea buses

Boats and ships of all sizes shuttle between the European and Asian shores, operating to summer (mid June-mid Sept) and winter timetables. Timetables are available from all ferry terminals; departure times are also posted online.

The main services run between Eminönü, Karaköy and Beşiktaş on the European side, and Üsküdar and Kadıköy on the Asian shore. These once-white ferries (*vapur*), capable of carrying hundreds of passengers, are soon to be replaced with a newer fleet. Departures are every 15 minutes or so.

There are also regular services running up the Golden Horn to Eyüp from Üsküdar via Eminönü. Less frequent commuter services criss-cross the Bosphorus, starting from Eminönü and calling at Haydarpaşa, Ortaköy, Arnavutköy, Bebek, Kandilli and beyond.

Ferries also depart from Eminönü and Kabataş to the Princes' Islands. The popular Bosphorus tour departs from Eminönü three times daily – *see p206*.

The modern catamarans (called *deniz otobüsleri* or 'sea buses') are faster but more expensive and generally restricted to commuter hours. You can pick up timetables from the ferry terminals or check online (*see below*).

Turkish Maritime Organisation
Türkiye Denizcilik İşletmeleri Şehir Hatları İşletmesi AŞ
Rıhtım Caddesi 4, Karaköy
(0212 251 5000/www.tdi.com.tr).

Istanbul Fast Ferry
Istanbul Deniz Otobüsleri AŞ
Kennedy Caddesi, Sahil Yolu,
Hızlı Feribot Iskelesi, Yenikapı
(0212 455 6900/www.ido.com.tr).

Bikes

Terrrible traffic, steep hills, slippery cobbles, and countless potholes make Istanbul very challenging for cyclists. However, the wide road alongside the Bosphorus north of Ortaköy is great for biking, with lovely views and a sea breeze. A hired bike is ideal for getting around the Princes' Islands where cars are banned.

If you're secure on two wheels, it may make sense to hire a motorbike from **Moto Villa** in Levent. All you need is a valid licence and a credit card. Your bike will be delivered to your hotel.

Moto Villa

Sülün Sokak 7, Levent (0212 280 3050/0555 267 0700/ www.villalevent.com). **Rates** from YTL45 per day; reduced weekly rates available. **Credit** AmEx, MC, V. Ask for Vasfı or Hakan Bozkurt, who both speak English.

Walking

The main tourist hubs of Sultanahmet, the Bazaar Quarter and Beyoğlu are all perfect for exploring on foot. There are very few main roads, while the narrow, sloping back-streets are better suited to pedestrians than cars. Pay attention when crossing roads, as drivers often jump lights.

Taxis

You won't have a problem finding a taxi, day or night. Licensed taxis are bright yellow, with a roof-mounted *taksi* sign. They're all metered, and relatively cheap by European standards. If the meter isn't running, get out.

During the day, the meter displays the word *gündüz* (day rate); the clock should start with YTL1.50. From midnight to 6am the *gece* (night) rate kicks in, adding 50 per cent to the fare. The day rate is YTL1.50 per mile. A trip

between Sultanahmet and Taksim Square costs YTL5-YTL6. There's no room for haggling and no need to tip. Cabbies are not necessarily streetwise. It's not unusual for your driver to ask you, other drivers or passers-by the way. If you cross the Bosphorus bridges, the toll (YTL4) will be added to the fare.

Driving

Driving is not recommended. Heavy congestion doesn't stop speeding, although the limit is 50kmh (30mph), rising to 120kmh (75mph) on motorways. Seat belts are the law, but observance of regulations is laughable. Street parking is difficult and not always legal, in which case you're liable to get towed. Use the plentiful car parks; you may have to leave the keys so that cars can be shuffled.

Paperwork

If you take your own car to Turkey, prepare to be entangled in red tape. Drivers must provide registration documents and a valid international driving licence at point of entry. Cars, minibuses, caravans, and motorbikes can be taken into Turkey for up to six months without a *carnet de passage* or *triptyque*. Your vehicle is registered in your passport and you're issued a certificate that should be carried at all times along with your driving licence and passport. If you stay in Turkey for more than six months, you must leave and re-enter the country, or apply to the Turkish Touring & Automobile Association for a *triptyque*. You won't be allowed to visit another country without taking your vehicle, unless you cancel the registration at the local customs office. Drivers from Europe also need a Green Card,

which is available from your insurance company.

A rarely enforced law requires all cars to be equipped with a fire extinguisher, first-aid kit and two triangles.

Turkish Touring & Automobile Association

Türkiye Turing ve Otomobil Kurumu
1 Sanayi Sitesi Yanı, Seyrantepe, 4 Levent (0212 282 8140). Turkey's equivalent of the AA.

Breakdown services

Gökşenler

Atatürk Oto Sarayı Sitesi 2, Kısım. Gökşenler Plaza 213, Maslak (0212 276 3640). **Open** 8.30am-6.30pm Mon-Fri; 8.30am-3.30pm Sun. **Credit** MC, V. 24-hour emergency service.

Istanbul Traffic Foundation

0212 289 9800. 24-hour towing services.

Car hire

Rental rates generally include VAT, insurance with third-party liability, and unlimited mileage, but are still relatively high. The rates below include VAT and insurance.

Avis

Abdülhakhamit Caddesi 72/A, off Cumhuriyet Caddesi, Taksim (0212 297 9610/ www.avis.com.tr). **Open** 9am-7pm daily. **Rates** YTL105-YTL195 per day. **Credit** AmEx, DC, MC, V. **Other locations**: *Atatürk Airport (0212 465 3455/56).*

Budget

Cumhuriyet Caddesi 19, Taksim (0212 235 3232/www.budget.com). **Open** 8.30am-7pm daily. **Rates** YTL60-YTL105/day. **Credit** AmEx, MC, V. **Other locations**: *Atatürk Airport (0212 465 5807).*

Europcar

Topçu Caddesi 1, off Cumhuriyet Caddesi, Taksim (0212 254 7710/ www.europcar.com.tr). **Open** 8.30am-7pm daily. **Rates** YTL75-YTL240/ day. **Credit** AmEx, DC, MC, V. **Other locations**: *Atatürk Airport (0212 465 3695).*

Directory

Resources A-Z

Addresses

When writing an address, the house number comes after the street name, with a slash separating the flat number. If it's on a side street (*sokak*), the custom is to include the nearest main street or avenue (*caddesi*). This main street is usually written first. So the address of Mehmet Aksoy, who lives in Flat 7 at 14 Matrar Sokak, off Sıraselviler Street, in the district of Cihangir, will be written like this:

Mehmet Aksoy
Sıraseviler Caddesi
Matar Sokak 14/7
Cirhangir
Istanbul

Business services

The largest city in Turkey, Istanbul is the centre for manufacturing and business. Although it is alive with opportunity, the city is also fraught with difficulties for business. For foreign investors, the traditional view of Turkey as a high-risk market has been replaced with the perception that it's a market well worth courting. But, of the many foreign companies that have successfully entered the Turkish market, few have done so alone. Foreign concerns have either bought controlling interests in local businesses, or work with Turkish partners. Corruption and interminable bureaucracy make it essential to have an efficient local representative, preferably with plenty of *torpil* ('influence').

Practicalities

Turkish employees work long hours and take few holidays, but seem to have inherited their administrative methods from the Byzantines. Things are slowly changing, but official paperwork still takes forever to complete, while the vocabulary of the average civil servant more often than not seems to consist entirely of negatives. Most foreign companies farm out tasks such as getting work permits and residence permits to local lawyers or accountants. Dealings with private-sector business are less fraught, and the AKP government has been trying to ease red tape to encourage more foreign investment.

Accountants

Deloitte & Touche *Dereboyu Sokak 24, Sun Plaza, floors 23-24, Maslak (0212 366 6000/www. deloitte.com).*

PricewaterhouseCoopers *Ninth floor, B Blok, BJK Plaza, Süleyman Seba Caddesi 48, Akaretler, Beşiktaş (0212 326 6060/www.pwcglobal.com).*

Business organisations

Foreign Economic Relations Board
Dış Ekonomik İlişkiler Kurulu *Ninth floor, Odakule I4 Merkezi, İstiklal Caddesi 286, Beyoğlu (0212 270 7386).* **Open** 9am-6pm Mon-Fri. **Map** p248 N3.
Organises joint business councils between Turkey and 56 countries worldwide. Also has a small library and resource centre.

TUGEV Istanbul Convention & Visitors Bureau
Istanbul Kongre ve Ziyaretçi Bürosu *BürosuHalaskargazi Caddesi 297/5, Şişli (0212 343 0701/ istanbul@ icvb.org).* **Open** 9am-5.30pm Mon-Fri. This non-profit provides information and services related to conventions and meetings in Istanbul.

Courier services

DHL *Yalçın Koreş Caddesi 20, Güneşli (0212 478 1225).* **Open** 9am-6pm Mon-Sat. International service only. Customer services 24 hours daily.

UPS *A Blok, Ambarlar Caddesi 6, Zeytinburnu (0212 413 2222/ www.ups.com).* **Open** 8.30am-7.45pm Mon-Fri; 8.30am-5pm Sat. International and national deliveries.

Federal Express *Fabrikalar Caddesi Tasoca35 Yolu 19 Mahmutbey (0212 444 0505/ www.fedex.com).* **Open** 8am-11pm Mon-Fri; 8am-8pm Sat. International service only.

Legal & consulting services

Ertan & Oran *Adnan Saygun Caddesi, Belediye Sitesi D1 Blok, Daire 82, Ulus (0212 225 0952/ ayhanoran@superonline.com).* **Open** 9am-6pm Mon-Fri. A consultancy and law firm that specialises in commercial,

Travel advice

For current information on travel to a specific country – including the latest news on health issues, safety and security, local laws and customs – contact your home country's government department of foreign affairs. Most have websites with useful advice for would-be travellers.

Australia
www.smartraveller.gov.au
Canada
www.voyage.gc.ca
New Zealand
www.safetravel.govt.nz

Republic of Ireland
http://foreignaffairs.gov.ie
UK
www.fco.gov.uk/travel
USA
http://travel.state.gov

corporate, international trade and maritime law.

IBS *Agahamami Caddesi, Aga Han 17/6, Cihangir, Beyoglu (0212 252 2460/www.ibsresearch.com).* **Open** 9am-6pm Mon-Fri. English-owned and run. Producers of the comprehensive, indispensable guide *Doing Business in Turkey.*

Wordsmith *Meşrutiyet Caddesi 126/7, Taksim. (0212 245 7050).* **Open** 9am-6pm Mon-Fri. Advertising, promotional films and translation.

Consulates

All foreign embassies are located in Ankara, but many countries also have a consulate in Istanbul.

Australian Consulate
Askerocağı Caddesi 15, Süzer Plaza 2nd Floor, Şişli (0212 243 1333-36/www.dfat.gov.au). **Open** 8.30am-12.30pm, 1.30-5pm Mon-Fri.

Canadian Consulate
Istiklal Caddesi 373/5, Beyoğlu (0212 251 9838). **Open** 9.30am-12.30pm, 1.30-5.30pm Mon-Thur; 9.30am-1pm Fri. **Map** p248 M4.

Republic of Ireland Honorary Consulate
Merter İş Merkezi 2/13, General Ali Rıza Gürun Caddesi, Merter (0212 259 6979). **Open** 9am-5pm Mon-Fri.

New Zealand Honorary Consulate
Inönü Caddesi 92/3, Gümüşsuyu, Taksim (0212 244 0272). **Open** 9am-7pm Mon-Fri. **Map** p247 P2.

UK Consulate
Meşrutiyet Caddesi 34, Tepebaşı, Beyoğlu (0212 334 6400/www.british embassy.org.tr). **Open** 8.30am-1pm; 2-4.45pm Mon-Fri. **Map** p248 M3.

US Consulate
Kaplıcalar Mevkii Sokak 2,Istinye Mahallesi, Istinye (0212 335 9000/ 340 4444 visas/www.usisist.gov.tr). **Open** 8am-noon, 1-4.30pm Mon-Fri,

Customs

Foreign visitors can import up to one 100cc (or two 75cc) bottle(s) of alcohol (including wine), 200 cigarettes, 50 cigarillos and ten cigars. You may be asked to register electronic equipment to ensure

it leaves Turkey with you. It's illegal to possess or export antiquities. You may need proof of purchase for a carpet. For more details, visit www.gumruk.gov.tr or call 0212 465 5244/45.

Disabled access

Hilly Istanbul is tough on anyone with a mobility problem. Roads and pavements are narrow, bumpy, and often cobbled, kerbs are high, and stairs ubiquitous. However, public transport is more accessible than before: the new metro has elevators, the light railway and trams are accessible; and 450 'low-riding' Mercedes buses have been provided to facilitate disabled access. Two of these buses (painted white and light blue) are designed for wheelchairs; they operate along the Topkapı-Emirgan (222) and Pendik-Kadıköy (28T) routes. A fleet of new ferries, to be introduced by 2008, will extend disabled access to maritime travel.

Apart from a handful of top hotels, few buildings make any provisions for the disabled, although Mayor Kadir Topbaş has put this issue high on his agenda.

Drugs

Turkey is a major transit point for heroin smugglers. The use of marijuana, cocaine and ecstasy is also on the rise. Enforcement is uneven, but heavy-handed; police conduct random sweeps of bars and nightclubs in Taksim and Beyoğlu. You may be body-searched and checked for needle tracks. Sentencing for drug offences is mild by Americanstandards, but harsh compared to Europe. Carry ID at all times, especially if you're out on the town.

Electricity & gas

Electricity in Turkey runs on 220 volts. Plugs have two round pins. Adaptors for UK appliances are readily available at hardware shops and electricians. Transformers are required for US 110-volt appliances. There are frequent, brief power cuts (more often in winter), so it's not a bad idea to bring a torch.

Emergencies

Police 155
Fire 110
Ambulance 112

Health

No vaccinations are required for Istanbul, although cases of rabies were reported as recently as 1999. Avoid tap water; cheap bottled water is readily available.

Hospitals & doctors

Turkey's health services suffer from an overstretched, underfunded public sector. There is no GP system, state hospitals are jammed, and underpaid hospital doctors often have to take on private patients. In contrast, private hospitals have state-of-the-art equipment, look like five-star hotels, and milk their patients royally. If you need medical aid, the simplest solution (especially if you have insurance) is to go straight to a private hospital, where you'll get immediate attention and are pretty sure to find English speakers. Many private hospitals also run dental clinics.

American Hospital
Amerikan Hastanesi
Güzelbahçe Sokak 20, Nişantaşı (0212 311 2000/www.amerikan hastanesi.com.tr). **Credit** AmEx, MC, V.
Well equipped and well staffed, the American Hospital also has a dental clinic.

Directory

European Florence Nightingale Hospital

Hastanesi Fulya Sağlık Tesisleri, Cahit Yalçım Sokak 1, off Mehmetçik Caddesi, Mecidiyeköy (0212 212 8811/444 0436 /www.florence. com.tr). **Credit** AmEx, MC, V.
Modern and well equipped, specialises in treating children.

German Hospital

Sıraselviler Caddesi 119, Cihangir, Taksim (0212 293 2150/www.alman hastanesi.com.tr). **Credit** AmEx, MC, V. **Map** p249 O3.
Part of the Universal Hospitals Group, it incorporates an eye hospital and dental clinic.

International Hospital

Istanbul Caddesi 82, Yeşilköy (0212 663 3000/www.international hospital.com.tr). **Credit** AmEx, DC, MC, V.
Five minutes from the airport, it has cutting-edge technology, eye and dental clinics.

Taksim State Emergency Hospital

Taksim Ilkyardım Hastanesi Sıraselviler Caddesi 112, Cihangir, Taksim (0212 252 4300). **No** credit cards. **Map** p249 O3.
A state-run hospital that recently got a much-needed overhaul. It only deals with emergencies.

Pharmacies

Pharmacies (*eczane*) are plentiful. Pharmacists are licensed to measure blood pressure, give injections, clean and bandage minor injuries, and suggest medication for minor ailments – many prescription medicines are available over the counter in Turkey. However, few pharmacists speak English. Opening hours are typically from 9am-7pm Mon-Sat. Every neighbourhood also has a duty pharmacy (*nöbetçi*) that is open all night and on Sundays.

Insurance

Turkey is not covered by EU mutual health insurance schemes, so visitors are advised to get private insurance policy. Anyone with a full residence permit is entitled to national health care.

Internet

Istanbul has embraced internet culture. The number of public terminals and Internet cafés has sky-rocketed. Particularly around Sultanahmet, you'll find most hotels offer Internet access and many travel agents have a couple of online computers. Wi-fi access is available in most upscale cafés and restaurants, including Gloria Jeans and Starbucks.

The majority of phone sockets take the US-style RJ11 plug, although a few older hotels use a Turkish model for which there don't seem to be any adaptors.

Internet access kits are sold at most large music/media and computer shops. The following are reputable providers with English-speaking technical staff and back-up services.

Superonline

0212 473 7475/www.superonline.com

Turknet

0212 444 0077/www.turk.net

Netone

0212 355 1700/www.netone.net.tr

Internet cafés

There are also many internet cafés in Sultanahmet, especially on and round Divan Yolu.

Robin Hood Internet Café

Yeniçarşı Caddesi 8/4, Galatasaray, Beyoğlu (0212 244 8959). **Open** 9.30am-11pm daily. **Rates** YTL2/hr. **No credit cards**.
This pristine, fourth-floor café has 30 computers. Provides printing, fax, and scanning services, plus English-speaking technical support. No smoking.

Libraries

While there are excellent Spanish and French libraries in Beyoğlu, there isn't a single English-language library open to the public since the closure of the British Council library after the 2003 bombing. Your

best bet for English-language resources is to visit Bilgi or Boğaziçi university.

Istanbul Library/Çelik Gülersoy Foundation

Ayasofya Pansiyonları, Soğukçeşme Sokak, Sultanahmet (0212 512 5730). **Open** 9am-noon, 1-4.30pm Mon-Fri. **Map** p243 N10.
Antique and modern books on Istanbul in several languages, stored in an Ottoman house beside Topkapı Palace. Used mainly by academics and specialists.

Lost property

To report a crime or lost property, go to the Tourist Police station (0212 527 4503) opposite Yerebatan Sarnıcı in Sultanahmet. Most officers speak English or German. If your passport is lost or stolen, you generally have to fill out a police report before the consulate will deal with you.

Media

In the mid 1980s, there were only two TV channels, and a handful of radio stations, all state owned. Then along came Star TV, beamed in from Germany, brazenly flouting regulations on private media ownership. (The owner of Star TV happened to be the brother of the Turkish president). Soon afterwards, the government loosened up media laws. The ensuing scramble saw the emergence of several huge, obscenely influential media conglomerates. One media mogul, Aydın Doğan, has stakes in three of Turkey's four major newspapers and its biggest magazine publishing house. He also owns several TV channels, a bank, and an internet portal, making Rupert Murdoch look like small fry.

Newspapers

National newspapers fall into two broad categories, secular and pro-Islamic. The secular press is monopolised by two empires – the Doğan and Sabah groups; between them, they account for around 60 per cent of the market. By European standards, newspaper circulation figures are pitiful, so ruthless publishers happily employ every gimmick imaginable to boost their sales.

The most highbrow papers are *Cumhuriyet* (Republic), a foundering left-of-centre paper , and *Radikal*, a Doğan title. Competition comes from three big hitters: *Hürriyet*, *Sabah* and *Milliyet*, indistinguishable popular dailies that occupy the political centre. Journalistic standards are undermined by low pay. The real news comes from the columnists – usually at least one per page.

The main pro-Islamic daily is *Zaman*, distinguished by surprisingly good coverage of international literature and film, and the first Turkish newspaper to go online. By far the worst Islamic paper is the hate-mongering *Akit*, with its habit of insinuating that successful business leaders are closet Jews or Christians.

Weekly satirical comics sell well. Popular titles include *Gır Gır*, *Penguen* and *LeMan*. No subject is taboo, and the humour, while crude, is usually on the mark.

Magazines

Most magazines are ephemeral unless backed by one of the big media groups. Established leaders are *Tempo* and *Aktüel*, which mix news, fashion and gossip. There's a slew of licensed international titles, including *Time Out Istanbul*.

English-language media

For such a cosmopolitan city, Istanbul is low on foreign-language publications. The only daily English newspaper is the semi-literate *Turkish Daily News*, which has reasonable coverage of domestic politics, but suffers from indigestible features and soapbox columnists. The monthly *Turkish Business World* does what it says on the cover, but reads suspiciously like advertorial. The new *Peru Weekly* (*Beyoğlu Gazetesi*), sold by street vendors, at bookstores and newsstands, has several pages of English summary of local news.

For news, reviews and up-to-date listings pick up the monthly *Time Out Istanbul*, which combines locally produced content with music and film reviews from the London edition. Our competitor *Istanbul: The Guide* also includes hotel, restaurant and club reviews, but only appears every other month.

Foreign press

Foreign newspapers and magazines are easy to find, but rarely arrive before late afternoon. The best places to look are the news stands in Sultanahmet and around Taksim Square, or the bookshops on Istiklal Caddesi.

Radio

The airwaves over Istanbul are so crammed with broadcasts that it's practically impossible to pick up any station without overlapping interference. Stations generally offer either Turkish or foreign music, but rarely both. One exception is Açık Radyo (94.9), which intercuts topical talk shows (often in English) with world music (*see p31* **On the radio**). Stations offering dance and pop music include Kiss FM (90.3), Radio Oxygen (95.9), Metro FM (97.2), Capital Radio (99.5), Power FM (100) and Number One FM (102.5). Radyo Blue (94.5) specialises in Latin and jazz, and Energy FM (102) in jazz. Radyo Eksen is the best channel for alternative music. For Turkish music, try Kral FM (92.0), Best FM (98.4) and Lokum FM (89.0). For Western classical music tune into ITU Radyosu (103.8). You can pick up the BBC news in English on NTV Radyo (102.8) at 6pm daily, and at 7am and 10.30pm Monday to Friday.

Television

Amazingly for a country with no private TV before 1991, Turkey now has 30 national channels, and countless more regional stations. Perhaps unsurprisingly, production values are low. The exceptions are CNN Turk and NTV, which feature excellent news, documentary and sports programmes. Cable TV is available in many areas, offering improved reception of terrestrial channels, plus BBC Prime, CNN, Discovery, Eurosport, and MTV. Digital TV is represented by Digitürk, which carries programming from Europe and the US, plus all the biggest Turkish TV and radio stations.

Money

Currency

Local currency is the Turkish lira, or YTL. High inflation (which hovered around 70-80 per cent for years) was down to a modest 9-10 per cent in 2006. After taming inflation with IMF help, Turkey lopped six zeros off its currency; in 2005 the New Turkish Lira (Yeni Türk Lirası, or YTL) was introduced. YTL banknotes come in denominations of 5, 10, 20, 50, and 100 .

ATMs

Cashpoints are common. Most machines will accept cards linked into the Cirrus or Plus networks, and supply Turkish lira or cash advances on major credit cards, provided you know your PIN number.

Banks

Most banks provide telephone and internet banking, which can be less frustrating than shabby counter service. Non-residents can open a savings account at a Turkish bank in any currency: just go to any branch with your passport. You'll be asked to sign a routine account agreement. Be sure to choose a branch that near your place of residence or work, because you'll only be able to draw cash from this branch without incurring charges. Cash can be deposited at any branch. With a current account, you can also apply for an ATM card. Getting a credit card isn't so easy: you need a residence permit, employment, proof of income, and a Turkish guarantor, as well as patience.

Akbank *www.akbank.com.*
Citibank *www.citibank.com.tr.*
Garanti Bank *www.garantibank.com.tr.*
HSBC *www.hsbc.com.tr.*
Yapı Kredi Bank *www.yapikredi.com.tr.*

Money transfer

Most banks will accept transfers even if you don't have an account. The drawback is that the money doesn't always arrive instantly, and the bank will block the money for up to 20 days. There is a way around this: you can withdraw the money in Turkish lira at the bank's discretionary rates, or by paying a hefty commission. The quicker and more reliable alternative is to use Western Union Money Transfer. This service is now offered by all branches of Denizbank, Dışbank, Oyak Bank, Finansbank and Ziraat Bankası. If you're expecting to receive money, just turn up at any branch of these banks with your passport and transfer details (time and amount of transfer, plus 'money transfer control number'). You should be able to draw the money instantly in dollars, euros or YTL.

Bureaux de change

Many shops and restaurants accept payment in US dollars, sterling or euros, but there are dozens of exchange bureaux (*döviz bürosu*) in the main tourist and shopping districts. These are easier to deal with than banks, where transactions can take forever and exchange rates are generally lower. Bureaux de change are open long hours, generally from from 9am to 7.30pm Monday to Saturday. Some exchange offices also open on Sundays, but they tend to offer considerably worse exchange rates.

Çetin Döviz
İstiklal Caddesi 39, Beyoğlu (0212 252 6428). **Open** 9am-8pm daily. **Map** p249 O2.

Çözüm Döviz
İstiklal Caddesi 53, Beyoğlu (0212 244 6271). **Open** 9am-7.30pm Mon-Sat; 11am-6pm Sun. **Map** p249 O2.

Klas Döviz
Sıraselviler Caddesi 51, Taksim (0212 249 3550). **Open** 8.30am-10pm daily. **Map** p249 O2.

Credit cards

Turkey has seen a big credit-card boom in recent years. Banks have hooked up with the retail sector to cajole consumers into spending money they don't have, while the government is promoting plastic in the hope of curbing the vast black economy. The good news for visitors is that major credit cards are widely accepted, but it's advisable to carry some cash in case.

American Express
0212 444 2525/ www.americanexpress.com.tr. Represented in Turkey by Akbank, AmEx is far less widely accepted than Mastercard or Visa because of high commission charges.

Mastercard
00 800 13 887 0903.

Visa
00 800 13 535 0900.

Travellers' cheques

Travellers' cheques can be cashed at banks or post offices, but are usually not accepted at exchange bureaux. You always need to have your passport with you to cash cheques. Banks charge different commissions, and some charge none at all; but the post office usually offers the best deal.

Opening hours

Opening hours are extremely variable in Istanbul, but here are some general guidelines:
Banks 9am-12.30pm, 1.30-5pm Mon-Fri.
Bars 11am or noon-2am daily.
Businesses 9am-6pm Mon-Fri.
Municipal offices 8am-12.30pm, 1.30-5.30pm Mon-Fri.
Museums 8.30am-5.30pm Tue-Sun.
Petrol stations 24 hrs daily.
Post offices see below.
Shops 10am-8pm Mon-Sat. In main shopping areas shops stay open until 10pm and also open on Sunday. Grocery stores (*bakkals*) and supermarkets are open 9am-10pm daily.

Police & security

Crime is low and physical violence (football supporters aside) is rare in Istanbul. The main thing to beware of is bag-snatching, especially around tourist areas like Sultanahmet, or crowded places such as Eminönü and Beyoğlu.

Single women can get hassled, but this is generally confined to verbal comments or staring (*see p228*). That said, women should not wander around Beyoğlu or Taksim late at night unaccompanied. Steer clear of Tarlabaşı, one of Istanbul's seedier districts, and remember that it's illegal not to carry a photo ID with you at all times.

The police have a very bad reputation for incompetence, excessive use of force, and an appetite for back-handers – which they have generally deserved. Determination to change this image has resulted in a major PR drive: the new police website (www.iem.gov.tr) has an exhaustive catalogue of services in ten languages.

Tourist police
Yerebatan Caddesi 6, Sultanahmet (0212 527 4503). Tram Sultanahmet. **Open** 24 hrs daily. **Map** p243 N10.
The place to report thefts, losses, or scams. Most officers speak English.

Post

Post offices are recognisable by their distinctive yellow and black PTT signs. Poste restante mail should be sent to the central post office at Sirkeci, addressed as follows:
Recipient's name
Poste Restante
Büyük Postane
Büyük Postane Caddesi
Sirkeci
Istanbul

To collect mail from poste restante, you need to bring your passport, and will have to pay a small fee for each letter that you receive.

Mosque etiquette

At least half of Istanbul's major sights are mosques. Non-Muslims are welcome to visit any of them but should steer clear of busy prayer times, of which noon – and especially Friday noon – is the main one. Note that prayer times vary throughout the year, so noon prayers don't take place exactly on the stroke of midday, but can fall anywhere between 11.30am and 1.30pm.

Dress modestly: no shorts, short skirts or bare shoulders. This is especially vital for visits to mosques out of the tourist loop, such as places in conservative areas like Fatih, Fener and Balat. Shoes must be removed, although in some places cloth covers are provided to slip over your footwear. Women will be given a headscarf to cover their hair if they haven't brought their own. Photography is usually allowed, but don't point your camera at people at prayer.

Postage rates

Stamps can only be bought at post offices. Postcards cost YTL0.70 to Europe, YTL0.80 to the US and Australia. Airmail letters up to 50g cost YTL1.50 to Europe, YTL1.75 to the US and Australia.

For parcels, airmail rates start at YTL39 to the UK, YTL38 to the US, and YTL45 to Australia for the first kilogramme, with an extra YTL8 , YTL17 and YTL24 respectively for every additional kilogramme. Rates for surface mail are YTL34 to the UK, YTL24 to the US and YTL29 to Australia.

The contents of all parcels will be inspected at the post office, so it's best not to seal them and bring tape with you.

Major post offices

Beyoğlu
Yeniçarşı Caddesi 4A, Galatasaray, Beyoğlu (0212 251 5150/www.ptt. gov.tr). **Open** 8.30am-5pm Mon-Fri; 8.30am-5pm Sun. **Map** p248 N3.

Sirkeci
Büyük Postane, Büyük Postane Caddesi, Sirkeci (0212 526 1200/ www.ptt.gov.tr). **Open** 8.30am-5.30pm daily. **Map** p243 N9.

Taksim
Cumhuriyet Caddesi 2, Taksim (0212 243 0284/www.ptt.gov.tr). **Open** 8.30am-12.30pm, 1.30-5.30pm Mon-Sat. **Map** p249 P2.

Religion

Istanbul may be a city of mosques, but there is a multitude of places to worship. After all, Istanbul was once a centre of a Christian empire, and is still the home of the Greek and Armenian Orthodox Patriarchates. Istanbul is also a city with a strong Jewish tradition.

Christian

Christ Church (Anglican)
Serdari Ekrem Sokak 82, Tünel, Beyoğlu (0212 251 5616). **Services** 9am, 6pm Mon-Sat; 9am,10am Sun. **Map** p248 N5.

Union Church of Istanbul (Protestant)
Postacılar Sokak, Beyoğlu (0212 244 5212). **Services** 9.30am, 11am, 1.30pm Sun. **Map** p248 N4.

St Anthony's (Catholic)
İstiklal Caddesi 325, Beyoğlu (0212 244 0935). **Open** 8am-7.30pm Mon-Sat, 9am-12.30pm and 3-7.30pm Sun. **Services** English 8am Mon-Sat, 10am Sun. **Map** p248 N3.

Haghia Triada (Greek Orthodox)
Meşelik Sokak 11/1, Taksim (0212 244 1358). **Services** *Short* 8.30am, 5pm daily (4pm in winter). *Full-length* 9am Sun. **Map** p249 O2.

Üç Horon (Gregorian Armenian)
Balık Pazarı, Sahne Sokak 24, Beyoğlu (0212 244 1382). **Open** 9am-5pm daily. **Services** 9.30am-1pm Tue; 9am-1pm Sun. **Map** p248 N3.

Jewish

Security at the Istanbul's synagogues has been tighter than ever since two suicide bombings on the Bet Israel and Neve Shalom synagogues in November 2003. To visit, you must first obtain permission. Call the office of the Chief Rabbinate for further information. Prayers are usually held daily at 7.30am, with Shabbat services at 8am. Friday evening services take place at sunset.

Chief Rabbinate
Yeminiçi Sokak 23, Tünel, (0212 293 8794/5). **Open** 9am-5pm Mon-Thur; 9am-1pm Fri.

Removals

Professional movers are pricey in Istanbul. The cheapest way to move furniture is to hire a truck. Ask your local grocer (*bakkal*) or greengrocer (*manav*) to help make arrangements. Agree on a price first (you shouldn't pay more than YTL45-YTL55), taking into account the number of stairs involved, and be sure to tip the movers afterwards.

Sumerman International
Menekşe Sokak 1, Tarabya (0212 223 5818/www.sumerman.com). English spoken.

Smoking

Smoking bans are slowly creeping in: first it was public transport, now it's public offices, banks, shops, and even

Directory

private offices. Offenders are supposedly liable to fines of up to YTL500. In practice, this is rarely enforced and only a few restaurants and cafés offer non-smoking sections. Foreign cigarettes cost around YTL3.50-YTL4 for 20, while the best domestic brand, Tekel 2000, goes for even less.

Study

Language courses

Turkish is taught at various private schools and colleges; many also offer individual tuition.You can also find private tutors in the classified ads in the *Turkish Daily News*.

Bilgi University

Kurtuluşderesi Caddesi 47, Dolapdere (0212 444 0428/ www.bilgi-egitim.com). **Open** 10am-6pm daily. Ten-week, 40-hour courses begin in January, April and October and cost YTL575.

English First (Turkish Department)

Aydın Sokak 12, off Korukent Yolu, Levent (0212 282 9064/www.turkish lesson.com). **Open** 9am-10pm Mon-Fri; 9am-5pm Sat, Sun.
10-week courses cost YTL740 + VAT.

Taksim Dilmer Language Teaching Centre

Tarık Zafer Tunaya Sokak 18, off İnönü Caddesi, Taksim (0212 292 9696/www.dilmer.com). **Open** 9am-8pm Mon-Fri; 9am-5pm Sat, Sun. **Map** p247 Q2.
Morning, afternoon, evening or weekend classes of no more than 14 students. A four-week, 80-hour course costs YTL518; an eight-week 96-hour course is YTL622.

Telephones

Istanbul's districts have different area codes: 0212 for Europe; 0216 for Asia. You must use the code whenever you call the opposite shore, but when dialling from abroad omit the zero. The country code for Turkey is 90. Call 118 for directory inquiries, 115 for the international operator.

Public phones

Public phones now operate with pre-paid cards (*telefon kartı*). There are two types: a floppy version, or a rigid 'smart card'. Some newer phones also take credit cards. Phone cards can be bought at post offices or, at a small premium, from street vendors and kiosks. They come in units of 30 (YTL2.15), 60 (YTL4.30), 100 (YTL7.20) and 120 (YTL8.60). Metered calls (*kontörlü*) can be placed at post offices or private phone and fax offices (*telefon ofisi*), but they charge over the odds.

Public phone rates are about YTL1.50 a minute to the UK and US, YTL2.25 to Australia. Reduced rates for international calls operate from 10pm to 9am Monday to Saturday, and all day Sunday and holidays. For local and national calls, cheap time is 8pm to 8am midweek and all weekend.

Mobile phones

There are three GSM networks: Turkcell, Telsim, and Avea. If you bring your UK mobile, you'll have no problem using your phone as long as you've set up a roaming facility. However, because the Turkish system operates on 900 MHz, US mobile phones won't work.

A cheaper option is to invest in a local SIM card, or *hazır kart*, available through all the GSM operators. Find an authorised dealer (Turkcell is the most popular), present a photocopy of your passport, and pay the subscription fee (around YTL30-YTL40), which includes 100 units, or roughly 25 minutes of talk-time within Turkey. Top-up cards are sold all over the place (look for the *hazır kart* sign) in units of 100 (YTL12.50), 250 (YTL28), 500 (YTL53), or 1000 (YTL98).

Getting a contract mobile phone is tricky and expensive, thanks to a 40 per cent tax.

You'll need a residence permit plus a Turkish guarantor prepared to stump up $900.

Time

Turkey is two hours ahead of Greenwich Mean Time (GMT) and seven hours ahead of New York. There is no Turkish equivalent of am and pm, so the 24-hour clock is used. Daylight-saving runs from the last Sunday in March to the last Sunday in October. This creates a three-hour time difference between Turkey and the UK in October only.

Tipping

Although not obligatory, the rule of thumb is to leave about ten per cent of the bill at cafés and restaurants. Service is occasionally included, in which case it'll say *servis dahil* at the bottom of the bill. If in doubt ask: '*Servis dahil mi?*' Tipping hotel staff, porters and hairdressers is discretionary, but YTL1-YTL2 is the norm. Hamam attendants expect more like 25 per cent. It's not necessary to tip taxi drivers.

Toilets

Public toilets are plentiful. They'll be signposted 'WC' (when asking, use the term *tuvalet*); the gents' is Bay; the ladies' is Bayan. Public facilities usually consist of a hole in the floor. Toilet paper in these places is a rarity, so carry a pack of tissues (*selpak*). City plumbing cannot cope with toilet paper, so use the bin provided. Hotels, bars and restaurants all have Western-style (*alafranga*) toilets.

Tourist information

The Ministry of Culture and Tourism has tourist information kiosks, where staff speak English, all over town.

Atatürk Airport
International Arrivals (0212 465 3151-3547). **Open** 24 hrs daily.

Beyazıt
Beyazıt Square (0212 522 4902). **Open** 9am-6pm daily. **Map** p242 K10.

Hilton Hotel
Cumhuriyet Caddesi, Şişli (0212 233 0592). **Open** 9am-5pm daily. **Map** p247 P1.

Karaköy Seaport
Kemankeş Caddesi, Karaköy (0212 249 5776). **Open** 9am-5pm Mon-Sat. **Map** p246 N6.

Sirkeci Station
Istasyon Caddesi, Sirkeci (0212 511 5888). **Open** 9am-5pm daily. **Map** p243 N8.

Sultanahmet Square
Divan Yolu 3 (0212 518 1802). **Open** 9am-5pm daily. **Map** p243 N10.

International Turkish tourist offices

Australia *Room 17, Level 3, 428 St George Street, Sydney NSW 2000 (02 9223 3055/ 9223 3204).*

Canada *Constitution Square, Suite 801, 360 Albert Street, Ottawa, Ontario K1R 7X7 (613 230 8654/ 230 3683).*

UK *1st floor, 170-173 Piccadilly, London W1V 9EJ (020-7629 7771/7491 0773).*

USA *821 UN Plaza, New York, NY 10017 (212 687 2194/599 7568/www.tourismturkey.org).*

Visas

Visas are required by most nationalities; they can be bought at the airport upon arrival. At press time, rates were as follows: UK $16 (YTL24); USA $26 (YTL39); Canada $75 (YTL110); Australia $70 (YTL105); Ireland $23 (YTL34). New Zealanders don't need a visa. Fees must be paid in foreign currency; Turkish lira, credit cards or travellers' cheques are not accepted. Visas are valid for three months. Overstaying your visa, even by a single day, will earn you a fine of around YTL150 ($100) when you finally leave the country.

When to go

Between December and March Istanbul is cold, grey and blustery. Temperatures average 5C (42F), but humidity and windchill make it feel much colder. Sleet and snow showers are not uncommon; the city is usually buried under several feet of snow at least once every winter – a magical sight, even if it means life grinds to a halt.

Summers can be oppressive; temperatures average 25-30C (78-88F) from June to August, occasionally rising beyond 35C (104F). The heat and humidity can be draining during the day, but when things cool down at sunset city dwellers descend to the Bosphorus to enjoy languid evenings at waterfront cafés.

The best weather is in spring and autumn, when days are temperate and evenings mild. Occasionally, *poyraz*, a chill Balkan wind, and *lodos*, hot, humid gusts from the south, can result in a 'four seasons in a single day' effect. Both spring and autumn are busy festival seasons. For average temperatures, *see p228*.

Public & religious holidays

Turkey's five secular public holidays last one day each. Banks, offices and post offices are closed, but many shops stay open and public transport runs as usual.

Religious holidays are different. They last three or four days; if these happen to be midweek, the government often extends the holiday to cover the whole working week. The city shuts down as Istanbullus flock to the country. Coaches and flights are jammed, so book ahead if your travel plans coincide.

Observance of **Ramazan**, the Islamic month of fasting, is widespread. Many Turks abstain from food, drink and cigarettes between sunrise and sunset. This has little impact on visitors, as most bars and restaurants remain open, but it's bad form to flaunt your non-participation by smoking or eating in the street, especially in religious districts, such as Fatih and Üsküdar. Here, Ramazan nights are the busiest of the year. At sundown, eateries are packed with large groups breaking their fast together with *iftar* ('breakfast'). Sultanahmet Square turns into an extravaganza of food and music at twilight – a revival of an old Ottoman tradition. The end of Ramazan is marked by the three-day Şeker Bayramı, or 'Sugar Holiday', when sweets are traditionally given to friends and family.

The main event in the Islamic calendar is Kurban Bayramı (the Feast of the Sacrifice), which marks Abraham's near-sacrifice of Isaac. While Isaac escaped the knife, the local livestock aren't so lucky. Traditionally, families buy a *kurban*, which could be a sheep, bull, goat or camel, which they sacrifice on the first or second day of the feast. The meat is shared with relatives, neighbours and the poor. There are now stricter regulations on slaughtering sites and methods, which has reduced the bloodbath effect, but the faint-hearted are advised to keep away from mosques around this time.

Islamic religious holidays are based on a lunar calendar, approximately 11 days shorter than the Gregorian (Western) calendar. Consequently, Islamic holidays shift forward by ten or 12 days each year.

New Year's Day (*Yılbaşı Günü*) 1 Jan.

The Feast of the Sacrifice (*Kurban Bayramı*) 20-23 Dec 2007; 8-11 Dec 2008.

National Sovereignty & Children's Day (*Ulusal Egemenlik ve Çocuk Bayramı*) 23 Apr.

Youth & Sports Day (*Gençlik ve Spor Bayramı*) 19 May.
Victory Day (*Zafer Bayramı*) 30 Aug.
Republic Day (*Cumhuriyet Bayramı*) 29 Oct.
Ramazan Holiday (*Ramazan Bayramı*) 12-14 Oct 2007; 30 Sept-2 Oct 2008.

Women

Few special rules apply for women in Istanbul. With some provisos, you needn't dress any differently than at home, certainly not in the more European areas such as Beyoğlu and points north. Probably best to leave the micro minis and short shorts at home, though. To avoid being stared at, wear trousers or skirts that come to the knee. And in more conservative areas, and particularly in mosques and churches, keep your shoulders covered.

In touristy areas like Sultanahmet you may get hit on. It's usually harmless and nothing more than you would expect in Italy or Greece, but all the same it can be annoying. It's also generally easy to shrug off. Avoid eye contact; don't beam wide smiles. Don't respond to invitations, come-ons or obnoxious comments. If a man is persistent and in your face, try saying '*Ayıp*', literally 'shame on you'. Chances are someone will intervene on your behalf. It seldom extends beyond that, but should you need help, the word is '*İmdat*'.

Working in Istanbul

Finding a job is not as easy as it once was. There's a large market for native-speaking English teachers, but most schools and universities now require an internationally recognised teaching qualification. Many foreigners work as journalists for local English-language publications, tour guides, or bar managers. Many work on tourist visas, hopping to North Cyprus or Greece every three months to renew their visa. This is, of course, illegal, but people get away with it for years.

Work permits

Work permits can only be obtained through a sponsoring employer. In principle, your job should only be doable by a foreigner. Getting the permit is a long, painfully bureaucratic process. First, the employer submits an application for authorisation to the Treasury in Ankara. This can take a couple of months. You then submit your own application to the Turkish Consulate General in your country of residence (which shouldn't be Turkey) and wait about six weeks for it to be processed. When it's ready, you must collect it from the consulate in person with your passport. Back in Turkey, you still need a residence permit (*see below*).

Residence permits

If you have a work permit, you're automatically entitled to residence as long as your permit is valid. Otherwise, residence applications should be filed with the Turkish Consulate General in your country of residence. The laborious application procedure for British passport holders is detailed online at www.turkconsulate-london.com. You'll need photocopies of your passport, bank statements, proof of income, photographs, a completed application form and covering letter. Applications take about eight weeks to process. You must pick up your visa in person.

Upon arrival in Istanbul, you must register with the Foreigners' Branch of the Police Department (Emniyet Müdürlüğü Yabancılar Şubesi) on Vatan Caddesi (Aksaray) within one month of the visa/work permit being issued. Queues are lengthy and the process is tedious. Go armed with a book, patience, a pile of cash and if possible, a local who knows the ropes. Residence permits are valid for one or two years; you can also apply for a five-year permit. Expect to pay upwards of YTL225.

Alternatively, use the time-honoured method of getting a work permit: get hitched to a Turkish national.

Average temperatures

Month	Minimum °C	Maximum °C
January	3	8
February	2	9
March	3	11
April	7	16
May	12	21
June	16	25
July	18	28
August	19	28
September	16	24
October	13	20
November	9	15
December	5	11

Vocabulary

A bit of Turkish goes a long way and making the effort to use a few phrases will be greatly appreciated. For information on language courses *see p226*.

Pronunciation

All words are written phonetically and except ğ there are no silent letters; so post office, *postane*, is pronounced 'post-a-neh'. Syllables are articulated with equal stress. The key is to master the pronunciation of the few letters and vowels that differ from English:

c – like the 'j' in jam; so cami (mosque) is 'jami'
ç – like the 'ch' in chip, so çiçek (flower) is 'chi-check'
ğ – silent, but lengthens preceding vowel
ı – an 'uh', like the 'a' in cinema
ö – like the 'ir' in girdle
ş – like the 'sh' in shop, so şiş (as in kebab) is pronounced 'shish'
ü – as in the French 'tu'

Accommodation

air-conditioning klima
bathroom banyo
bed yatak
bed & breakfast pansiyon
breakfast kahvaltı
double bed çift kişilik yatak
hotel otel
no vacancies yer yok
room oda
shower duş
soap sabun
tax/VAT vergi/KDV
towel havlu
vacancy yer var

Days of the week

Monday pazartesi
Tuesday salı
Wednesday çarşamba
Thursday perşembe
Friday cuma
Saturday cumartesi
Sunday pazar

Emergencies

accident kaza
ambulance ambülans
doctor doktor
fire yangın
help! imdat!
hospital hastane
medication ilaç
pharmacy eczane
police polis
sick hasta

Essentials

a lot/very/too çok
and ve
bad/badly kötü
big büyük
but ama/fakat
good/well iyi
I don't speak Turkish Türkçe bilmiyorum
I don't understand anlayamadım
leave me alone (quite forceful) beni rahat bırak
Mr/Mrs bey/hanım (with first name)
no hayır
OK tamam
or veya
please lütfen
slow(ly) yavaş
small küçük
sorry pardon
thank you teşekkürler/mersi/sağol
yes evet
this/that bu/şu

Getting around

airport havalimanı
bus otobüs
bus/coach station otogar
car park otopark
entrance giriş
exit çıkış
left sol
map harita
no parking park yapılmaz
petrol benzin
platform peron
right sağ
road yol
station gar
street sokak
train tren

Greetings

good morning günaydın
good afternoon/goodbye iyi günler
good evening/goodbye iyi akşamlar
good night/goodbye iyi geceler
goodbye güle güle (to the person leaving)
hello merhaba
see you görüşmek üzere

Questions

do you have change? bozuk paranız var mı?
do you speak English? ingilizce biliyor musunuz?
how? nasıl?
what? ne?
when? ne zaman?
where? nerede?
where to? nereye?
which (one)? hangi(si)?
who? kim?
why? niye/niçin/neden?

Shopping

bank banka
cheap ucuz
credit card kredi kartı
expensive pahalı
how many? kaç tane?
how much (price)? kaç para?
I would like....istiyorum...
is there/are there any? var mı?
post office postane/PTT
price fiyat
stamp pul
till receipt fiş

Sightseeing

castle kale
church kilise
closed kapalı
free bedava/ücretsiz
open açık
mosque cami
museum müze
palace saray
reduced price indirimli
ticket bilet

Time

at what time? saat kaçta gün
hour saat
minute dakika
month ay
today bugün
tomorrow yarın
week hafta
what time is it? saat kaç?
when? ne zaman?
yesterday dün

Numbers

0 sıfır; 1 bir; 2 iki; 3 üç; 4 dört; 5 beş; 6 altı; 7 yedi; 8 sekiz; 9 dokuz; 10 on; 11 onbir; 12 oniki; 20 yirmi; 21 yirmibir; 22 yirmiiki; 30 otuz; 40 kırk; 50 elli; 60 altmış; 70 yetmiş; 80 seksen; 90 doksan; 100 yüz; 1,000 bin; 1,000,000 milyon; 1,000,000,000 milyar

Further reference

Books

Istanbul has a lively literary scene. Authors whose work has been translated include Turkey's national poet, **Nazım Hikmet**, and award-winning fiction writers **Orhan Pamuk** and **Yaşar Kemal**. Most of the titles listed here are available in Istanbul.

Fiction

Ali, Tariq *The Stone Woman* (2000) Historical novel by former Trotskyist activist in which an Ottoman noble family observes the decay of the empire.
Christie, Agatha *Murder on the Orient Express* (1934) The fabled train is stuck in a snowdrift on the Turkish border when one of the passengers is bumped off.
de Souza, Daniel *Under A Crescent Moon (1989)* True-life tale of a guy banged up in Istanbul for drug smuggling.
Greene, Graham *Stamboul Train* (1932) Lesser yarn about a bunch of characters crossing central Europe on the Orient Express. Greene's advance wouldn't stretch beyond Cologne, so all the eastern detail was cribbed from Baedeker.
Kemal, Yashar *Memed, My Hawk* (1961) The book that established Kemal as one of Turkey's greatest contemporary writers is a gritty insight into Turkish rural life.
Nadel, Barbara *Harem* (2002) Taking on prostitution and mafia violence, this crime novel from the Inspector Ikmen series has won few friends in the Istanbul tourist board.
Pamuk, Orhan *Snow* (2005) A sensation in his native Istanbul, Pamuk scooped the Nobel Prize in 2006 (*see p97*). This poetic novel is set in the border town of Kars.
Unsworth, Barry *The Rage of the Vulture* (1982) Booker Prize-winner Unsworth once taught English in Istanbul. His detailed imagery enriches this tale of political intrigue, as the 'vultures of Europe' circle the dying Ottoman empire.

Non-fiction

Beck, Christa & Fausting, Christiane *Istanbul: An Architectural Guide* (1997) Excellent gazetteer of nearly 100 of the city's most significant buildings.

Hellier, Chris & Venturi, Franscesco *Splendors of Istanbul: Houses and Palaces along the Bosphorus* (1993) Glossy photos of the interiors of improbably lavish waterside mansions.
Hull, Alastair & Luczyc-Wyhowska, Jose *Kilims: The Complete Guide* (2000) Lavish but practical large format paperback.
Hutchings, Roger & Rugman, Jonathan *Atatürk's Children: Turkey and the Kurds* (2001) One of the best books on an explosive national issue – the conflict in the country's south-east.
Kinzer, Stephen *Crescent and Star* (2002) Opinionated and engaging account of contemporary Turkey by the former New York Times correspondent for Istanbul.
Mango, Andrew *Atatürk* (2002) Latest in a long line of Atatürk bios, with a strong narrative drive.
Mansel, Philip *Constantinople: City of the World's Desire* (1996) Grand discourse on the rise and fall of the imperial capital.
Norwich, John Julius *A Short History of Byzantium* (1998) An authoritative tour of the Byzantine Empire's 1,123-year history, which captures every tawdry and riveting detail at a galloping pace.
Orga, Irfan *Portrait of a Turkish Family* (1989) A haunting autobiography that follows a wealthy Istanbul family's demise following World War I, offering insight into Turkey's uneasy transition from crumbling empire to republic.
Pope, Hugh & Nicole *Turkey Unveiled* (2000) Balanced assessment of the contemporary political and cultural landscape by two long-term Istanbul journalists.
Procopius *The Secret History* (1982) The first-century Byzantine historian wrote the official biography of Justinian; in these salacious diaries, he gives his own, uncensored account of the tyrannical emperor.

Travel

Freely, John & Sumner-Boyd, Hilary *Strolling Through Istanbul* (2003) An enlightening companion for city wandering, with an emphasis on history and architecture from the Byzantine to the Ottoman age. Itineraries are provided.
Kelly, Laurence (ed) *Istanbul: A Traveller's Companion* (1987) Historical writings and travellers' tales covering places, people, courtly life, and social diversions.

Montagu, Mary Wortley *Turkish Embassy Letters* (1763) London socialite Lady Montagu was a diplomatic wife in Istanbul from 1716-18 and an amusing correspondent, equally at home with court politics and harem gossip.

Film

Istanbul has yet to be accurately or exhautively immortalised on celluloid for an international audience. Instead, it's made a few brief cameo appearances to add a dash of Oriental spice to some otherwise bland cinematic fare. For Turkish films *see p192*.

Journey Into Fear (Norman Foster, 1942) World War II spy thriller co-written, produced by and starring Orson Welles as intelligence officer Colonel Hakkı. Lead Joseph Cotten was paired with Welles again seven years later for The Third Man. Though not as well known, this is every bit as good.
Istanbul (Joseph Pevney, 1957) Suspected diamond smuggler (Errol Flynn) returns to Istanbul to find his old flame, whom he thought was dead, is still alive.
From Russia with Love (Terence Young, 1962) 'He seems fit enough. Have him report to me in Istanbul in 24 hours.' 007 casually dispatches Eastern Bloc assailants in various tourist spots and gets to shag two wrestling gypsies.
America, America (Elia Kazan, 1963) Autobiographical film (Kazan was born in Istanbul) picturing the working-class neighbourhoods of Istanbul through the eyes of the director's uncle, as he journeys from Anatolia to the New World.
Topkapı (Jules Dassin, 1964) Caper movie in which a small-time con-man (Peter Ustinov) gets mixed up in a big-time jewellery heist. Good fun, and Istanbul looks stunning.
Murder on the Orient Express (Sidney Lumet, 1974) Albert Finney, Lauren Bacall, Ingrid Bergman, Sean Connery and John Gielgud ham it up something rotten.
Midnight Express (Alan Parker, 1978) Still misshaping views of Turkey and the Turks thirty years on. A great movie? Perhaps, but an inexcusably racist one.
Pascali's Island (James Dearden, 1988) Based on a novel by Barry Unsworth. Pascali (Ben Kingsley) is a spy for the Ottoman sultanate.

Although entirely shot in Greece, it successfully captures the period.
Hamam (Ferzan Ozpetek, 1996) Italian man visits Istanbul, repairs bathhouse, falls for local boy. A gorgeously photographed, lushly scored ethno-homo romp.
The World Is Not Enough (Michael Apted, 1999) Bond is back. In Istanbul. Except he wasn't. Brosnan and co stayed away because of PKK activity; his dip into the Bosphorus was computer-generated.
The Accidental Spy (Teddy Chen, 2000) Jackie Chan takes on Istanbul!
In This World (Michael Winterbottom, 2002) Award-winning account of two Afghans smuggled across countless borders between Pakistan and Britain, featuring dingy sweat-shop scenes in Istanbul.

Music

Rock and pop releases on local labels are not widely available outside Turkey, but traditional Turkish music can be tracked down in the world music sections of specialist stores. Two fine labels are Kalan Music (www.kalan.com) and Traditional Crossroads (www.rootsworld.com). Golden Horn (www.goldenhorn.com), based in California, has a decent catalogue of traditional Turkish music and jazz.

For more on Turkish music *see p186*; for places to buy CDs and tapes *see p159*.

Fasıl

There are surprisingly few *fasıl* recordings on the market. Generally, the older the recording, the better. Look out for albums by Müzeyyen Senar and Zeki Müren, reissues by Hamiyet Yüceses and Safiye Ayla, or newcomer Muazzez Ersoy's interpretations of standards and soundtracks.

Zeki Müren *1955-63 Recordings* (Kalan) Double CD of gorgeous melodies complemented by Müren's gender-bending alto voice.

Folk music

Bosphorus *Balkan Dusleri* (Ada Müzik) Turkish classical musicians revive the Istanbul Greek repertoire.

Ali Ekber Çiçek *Klasikleri* (Mega Müzik) One of the most respected exponents of the saz.
Mehmet Erenler *Mehmet Erenler ve Bozlaklari* (Folk Müzik Center) Anything by saz maestro Erenler is worth picking up.
Neşet Ertaş (Kalan) An eight-CD collection of work by Ertaş, a cult figure on the Turkish folk scene, now resident in Germany.
Muhabbet *Volumes 1-7* (Kalan) Fantastic *aşık* – Alevi mystical songs – performed by top names like Arif Sağ, Yavuz Top and Musa Eroğlu.

Ottoman, classical & court music

Erol Deran *Solo Kanun* (Mega) This is what Turkish classical music should be: subtle and virtuosic.
Emirgan Assemble *Klasik Osmanlı Müziği* (Kalan) A sampler of Ottoman instrumental works, featuring *kemençe, ud, kanun, ney* and percussion.
Kani Karaca *Kani Karaca* (Kalan) Something of a national treasure, Karaca is a *hafız*, someone who can recite the Koran from memory, with voice bound to raise goosebumps.
Various *Gazeller 1&2* (Kalan) Amazing archival recordings of traditional vocal improvisations, rescued from ancient 78rpm vinyl.
Various *Lalezar* (Istanbul Büyük Belediye) Four-CD set of Ottoman music, including compositions by sultans and imperial dance music.

Rock & pop

Sezen Aksu *Serçe* (EMI) The glitzy queen of pop churns out an album every two years, but this, her 1978 debut, is still her best.
Baba Zulu Uç *Psyche-Belly Dance* (Doublemoon) Ghastly psychedelic art rock, complete with wacky lyrics.
Ceza *Med Cezir* (Hammer Müzik) Ceza's intense lyrical flurries kick-started the Turkish hip-hop scene.
Cem Karaca *Best of* (Yavuz ve Burç Plakçilik) Around since the 1960s, this old crooner is still a regular performer around town.
Erkin Koray *Şaşkın* (Kalite Ticaret) Great intro to Turkish psychedelia by one of its leading lights.
Barış Mançolo *Mançoloği* (Stereo) Anatolian rocker turned TV celeb whose early death immortalised him as a legend of Turkish rock.
Erkan Oğur *Fuad* (Kalan) An extraordinary and strangely unsung talent, Erkan brings jazz and blues to Turkish instruments and melodies – or vice versa.
Tarkan *Dudu* (Istanbul Plak) Love him or hate him, you can't escape him. The sultry prince of

pop is the sound of Istanbul for a huge percentage of its population.
Various *East2West* (Doublemoon) An eclectic, jazz-soaked sampler from the Doublemoon label.

Roma (Gypsy)

Ciguli *Ciguli* (Dost) Accordion-led recording that catapulted Ahmet Ciguli from street musician to star.
Roman Oyun Havaları *Volumes 1 & 2* (EMI-Kent) Istanbul's top Roma session musicians thump out much-loved dance tunes.
Mustafa Kandıralı *Caz Roman* (World Network) The 'Benny Goodman of Turkey', with cameos from other famous fasıl musicians.
Selim Sesler & Grup Trakya *The Road to Keşan* (Traditional Crossroads) Songs and dances from Keşan, a Roma town on the Turkish-Greek border. Excellent sleeve notes.

Sufi religious

Asitane *Simurg* (Istanbul Ajans) A young ensemble featuring *tanbur, kemençe, ney* and *bendir*.
Mercan Dede *Secret Tribe Nar* (Doublemoon) Mercan Dede (aka DJ Arkın Allen) splices traditional mystic instruments with electronica.
Doğan Ergin *Sufi Music of Turkey Vol 2* (Mega) Ephemeral, meditative improvisations on the Ü (flute).
Music of the Whirling Dervishes *Sufi Music of Turkey* (Mega) Music to twirl by.
Various Mevlana *Dede Efendi* (Kalan) 1963 recording featuring some of the finest performers of the genre, including Kani Karaca.

Websites

Great Buildings Online *www.greatbuildings.com* Take a virtual tour of Haghia Sophia or explore Sinan's masterpieces.
Istanbul Foundation for Culture & Arts *www.istfest.org* Information and online booking for Istanbul's film, jazz, music and theatre festivals.
Istanbul City Guide *www.istanbulcityguide.com* English-language listings updated daily, plus features and news.
The Turkish Daily News *www.turkishdailynews.com* Headline news, political commentary, business and sport.
Turkish Music Club *www.turkishmusic.com* All manner of Turkish music for sale.
The World Factbook – Turkey *www.cia.gov/cia/publications/factbook/geos/tu.html* The CIA's factual take on Turkey, from politics to people.

Index

Note: page numbers in **bold** indicate section(s) giving key information on a topic; *italics* indicate photographs.

Accommodation

Restaurants

DISCOVER MORE CITIES

Tell us what you think and you could win £100-worth of City Guides

Your opinions are important to us and we'd like to know what you like and what you don't like about the Time Out City Guides

For your chance to win, simply fill in our short survey at
timeout.com/guidesfeedback

Every month a reader will win £100 to spend on the Time Out City Guides of their choice – a great start to discovering new cities and you'll have extra cash to enjoy your trip!

Place of Interest and/or Entertainment	
Railway Station	
Park	
College/Hospital	
Pedestrian Streets	
Steps	
Area Name	GALATA
Church	✚
Mosque	☪
Post Office	✉
Tram Stops	●
Metro Station	Ⓜ

Maps

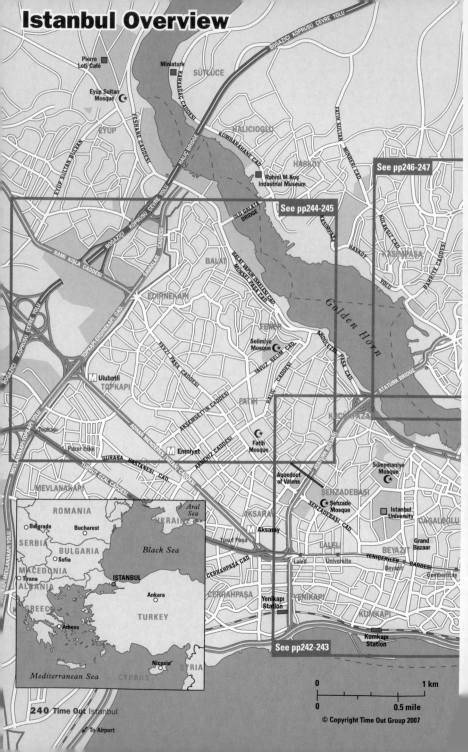

Istanbul Overview

Pierre
Loti Café

Miniaturk

SÜTLÜCE

Eyüp Sultan
Mosque

EYÜP

HALICIOĞLU

HASKÖY

See pp246-247

Rahmi M.Koç
Industrial Museum

OLD GALATA
BRIDGE

See pp244-245

KASIMPAŞA

KASIMPAŞA

BALAT

FENER

Golden Horn

Selimiye
Mosque

ATATÜRK BRIDGE

EDIRNEKAPI

M Ulubatlı

TOPKAPI

FATIH

KÜÇÜKPAZAR

Topkapı

Fatih
Mosque

M Emniyet

Süleymaniye
Mosque

Pazar Tekke

Aqueduct
of Valens

ŞEHZADEBAŞI

Istanbul
University

ÇAĞALOĞLU

Şehzade
Mosque

Grand
Bazaar

[Inset map]

ROMANIA

Aral
Sea

Belgrade   Bucharest

UKRAINE

SERBIA

BULGARIA

Black Sea

Sofia

MACEDONIA

Tirana

ISTANBUL

Ankara

GREECE

TURKEY

Athens

Nicosia

CYPRUS

SYRIA

Mediterranean Sea

MEVLANAKAPI

CERRAHPAŞA

AKSARAY

M Aksaray

Yusuf Paşa

LALELI

Laleli

BEYAZIT

Üniversite

Beyazıt

Çemberlitaş

YENİÇERİLER CADDESİ

Yenikapı
Station

YENİKAPI

KUMKAPI

Kumkapı
Station

See pp242-243

0		1 km
0	0.5 mile	

To Airport

© Copyright Time Out Group 2007

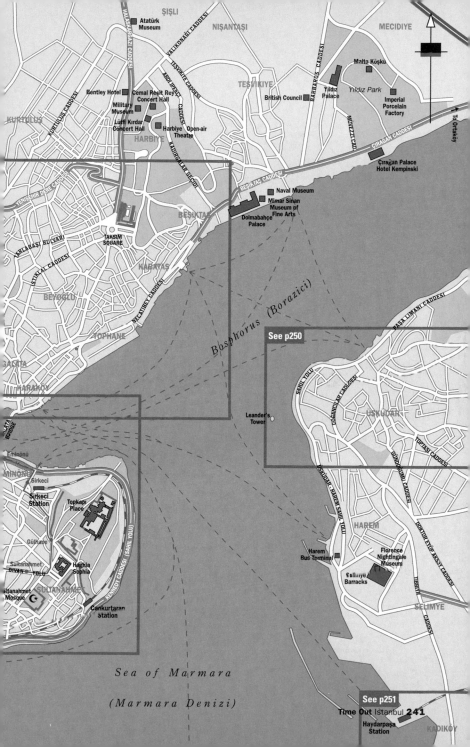

SISLI

NISANTASI

MECIDIYE

Atatürk
Museum

TESVIKIYE

Malta Köşkü

Yıldız Park

Bentley Hotel
Cemal Reşit Rey
Concert Hall
Military
Museum
Lütfi Kırdar
Concert Hall
Harbiye Open-air
Theatre

British Council

Yıldız
Palace

Imperial
Porcelain
Factory

KURTULUS

HARBIYE

To Ortaköy

Çırağan Palace
Hotel Kempinski

BEŞIKTAŞ

Naval Museum
Mimar Sinan
Museum of
Fine Arts
Dolmabahçe
Palace

TAKSIM
SQUARE

KABATAS

Bosphorus (Borazici)

BEYOĞLU

TOPHANE

See p250

PAŞA LIMANI CADDESI

ÜSKÜDAR

GALATA

KARAKÖY

Leander's
Tower

Eminönü

MINÖNÜ

Sirkeci

Sirkeci
Station

Topkapı
Place

Gülhane

Sultanahmet

DIVAN YOLU

Haghia
Sophia

Sultanahmet
Mosque

Cankurtaran
Station

HAREM

Harem
Bus Terminal

Florence
Nightingale
Museum

Selimiye
Barracks

SELIMYE

Sea of Marmara

(Marmara Denizi)

Haydarpaşa
Station

KADIKÖY

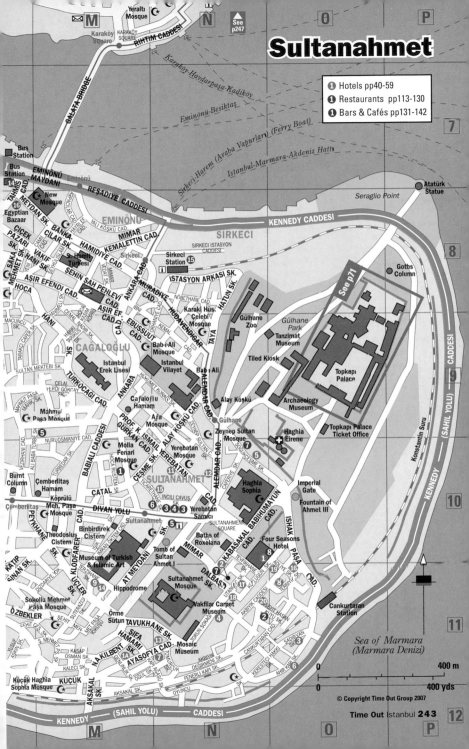

Sultanahmet

See p247

1 Hotels pp40-59
1 Restaurants pp113-130
1 Bars & Cafés pp131-142

Karaköy Square

Yeraltı Mosque

Karaköy Square

RIHTIM CADDESI

GALATA BRIDGE

Karaköy-Haydarpaşa-Kadiköy

Eminönü-Beşiktaş

Sirkeci-Harem (Araba Vapurları) (Ferry Boat)

Istanbul-Marmara-Akdeniz Hattı

Seraglio Point

Atatürk Statue

Bus Station

Bus Station

EMİNÖNÜ MAYDANI

Eminönü

New Mosque

MEYDAN SK. BANKA

Egyptian Bazaar

ÇİÇEK PAZARI

ÇILAR SK.

RESADIYE CADDESI

EMİNÖNÜ

YALI KÖŞKÜ CAD.

MIMAR

HAMIDIYE CAD.

KEMALETTIN CAD.

Hamit Türbesi

SEHIN SAH PEHLEVI

AŞİR EFENDI CAD.

AŞIR EF. CAD.

EBUSSUUT CAD.

KENNEDY CADDESI

SIRKECI

SIRKECI ISTASYON CADDESI

Sirkeci

ISTASYON ARKASI SK.

Sirkeci Station

Goths Column

NÖBETHANE CAD.

Karaki Hüs. Çelebi Mosque

Gülhane Zoo

Gülhane Park

Tanzimat Museum

See p71

HOCA

HANI

ÇAĞALOĞLU

Istanbul Erek Lisesi

Bab-ı Ali Mosque

Istanbul Vilayet

Bab-ı Ali

Tiled Kiosk

Topkapı Palace

MACUNCU

SULTAN MEKTEBI SK.

TURKOCAĞI CAD.

ANKARA

Cağaloğlu Hamam

Afa Mosque

ALAY KÖŞKÜ CAD.

Alay Köşkü

Archaeology Museum

Topkapı Palace Ticket Office

NURUOSMANIYE CAD.

BABIALI CADDESI

PROF. K. ISMAIL GÜRKAN CAD.

Molla Fenari Mosque

Yerebatan Mosque

Zeynep Sultan Mosque

Haghia Eirene

Imperial Gate

Burnt Column

Çemberlitaş Hamam

Köprülü Men. Paşa Mosque

Çemberlitaş

DIVAN YOLU

SULTANAHMET

TİCARETHANE SK.

INCILI ÇAVUS SK.

Haghia Sophia

Fountain of Ahmet III

PEYKHANE

Theodosius Cistern

Binbirdirek Cistern

Sultanahmet

Yerebatan Sarnıcı

SULTANAHMEN SQUARE

Baths of Roxelana

KABASAKAL CAD.

BABIHUMAYUN CAD.

Four Seasons Hotel

KATİP

KLODFARER CAD.

SINAN SK.

UĞLER

Museum of Turkish & Islamic Art

AT MEYDANI

Tomb of Sultan Ahmet I

MIMAR

DALBAŞ

TEVKIFHANE

ISHAK PAŞA CAD.

ÖZBEKLER

Sokollu Mehmet Paşa Mosque

Hippodrome

Sultanahmet Mosque

Vakiflar Carpet Museum

Örme Sütun

Cankurtaran Station

TAVUKHANE SK.

ŞIFA HAMAMI

AYASOFYA CAD.

Mosaic Museum

Sea of Marmara
(Marmara Denizi)

Küçük Haghia Sophia Mosque

KUÇUK

AKSAKAL SK.

AKSAKAL SK.

OYUNCU

KENNEDY (SAHIL YOLU) CADDESI

400 m

400 yds

© Copyright Time Out Group 2007

Time Out Istanbul **243**

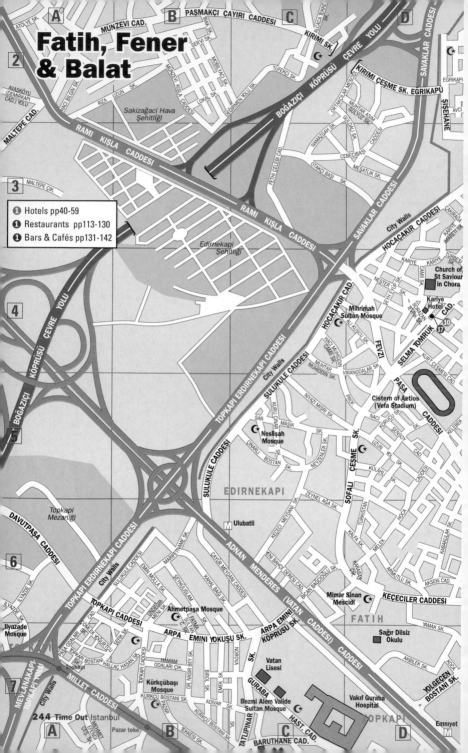

OLD GALATA BRIDGE

OKMEYDANI CAD.

AYNALI KAVAK CAD.

KASIMPAŞA HASKÖY YOLU

2

Aynalı Kavak Kasrı

Museví Hastanesi

Church of Hiresdagabet

Balat Vapur İskelesi

Camialtı Shipyard

0   400 m

0   400 yds

© Copyright Time Out Group 2007

İlkokulu

DEMIRHISAR CADDESI

AVYANSARAY CAD.

DERVIŞZADE CAD.

CINCINLI ÇEŞME

3

_G o l d e n   H o r n_

BALAT VAPUR

MÜRSEL PAŞA CADDESI

St Stephen of the Bulgars

İSKELESI CADDESI

FENER

Ahrida Synagogue

Yatagan Mosque

Koca Mustafa Paşa Mosque

KAYA CAD.

MIRAÇ SK.

ZÜLÜFLÜ SK.

FETHİYE CAD.

Fethiye Mosque

Draman Mosque

Kefeli Mosque

TATLICI SK.

Church of Panaghia Mouchliotissa

Fener Vapur İskelesi

_(H a l i ç)_

4

Ismail Efendi Mosque

ABDÜLEZEL PAŞA

Orthodox Patriarchate (Church of St George)

Aykapı İskelesi

Vasıf Çınar İlkokulu

Murat Mulla Halk Kütüphanesi

MURAT MOLLA CAD.

MAMYASIZADE CADDESI

Ismail Ağa Mosque

Çukurbostan Mosque

Selim I Mosque

SELIM CAD.

CAMCI ÇEŞ.

CIBALI SET SK.

MIRALAY NAZIM BEY CAD.

HALIÇ CADDESI

Gül Mosque

TABAK YUNUS SK.

5

Cistern of Aspar

DARÜSSAFAKA

YAVUZ

Hacı Ferhat Mosque

Library

Darüşşafaka Lisesi

FEVZI PAŞA CAD.

Zincirlikuyu Mosque (Atik Ali Paşa)

YAVUZ SELIM

CADDESI

Kumrulu Mosque

Altay Mosque

N. Mehmet Paşa Mosque

Mesih Ali Paşa Mosque

MÜTERCİM ASIM SK.

Fatih Sarnıçlar

HALIÇ CADDESI

6

Hırka-i Şerif Mosque

KEÇECİLER CAD.

HIRKAI ŞERIF CAD.

FEVZI PAŞA

AKŞEMSETTIN CADDESI

BALI PAŞA

Bali Paşa Mosque

HOCA EFENDI SK.

KINALIZADE SK.

İSLAMBOL CADDESI

Yeni Doğan Mosque

Eski İmaret Mosque

Eski Mahe Mosque

See p242

ZEYREK MEHMET PAŞA CAD.

Zeyrek Mosque

AKDENIZ CADDESI

Fatih Mosque

HALICILAR CAD.

7

İTYAİYE CADDESI

ATATÜRK BULVARI

Time Out Istanbul **245**

Beyoğlu

See
p242

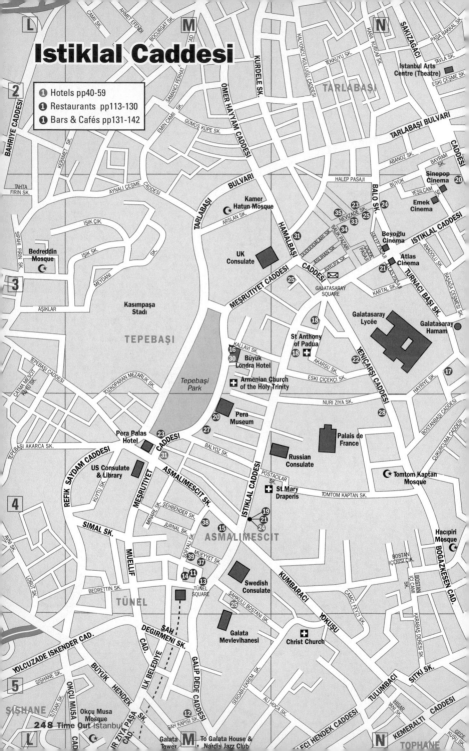

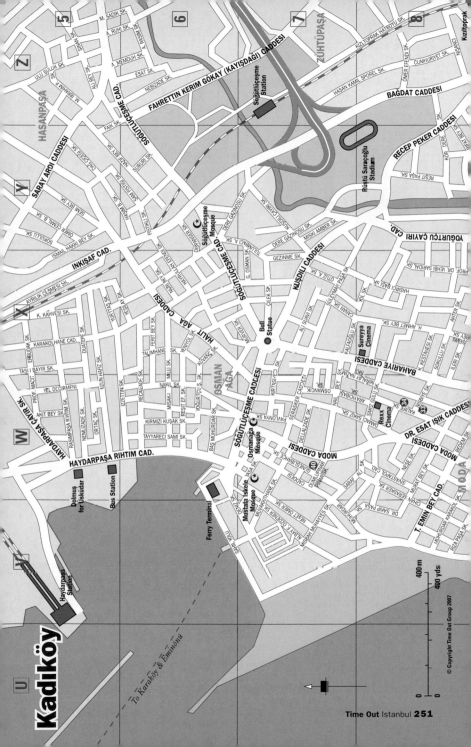

Kadıköy

Street index

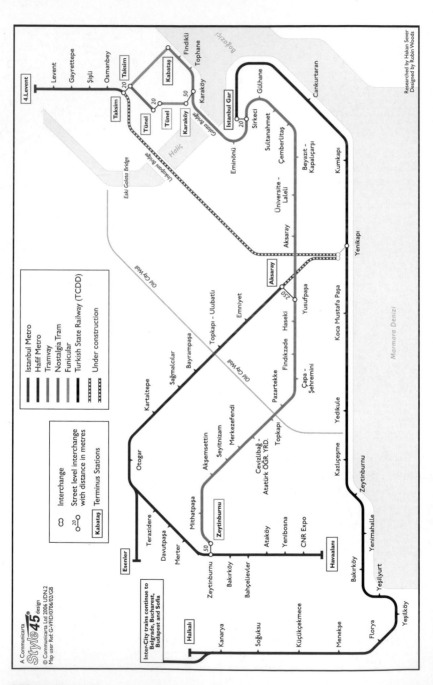